In Conversation with God
Meditations for each day of the year

Volume Seven

Feasts: July – December

Francis Fernandez

In Conversation
with God
Meditations for each day of the year

Volume Seven
Feasts: July – December

SCEPTER
London – New York

This edition of *In Conversation with God – Volume 7* is published:
in England by Scepter (U.K.) Ltd., 21 Hinton Avenue, Hounslow
    TW4 6AP; e-mail: scepter@pobox.com;
in the United States by Scepter Publishers Inc.; 800-322-8773; e-
    mail: info@scepterpublishers.org; www.scepterpublishers.org

This is a translation of *Hablar con Dios – Vol VII*, first published in
1991 by Ediciones Palabra, Madrid, and in 1993 by Scepter.

With ecclesiastical approval

© Original — Fomento de Fundaciones (Fundación Internacional),
Madrid, 1991
© Translation — Scepter, London, 1993
© This edition — Scepter, London, 2019

British Library Cataloguing in Publication Data

Fernandez-Carvajal, Francis
In Conversation with God — Volume 7
Feasts: July – December
1. Christian life — Daily Readings
I Title   II Hablar con Dios *English*
242'.2

ISBN Volume 7	978-0-906138-36-6
ISBN Volume 6	978-0-906138-25-0
ISBN Volume 5	978-0-906138-24-3
ISBN Volume 4	978-0-906138-23-6
ISBN Volume 3	978-0-906138-22-9
ISBN Volume 2	978-0-906138-21-2
ISBN Volume 1	978-0-906138-20-5
ISBN Complete set	978-0-906138-19-9

Cover design & typeset in England by KIP Intermedia, and printed in
China.

CONTENTS

3 JULY
1. Saint Thomas   **17**
1.1 The absence of Thomas.
1.2 His disbelief.
1.3 His faith.

11 JULY
2. Saint Benedict   **23**
2.1 The Christian roots of Europe.
2.2 The need for a new evangelization.
2.3 The task of all – to do our part.

16 JULY
3. Our Lady of Mount Carmel   **29**
3.1 Love for Our Lady: scapular of Mount Carmel.
3.2 The special help and graces from Our Lady at the
    hour of death.
3.3 The scapular: a symbol of *the wedding garment*.

22 JULY
4. Saint Mary Magdalene   **35**
4.1 Mary Magdalene exemplifies our seeking God at
    every moment.
4.2 She recognizes Jesus when he calls her by her name.
    Her joy before the risen Christ.
4.3 Mary Magdalene is sent by our Lord to the Apostles.
    The joy of the apostolate.

25 JULY
5. Saint James   42
5.1 To drink from the cup of the Lord.
5.2 Not becoming discouraged by personal weaknesses
     by seeking the Lord's strength.
5.3 Approaching Our Lady during difficulties.

26 JULY
6. Saints Joachim and Anne   49
6.1 The home of the Blessed Virgin's parents.
6.2 Christian families.
6.3 The education of the children. Family prayer.

29 JULY
7. Saint Martha   54
7.1 Love for the Master and confidence in His help.
7.2 The most Holy Humanity of Jesus.
7.3 Friendship with our Lord makes the way easy for us.

31 JULY
8. Saint Ignatius of Loyola   61
8.1 The influence of spiritual reading on the conversion
     of St Ignatius.
8.2 The importance of spiritual reading.
8.3 Vigilance over printed material. A way of doing
     spiritual reading.

1 AUGUST
9. Saint Alphonsus Liguori   67
9.1 Devotion to Our Lady.
9.2 The mediation of Our Lady.
9.3 The efficacy of this mediation.

Contents

4 AUGUST
10. Saint John Vianney   73
10.1 Holy priests. Love for the priesthood.
10.2 The need for the priest. Prayer and mortification for
     priests.
10.3 Appreciation for and great confidence in the prayer
     of the priest.

5 AUGUST
11. Our Lady of the Snows   79
11.1 The origin of the Roman basilica dedicated to the
     Mother of God.
11.2 Mother of God and our Mother.
11.3 Mary: *the conduit* of all the graces we receive.

6 AUGUST
12. The Transfiguration   85
12.1 The Lord strengthens the disciples before his
     Passion and Death.
12.2 God will be our reward.
12.3 The Lord helps us bear our greatest burdens.

8 AUGUST
13. Saint Dominic   91
13.1 The need for good doctrine.
13.2 The Rosary is a *powerful weapon*.
13.3 The consideration of the mysteries of the Rosary.

14 AUGUST
14. Vigil of the Assumption of Our Lady   97
14.1 Our Lady, *Ark of the New Covenant*.
14.2 The hope of heaven.
14.3 Being faithful is worth while.

15 AUGUST
15. The Assumption of the Blessed Virgin Mary   103
15.1 Mary is taken into heaven, body and soul.
15.2 Our Blessed Mother intercedes from heaven and
       provides for her children.
15.3 Our Lady's Assumption, hope of our own resurrection.

21 AUGUST
16. Saint Pius X   110
16.1 Giving doctrine whenever possible.
16.2 Serenity and good humour in the face of difficulties.
16.3 Love for the Church and for the Pope.

22 AUGUST
17. Our Lady, Queen and Mother   116
17.1 Mary, Queen of heaven and earth.
17.2 The royal titles of Our Lady.
17.3 The Queenship of Mary over Heaven, earth, and
       Purgatory.

24 AUGUST
18. Saint Bartholomew   123
18.1 The encounter with Jesus.
18.2 Praise from the Lord. The virtue of sincerity.
18.3 The virtue of simplicity.

27 AUGUST
19. Saint Monica   129
19.1 St Monica prays for her son, Augustine, to be
       converted.
19.2 Transmitting the faith in the family.
19.3 Prayer as a family.

28 AUGUST
20. Saint Augustine   **135**
20.1 Life should be a continual conversion.
20.2 To begin and begin again.
20.3 The importance of little things. Our Lady and
    conversion.

29 AUGUST
21. The Martyrdom of Saint John the Baptist   **141**
21.1 The fortitude of St John the Baptist.
21.2 The Baptist's martyrdom.
21.3 Joyfully bearing difficulties in faithfully following
    Christ.

8 SEPTEMBER
22. The Birthday of Our Lady   **147**
22.1 Joy over the birth of Our Lady.
22.2 Mary's birth leads us to deep respect for every
    human being.
22.3 The value of ordinary things.

14 SEPTEMBER
23. The Exaltation of the Holy Cross   **154**
23.1 The origin of the feast day.
23.2 The Lord blesses those he loves with the Cross.
23.3 The fruit of the Cross.

15 SEPTEMBER
24. Our Lady of Sorrows   **160**
24.1 Mary's suffering is united to Christ's suffering.
24.2 The co-redemption of Our Lady.
24.3 Sanctifying our sufferings through Our Lady,
    Comforter of the Afflicted.

21 SEPTEMBER
25. Saint Matthew   **167**
25.1 St Matthew's correspondence to the Lord.
25.2 The joy of our vocation.
25.3 Our essentially apostolic vocation.

24 SEPTEMBER
26. Our Lady of Ransom   **173**
26.1 Mary as intercessor for the persecuted and those
     bound by sin.
26.2 She reserves many graces for us.
26.3 To count always on her divine Motherhood.

29 SEPTEMBER – I
27. Saint Michael the Archangel   **178**
27.1 The mission of the Archangels.
27.2 The Archangel Michael helps us fight the devil.
27.3 Petitioning the Holy Archangel for his continual
     protection of the Church.

29 SEPTEMBER – II
28. Saint Gabriel the Archangel   **184**
28.1 St Gabriel, the *Power of God*.
28.2 The Archangel foretells the child to be born. The
     value of each infant.
28.3 Children are a reason for rejoicing.

29 SEPTEMBER – III
29. Saint Raphael the Archangel   **190**
29.1 St Raphael the Archangel in Sacred Scripture.
29.2 Personal vocation.
29.3 To help others find the path of vocation.

2 OCTOBER
30. The Holy Guardian Angels **196**
30.1 The existence of the guardian angels.
30.2 The Guardian Angels' continuous service.
30.3 The Guardian Angels, our dearest friends.

4 OCTOBER
31. Saint Francis of Assisi **202**
31.1 The poverty of St Francis and the practice of this
virtue for the ordinary Christian.
31.2 The special need of the virtue of poverty today and
some ways to practise it.
31.3 The benefits of having limited material means.

THANKSGIVING DAY
32. Day of Thanksgiving and Petition **209**
32.1 Prayer in imitation of Christ.
32.2 There is a great deal to be thankful for.
32.3 Asking with confidence and entrusting our requests
to Our Lady.

7 OCTOBER
33. Our Lady of the Rosary **215**
33.1 The Rosary, a *powerful weapon* in the apostolate.
33.2 Contemplating the mysteries of the Rosary.
33.3 The Litany of Loreto.

12 OCTOBER
34. Our Lady of the Pillar **222**
34.1 Devotion to Our Lady of the Pillar.
34.2 Counting on Mary's help to prepare the way for our
personal apostolate.
34.3 Practising faith and charity in doing apostolate.

15 OCTOBER
35. Saint Teresa of Avila   **228**
35.1 The need for prayer and its primary importance in
     Christian life.
35.2 Dealing with Jesus; his most Sacred Humanity.
35.3 Difficulties in mental prayer.

18 OCTOBER
36. Saint Luke   **235**
36.1 The Gospel of St Luke and striving for perfection in
     our work.
36.2 The Evangelist's message. The painter of the Virgin.
36.3 Reading the Holy Gospel with reverence.

28 OCTOBER
37. Saints Simon and Jude   **241**
37.1 The Apostles seek no personal glory.
37.2 The faith of the Apostles and our faith.
37.3 Love for Jesus in order to follow Him closely.

1 NOVEMBER
38. The Feast of All Saints   **248**
38.1 Sanctification through ordinary life.
38.2 The universal call to holiness.
38.3 Christ is the measure and model of holiness.

2 NOVEMBER
39. The Commemoration of All Souls   **255**
39.1 Purgatory is a place of purification.
39.2 Close union with the souls in Purgatory through
     suffrages.
39.3 Personal purification on earth and the desire to
     bypass Purgatory.

Contents

9 NOVEMBER
40. The Dedication of the Lateran Basilica **261**
40.1 Churches, a symbol of God's presence.
40.2 Jesus Christ is truly present in our churches.
40.3 Divine grace makes us living temples of God.

21 NOVEMBER
41. The Presentation of the Blessed Virgin Mary **267**
41.1 The significance of this feast day.
41.2 Full dedication and correspondence with grace.
41.3 Renewing our dedication through following the
     example of the Blessed Virgin.

30 NOVEMBER
42. Saint Andrew **274**
42.1 Andrew's first encounter with Christ.
42.2 The apostolate of friendship.
42.3 The call of vocation. Detachment and promptness in
     following the Lord.

IMMACULATE CONCEPTION NOVENA – DAY 1
43. Morning Star **281**
43.1 Mary is prefigured in the Old Testament.
43.2 Our Lady illuminates our way and guides us.
43.3 Our Lady, Star of the Sea.

IMMACULATE CONCEPTION NOVENA – DAY 2
44. House of Gold **288**
44.1 Through the Holy Spirit God dwells in our Blessed
     Mother.
44.2 The gifts of Understanding, Knowledge and
     Wisdom in Our Lady.
44.3 The gifts of Counsel, Piety, Fortitude and Fear of
     the Lord.

IMMACULATE CONCEPTION NOVENA – DAY 3
45. Handmaid of the Lord   **295**
45.1 The vocation of Mary.
45.2 God calls each one of us.
45.3 Discerning the Will of God.

3 DECEMBER
46. Saint Francis Xavier   **302**
46.1 The apostolic zeal of St Francis Xavier
46.2 Winning new apostles for Christ.
46.3 Apostolic efficacy in our life.

IMMACULATE CONCEPTION NOVENA – DAY 4
47. Cause of Our Joy   **309**
47.1 Mary brings authentic joy into the world.
47.2 Mary teaches us how to bring joy to others.
47.3 Casting all sadness far from us.

IMMACULATE CONCEPTION NOVENA – DAY 5
48. Mystical Rose   **316**
48.1 Having Jesus abide at our side always through a life
     of prayer.
48.2 Learning how to pray.
48.3 Vocal prayers and the Rosary.

IMMACULATE CONCEPTION NOVENA – DAY 6
49. Mother Most Amiable   **323**
49.1 Jesus gives us his Mother to be our own.
49.2 Mother most amiable and most merciful.
49.3 Learning to communicate more and better with our
     Mother.

Contents

6 DECEMBER
50. Saint Nicholas of Bari **330**
50.1 St Nicholas and the all the saints are friends of God
and our intercessors.
50.2 The need for human and material means.
50.3 Generosity and detachment in the use of material
goods. Seeking the patronage of St Nicholas.

IMMACULATE CONCEPTION NOVENA – DAY 7
51. Refuge of Sinners **337**
51.1 Mary's protection in the Sacrament of Penance.
51.2 Mother most merciful.
51.3 Mary is our refuge.

IMMACULATE CONCEPTION NOVENA – DAY 8
52. Gate of Heaven **344**
52.1 We find Jesus through Mary.
52.2 The intercession of Our Lady.
52.3 Devotion to Our Lady, a sign of predestination.

THE IMMACULATE CONCEPTION – 8 DECEMBER
53. The Immaculate Conception of Our Lady **351**
53.1 The Blessed Virgin and the mystery of Christ.
53.2 Her fulness of grace was received at the moment of
her Immaculate Conception.
53.3 Having devotion to Our Lady in order to imitate her.

10 DECEMBER
54. Our Lady of Loreto **357**
54.1 The Holy House of Loreto.
54.2 The home of Nazareth, model of Christian homes.
54.3 Making life agreeable for those we live with.

12 DECEMBER
55. Our Lady of Guadalupe   **364**
55.1 The apparition of the Blessed Virgin to Juan Diego.
55.2 Our Lady prepares the souls of our friends.
55.3 Taking advantage of every opportunity of
     contributing to re-evangelisation.

Index to quotations   **373**

Subject Index   **385**

Epilogue – From the Publishers   **399**

3 July

1. SAINT THOMAS

Apostle
Feast

Thomas is known for his disbelief in Christ's Resurrection prior to the apparition of Jesus to the Apostles. The stunning encounter provides us with an occasion for strengthening our own confidence in the historical fact of God's definitive conquest over death.

The Gospels offer us the clearest insights into the life of St Thomas. We know through tradition that he evangelized India. The mortal remains of the once incredulous Apostle were moved to Edessus on July 3 in the sixth century and ever since then his feast day has been celebrated on this day.

1.1 The absence of Thomas.

When Jesus, called by the sisters of the sick Lazarus, was getting ready to set out for Judaea where the Jews awaited him with all their deceit and hatred, Thomas said to the other disciples: *Let us also go, that we may die with him.*[1] These are the apostle's first words as recorded by St John. The Lord will in the end gratefully accept his courageous and generous gesture.

Later, during the final discourse of the Last Supper, Thomas asked the Master a question which elicited one of the Lord's great definitions of himself: *Lord, we don't know where you are going; how can we know the way?* Jesus answered him with those words on which we have so often meditated: *I am the Way, the Truth, and the Life; no one comes to the Father, but by me.*[2]

---

[1] John 11:16
[2] John 14:5-6

On the very afternoon of Easter Sunday, Jesus appeared to his disciples. He came upon them without having to open the doors, since his body had already been glorified. Jesus showed them his hands and his side to dispel any thoughts that he was only a spirit. The disciples were fully convinced that Jesus stood before them and that he had truly risen. Jesus greeted them twice in the customary way among the Jews, using the same accent he had lent to these words so many times in the past. Even though the Apostles were little inclined to admit whatever went beyond the horizon of their personal experience and their own way of seeing things, they could not harbour any doubt that they were really seeing and hearing the Master. As a result of this friendly and cordial conversation, the Apostles get over their fear and shame for having abandoned their Friend when He was most in need. Thus, Jesus restores his friendly relationship with the Apostles before he confers on them supernatural powers.[3] Thomas, however, is not with them. He is the only one missing. Why is he absent? Is it only a coincidence? It could be that St John the Evangelist, who narrates the scene in great detail, kept silent out of consideration for one who, after seeing Christ on the cross, not only suffered like the others, but may have gone off on his own, engulfed in a particular discouragement.[4]

Through the accounts of St Matthew and of St Mark, we know that Jesus told the apostles to leave right away for Galilee, where they were to behold him glorified. Why, then, did they stay eight more days in Jerusalem when there was nothing to keep them there? Perhaps they did not want to go without Thomas for whom they began to search immediately. They must have sought to convince him in a

---

[3] cf *The Navarre Bible,* note to John 20:19-20
[4] cf O. Hophan, *The Apostles,* Madrid 1982

thousand different ways that the Master would again be awaiting them beside the Sea of Tiberias. When at last they found Thomas, they exclaimed to him with irrepressible joy: *We have seen the Lord!*[5] They repeated it to him over and over again. They try everything to win Thomas back for Christ. Surely the Lord – the Good Shepherd who always seeks us out, each one of us – must have approved of this delay. Thomas must have thanked them for all their efforts on his behalf and for not having left him behind in Jerusalem, stubborn as he was! It is a lesson that can help us today to examine the quality of our fraternity and of our fortitude in dealing with our brother Christians who, like us, at any moment are quite capable of falling into discouragement and loneliness. We cannot abandon them.

1.2 His disbelief.

Bring your hand and feel the place of the nails, and do not be unbelieving but believing.[6]

The discouragement and disbelief of Thomas were not easy to overcome. At the insistence of the other apostles, he responds: *Unless I see the holes the nails made in his hands and can put my finger into the holes they made, and unless I can put my hand into his side, I refuse to believe.*[7] These words seem like a definitive, quite final answer. They are a harsh reply to the concern of his friends. But without a doubt the joy of the others opened the door to hope for him. How cheerful they must have been! For this reason he returned to their company for good. Thomas' dark stubbornness contrasts starkly with Jesus' magnanimity and his tremendous love for each person. The Lord would not permit any of his own to be lost: He has already prayed

---

[5] John 20:24
[6] *Communion Antiphon:* cf John 20:27
[7] John 20:25

for his disciples at the Last Supper and his prayer is always efficacious.[8] He personally intervenes and speaks even before Thomas does. St John relates: *Eight days later his disciples were again in the house and Thomas was with them.* At least they had succeeded in keeping him in their company. *When the doors were shut, Jesus came in and stood among them. 'Peace be with you,' he said. Then he addressed Thomas: 'Put your finger here, and see my hands; and put out your hand, and place it in my side; do not be unbelieving, but believe.'*[9]

It is inspiring to consider that the Lord will never leave us as long as we do not leave him first, since He has prayed for us also.[10] Those whom God has placed at our side will not fail to help us either. If at some point we find ourselves in the dark, no matter what the state of our soul we will be able to lean on the faith and example of the others and on the strength of their charity. We have the duty of attending to and looking out for those the Lord has placed at our side, those who share our same faith and ideals, if they are having a rough time. Living responsibility for the faithfulness of others will always be a great help for our own faithfulness. *Everything will go much better, and we will be happier, if we decide always to get to know better – so as to be able to love them more – the truth about the people to whom we are bound by ties of permanent responsibility. The surest guarantee of fidelity is to think about one's own responsibilities, to meditate on the influence that our example has on others, and to consider the harm that deserting them can cause. We should always maintain supernatural perspective: God is faithful and does not permit us*

---

[8] cf John 17:9
[9] John 20:26-27
[10] cf John 17:20

to be tempted beyond our strength (1 Cor 10:13).[11] The Lord will never give up on us. May we in our turn never give up on our neighbours. Let us remember that everyone, including ourselves, is susceptible to phases of blindness or discouragement. No one in our family or among our friends is ever to be considered lost since we count on the powerful help of charity, prayer, and grace which in such circumstances take on so many different manifestations.

1.3 His faith.

When Thomas encountered the risen Jesus, he opened up his heart: *My Lord and my God!* he exclaimed, moved to the very depths of his being. At the one and same time his reaction is an act of faith, of surrender, and of love. He openly confesses that Jesus is God and recognizes him as his Lord. Jesus answers him: *You believe because you can see me. Happy are those who have not seen and yet believe.*[12] St John Paul II commented: *This is the faith we should renew, following in the wake of innumerable Christian generations who for two thousand years have confessed Christ, the invisible Lord, even to the point of martyrdom. Like the many who have preceded us we should make the words of St Peter in his first Letter our own: 'You have not seen him, yet love him; now believing in him without seeing him, you feel an indescribable joy' (1 Pet 1:8). This is genuine faith – absolute dedication to things unseen, yet capable of ennobling and crowning an entire life.*[13]

From the moment of that encounter with Christ Thomas was a different man thanks in large part to the fraternal charity of the other apostles. His faithfulness to the Master was to be forever firm and unshakable, even

---

[11] J. Abad, *Fidelity,* Madrid 1987

[12] John 20:29

[13] John Paul II, *Address,* 9 April 1983

though it had once seemed impossible to maintain. Perhaps his spontaneous declaration of faith has frequently helped us make an act of faith – *My Lord and my God!* – as we pass before the tabernacle or during the consecration of the Mass. The example of Thomas stands out today as a reason for increased confidence in the Lord, who will never leave us; and for hope, if by the Will of God those closest to us go through times of wavering in their fidelity to him. The reassurance we offer then, together with the grace of God, will work miracles in such a situation.

Today we ask our Lord in the words of the Liturgy: *Grant us the grace to celebrate the feast of your Apostle Thomas with joy. Through his intercession may our lives be filled with faith in Jesus Christ your Son, whom your apostle recognized as his Lord and God.*

The Blessed Virgin, who was so close to the apostles during those days, attentively followed the evolution of Thomas' faith. Perhaps she was the one who stopped him from deserting altogether. Today we confide our fidelity and that of the ones God has placed under our care to Our Lady. Virgin most faithful... pray for them... pray for me.

11 July

2. SAINT BENEDICT

Patron Saint of Europe
Memorial

Benedict was born in Nursia, Italy about the year 480. After receiving an excellent education in Rome, he returned to Subiaco to live the life of a monk with some disciples he gathered together. He then established the famous monastery Montecassino and wrote his *Rule* for the monastic life. The volume continued to influence constitutions for religious life today. It has earned for Benedict the title 'The Father of Western Monasticism'. He died at Montecassino on March 21, 547. Since the end of the Eighth Century his feast has been celebrated on July 11. Benedict was proclaimed Patron Saint of Europe in 1964 for his enormous influence in establishing Christianity on the continent.

2.1 The Christian roots of Europe.

During the fifteenth centennial commemoration of St Benedict's birth, St John Paul II recalled the *gigantic contribution* this saint made toward the formation of Europe.[1] It was a time when *the Church, civil society and Christian culture itself were in great danger. Through his sanctity and singular accomplishments, St Benedict gave testimony of the perennial youth of the Church.* Furthermore, *He and his followers drew the barbarians from paganism toward a civilized and truly enhanced way of life. The Benedictines guided them in building a peaceful, virtuous and productive society interwoven by bonds of fraternal concord.*[2]

---

[1] John Paul II, *Address,* 1 January 1980
[2] Pius XII, Encyclical, *Fulgens radiatur,* 21 March 1947

Benedict contributed hugely towards forming the essentially Christian soul and roots of Europe. Without Christianity neither our common culture nor our way of being can be explained or understood.[3] European identity itself is not intelligible without Christianity since *herein we find the common roots that have brought continental civilization to maturity – Europe's dynamism, activity and capacity for constructive expansion to other continents as well; in a word, all that constitutes her glory.*[4]

Today we have the misfortune of seeing a concerted and systematic effort to do away with the deeply Christian meaning of our existence, its most essential aspect. *On the one hand, the almost exclusive orientation towards the consumption of material goods robs human life of its deepest meaning. On the other hand, work often becomes an alienating experience, a constraint for man, subjected as it is to collectivism, since it is precipitously separated from prayer and deprived of its supernatural dimension.*[5] At times it seems as though entire nations are heading toward a new barbarism considerably worse than any other in history. Practical materialism *is now aggressively imposed on everyone in subtle ways. The most sacred principles that were a sure guide of individual and social behaviour – the sanctity of human life, the indissolubility of marriage, the authentic significance of human sexuality, the upright use of material goods made available by progress – are being displaced by false pretexts of freedom.*[6] It is not an exaggeration to realize that without the appropriate remedy the ideas crystallizing in many places will give way to a new pagan society. Due to the influence of a laicism which

---

[3] cf L. Suarez, *Christian roots of Europe*, Madrid 1986
[4] John Paul II, *Address*, 9 November 1982
[5] *idem*, *Address*, 23 March 1980
[6] *idem*, *Address*, 29 September 1979

prescinds from any relation to God, the rights and duties of citizens are established in civil codes devised without any relation to objective moral law. This transformation is made compatible with an appearance of goodness that only deceives people deprived of religious formation or those who have already lost all awareness of human dignity.

In the face of this situation, St John Paul II has called us all on various occasions to a new evangelization of Western Europe and the world. Today, on the feast of St Benedict, let us examine our Christian perspective on life and the apostolic spirit that should inspire all our acts. Let us not forget that *as the third millenium of the Redemption draws near, God is preparing a great springtime for Christianity and we can already see its first signs.*[7] He wants us to be protagonists of this rebirth of the Faith. We will experience the joy of making Christ known among our families, our friends and colleagues... The Lord will reward our efforts with abundant graces so as to lead us to a greater intimacy with him.

2.2 The need for a new evangelization.

Confronted with a seemingly unsympathetic environment, many Christians have preferred to abstain from expressing whatever might clash with popular 'modern' or 'progressive' trends. One contemporary writer warns: *If for the sake of preserving friendships we decide to put bothersome issues in a parenthesis as it were, we surely run the risk of burying within ourselves that which is most essential to us,*[8] that is, the truth and meaning behind daily living.

No Christian can remain on the fringes of the great human questions confronting the world. *We cannot simply fold our arms when a subtle persecution condemns the*

---

[7] *idem,* Encyclical, *Redemptor missio,* 7 September 1990
[8] J. Guitton, *Silence on the essentials,* Valencia 1988

Church to die of neglect, putting it outside the sphere of public life, and above all obstructing its part in education, culture and family life.

These are not our rights; they are God's rights. He has entrusted them to us Catholics so that we may exercise them![9]

As this opposition becomes increasingly evident we have to realize the urgency of re-Christianizing the world, in particular the specific area, perhaps small, in which our own life unfolds. *Each one of us has seriously to ask: What can I do in my city, in my work place, my university, and any other environment I am in, to help Christ reign more effectively in souls? Consider this question in the presence of God, ask advice and pray. Then, set out with holy determination to win that particular domain for God.*[10]

The task of re-evangelizing the West is not within reach only of those with particular status or influence in public life. It is the responsibility of everyone. We will carry out the evangelization which this world of ours is so sorely in need of when we live as God wants, when mothers and fathers teach by example – generosity in the number of their children, their relationships with hired help and neighbours... – and when they show their children detachment from personal things, a sense of duty, temperance and a spirit of sacrifice in caring for the elderly and needy... Preachers and catechists cooperate in the re-Christianization of society by tirelessly teaching the complete message of Christ, without adding to it or leaving anything out; high schools, taking into account their foundational objectives, by truly educating students in the Christian spirit; businessmen, by avoiding immoral practices like unjust commissions, taking unfair advantage

---

[9] St. J. Escrivá, *Furrow,* 310
[10] A. del Portillo, *Letter,* 2 October 1985

of confidential information or contacts, or inserting advertisements in the news media that propagate ideas contrary to the faith... even if this entails certain economic disadvantages; and doctors, by refraining from medical procedures contrary to God's Law. As always our personal apostolate of friendship is fruitful in all circumstances.

2.3 The task of all – to do our part.

An ancient proverb proclaims *it is better to light one candle than to curse the darkness.* Complaining about the evils in society is not appropriate behaviour for the sons and daughters of God. If each Christian decides to carry out the task at hand to completion, we will change the world as the first Christians did. They were few, but they had a living and operative faith.

It's a big mistake not to do anything with the excuse perhaps that one can do so little. A letter in appreciation of a good article can encourage an editor or journalist to publish others along the same lines. Recommending a good book can be an occasion for the Holy Spirit to act in transforming a soul. Calmly speaking up to clarify a matter of doctrine can confirm someone in a point of faith... With the grace of God all of our actions can have unsuspected repercussions.

We have to realize that doing good is always more attractive than doing evil. To reach our goals we also need to count on the help of the Blessed Virgin Mary and the Holy Guardian Angels, and on the fortitude we derive from the Communion of Saints which affects even those souls most alienated from God. There are many reasons for being optimistic; *with a supernatural optimism, its roots sunk in the faith, nourished by hope and given wings by love. We have to imbue all strata of society with a Christian spirit. We cannot be satisfied with mere good desires. Each and every person, there where he works, can find God in his task, and needs to be concerned – through his prayer, mortification, and professional work well-finished – to sanctify himself and his work, and to sanctify others in the Truth so that Christ may be proclaimed Lord of all earthly activities.*[11] We can take advantage of every occasion, including business or recreational trips as did the first Christians who, *travelling, or settling in regions where Christ had not been proclaimed, bore courageous witness to their faith and founded the first communities.*[12]

Today we entrust St Benedict with this common task of re-Christianizing society. We ask his help to proclaim *the perennial youth of the Church* by our words and deeds. Above all we ask him to gain for us an increase in personal holiness, the foundation of all apostolate worthy of the name. *I see dawning* – St John Paul II pointed out – *a new missionary age, which will become a radiant day bearing an abundant harvest, if all Christians, missionaries and young Churches in particular, respond with generosity and holiness to the calls and challenges of our times.*[13]

Holy Mary, Queen of Europe and of the world, pray for all those who continue each day on their way towards Christ... pray for us.

---

[11] *idem, Letter,* 25 December 1985, 10
[12] John Paul II, Encyclical, *Redemptoris missio,* 82
[13] *ibid,* 92

16 July

3. OUR LADY OF MOUNT CARMEL

Memorial

The feast we celebrate today began in 1726. It commemorates the apparition of the Blessed Virgin on July 16, 1251 to St Simon Stock, the first General of the Carmelite Order.

Mary promised special blessings and indulgences throughout the centuries for all those who wear her scapular. This devotion began in England and has received the solemn approval of the Church and the constant blessings of the Popes.

Our Lady of Mount Carmel is the Patroness of sailors. She is always our sure haven in the midst of the storms of life.

3.1 Love for the Virgin and the scapular of Mount Carmel.

Devotion to Our Lady of Mount Carmel began with the Carmelite Order whose oldest tradition connects it with the following apparition in the Book of Kings: *Behold, a little cloud like a man's hand is rising out of the sea.*[1] People could see it from the summit of Mount Carmel while the prophet Elizah was beseeching the Lord to put an end to a long drought. The cloud quickly spread to cover the sky and brought abundant rain to the parched earth. Scripture scholars see this rain cloud as a type of the Blessed Virgin Mary.[2] By bringing the Saviour into the world she bore the living water to quench the thirst of all humanity, and she continually brings us countless graces.

The Blessed Virgin appeared to St Simon Stock on July 16, 1251. At that time she promised special graces and

---

[1] 1 Kings 18:44
[2] cf Professors of Salamanca, *Bible Commentary,* Madrid 1961

blessings to those who would wear the scapular. This devotion *has brought down a copious stream of spiritual and temporal graces upon the earth.*[3] The Church periodically renews her approval of this powerful devotion besides granting numerous other spiritual benefits. For centuries, Christians have sought refuge in this special protection of Our Lady. *Wear on your breast the holy scapular of Mount Carmel. There are many excellent Marian devotions, but few are as deep-rooted among the faithful and so richly blessed by the popes. Besides, how motherly is the sabbatine privilege.*[4]

Our Lady promised the grace to repent during the final moments of life to those who live and die wearing the scapular, or the blessed medal with the Sacred Heart and the Blessed Virgin of Carmel that can stand in its stead.[5] Among the other graces and indulgences, the so-called *sabbatine privilege* consists in our release from Purgatory on the Saturday following our death.[6] Truly, *by her maternal charity Mary cares for the brethren of her Son who still journey on earth surrounded by dangers and difficulties until such time as they are led into the eternal happiness of their true homeland...*[7] May we not forgo approaching Our Lady many times each day so that she may help and protect us. The scapular itself can frequently remind us that we are under the watchful vigilance of our heavenly mother, and that she is our own since we are her children who have cost her so dear.

---

[3] Pius XII, *Address,* 6 August 1950
[4] St. J. Escrivá, *The Way,* 500
[5] cf Innocent IV, Bull, *Ex parte dilectorum,* 13 January 1252
[6] cf John XXII, Bull, *Sacratissimo uticulmine,* 3 March 1322
[7] Second Vatican Council, *Lumen gentium,* 62

3.2 The special help and graces from Our Lady at the hour of death.

In this devotion we express a personal dedication of ourselves and all that is ours to Our Lady, since *during the apparition in which the most Holy Virgin gave the scapular to St Simon Stock the Mother of God manifested herself as 'Mother of divine grace' and also as 'Mother most lovable' who protects her children throughout life and at the moment of death.*

The Christian faithful are accustomed to venerating Our Lady of Mount Carmel through devotion to the holy scapular. She, the Mother of God and our mother, offers us the following pledge in reward for our commitment to her: 'Throughout life I protect; at the hour of death I lend assistance; and after death I save.' [8] She is *our life, our sweetness and our hope* as we have so often recited in reciting the Hail Holy Queen.

The scapular devotion is a manifestation of our confidence in the maternal aid of the Blessed Virgin. In the same way that trophies and medals are used to signify friendship, remembrance or triumph, we give a heartfelt significance to the scapular so as frequently to remind ourselves of our love for our Mother Mary and of her watchful protection. She takes us by the hand and leads us along by *a sure path* every day of our life. She helps us to overcome every difficulty and temptation and will never abandon us *since it is her practice to favour those who long to be protected by her.* [9]

Some day the hour of our definitive encounter with God will arrive. Then we will need her protection and help more than ever. Devotion to Our Lady of Mount Carmel and to her holy scapular is a sure sign of hope in heaven since our

---

[8] Card. Goma, *The Blessed Virgin Mary,* Barcelona 1947

[9] St Teresa of Avila, *Foundations,* 23,4

Blessed Mother prolongs her maternal protection after our death. Such a broad privilege fills our hearts with consolation. *Mary guides us toward the eternal future; she helps us desire and discover it. She gives us her hope, assurance and desire. Inspired by such a splendid reality and with unspeakable joy we can persevere in our humble and perhaps wearisome earthly pilgrimage. Mary will light up our way and transform it into a sure path to Paradise – 'iter para tutum'.*[10] There with the grace of God we will one day see her.

When Cardinal Medici was elected Pope in 1605 he took the name Leo XI. While vesting him in the papal garments his attendants wanted to remove a large scapular of Our Lady of Mount Carmel which he wore with his clothes. At that moment the Pope told those who were helping him to vest: 'Leave me Mary, so that Mary won't leave me.' We do not want to leave her either since we are so much in need of her help. That is why we always wear her scapular. Let us tell her now that whenever the final moments of our life arrive we will abandon ourselves into her loving arms. We have so often asked her to pray for us *now and at the hour of our death* that she will never forget to grant our request.

During his visit to Santiago de Compostela in Spain, St John Paul II expressed this desire for all the faithful: *May Our Lady of Mount Carmel be with you always. May she be the Star that guides you and never disappears from your horizon. May she lead you now, throughout your life and at its completion to a safe haven.*[11] Hand in hand with Mary we will arrive in her Son's presence. If we need further purification she will hasten us toward the moment when we are completely purified and can enjoy the eternal vision of God.

---

[10] Bl. Paul VI, *Address,* 15 August 1966
[11] John Paul II, *Address,* 9 November 1982

In the Middle Ages Our Lady of Mount Carmel used to be shown surrounded by souls engulfed in the flames of Purgatory, in order to depict her special intercession for those undergoing the purification they need.[12] *The Virgin serves the souls in Purgatory well because she secures them relief,*[13] as St Vincent Ferrer frequently preached. Our love for her will help us to be purified in our present life so we can be with her Son immediately after death.

3.3 The scapular is a symbol of the wedding garment.

The scapular is also an image of *the wedding garment,* divine grace, that must always clothe our soul.

While speaking to young people in a parish in Rome appropriately dedicated to Our Lady of Mount Carmel, St John Paul II recalled in an intimate way the special help and protection he himself received from the Blessed Mother through his devotion to Our Lady of Mount Carmel. *I should tell you* – he said to them – *that in my youth, when I was about your age, she helped me a great deal. I cannot say to what degree exactly, but I believe it was to a very great extent. She helped me to gain the grace proper to my age in life, the grace to understand my vocation.*

He reminded his listeners that the mission of Our Lady, the one prefigured long ago in the Old Testament and which begins on *Mount Carmel in the Holy Land, is associated with a piece of clothing. This garment is called the holy scapular. I owe a great deal in my early youth to my devotion to the Carmelite scapular. A mother's constant diligence and concern for the clothes of her children is beautiful to see. She always wants them well-dressed. When her children's garments are torn the mother makes an*

---

[12] cf M. Trens, Mary: Iconography of the Virgin in Spanish art, Madrid 1946

[13] St Vincent Ferrer, Sermon on the Nativity, II

effort to repair them. The Blessed Mother of Mount Carmel and of the holy scapular speaks to us of her maternal care, her concern to clothe us spiritually with the grace of God and to help us always keep our garments white.

The Pope made mention in his Address of the white garment the first-century catechumens wore as a symbol of the sanctifying grace they would receive with Baptism. After exhorting the young people to strive always to keep their souls clean, he concluded: *Be vigilant to correspond to your good Mother who is concerned about how you go about dressed, especially with respect to the garment of grace that her daughters and sons should always wear.*[14] This is the *wedding garment* that we will one day present for our final espousal to enter everlasting life.

The scapular of Mount Carmel can help us to love our Mother in heaven more. It is a special reminder for us that we are dedicated to her and that in whatever moment of trouble, in the midst of temptation, we can count on her help. Having her so close to us will permit us to be strong. In the words of the Opening Prayer for today's feast, we ask Our Lord: *'Recordare, virgo Mater Dei...ut loquaris pro nobis bona'. Remember, Blessed Virgin Mother of God...to speak well on our behalf before the Lord,*[15] especially on the days when we have not been as faithful as God expects his children to be.

---

[14] John Paul II, *Address*, 15 January 1989
[15] *Graduale Romanum, in loc*, p.580

22 July

4. SAINT MARY MAGDALENE

Memorial

Mary was originally from Magdala, a small city of Galilee on the northwest shore of Lake Tiberias. She was one of a group of women who followed Jesus and cared for him out of their own possessions. Mary Magdalene was present with Jesus on Calvary and she was the second one, after the Blessed Mother, to behold the risen Saviour on Easter morning. She recognized Him when on Our Lord called her by name.

Devotion to this most constant follower of Christ spread throughout the Western world during the Middle Ages. Most probably she is not the same Mary who out of sincere contrition pours out precious ointment on our Lord's feet at the home of Simon the Pharisee.

4.1 Mary Magdalene exemplifies our search for God at every moment.

O God, you are my God and for you I long. For you my soul is thirsting. My soul pines for you like the dry, parched earth.[1] We read these words in the Responsorial Psalm of today's Mass and they remind us of the steadfast faith of Mary Magdalene. After nearly twenty centuries the delicacy, fidelity and love of this stalwart follower of Jesus are still deeply moving.

St John narrates for us in the Gospel of the Mass how this woman set out for the tomb as soon as the Sabbath rest permitted, *when it was still dark,*[2] to go to find the dead body of our Lord. Some time previously he had freed her

---

[1] *Responsorial Psalm:* Ps 62:2
[2] John 20:1-2

of an evil spirit,[3] and grace quickly bore fruit in her soul.
She followed the Master faithfully on some of his apostolic
journeys and served him generously with all her possessions. During the terrible moments of the crucifixion she
remained on Calvary near the one who cured her of all that
was wrong in her life.[4] Furthermore when they lay Jesus in
the tomb she stayed close and kept him company as we
may have done at some point on the occasion of a loved
one's death. St Matthew attests to her courage: *Mary
Magdalene and the other Mary were seated there in front
of the tomb.*[5]

When the Sabbath was over, *as the first day of the
week began to dawn,*[6] she set out with the other holy
women for the place where the dead body of Jesus was
lying, in order to anoint it. But the Lord was no longer
there. He had risen! She saw the heavy stone rolled away
and the tomb empty. *Then she began to run to Simon and
the other disciple whom Jesus loved and said to them:
'They have taken the Lord out of the tomb, and we do not
know where they have laid him.'*[7] Peter and John went running toward the empty sepulchre. St John tells us that this
moment was crucial in his life: *he saw and believed.*[8] Both
apostles *went back to their home again,*[9] but Mary stayed
there weeping, in the absence of the Master's Body. With
unspeakable sadness, still not believing in the Resurrection,
she perseveres in her vigil, not wanting to tear herself away
from the place where she last saw our Saviour.

Today we consider *the intensity of the love burning in*

---

[3] Luke 8:2
[4] cf Matt 27:56
[5] Matt 27:61
[6] cf Matt 28:1
[7] John 20:2
[8] cf John 20:8
[9] John 20:10

the heart of the woman who did not leave the tomb, although the disciples had already gone away. She continued to seek the one she had failed to find. She sought for him in tears and, inflamed with the fire of love, was burning with longing to see the One she thought they had taken away. Because Mary Magdalene remained there with the expectation of finding him, she was the only one to then encounter him. Perseverance strengthens good deeds and as the voice of Truth informs us: 'Whoever perseveres to the end will be saved.'[10] Let us not stop seeking Jesus in every circumstance of our lives; even during those moments in which, if the Lord so permits, discouragement or darkness penetrate our soul. Let us never forget that he is always very much in touch with the events of our life though we may not be aware of him. He is always close at hand, for as the Apostle assures us – *'Dominus prope est!'* – the Lord is near. *I shall walk with him, therefore, quite confidently, for the Lord is my Father... and with his help I shall fulfil his most lovable Will, even if I find it hard.*[11]

4.2 She recognizes Jesus when he calls her by her name. Her joy before the risen Christ.

Through her perseverance and great love in seeking him, Mary Magdalene received the grace of being the first person to whom Christ appeared.[12] At first she didn't recognize him, despite his being right beside her. St John tells us *she turned around and saw Jesus standing there, but she did not know that it was Jesus.*[13] Even though He spoke to her, she didn't immediately realize it was Christ – alive! – there at her side. *Woman* – the Lord said to her –

---

[10] *Liturgy of the Hours,* Second Reading, St Gregory the Great, *Homilies on the Gospels,* 25,1-2

[11] St. J. Escrivá, *Furrow,* 53

[12] cf Mark 16:9

[13] John 20:14

why are you weeping? Who is it you are seeking?[14] Mary's
tears prevented her from seeing the Master, who, we guess,
was smiling, being happy over the encounter. He glances at
us too, as we continue to seek him out in the midst of all
the circumstances and events of our lives, for Christ is the
same now as then. *Supposing him to be the gardener, she
said to him: 'Sir, if you have removed him, tell me where
you have laid him, and I will go and take him away'.*[15]
Then Jesus called her by name the way he used to: *Jesus
said to her: Mary.*[16] The dark clouds oppressing her heart
for the last three days all of a sudden were dispersed. *How
many interior sufferings, how many torments of the spirit
caused by great love and apparently without consolation
are frequently dissolved* – and how often! – *like the surf of
a wave, at one word from Jesus.*[17] And like a river bursting
its banks, as if it had all been a nightmare, Mary looks at
him and says *'Rabboni!' (which means Teacher).*[18] As
though the connotation of this familiar term were a moving
reality incapable of translation, St John wanted to leave us
the precise Hebrew word the Magdalene often used to
address Christ.

She sought him among the dead – comments St
Augustine – *and he presented himself alive. How is it He is
alive? He calls her by name, 'Mary', and she responds the
instant she hears her name spoken: 'Rabboni'. The
gardener could have said, 'Who is it you seek? Why are
you crying?' 'Mary', on the other hand, only Christ could
have said in that way. He called her by her name, the same
One who called her to the kingdom of heaven. He spoke the
name – Mary – He had written in the Book of Life, and she*

---

[14] John 20:15
[15] John 20:15
[16] John 20:16
[17] M.J. Indart, *Jesus in his world*, Barcelona 1963
[18] John 20:16

– 'Rabboni' – which means 'Teacher'. She already recognized the one who had illuminated her so that she could recognize him: she already saw Christ in the one in whom before she perceived a gardener. The Lord said to her: 'Do not touch me for I have not yet ascended to my Father' (John 20:17).[19]

How our burdens disappear when we make an effort to discover Jesus alive and glorious at our side, calling us by our name! What a great joy for us to be on familiar terms with Christ and to be able to call on him in the particular way He knows so well. Prayer – dialogue with the Lord – is our most profound blessing and the foundation of our entire life. May we never stop seeking his company, even if at times we do not perceive his presence. If we persevere in prayer He will always come out to meet us, calling us by our name. Closely united to Jesus we will recover our peace and joy. One word from Him will restore our hope and renew our desire to begin again. Let us never forget in any situation that *the Lord's triumph on the day of the Resurrection is final. Where are the soldiers the rulers put on guard? Where are the seals they affixed to the stone of the tomb? Where are those who condemned the Master and those who crucified Jesus? He is victorious, and these poor wretches have fled away...*

Be filled with hope: Jesus Christ is always victorious.[20] He conquers even in the battles of our own life. He triumphs over those defects and weaknesses of ours which at times seem insurmountable.

4.3 Mary Magdalene is sent by our Lord to the Apostles. The joy of the apostolate.

After consoling Mary, Jesus gave her a message for

---

[19] St Augustine, *Sermon 246*, 3-4
[20] St. J. Escrivá, *The Forge*, 660

the apostles whom he very affectionately called *brothers*.
Then *Mary went and said to the disciples, 'I have seen the
Lord'*; and she told them all that had happened.[21] We can
imagine Mary's joy upon saying the words: *I have seen the
Lord!* This is the joy and happiness of all apostolate worthy
of the name in which we proclaim to others in countless
ways the fact that Jesus is alive today. St Thomas Aquinas
comments: *Through this woman, who was eminently
steadfast in finding out about the burial place of Christ, is
prefigured every person who yearns to know divine truth
and is therefore well-disposed to pass on the knowledge of
such a grace to others, just as Mary announced it to the
disciples so that she could not be reprimanded for hiding
her talent.* The Angelic doctor concludes: *God has not
granted us this joy in order for you to hide it in the
recesses of your hearts, but to share it with those who are
capable of love,*[22] unfurling it to the four winds. Whoever
finds Christ, finds him for everyone. The news of the
resurrection spread like wildfire during the first centuries:
Christians were conscious of being bearers of the *Good
News*. The disciples rejoiced over the One who died for us
and rose again on the third day *as He said.* They were
happy people in the midst of a sad world. Their joy, like
ours, stems from always being near the living Christ.
Apostolate is always the communication of this joyful
message, the most cheerful message of all.

Today we ask St Mary Magdalene to gain for us a
share in her loving perseverance in seeking the Lord: *O
God, whose Only Begotten Son entrusted Mary Magdalene
before all others with announcing the great joy of the
Resurrection, grant, we pray, that through her intercession
and example we may proclaim the living Christ and come*

---

[21] cf John 20:18
[22] St Thomas, in *Catena Aurea*, VIII, p.400

to see him reigning in your glory.[23] In heaven we will also contemplate Mary, the Mother of God and our Mother, who has never left our side. With a special joy we shall see all those to whom we shall have so often borne witness through our friendship that the risen Christ continues to be present among us.

[23] *Collect* of the Mass

25 July

5. SAINT JAMES

Apostle

Feast

James, from Bethsaida, was the son of Zebedee and the brother of John. He was one of the three disciples to witness the Transfiguration and the agony in the Garden besides other important events of our Saviour's public life. He and his brother's impetuous zeal caused the Lord to name them the *Sons of Thunder*.

James developed his apostolate in Judaea and Samaria. According to tradition he preached the Gospel in Spain. On his return to Palestine about the year 44, he became the first Apostle to suffer martyrdom, at the order of Herod Agrippa. His mortal remains were later brought to Santiago de Compostela, in Spain, which became a popular medieval pilgrimage site and a sanctuary of the Faith for all of Europe.

5.1 To drink from the cup of the Lord.

Walking by the Sea of Galilee, Jesus saw James and John, the sons of Zebedee, mending their nets, and called to them, giving them the name 'Boanerges' which means 'Sons of Thunder'.[1]

It all began when a few fishermen on Lake Tiberias were called by Jesus of Nazareth to follow him. They responded to Jesus' call, followed him, and lived with him for nearly three years. They shared his daily life and were witnesses of his prayer, his mercy toward sinners and those who suffer, and his power. They listened attentively to his words, the like of which they never heard before.

---

[1] cf Matt 4:18-21; Mark 3:17

In the three years they spent together, the disciples experienced a reality that was to possess them forever; in a word, 'life with Jesus'. It was an experience that broke the threads of their prior existence; they had to leave everything – their family, their trade, and their possessions – to follow Him. In short, they were introduced to a new way of living.[2]

One day Jesus invited James to follow him. He was the brother of John and the son of Salome, a woman who served Jesus with all she had and ultimately was present on Calvary. James knew Jesus before he was called. Together with Peter and his brother, this apostle enjoyed a special predilection from our Lord. He was one of the three present at the Transfiguration on Mount Tabor.[3] He was present at the raising of Jairus' daughter too, and was one of the three who accompanied the Master in Gethsemane toward the beginning of the Passion.[4] Our Lord was so taken by the impetuous zeal of James and John that he nicknamed them *Boanerges*, the sons of thunder.

The Gospel of the Mass narrates for us a singular event in the life of this Apostle. Jesus had just finished speaking about his impending Passion and death in the Holy City: *Behold we are going up to Jerusalem* – He told them – *and the Son of Man will be given over to the chief priests and the scribes, and they will condemn him to death, and deliver him over to the Gentiles to be mocked and scourged and crucified, and he will be raised on the third day.*[5] Our Lord feels the need to share with his disciples the innermost sentiments that fill his soul. *Then the mother of the sons of Zebedee drew near to him with*

[2] C. Caffarra, *Living in Christ,* Ignatius 1987, pp.15-16
[3] Matt 17:1 ff
[4] Matt 26:37
[5] Matt 20:17-19

her sons and bowed down at his feet to make a request.[6]
She asks him to reserve two eminent places for her sons in
his seemingly imminent kingdom. Jesus turns to the
brothers and asks them if they can share the same fate with
him. He offers them *his cup.* To offer another one's own
chalice to drink from was considered a great sign of friendship in antiquity. They immediately respond: *We can!*[7]
*These words express generous docility. They reflect an
attitude that belongs to all the young at heart and to all
Christians, especially those who are willing to be apostles
of the 'Good News'.*[8] Jesus accepts the generous response
of the two disciples straightaway and tells them: *Yes, you
will drink from my cup,*[9] you will participate in my sufferings, and you will complete my Passion in your own
bodies. Soon thereafter, in the year 44 A.D., James was to
die by decapitation. John was tried with innumerable
sufferings and persecutions throughout his long life.

Ever since Christ redeemed us on the Cross all
Christian suffering consists in *drinking from the cup of the
Lord* through participation in his Passion, Death and
Resurrection. By means of our suffering, we complete in a
certain way his Passion that is thus prolonged in time with
its saving fruits.[10] Human suffering becomes redemptive
when it is closely associated with the ignominy the Lord
endured. In his mercy he lets us share his cup. In the face
of difficulties, sickness or pain, Jesus puts the same
question to us: *Can you drink from my cup?* If we are
united to him, we will respond positively and bear what is
humanly disagreeable for his sake. In union with Christ
even our pain and failure are converted into joy and peace.

---

[6] Matt 20:20
[7] Matt 20:22
[8] John Paul II, *Address,* 9 November 1982
[9] Acts 12:2
[10] cf Col 1:24

The great Christian revolution has been to convert pain into fruitful suffering, to turn a bad thing into something good. We have deprived the devil of this weapon, and with it we can conquer eternity.[11]

5.2 Not becoming discouraged by personal weaknesses. Seeking the Lord's strength.

From the time James made his not entirely noble ambitions known until the hour of his martyrdom there is a long interior development. That same zeal of his, earlier directed against the Samaritans who did not want to receive Jesus – *the people would not receive Him because his face was set toward Jerusalem*[12]– was later to be transformed into a zealous concern for souls. Little by little, without losing the vigour of his own personality, James learned that zeal for divine interests cannot be violent or bitter. The glory of God alone is the only worthwhile ambition. Clement of Alexandria relates how when the Apostle of Spain was taken before the tribunal to be judged, his integrity was so apparent that his accuser approached him afterwards to ask his pardon. James thought about it... and then embraced him, saying: *Peace be with you.*[13] The two of them together then received the crown of martyrdom.

While meditating on the life of the Apostle James, it helps a great deal for us to see evidence of his defects and those of the other eleven the Lord had chosen. They were not powerful, or wise or even simple. We see them at times being ambitious and argumentative,[14] and short of faith.[15] James, however, was to be the first apostle to be

---

[11] St. J. Escrivá, *Furrow,* 887
[12] Luke 9:53
[13] cf Clement of Alexandria, *Hypotyposes,* VII, quoted by Eusebius, *Ecclesiastical History,* 11,9
[14] Luke 22:24-47
[15] Matt 14:31

martyred.[16] Clearly, the help of God can work wonders in us. How thankful to God James will be in heaven for leading him along paths quite different from the ones he dreamed of earlier in life. Since the Lord is good, infinitely wise, and loving beyond what we can realize, on many occasions He does not give us what we ask for, but what is most appropriate for us and therefore the best.

Like the other Apostles, James has clear and undeniable defects and weaknesses that are clearly seen in the gospel accounts. Nevertheless, together with these shortcomings he had a great soul and a big heart. Jesus was always patient with him and the others too. The Master allowed them time for them to learn the lessons He imparted with divine wisdom and affection. *Let us examine* – writes St John Chrysostom – *how our Lord's way of questioning is equivalent to an exhortation and a stimulus. He does not say: Can you bear defeat? Are you capable of shedding your blood? His words are: 'Can you drink from the cup...' To encourage them to the task he adds: '...from which I am to drink?' The prospect of drinking from the Lord's very cup leads them to a more generous response. He gives the name 'baptism' to his Passion, to emphasize that his sufferings would be the cause of a great purification for the whole world.*[17]

The Lord has also called us. May we not give in to discouragement if our defects and weaknesses become manifest. If we approach Jesus for help, He will give us the courage to continue on our path with greater fidelity since He is ever patient and allows us the time we need to improve.

---

[16] cf Acts 12:2
[17] *Liturgy of the Hours, Second Reading*, St John Chrysostom, *Homilies on St Matthew's Gospel*, 65,3-4

5.3 Approaching the Virgin during difficulties.

In the *Second Reading* of the Mass St Paul reminds us: *We bear this treasure in vessels of clay so that it may be clearly seen that our power comes from God and not from ourselves.*[18] We are rather fragile creatures and not very constant, but nevertheless we are capable of bearing in ourselves an incomparable treasure since God works marvels in men despite their weaknesses. So as to show that it is He who acts and grants efficacy to our desires, the Lord wants *to choose the weak to confound the strong, and the vile and scorned of the world as well as those who are naught to destroy the things that are, lest any human flesh should pride itself before the Creator.*[19] Amazingly enough, one who was formerly a persecutor of the Church of God wrote these words, filled with humility.

We Christians, by bearing God in our soul, can live at the same time both *in heaven and on earth, divinised, but knowing that we are of the world and made of clay – an earthenware pot which Our Lord has deigned to use in his service – with the frailty that is typical of such fragile material. And when the vessel is cracked or broken, we will seek the seals that are put on pitchers in need of repair so that they may continue to be useful. Like the Prodigal Son we will say 'Father, I have sinned against You...'*[20]

God grants efficacy to those who have the humility to feel themselves as *vessels of clay,* the ones who bear in their own body the mortification of Jesus,[21] and who drink from the cup of the Passion which Jesus drank.

Tradition recalls the Apostle's preaching throughout Spain. His great zeal for souls led him to the very limits of

---

[18] 2 Cor 4:7
[19] 1 Cor 1:27-29
[20] S. Bernal, *Monsignor Josemaria Escrivá: A Profile of the Founder of Opus Dei*, Scepter, London 1977, p.342
[21] cf *Second Reading*: 2 Cor 4:10

the known world. We also learn from accounts passed on
to us of the difficulties he encountered in the beginnings of
his evangelizing, and how Our Lady appeared to him to
offer encouragement. It is possible that we too may feel
disheartened on occasion and baffled by the obstacles that
obstruct our desires to bring other souls to Christ. We may
also encounter misunderstanding, mockery and opposition
of all sorts, but Jesus never will never abandon us. We will
approach the Lord and be able to tell him with the
confidence of St Paul: *We are sore pressed, but not
destitute; we endure persecution, but are not forsaken; we
are cast down, but never perish...*[22] We shall also seek the
intercession of our Mother Mary. In her we will find the
courage and joy to proceed on our way like the Apostle
James.

---

[22] *Second Reading*: 2 Cor 4:8

26 JULY

6. SAINTS JOACHIM AND ANNE

Parents of the Blessed Virgin Mary
Memorial

An ancient tradition from the second century attributes the names of Joachim and Anne to the parents of the Blessed Virgin. Devotion to them is a prolongation of the piety with which the faithful have always approached the intercession of their daughter our Mother Mary. Pope Leo XIII created this joint feast, which was celebrated individually up until the most recent liturgical reform.

6.1 The home of the Virgin's parents.

Let us praise Joachim and Anne, to whom, in their generation, the Lord gave him who was a blessing for all the nations.[1]

A very ancient tradition has preserved for us the names of Mary's parents, who were, *in their time and historical circumstances, a precious foundational stone in the fulfilment of the salvation of mankind.*[2] Through them, the blessing that God promised Abraham and his descendants has reached us, since we received the Saviour through their cooperation. St John Damascene affirms that we know the blessed couple by their fruits: the Virgin Mary is the resplendent fruit they gave to humanity. Saint Anne conceived her, most pure and immaculate, in her womb. *Oh, most beautiful, most lovable child!* – the holy Doctor exclaims – *Oh, daughter of Adam and Mother of God! Blessed be the womb that bore you! Blessed be the arms that held you, the lips that had the privilege of kissing*

---

[1] *Entrance Antiphon*
[2] John Paul II, *Address*, 26 July 1983

you...[3] Saints Joachim and Anne had the immense privilege of caring for the Mother of God in their own home. The Lord must have poured out many graces on them throughout this time. St Teresa of Avila, who used to put the monasteries she founded under the protection of St Joseph and St Anne, argues: *The mercy of God is so great he will never fail to favour the homes of his glorious grandmother.*[4] Jesus descended directly from the maternal side of the faithful parents whose feast we celebrate today.

We can entrust the mother and father of Our Lady with all our needs, especially the ones that have to do with the sanctity of our homes. *Lord, God of our fathers* – we pray in the Liturgy of the Mass – *you gave Saints Joachim and Anne the privilege of being the parents of Mary, the mother of your Incarnate Son. May their prayers help us to attain the salvation you have promised to your people.*[5] Help us to be vigilant on behalf of those you have put under our care. Teach us how to create a human and supernatural tone for our surroundings, in which it will be easier to find you, our last end and our treasure.

6.2 Christian families.

St John Paul II taught that Saints Joachim and Anne are *a constant source of inspiration in everyday family and social life. Pass on to one another* – he exhorts – *from one generation to the next, the entire spiritual legacy of Christian life including prayer.*[6] Mary received the treasure of traditions of the House of David, which had been passed on for generations, from her parents at home. Here Our Lady learned to address her Father God with profound

---

[3] *Liturgy of the Hours*, St John Damascene, *About the Nativity of the Virgin*
[4] cf M. Auclair, *Teresa of Avila*, p.316
[5] *Opening Prayer*
[6] John Paul II, *Address*, 21 June 1983

reverence. In this home she learned of the prophecies referring to the coming of the Messiah – the place of his birth...

Mary surely remembered the home of her parents when it came time to set up her own home when Jesus was to be born. The Lord then learned from his mother popular ways of speaking and sayings full of wisdom which he later employed in his preaching. The child Jesus piously heard from her motherly lips the first prayers the Hebrews taught their children as soon as they could speak. What a good teacher Our Lady must have been! With what tenderness did she reflect the richness of her own soul so full of grace. It is likely that we also have received the inestimable gift of Faith and countless good customs from ancestors who have conserved and transmitted them in turn as a treasure. At the same time, we have the gracious duty of maintaining this living patrimony in order to pass it on to others.

Currently, when attacks against the family seem stronger than ever, we will need to practise fortitude to conserve the inheritance we have received. We are also called to enrich it through our faith and our struggle to live all of the human virtues. It is our duty to make God present in our homes too by means of those everyday Christian customs; blessings at meals, night prayers with the youngest children..., reading some passage from the Gospel with the oldest, saying a brief prayer for the deceased, remembering the intentions of the family and of the Pope, attending Mass together on Sundays... and reciting the Rosary, the prayer the Roman Pontiffs have so often recommended as a family prayer. It can be said in keeping with the family schedule or at times while travelling ... It is not necessary to have many family acts of piety, but it would be unnatural for a family of all, or mostly all, believers not to have some. Parents who pray with their children have an easier time finding a way to their hearts. Also, young people never forget the help of their parents in teaching them to pray and go to the Virgin for all kinds of needs. How thankful we are for the prayers our parents taught us as children and for the practical ways we can have recourse to Jesus in the Blessed Sacrament...! Without a doubt these lessons are the greatest inheritance we could receive.

The present circumstances in society call for families to be coherent in their beliefs and generous in their behaviour. It will be very pleasing to our Mother Mary for us to renew the resolution we have often made to try to be instruments of unity among the various members of our family, mostly through our cheerful deeds of service and the small daily sacrifices we make to help the others. Such a determination will lead us to pray for the person in the family who needs it most, to give the weakest or the member who is perhaps weakening greater attention, and to be especially affectionate with whichever one may be sick or troubled.

6.3 The education of the children. Family prayer.

Saints Joachim and Anne must often have thought God was asking something great from their daughter who showed herself to be so humanly and supernaturally gifted. They offered her up to God, as the Hebrews used to do with their offspring. Parents who strengthen their love for each other through prayer will respect the will of God for their children. Their love will be strengthened even more if these receive a vocation of full dedication to God. Often they will ask our Lord for this grace and desire it, since as St Josemaría Escrivá used to say: *Giving up one's children to the service of God is not a sacrifice: It is an honour and a joy,*[7] the greatest honour and the greatest joy. The children *will experience the beauty of dedicating their*

---

[7] St. J. Escrivá, *Furrow,* 22

energies to the kingdom of God, since in many ways they have already learned to do so through their family life.

Love which leads to marriage can also be a marvellous divine way, a vocation, a path for a complete dedication to our God.[8] This love must be efficacious and operative regarding its fruit, the children. True love will be clearly seen in the effort to teach them how to be hard-working, temperate and educated in the fullest sense of the word... and in this way to be good Christians. May the human virtues take root in them: strength of character, sobriety in the use of material goods, responsibility, generosity, industriousness... and may they learn to spend money frugally, keeping in mind the want many in the world presently suffer.

True love for the children will lead parents to take an interest in the school they attend, particularly their religious training, since their very salvation may depend on it. This same love will move parents to look for a suitable place for vacation and leisure time – often sacrificing personal tastes and interests and avoiding those surroundings that make the practice of a truly Christian life difficult. Parents should never forget that they are administrators of an immense treasure for God. As Christians, they form a family in which Christ is present.

Today we ask Saints Joachim and Anne to help us make our Christian homes places where God can easily be found. Let us approach our Lady's intercession too. St John Paul II encouraged us: *United together, let us raise our hearts to Mary. Through your mediation, daughter and Mother, show yourself to be the Mother of us all. Offer up our prayer so that Christ, who has become your Son, may kindly accept it.*[9]

---

[8] *Conversations with Monsignor Escrivá*, 121
[9] John Paul II, *Address*, 10 December 1978

29 July

7. SAINT MARTHA

Memorial

Martha lived with her sister and brother, Mary and Lazarus, in Bethany near Jerusalem. Toward the end of his public life the Lord would often stay at the home of these close friends. Strong bonds of affection closely unite the three to Jesus.

7.1 Love for the Master and confidence in his help.

The feast of St Martha is another occasion for us to enter into the home that was so often graced by the presence of Jesus in Bethany. There in the family formed by Martha, Mary and Lazarus, the Lord found affection and also rest for his body, tired out as it often was by never-ending travels through outlying towns and cities. Jesus sought refuge among his friends, especially during those final days when he more frequently encountered misunderstanding and scorn, particularly from the Pharisees The sentiments of the Master towards his friends at Bethany are expressed by St John in his Gospel account: *Now Jesus loved Martha, and her sister and Lazarus.*[1] They were indeed true friends!

The Gospel of the Mass[2] recounts Jesus' visit to the home of this family four days after Lazarus had died. Before He arrived there, when Lazarus was already gravely ill, the sisters, full of confidence, had sent the Master this message: *Lord, behold, the one whom you love is sick.*[3] Jesus, then in Galilee, a few days journey away, *when he*

---

[1] John 11:5
[2] John 11:17-27
[3] John 11:3

heard that he was sick, he remained two more days in the same place. Then afterwards, He said to his disciples: 'Let us go into Judaea'.[4] When He arrived, Lazarus had already been four days in the tomb.

Martha, always attentive and active, realized probably even before Jesus reached the house that he was getting close, and went out immediately to greet him. Despite the Lord's apparent lack of response to their plea for help, her love and confidence had not been diminished. *Lord –* Martha tells him – *if you were here, my brother would not have died.*[5] She upbraids him with great sensitivity for not having arrived earlier. Martha was hoping for her brother's cure when he was still sick. And Jesus, with a friendly gesture, perhaps with a smile on his lips, surprised her: *Your brother will rise again,* he says.[6] Martha receives these words of consolation, but understanding the final resurrection by his words she answers him: *I know that he will rise again at the resurrection on the last day.*[7] The response provokes an amazing declaration from Jesus regarding his divinity: *I am the Resurrection and the Life; he who believes in me, though he die, shall live, and whoever lives and believes in me shall never die.*[8] And he asks her: *Do you believe this?* Who could resist the sovereign authority of this declaration? *I am the Resurrection and the Life...I....* I am the reason for being of all that exists. Jesus is the Life, not only the Life that begins hereafter, but also the present one in which supernatural grace works in our souls while we are still wayfarers. These extraordinary words assure us and draw us closer and closer to Christ. They lead us to make Martha's

---

[4] John 11:67
[5] John 11:21
[6] John 11:23
[7] John 11:24
[8] John 11:25

response our own: *I believe you are the Christ, the Son of God, come into the world.*[9] Moments later, the Lord was to raise Lazarus from the dead.

We admire Martha's faith and want to imitate her in her trusting friendship with the Master. *Have you seen the affection and confidence with which Christ's friends treat him? In a completely natural way the sisters of Lazarus 'blame' Jesus for being away: 'We told you! If only you'd been here!'*

Speak to him with calm confidence: 'Teach us to treat you with the loving friendliness of Martha, Mary and Lazarus, as the first twelve treated you, even though at first they followed you perhaps for not very supernatural reasons'.[10]

7.2 The most Holy Humanity of Jesus.

Some time later, around the time of the Passover, Jesus visited these friends again: *Six days before the Passover, Jesus went to Bethany, where Lazarus lived, whom Jesus raised from the dead. There they made him a supper; Martha served, and Lazarus was one of those at table with him.*[11]

Martha served.... With what grateful love she must have done it. The Messiah was in her house; God was in need of her services. She was able to wait on him. God became man in order to identify with our human needs, so that we might learn to love him through his most Sacred Humanity and be able to become his intimate friends. We need to consider, time and time again, that the same Jesus of Nazareth, of Capharnaum and of Bethany eagerly awaits us in the nearest tabernacle. He is *in need* of our attention

---

[9] John 11:27
[10] St. J. Escrivá, *The Forge*, 495
[11] John 12:1-2

and services. *It is true that I always call our tabernacle Bethany. Become a friend of the Master's friends – Lazarus, Martha and Mary – and then you will no longer ask me why I call each of our tabernacles Bethany.*[12] There Christ is sacramentally present. We cannot remain indifferent. We need to visit him each day and keep him company, without hurry and without anxiety, during those precious moments of thanksgiving after we receive Holy Communion. How profitable this time can be for us!

St Thomas teaches that the Incarnation was the most effective and beneficial way for God to redeem mankind.[13] He adduces the following reasons: as far as faith is concerned – it became easier to believe, since God himself was the one speaking; as far as hope – by the great proof of his salvific will that this act of revelation represents; as far as charity – since *greater love than this no man has, that he lay down his life for his friends;*[14] and as far as actual deeds of love – since God himself was going to be our model. By taking on human flesh, God shows the tremendous value of every human creature; through his humility, he cures our pride...

Through the Sacred Humanity of Jesus, the love of God assumed human form for us. This act gently opens to us the way up an inclined plane that leads to union with God our Father. Therefore Christian life consists in loving, imitating and following Christ. We should be inspired by the example of his life and by our friendship with him.

Our sanctification should not have as its main focus the struggle against sin, something negative. It is not a question of avoiding evil, but of loving and imitating the

---

[12] St. J. Escrivá, *The Way,* 322
[13] cf St Thomas, *Summa Theologiae,* II, 1, 2
[14] John 15:13

Master who *passes by doing good...*[15] Christian life is
profoundly human. Our hearts have an important role in
the work of our sanctification since God has deigned to
become man. If we are lacking in affectionate care in our
life of piety and recklessly allow our heart free reign
among creatures, our personal friendship with the Master
will suffer and our strength of will not be enough for us to
push ahead on the narrow path of holiness. Therefore, we
need to make an effort to be always aware He is at our
side. We can use our imagination to represent the living
Christ, who was born in Bethlehem, worked in Nazareth,
and had friends whose company he sought out and truly
appreciated during his earthly life.

May we learn from Christ's friends to deal with him
from the standpoint of immense respect, since our Lord is
God. At the same time may we have recourse to him with
great confidence because He is our everyday Friend who
continually seeks us out and desires our company.

7.3 Friendship with our Lord makes the way easy for us.

On another occasion Jesus and his disciples stopped at
the house of his friends in Bethany en route to Jerusalem.
The two sisters were disposed to prepare what is necessary
to provide hospitality for the Master and those who were
accompanying him. But Mary, perhaps shortly after Jesus
arrived, sat down at his feet and *listened to his teaching*[16]
while Martha went on alone with the housework. Mary put
aside everything still left to do and gave all of her attention
to the Master. *The familiarity with which she settles down
at his feet, her habit of listening to him, and her hunger to
hear his words show that this is not a first encounter, but*

---

[15] Acts 10:38
[16] Luke 10:39

that there is a rare sympathy here.[17]

Martha was certainly not indifferent to the words of Jesus. She too was paying attention to him, but she was more occupied with the domestic chores. Without her realizing it, Jesus moves the conversation onto a higher plane. The very means at hand to attend him well absorb her. Left this way on her own, she begins to grow uneasy and perhaps feeling she is overburdened with work. In the meantime, she contemplates her sister at the feet of Jesus. Maybe a little upset, but with great confidence, she goes before Jesus, St Luke recounts, and addresses him: *Lord, don't you care that my sister has left me to serve alone? Tell her then to help me.*[18] How trustingly Martha approaches our Lord!

Jesus responds in the familiar tone the repetition of her name seems to indicate: *Martha, Martha* – he tells her – *you are worried and concerned about many things; only one thing is necessary.*[19] Mary, who most assuredly would have been willing to help her sister, did not in the midst of everything forget what was most essential: to have Christ at the centre of her attention and of her life. Our Lord does not praise Mary's entire disposition, but precisely the most important part of it – her love.

Not even the *the things of the Lord* should make us forget the *Lord of all things.* Martha would never forget the Lord's friendly counsel. Indispensable as her work was, her care not to relegate Christ to second place should have been even greater.

Concretely, our activities and concerns that refer directly to the Lord's service should never cause us to forget the *one thing needful,* the Person of Christ. In our

---

[17] M.J. Indart, *Jesus in his world*
[18] Luke 10:40
[19] Luke 10:41-42

ordinary life we need to keep in mind that matters which seem terribly important, like work, financial gain and social relations should never take precedence over the family itself. These means are worth little if family life suffers. Only in extraordinary situations may it be necessary for the head of the family to work far away from the home as in the case of immigrants or sailors. If a father or mother earns more money but neglects the children, what good can this result?

The Blessed Virgin, who enjoys the ineffable presence of Christ in heaven forever, will gain for us the grace of better appreciating an active friendship with the Master. She will teach us to take diligent care of the things of the Lord without forgetting the Lord of all. She will intercede for us before Jesus so that we may learn never to value the family itself less than those noble gains we seek for its sake.

31 JULY

8. ST IGNATIUS OF LOYOLA

Memorial

Ignatius was born in Loyola in 1491 and pursued a career
in the military. Wounded during the defence of Pamplona, he
was transported to his own part of the country to recuperate.
During his convalescence, he read a life of Christ and certain
lives of the saints which lead to his profound conversion.

He set out for Paris to study theology. There he gathered
together his first followers. With them he later founded in
Rome the Society of Jesus. He died in the Eternal City in
1556.

8.1 The influence of spiritual reading on the conversion of St Ignatius.

St Ignatius of Loyola recalls in his *Autobiography: Up
until the age of twenty-six I was carried away with the
vanities of the world. Above all, I found delight in the
military profession and had in my activities a great and
vain desire of winning honour.*[1] After receiving a leg
wound during the defence of the city of Pamplona, he was
taken on a stretcher to his homeland where he lay for some
time on the verge of death. After a long period of recovery,
he regained his health. During this time though, *since he
very much enjoyed reading the worldly and fantastic books
of chivalry, he asked for some of them so that they might
help him to pass the time. As none of that kind could be
found in the house, they brought him a 'Life of Christ' and
a book on the lives of the saints.*[2] He was very much

---

[1] St Ignatius of Loyola, *Autobiography,* Madrid 1963, I, 1
[2] *ibid,* I, 5

intrigued by these readings, reflected on them during the long time he had to stay in bed, and *while reading about the life of our Lord and of the saints, he stopped to consider in his own mind: 'What would happen if I carried out this thing St Francis did, and that other St Dominic?' And so, he thought long and hard about all their good works.*[3]

He became happy when he set out to follow the example of the saints, and sad when he abandoned these inclinations. *Gaining not a little light from this lesson, he began to think more sincerely about his past life and how much penance he had to do for it.*[4] In this way, little by little, God entered into his soul. From a valiant henchman of an earthly lord *he grew into a heroic knight of the Eternal King, Jesus Christ. The wound he suffered in Pamplona, the readings, his long recovery in Loyola, his reflection and meditation in cooperation with grace, and the different states his soul passed through in this period brought about a radical conversion in his life. From the dreams of a worldly life to full consecration to Christ at the feet of our Lady of Montserrat, he further matured on his retreat in Manresa.*[5]

The Lord used the reading of St Ignatius as an instrument for his conversion. He penetrates the depths of many souls in like fashion. Truly, *Reading has made many saints.*[6] Through reading, we build up our understanding of Christian doctrine and also gain insights for our daily conversation with God. *'By reading'* – you wrote me – *'I build up a store of fuel. It seems a lifeless pile, but I often find that my mind spontaneously draws from it material*

---

[3] *ibid*, I, 7
[4] *ibid*, I, 7
[5] John Paul II, *Message for the Ignatian Year*, 31 July 1990
[6] St. J. Escrivá, *The Way*, 116

*which fills my prayer with life and inflames my thanks-
giving after Communion'.*[7] A good spiritual reading book is
comparable to a good friend. It is difficult to put it down
since it shows us the road that leads to God and provides
impetus for us on the way.

8.2 The importance of spiritual reading.

Spiritual reading takes on particular importance in our
time since ordinarily it is one of the most important means
of acquiring good doctrine to nourish our piety and to
enable us to proclaim the Faith in a world engulfed by
profound ignorance. It is not uncommon in our daily
conversation with friends, relatives and acquaintances to
encounter people oblivious of the most elementary notions
of the faith and of the most fundamental criteria with
which to form judgments about the problems of the world.

St John Chrysostom's regret over religious ignorance
among Christians during the first centuries of the Church is
still applicable today: *At times we dedicate all our efforts
not only to what is superfluous but also to what is useless
or even harmful, while we abandon the study of Sacred
Scripture. Many people who are completely enthused over
the horse races can quickly come up with the name,
pedigree, race, nation, and training of the horses; their age,
which horse would win the race against some other one,
and an individual horse's potential to pass the winning-
post first, when mounted by a given rider, all spring
immediately to mind... If, however, we ask them the number
of St Paul's Epistles, they are incapable of an answer.*[8] The
Lord urges us to light up the darkness of so many who are
ignorant of the fundamental truths of faith and morals with

---

[7] *ibid*, 117
[8] St John Chrysostom, *Homilies on certain passages from the New
Testament*, I, 1

the light of Catholic doctrine .

When the media bombard us every day with images which in themselves do not draw us closer to God and often tend to separate us from him, a few moments of reflection on a suitable reading to remind us of the meaning of life in the light of our supernatural last end and the teachings of the Church become urgent.[9] A good book can turn into an excellent friend: *It puts before our eyes the example of the saints, shakes off our indifference, reminds us of God's judgments, discourses on eternity, dissipates the false illusions of the world, responds to the false pretexts of self-love and provides a means for us to resist our disordered passions. It acts as a discreet counsellor to warn us and as a friend who will never deceive us...*[10]

We can apply the words of Sacred Scripture regarding a good friendship to our spiritual reading: We can truly say that when we find a good book we have found a treasure.[11] Such a find can be decisive in a person's life, as in the case of St Ignatius of Loyola and of so many other Christians. For this reason recommending good books is a way of spiritually enriching our friends, an excellent form of apostolate.

8.3 Vigilance over printed material. A way of doing spiritual reading.

Thus says the Lord: I have come to cast fire on the earth and how I wish that it were kindled![12]

To spread the love of God throughout the whole world we need to have it in our hearts like St Ignatius. Spiritual reading provides insights for our interior life, sets living

---

[9] cf E. Boylan, *This Tremendous Lover,* pp.11-112
[10] Berthier, quoted by A. Royo Maria in *Theology of Christian perfection,* Madrid 1962, p.737
[11] cf Sir 6:14
[12] *Communion Antiphon*: Luke 12:49

examples of virtue before us, sparks our desires of loving God, and is a great help for prayer besides being an excellent means of good doctrinal formation. Many specific teachings on spiritual reading are found in the Fathers of the Church. St Jerome, for example, suggests we read some verses from Sacred Scripture every day, as well as *the spiritual works of learned men, always taking care that they are doctrinally sound. Truly, one cannot search for gold in the mud.*[13]

Spiritual reading must be done with carefully chosen books in order to provide us with appropriate nourishment, given the personal circumstances of our soul. As on so many other occasions, the help we receive in spiritual direction can be inestimable. In general, it is better to choose books that expound the fundamentals of the faith or help us contemplate the life of Christ, rather than works on *new theological problems,* they being probably of interest only to specialists in the field.

To carry out the spiritual reading fruitfully, we should read fifteen minutes every day for example, including some passages from the New Testament. We should read slowly, with attention and recollection; *stopping to consider, to ruminate, to think about and savour the truths that affect us most intimately. Engrave these words upon your soul and then draw up resolutions and affections that lead us to love God more.*[14] St Peter of Alcantara used to give similar advice: Spiritual reading *should not be hurried or rushed, but done attentively and with calm. We apply our intelligence to understand and above all our will to relish what we read. Before a passage that is particularly moving, pause a moment to consider it more deeply with our Lord.*[15]

---

[13] St Jerome, *Epistle,* 54,10
[14] St John Euden, *Royaume de Jesus,* II, 15, 196
[15] St Peter of Alcantara, *Treatise on Prayer and Meditation,* I, 7

Continuity with the same book helps a great deal. It can be helpful to take the volume along with us when we are away on weekends, professional trips, etc., as we do with other perhaps more sizable, but less significant works. *During certain periods it can be helpful to re-read those books which were of great benefit to our soul in years gone by. Life is short, and therefore we can well be content with going back to the readings that truly lead us to God and not waste our time on lifeless and unprofitable selections.*[16]

We ask St Ignatius to help us from heaven to derive abundant fruit from our daily spiritual reading so that we might render a greater service to God.

Father, you gave St Ignatius of Loyola to your Church to bring greater glory to your name. May we follow his example on earth and come to share the crown of eternal life in heaven.

---

[16] R. Garrigou-Lagrange, *The Three Ages of the Interior Life*, I

1 AUGUST

9. ST ALPHONSUS LIGUORI

Memorial

Alphonsus was born in Naples in 1696. He earned doctorates in both civil and canon law. Following his ordination, he founded the Redemptorists. To promote Christian life, he dedicated himself to preaching and wrote classical treatises on the Blessed Virgin, the Holy Eucharist and Moral Theology. He was later named a Doctor of the Church.

His long and simple life is an admirable example of diligent work and self-sacrificing concern to help others achieve eternal salvation. Alphonsus was named Bishop of Saint Agatha of Gotti, but after several years of service he renounced that office. He died in 1787 in the company of his spiritual sons in the town of Pagani near Naples.

9.1 Devotion to the Virgin Mary.

The Spirit of the Lord God is upon me, for he has anointed me and sent me to preach the good news to the poor, to heal the broken-hearted.[1]

The long life of St Alphonsus *was filled with uninterrupted work; as a missionary, bishop, theologian, spiritual writer, and founder and superior of a religious congregation.*[2] He lived during a period in which Christianity seemed to be in decline. The Lord led him into contact with the culturally impoverished and spiritually needy by way of the popular missions. He preached tirelessly, giving doctrine and encouraging everyone to personal prayer through his words and writings: *Prayer restores a lively spirit of optimism and hope in salvation to*

---

[1] Common of Pastors, *Entrance Antiphon*: Luke 4:18; cf Is 61:1
[2] John Paul II, Apostolic Letter, *Spiritus Domini*, 1 August 1987

souls. Among other insights he wrote: *God does not refuse anyone the grace of prayer; it is our means of acquiring help to overcome every concupiscence and temptation. I say, say again, and will always repeat as long as I'm alive – the saint emphasized – all our salvation comes from prayer. From this conclusion follows his famous axiom: He who prays is saved; he who does not pray is condemned.*[3] Prayer has always been the great remedy for all evils. This has been the continuous teaching of souls who have been very close to God. Personal dialogue with the Lord truly opens the gate of heaven for us.

St Alphonsus urged the faithful to centre their lives on the tabernacle. He gave special importance to the *Visit to the Blessed Sacrament* and wrote a short treatise to facilitate it.[4] For the depth of his sound doctrine, especially in matters of Moral Theology, he was named a *Doctor of the Church.*[5]

As concerned as he was about the instruction of consciences, the saint also clearly taught that the slide towards loss of faith often begins with lukewarmness and coldness in devotion to Our Lady. On the positive side, the return to Jesus begins through a great love for Mary. For this reason he spread devotion to her everywhere. He prepared an arsenal of *materials to preach and propagate devotion to the divine Mother* for all the faithful, but especially for priests. As the Church has perennially under-stood as well, *devotion to Mary for Alphonsus occupies a totally unique place in the economy of salvation. Mary is the Mediator of all graces and Co-Redemptrix, therefore our Mother, our Advocate and our Queen. Truly,*

---

[3] *ibid*

[4] St Alphonsus Liguori, *Visits to the Blessed Sacrament and to the Blessed Virgin*, 1934

[5] St Pius IX, Decree *Urbis et orbis,* 23 March 1871

Alphonsus was always, from the beginning of his life until his death, all Mary's.[6] Each one of us can fruitfully strive to be *all Mary's,* bringing her to mind in the midst of all our ordinary duties, no matter how trivial they may appear. May we never forget, above all if at some point we have the misfortune of straying from the path our Lord continually encourages us to follow, that *to Jesus we always go, and to him we always return, through Mary.*[7] She leads us quickly and surely into the presence of her Son.

9.2 The mediation of Our Lady.

St Alphonsus died at a ripe old age, one year into his nineties. The Lord permitted the last years of his life to be a time of purification. Among the trials he endured, the loss of his sight was particularly grievous. The saint would intersperse the long hours of his final days with prayer and by getting others to read to him from some pious book. One day, he became very enthused over a book they were reading to him. Failing to remember the author of the fine marvels he was hearing, he asked who had written those pious words so full of affection for Our Lady. The one at his side opened the book to the title page and read: *'The Glories of Mary' by Alphonsus Mary of Liguori.* The venerable man covered his face with both hands, lamenting the loss of his memory,[8] but rejoicing greatly over so beautiful a testimony of love for Our Lady. The Lord affectionately permitted him this consolation in the midst of so much darkness.

Alphonsus' theological knowledge as well as his personal experience led him to the conviction that the

---

[6] John Paul II, *loc cit*

[7] St. J. Escrivá, *The Way,* 495

[8] P. Ramons, in the prologue to *Glories of Mary,* Madrid 1941

spiritual life and its restoration in souls has to come about through the mediation of Mary. According to the divine plan God himself pre-established and is implementing in salvation history, Life with a capital 'L' comes to us through her. She is the shortest route, the easiest path, for us to return to God.

The saint affirms: *God wants all benefits coming from Christ to reach us through the Blessed Virgin.*[9] He cites the well-known phrase of St Bernard: *It is the Will of God that we should not receive anything which has not first passed through the hands of Mary.*[10] She is our principal intercessor in heaven, the one who gains for us all we need. Furthermore she often foresees our petitions, protects us and raises holy inspirations in our souls to incite us to live charity with greater refinement and to go to confession with the regularity we have scheduled. She gives us strength in moments of discouragement and comes to our defence in moments of temptation, as soon as we go to her. She is our great ally in the apostolate: More specifically, she permits our words to find room in the hearts of our friends, regardless of their lack of eloquence. The following has been the great discovery of many saints: With Mary, we reach the supernatural resolutions we propose for ourselves *sooner, more, and better.*

9.3 The efficacy of this mediation.

The role of *mediator* consists in uniting or joining together two extremes. Jesus Christ is the only and perfect mediator between God and men,[11] *since as both God and man He offers his own death, a sacrifice of infinite value,*

---

[9] cf Alphonsus Liguori, *Glories of Mary*, V, 3-4
[10] St Bernard, *Third Sermon for Christmas Eve*, 10
[11] cf I Tim 2:51

to reconcile mankind with God.[12] However this does not prevent the angels and saints, and in a singular way Our Lady, from acting as mediators too. *Mary's maternal duty for the sake of mankind in no way lessens or obscures the unique mediation of Christ, but actually shows forth its efficacy. All the salvific influence of the Blessed Virgin for men originates, not from some inner necessity, but from the divine pleasure. It shows forth from the superabundance of the merits of Christ, rests on His mediation, depends entirely on it and draws all its power from it.*[13]

The Blessed Virgin, the spiritual Mother of the daughters and sons of God, is especially our Mother since she presents our prayers and works to the Lord on our behalf and passes on the gifts of grace from God to us. She redirects any of our less than completely upright petitions so that they may be fruitful for us. As the Mother of God, Our Lady has a special place alongside the Blessed Trinity. As the Mother of mankind, she has the divine charge of caring for her pilgrim children who are still on the way to the home of our common Father.[14] We often encounter her in our everyday life and can enjoy the consolation of her presence. Where would we be without her constant vigilance over us and the assurance of her ever-outstretched hand?

Why are the prayers of Mary so efficacious in the sight of God? asks St Alphonsus rhetorically. He responds: *The prayers of the saints are the prayers of servants. The prayers of Mary are those of a Mother. From this stand-point they derive their authority and potency. Since Jesus loves his Mother immensely, it is impossible for to him to hear her prayer without being moved.* To prove it,

---

[12] cf St Thomas, *Summa Theologiae,* II, 26, 2

[13] Second Vatican Council, *Lumen gentium,* 60

[14] cf *ibid,* 62; John Paul II, Encyclical, *Redemptoris Mater,* 2 April 1987

Alphonsus recalls the wedding feast at Cana, where the
Lord worked his first miracle through the intercession of
our Lady. They had run out of wine and as a result the
bride and groom were in a tight corner. No one asked the
Blessed Virgin to intercede with her Son for the sake of the
disconcerted couple. In the end though, the heart of Mary
was moved to take upon herself the role of intercessor. She
asked the miracle from her Son, though no one else dared
to do so. The saint concludes: If *our Lady works like this
without her being asked, what might she do if we were
confidently to beseech her?*[15] How can she fail to hear our
petitions?

On today's feast we ask St Alphonsus Liguori to gain
for us the grace of loving our Lady here on earth as much
as he himself loved her. Let us seek to spread devotion to
her among our family and friends. With Mary at our side
we will reach our apostolic and spiritual goals *sooner,
more and better.*

---

[15] St Alphonsus Liguori, *Abbreviated Sermons*, Madrid 1952, 48

4 AUGUST

10. SAINT JOHN VIANNEY
The Curé d'Ars
Memorial

St John Vianney was born near Lyon in 1786. He overcame many difficulties prior to receiving ordination and was later entrusted with a parish in the village of Ars where he spent the next forty-two years. He excelled in active concern for souls and in the spirit of prayer and penance. Above all, he was exemplary in his tireless dedication to souls through the Sacrament of Confession.

He died in 1859, and was canonized and declared the patron saint of the clergy in 1929 by Pope Pius XI.

10.1 Holy priests. Their incomparable dignity. Love for the priesthood.

When John Baptist Mary Vianney was about to be sent to the small parish of Ars – a tiny place of two hundred and thirty inhabitants – the Vicar-General of the diocese told him: *There is not much love for God in that parish; you will have to try to introduce it.*[1] And that is precisely what he did; he set aflame those peasants and countless other souls besides with the love for the Lord he bore in his heart. He was not very learned, healthy or wealthy..., but his personal sanctity, his union with God, worked the required miracle. A few years later, great crowds from all the regions of France came to Ars. At times they had to wait for days to see the parish priest and go to confession. The great attraction was not curiosity to witness the miracles he made every attempt to hide, but the expectation

---

[1] F. Trochu, *The Curé d'Ars*, London 1951, p.101

of finding a saintly priest, *surprising in his penance, so familiar with God in prayer, outstanding for his peace and humility in the midst of popular acclaim, and above all, so intuitive in corresponding to the interior dispositions of souls and freeing them from their burdens, especially in the confessional.*[2] The Lord chose *as a model of pastors him who, alone, would only have been able to appear poor, weak and defenceless, worthy of scorn in the eyes of men (1 Cor 1:27-29). God rewarded him with his greatest gifts as a guide and doctor of souls.*[3]

On a certain occasion people asked a lawyer from Lyon returning from Ars what he had seen there. He answered: *I saw God in a man.*[4] Today we ask the Lord that we may be able to say the same of each priest on account of his holiness, his union with God and his concern for souls. In the sacrament of Holy Orders, the priest, according to St Paul, is constituted a minister of God and dispenser of his treasures.[5] These treasures include the divine Word for preaching, the Body and Blood of Christ he dispenses at Mass and in Holy Communion, and the grace of God in the administration of the other sacraments. The priest is entrusted with the divine task – *par excellence, the most divine of the divine works,* in the words of an early Father of the Church – no less than the salvation of souls. He is an ambassador, a mediator between God who is in heaven and man who is still on his way on earth. With one hand he accepts the treasures of divine mercy, and with the other distributes them with liberality. By the exercise of his mission as a mediator, the priest participates in the authority of Christ, who builds up,

---

[2] John Paul II, *Holy Thursday Letter to Priests*, 16 March 1986
[3] *ibid*
[4] Quoted by John Paul I, *Address*, 7 September 1978
[5] cf 1 Cor 4:1

sanctifies and governs his Body.[6] He *confects* the Eucharist, the holiest action man can carry out on earth.

What do people want and expect from the priest, the Minister of Christ, the living sign of the presence of the Good Shepherd? Bishop Alvaro del Portillo answers: *They need, desire and hope – perhaps without thus consciously reasoning out such a need or hope – for a priest who is a priest one hundred percent; a man who shows an ardent concern for them by opening up new horizons for their souls, who exercises his ministry without ceasing, and who has a big heart capable of understanding and loving everyone, though at times his concern may not be reciprocated. May he be a man who gives what he alone can give, with simplicity and joy, in season and out of season (2 Tim 4:2). God wants to disseminate to men, through him, the wealth of his grace and of his divine intimacy.*[7]

Today is an appropriate occasion to pray for the holiness of priests, especially those who in some way are placed by God to help us on our way toward him.

10.2 The need for priests. Prayer and mortification for priests.

The Curé d'Ars used frequently to say: *What a great thing it is to be a priest. If I were to understand this fully, I think I would die.*[8] God calls some men to this great dignity in order for them to serve their brothers. Nevertheless, *the salvific mission of the Church in the world is realized not only by ministers in virtue of the Sacrament of Orders, but also by all the lay faithful.*[9] Each one in his own profession

---

[6] cf Second Vatican Council, Decree *Presbyterorum ordinis,* 12

[7] A. del Portillo, *On the Priesthood,* p.66

[8] B. Nodet, Jean-Marie Vianney, *Curé d'Ars, sa pensée, son coeur,* Le Puy, ed Virgin, Brooklyn, NY 1934

[9] John Paul II, Apostolic Exhortation, *Christifideles laici,* 30 December 1988

and place in the world *shines as a light in the world.*[10] *By virtue of their Baptism and specific vocation, in the measure proper to each person, the lay faithful participate in the priestly, prophetic and kingly functions of Christ.*[11] Their participation is in no way limited to helping clerics, although sometimes they may do this. The real place of the laity is not the sacristy, but the family, business, fashion, sport..., fields of endeavour in which in their own right they must try to bring to God. The mission of the laity must lead them to imbue family, work and the social order with the Christian principles that raise these areas of human living to the supernatural order and thus make them more human; the laity's business is the dignity and primacy of the human person, social solidarity, the sanctity of marriage, responsible freedom, love for the truth, respect for justice on all levels, the spirit of service, and the practice of mutual understanding and of charity...

Precisely in order to exercise fully this prophetic, priestly and royal function of Christ, the baptized need the help of the ministerial priesthood that confers the gift of divine life received from Christ, Head of the Body, in a privileged and tangible way. The more Christian and conscious people are of their dignity and of their vital role in the Church, the more urgently they feel the need for priests who are truly priests.[12]

Today we ask Our Lord for holy, lovable and learned priests who treat souls like precious jewels of Jesus Christ and who know how to give up their own personal plans for the love of others. May they have a profound love for the Mass, the principal end of their ordination and the centre of their day. May they orient their best pastoral efforts, *like the Curé d'Ars, towards the explicit proclamation of the*

---

[10] cf Phil 2:15

[11] John Paul II, *loc cit*

[12] *idem, Retreat at Ars,* 6 October 1986

Faith, towards the forgiveness of sins and the Eucharist.[13]

10.3 The priest accompanies man in the name of the Lord. Appreciation for those who have given us so much. Having great confidence in the prayer of the priest.

God has placed the priest close to the lives of men that he be a dispenser of divine mercy. *Hardly is a man born when the priest regenerates him in Baptism, confers a more noble, precious, and supernatural life on him, and makes him a son of God and of the Church of Jesus Christ.* A priest strengthens and prepares souls to undergo spiritual combat by means of Confirmation.

When a child is just able to discern and appreciate the Bread of Angels, a gift from heaven, the priest feeds and fortifies him with this living and life-giving food. If a person has suffered the misfortune of falling from grace, the priest raises and reconciles him in the name of God through the sacrament of Penance. God may call him to found a family, to collaborate in the transmission of human life and thereby increase the number of faithful on earth and ultimately the ranks of the elect in heaven. The priest is present to bless his noble love and marriage. When the Christian is finally at the portals of eternity, he feels the need of fortitude and divine aid before appearing before the divine Judge. The priest anoints the failing members of the sick or dying Christian with the holy oils and thus comforts him.

The priest therefore accompanies the Christian throughout the pilgrimage of this life to the gates of heaven. He accompanies the body to its resting place in the grave with rites and prayers of immortal hope. And even beyond the threshold of eternity he aids the soul with Christian suffrages, if need there be of further purification and

---

[13] *ibid*, 14

alleviation. Thus, from the cradle to the grave, the priest is always a guide, a solace, a minister of salvation and a dispenser of grace and blessing at the side of the faithful.[14]

It is a matter of justice for the faithful to pray each day for priests, especially for those who have the charge of providing for our own spiritual needs, particularly today when we celebrate the feast of the Holy Curé d'Ars. From priests we receive the Bread of Angels and pardon of our sins. In the words of the St Josemaría Escrivá, they teach us how to have recourse to Christ, to meet him in the loving tribunal of Penance, and in the unbloody renewal of the Sacrifice of Calvary, the Mass.[15]

We unite ourselves to their prayers and intentions which habitually encompass the most pressing needs of the Church and souls. We also venerate them with affection since *no one is as truly our neighbour as the person who has healed our wounds. May we love the priests, seeing Our Lord in each one. Let us love the priest as we love our neighbour.*[16] We ask this grace of reverence through the intercession of the Curé d'Ars.

---

[14] Pius XI, Encyclical, *Ad catholici sacerdotii,* 20 December 1935, 21

[15] cf St. J. Escrivá, *In Love with the Church*, 43

[16] St Ambrose, *Treatise on St Luke's Gospel*, 7,84

5 AUGUST

11. OUR LADY OF THE SNOWS

Dedication of Saint Mary Major's Basilica
Optional Memorial

After the promulgation of the dogma of the divine Maternity of Mary at the Council of Ephesus (431), Pope Sixtus III consecrated a basilica in Rome in honour of the Blessed Virgin which was later called Saint Mary Major. It is the oldest church dedicated to our Mother Mary.

Today's feast is also known as *Our Lady of the Snows* due to an ancient legend about a Roman who asked the Blessed Virgin's guidance on how best to use his fortune. In the early hours of August 5th, Our Lady told him in a dream to build a church in her honour where snow was to appear on the Esquiline Hill. That same morning it seems that snow appeared miraculously on the site where the Basilica of Saint Mary Major now stands.

11.1 The origin of the Roman basilica dedicated to the Mother of God.

Today we celebrate the *Dedication* of the Basilica of Saint Mary Major in Rome, the oldest and most venerable church in the Western world consecrated to the Blessed Virgin. So many events in the history of the Church have taken place here. This Marian basilica is closely linked to the dogmatic definition of the divine Motherhood of Mary promulgated at the Council of Ephesus. It was built under her invocation on the site of an already existing church during the fourth century, shortly after the Council ended. The people of the city celebrated with enormous enthusiasm the official declaration of the truth they had long believed, and joy spread throughout the Church. The faithful raised the enormous basilica under her name in the Eternal City.

Their exultation extends to us today, when we praise Mary in a special way, as the Mother of God and our Mother.

According to pious legend, a Roman patrician named John and his wife mutually agreed to dedicate their estate to honour the Mother of God, but they did not know exactly how to do it. At this time, he and the Pope both had a dream in which Our Lady requested a beautiful church in her honour to be built on the part of the Esquiline hill that was to be covered with snow out of season on August 5. Although the legend is subsequent to the Basilica's construction, it has caused the feast to be known in many places as the feast of *Our Lady of the Snows*. A great many mountain enthusiasts also have her as their Patroness.

From time immemorial, the faithful in Rome have honoured our Mother in this basilica under the invocation *Salus Populi Romani...Health of the Roman People.* They come, as to a place where their petitions are always heard, to ask favours and graces. St John Paul II *paid a visit* to Our Lady here just after his election to the Pontificate. On that occasion, he said: *Mary is called to lead all people to the Redeemer, and to bear witness to him without words, through love alone, in a way that shows 'her motherly disposition'. She is called to draw even those who offer stubborn resistance, the ones for whom it is more difficult to believe in Christ's love. Her vocation is to bring each person closer to her Son.* At her feet, the Pope offered the Mother of God his whole life and deepest desires, a dedication we too can make, imitating him as good children imitate their parents: *Totus tuus ego sum et omnia mea tua sunt. Accipio te in mea omnia...I am all yours, and everything I have is yours. May you be my guide in everything.*[1] With her protection, we will advance with a sure step on our way.

---

[1] John Paul II, *Address,* 8 December 1978

11.2 Mother of God and our Mother.

The mystery of the Incarnation has allowed the Church to penetrate and shed ever more light on the mystery of the Mother of the Word Incarnate. The Council of Ephesus is of particular importance in this respect.[2] St Cyril relates how the promulgation of the Marian dogma profoundly moved all the Christians of the city. It stirs us now too, as we consider that the Mother of God is also our Mother. This ancient Father of the Church describes the events as follows: *From the first hours of the morning until evening, all the people of the city of Ephesus anxiously awaited the outcome. When it was known that the author of the blasphemies – Nestorius – had been deposed, all as one began to glorify God and acclaim the synod, since the enemy of the Faith had fallen. On leaving the church, we were accompanied to our homes by torch-light. It was night-time: The whole city was joyful and brilliantly lit up.*[3] The faith of the first Christians was strong and vibrant, as our own should grow to be.

In a homily given during the Council, St Cyril praised the Motherhood of our Lady: *Hail Mary, Mother of God, Blessed Virgin Mother, Morning Star... Hail Mary, most precious jewel of the whole world...*[4] St Thomas Aquinas affirms: *As the Mother of God, her dignity is in a certain sense infinite on account of the limitless Goodness of God. Similarly, greater dignity than hers there cannot be, just as there cannot be any greater than God.*[5] She is above all the angels and saints in dignity. After the Sacred Humanity of her Son, she is that part of creation which is the purest reflection of the glory of God. In her, as in no other

---

[2] *idem*, Encyclical, *Redemptoris Mater*, 25 March 1987
[3] St Cyril of Alexandria, *Epistles*, 24
[4] *idem, In Honour of Mary, Mother of God*
[5] St Thomas, *Summa Theologiae*, 1, q25, a6

creature, shines a participation in the divine gifts – Wisdom, Beauty, Goodness... *There is no stain in her. She is a reflection of eternal light, the immaculate mirror of the action of God and an image of his goodness.*[6]

May we keep in mind throughout the day her divine Motherhood, the root of all her graces, virtues and perfections. Holy Mary, Mother of God, pray for us... Keep us by your side and do not ever let go of us. Take care of us as mothers protect the weakest and most needy of their children.

11.3 Mary is *the conduit* of all the graces we receive.

St Bernard affirms that Mary is the conduit through whom we daily receive the grace we require. We can always turn to her, since *it is the Will of the Lord, who wants us to obtain everything at his Mother's hands, particularly when we find ourselves in the midst of special difficulties or temptations.*[7] We need to have recourse to her as often as we can, for our spiritual needs as for our bodily ones.

The spiritual Motherhood of Mary culminated next to her Son on Calvary. When all have fled, the Virgin remains *iuxta crucem Iesu... standing by the cross of Jesus,*[8] suffering and co-redeeming, in perfect conformity with the Will of God. *She is not a purely passive instrument in the hands of God, but cooperates in the salvation of men with free faith and obedience.*[9] She continues to exercise her loving maternity unremittingly, and now in heaven, *she has not given up this salvific activity, but through her constant intercession continues to obtain for us the gifts of eternal*

---

[6] cf Wis 7:25-26
[7] St Bernard, *Homily on the Nativity of the Blessed Virgin Mary*, 7
[8] John 19:25
[9] Second Vatican Council, *Lumen gentium,* 56

salvation.[10]

We thank God often for wanting to give us his very own Mother to draw close to in the Life of grace. Mary is our Mother, not only because she loves us as an earthly mother does or because she stands in her stead. The spiritual motherhood of Mary is superior to and more effective than any legal or affective bond. She really engenders us in the supernatural order. The power to become sons and daughters of God, to participate in the divine nature,[11] has been given to us thanks to the redemptive action of Christ, who forms us in His own likeness, a fashioning that comes to us through Mary. Just as God the Father has only one Son according to nature, and countless others according to grace, Mary has only one Son, but many sons and daughters of the supernatural order. Through her intercession, we receive all the spiritual nourishment we need every day, defence against our enemies and consolation in our sufferings.

In the eyes of Our Lady, *we never cease to be little ones. She shows us the way to the kingdom of heaven, which is for those who become like small children (Matt 19:14). We need to stay attentively by her side. How? By having constantly renewed recourse to her, telling her loving things, showing her our affection, pondering the scenes of her life on earth and sharing with her our struggles, successes, and failures.*

By thus sharing our life with her and contemplating the mysteries of her earthly existence, we discover the meaning of the traditional Marian prayers of the Church, as if we were reciting them for the first time. What are the 'Hail Mary' and 'Angelus' if not loving praises of her divine motherhood? When we say the Rosary, our minds

---

[10] cf *ibid*, 62
[11] cf 2 Pet 1:4

and hearts reflect on the mysteries of Mary's admirable life, which are at the same time the fundamental mysteries of our faith.

As the feasts of Our Lady come round each year, may we not be sparing in the details of affection we show her. We raise our hearts to her more often and ask her for what we need. We give thanks for her constant motherly care and entrust those we love to her. Naturally though, if we really want to act as good children, every day is a good occasion on which to express affection, for those who really love one another.[12]

In the words of an ancient hymn of the Church, we tell her today: *Monstra te esse matrem....Show us you are our Mother; and that the One who took blood in his veins to redeem us, hears our prayers on account of you.*[13]

---

[12] St. J. Escrivá, *Friends of God,* 290-291
[13] Hymn, *Ave Maris Stella*

6 AUGUST

12. THE TRANSFIGURATION

Feast

Today's feast has long been celebrated throughout the Eastern and Western Church on the same day. During the fifteenth century it was extended to the universal Church by Pope Calixtus III.

Twice during the Liturgical year we remember the Transfiguration in a special way. First, on the Second Sunday of Lent, to affirm the divinity of Christ before we commemorate his Passion. And second, today, as we recall the exaltation of Christ in anticipation of his eternal glory. This revelation prefigured the splendour of heaven where we will see God face to face. Through grace, we acquire the seed of eternal life during our present existence and begin to participate to a certain extent in the promise of salvation even now.

12.1 The Lord strengthens the disciples before his Passion and Death.

When Christ appears, we shall be like him, for we shall see him as he is.[1]

Jesus told his disciples of his forthcoming Passion and of the suffering He would undergo at the hands of the Jews and Gentiles. He exhorted them to follow him on the way of the Cross and of sacrifice.[2] A few days later, in Caesarea Philippi, He wants to strengthen their faith. St Thomas teaches that for one to advance directly along a particular path, it is important to know the destination beforehand, *just as the archer does not accurately launch an arrow*

---

[1] *Communion Antiphon*: 1 John 3:2
[2] cf Matt 16:24 ff

without first looking at the target. This is necessary, above all, when the road is rough and hazardous, and the path laborious. It is fitting, therefore, for Christ to reveal to his disciples the splendour of his glory, to become transfigured before them, since in the same glory he would one day transfigure his own.[3]

Our life is a roadway to heaven, but one that passes by way of the cross and through sacrifice. Until our final moments, we shall have to swim against the current. The tendency to make our dedication compatible with an easy and perhaps lukewarm existence, like that of so many whose minds are set exclusively on material well-being, may affect us too. *Haven't we frequently felt the temptation to let Christianity be comfortable, devoid of sacrifice, of having it conform to the easy-going and worldly ways of others? But that is not how Our Lord meant it to be. Christian life cannot dispense with the cross since it has no meaning without the hard, pressing weight of duty. If we were to attempt to remove the cross from our lives, we would be creating illusions for ourselves and weakening the Faith, since we would have transformed Sacred Tradition into a soft and complacent style of life.*[4] This is not the narrow path the Lord points out.

The disciples were profoundly shaken by the experience of witnessing the Passion. For this reason, the Lord leads three of them, the ones who were to accompany him in his agony in Gethsemane, to the summit of Mount Tabor, so that they can in part contemplate his glory. There He reveals himself in a glimpse, *in the sovereign glory he wanted to show these three, reflecting spiritual reality in a way compatible with human nature. Given the limitations of mortal flesh, it is impossible for them to see the ineffable*

---

[3] St Thomas, *Summa Theologiae*, 2, q45, a1
[4] Bl. Paul VI, *Address*, 8 April 1966

vision of God in all his majesty. That awesome sight is reserved in eternity for the clean of heart, those righteous souls who have merited eternal life.[5] This is the reward which awaits us, if we make an effort to be faithful each day.

The Lord wants to strengthen us with the hope of heaven too, especially if at some point the way becomes taxing, and discouragement causes us to falter. Thinking about the life of heaven will help us be strong and to persevere. May we not fail to keep before our eyes the final destination prepared for us by our Father God. Each day that passes draws us a little closer to it. For a Christian, the passing of time is in no way a tragedy. On the contrary, it shortens the distance we need to travel before our long-awaited and definitive meeting with God.

12.2 God will be our reward.

Jesus took Peter, James and John, *led them up a high mountain, and was transfigured before them, in such a way that his face shone like the sun, and his garments became as white as snow. And behold, there appeared to them Moses and Elijah talking with him.*[6] The vision gives the Apostles unspeakable happiness. Peter does his best to express it: *Lord, how good it is for us to be here! If you wish, I will make three booths here, one for you, one for Moses and one for Elijah.*[7] He is so happy that he was not thinking of himself or of James and John who accompanied him. St Mark, who records the teachings of St Peter, adds: *For he did not know what he way saying.*[8] He was still speaking when a shining cloud covered them and a voice from within the cloud said: *This is my beloved Son, with*

---

[5] St Leo the Great, *Homily on the Transfiguration*, 3
[6] Matt 17:1-3
[7] Matt 17:4
[8] cf Mark 9:6

whom I am well pleased: Hear him.[9]

Recalling these moments with the Lord on Mount Tabor was assuredly a tremendous help for the three\p disciples during the many trying circumstances to come later. St Peter would remember them throughout his life on earth. In a *Letter* written to the first Christians to strengthen them during a severe persecution, he affirms that the Apostles do not make Christ known on the false evidence of ingenious myths: *We are eyewitnesses of his majesty. For He was honoured and glorified by God the Father, and from out of the sublime brilliance a voice came down to him, speaking thus: 'This is my beloved Son in whom I am well pleased.' And we ourselves heard this voice come down from heaven, when we were with him on the holy mountain.*[10] The Lord let his divinity be momentarily perceived. The disciples were beside themselves and moved by a tremendous grace they would never forget. *The Transfiguration reveals Christ to them in a way they were not familiar with from ordinary life. He is present before them as the fulfilment of the Old Covenant, and above all, as the chosen Son of the Eternal Father, to whom absolute faith and total obedience are due.*[11] He is the one we should be seeking every day of our lives.

What will heaven be like, where if we are faithful we will see the glorified Christ, not for a few moments, but throughout all eternity? *My God, when will I love you for yourself alone? Although when we think about it, Lord, to desire everlasting reward is to desire you, for you give yourself as our reward.*[12]

---

[9] Matt 17:5
[10] 2 Peter 1:16-18
[11] St John Paul II, *Address,* 27 February 1983; cf *Address,* 27 May 1987
[12] St. J. Escrivá, *The Forge,* 1030

12.3 The Lord accompanies us to help us bear our greatest burdens.

Peter was still speaking when a shining cloud covered them, and a voice from within the cloud said to them: This is my beloved son, with whom I am well pleased: Listen to him.[13] How often have we not heard him in the intimacy of our hearts?

The mystery we celebrate today is a prefiguring of Christ's glory to come and of the glory we are invited to one day share with Him. As St Paul teaches: *The Spirit himself gives testimony to our spirit that we are sons of God. But if we are sons, we are heirs also; heirs indeed of God, and joint heirs with Christ, provided, however, we suffer with him, that we may also be glorified with him.*[14] The Apostle adds: *For I consider that the sufferings of this present time are not worth comparing to the glory that is to be revealed in us.*[15] Whatever small or great suffering we endure for Christ is nothing compared to what awaits us.

The Lord blesses with the Cross, especially when He plans to confer great graces. If at some point He leads us to experience his Cross more intensely, it is a sure sign that He considers us chosen children. Physical pain, humiliation, failure and family problems all may come. Then is not a time to become sad, though, but an occasion to seek the Lord and experience his paternal love and consolation. We will always have his help to convert apparent evils into blessings for the good of our soul and for the whole Church. *We no longer bear just any cross, but encounter the Cross of Christ, with the consolation that the Redeemer takes it upon himself to bear the weight.*[16] He is our

---

[13] Matt 17:5
[14] Rom 8:16-17
[15] Rom 8:18
[16] St. J. Escrivá, *Friends of God*, 132

inseparable Friend, the one who himself carries whatever is hardest to bear. Without him, however, any burden at all will sap our energy.

If we keep always in contact with Jesus nothing can ever harm us; neither economic ruin, nor imprisonment or serious illness, much less the small daily annoyances that tend to take away our peace if we are not on our guard. St Paul himself reminds the first Christians: *Now who is there to harm you if you are zealous for what is right? But even if you do suffer for righteousness' sake, you will be blessed.*[17]

Let us ask Our Lady to help us learn to offer with serenity the fatigue and tiredness each day brings with it, with our thoughts fixed on Christ, who accompanies us in this life and waits for us, glorified, at the end of the way. *And when that hour arrives when these mortal eyes close, grant us, Lord, a grander vision in order that we may behold your awesome face. May death lead us to a more splendid birth,*[18] the beginning of everlasting life.

---

[17] 1 Pet 3:13-14
[18] J. Maragall, *Spiritual Canticle,* Madrid 1985

8 August

13. SAINT DOMINIC

Memorial

St Dominic was born in Caleruega about the year 1170. He fought the Albigensian heresy with his preaching and exemplary life. He founded the Order of Preachers (Dominicans) and spread devotion to the Holy Rosary. He died in Bologna on August 6, 1221.

13.1 The need for good doctrine. The help of the Blessed Virgin.

At the beginning of the thirteenth century some sects were causing great harm in the Church, especially in the south of France. During a journey St Dominic made throughout that region in the company of his bishop, he was able to verify the damaging effects that novel doctrines were causing in the People of God on account of deficient formation, as has so often been the case. How much evil has ignorance brought about! During his tour the saint perceived the need to teach the truths of the Faith clearly and simply. With great zeal and love for souls he gave himself over fully to the task. Shortly thereafter, he decided to found a new religious order whose aim would be the spread of Christian doctrine and its defence against error throughout Christendom. In this way, the *Order of Preachers* was founded. The study of Truth was to be one of its fundamental tenets.[1] Ever since then, *Dominicans can be found in all kinds of apostolic activities in service to the Church, bringing truth to the minds of humanity. Like their*

---

[1] cf J. M. Macias, *St Domingo of Guzman,* Madrid 1979

founder, they put their particular charism into practice so as to illuminate the consciences of persons with the light of the Word of God.[2]

The task of transmitting the deposit of faith to everyone is currently as pressing a need as it was in Dominic's day. This is a mission of the entire Church and it is becoming more urgent than ever before.

St John Paul II periodically warned of the widespread ignorance of the most elementary truths of the Faith. There is contagion of numerous doctrinal errors, with detrimental consequences to souls; the lack of love and esteem for the Holy Eucharist, the neglect of Confession, a sacrament vitally necessary for obtaining God's pardon and for the formation of a person's conscience, the disregard for our supernatural last end, and a widespread relegation of faith to private life, stripping it of all public expression. Marriage is deprived of its natural meaning and dignity. Laws permissive of abortion declare the triumph of material ease and egoism over the most sacred value of human life. A decrease in the birthrate and an aging population have led one responsible European to speak of *demographic suicide* in Europe: It appears to be a serious symptom of profound spiritual impoverishment.[3]

Clearly, many are oblivious of our call to friendship with God, of sin, of eternal life, and of the Christian meaning of suffering. It is plain to see that the world becomes less human to the extent that it ceases to be Christian. A *wave of materialism,* the loss of supernatural perspective, also affects – and perhaps very profoundly – the people we see around us every day and whom the Lord perhaps puts under our care for one reason or another.

Let us consider in the presence of God today whether

---

[2] *ibid,* p.260
[3] cf John Paul II, *Address,* 11 October 1985

we are taking to heart the Pope's call to re-Christianize the world around us in our social milieu. May we consider whether we are making an effort to know the teachings of Jesus Christ in depth and to spread them. Do we rectify our personal, family, professional, social and political conduct accordingly? Are we trying to invigorate those external signs of religion and Christian life that so many are bent on disregarding – the scapular, blessings at meals and of our new house, having recourse to images of the Lord and of the Virgin, in our home and at our place of work?

13.2 The Rosary is a powerful weapon.

Like so many others after him, St Dominic depended on *a powerful weapon* to conquer in what at first appeared to be a losing battle:[4] *Great in the integrity of his doctrine, in the example of his virtue and in his apostolic labours, he dauntlessly declared war on the enemies of the Church, not by force of arms, but through burning faith in the Holy Rosary. He was the first to establish and personally spread this devotion with his sons, to the four corners of the earth.*[5] *The saint required his spiritual sons to frequently make use in their preaching of this form of prayer from which he drew so much profit. On the one hand, he knew of Mary's enormous influence with her Son, who always dispenses his graces through her hands. On the other, she is so naturally inclined to mercy and kindness, and so used to spontaneously helping those in need, that she cannot withhold her help from those who ask it. The Church always finds her to be 'Mother of divine grace' and 'Mother most merciful', and has long had the custom of greeting her as such, above all through the Holy Rosary. For this reason, the Roman Pontiffs have extolled devotion*

---

[4] cf St. J. Escrivá, *Holy Rosary,* p.7

[5] Leo XII, Encyclical, *Supremi apostolatus,* 1 September 1883

to the Marian Rosary with the highest praise, and have enriched it with indulgences.[6]

By filial instinct and on the explicit recommendation of the Popes, Christians have recourse to the Holy Rosary in both ordinary and extraordinary circumstances including public catastrophes, wars, heresies and important family problems. This powerful and perennial devotion is an excellent means of thanksgiving too. The advice of the most recent Popes is constant, particularly with respect to the family Rosary. The Second Vatican Council reminded the Christian faithful *to esteem those acts of piety for the Blessed Virgin Mary which the Magisterium has recommended throughout the centuries.*[7] Blessed Paul VI explicitly interpreted these words as referring to the Holy Rosary.[8]

Today, when humanity is in so much need, let us examine the quality of our love for and our confidence in Our Lady as expressed through this grace-laden devotion. Let us ask ourselves whether we turn to Our Mother in heaven with faith while we spread good doctrine around us, especially if any of those closest to us are straying from the Lord.

13.3 The consideration of the mysteries of the Holy Rosary.

If we try to pray the Holy Rosary with love every day, like St Dominic we will win many graces for ourselves and for those we want to lead to the Lord. In it, we consider the principal mysteries of our salvation, from the Annunciation of the Blessed Mother to the Resurrection and Ascension

---

[6] Benedict XV, Encyclical, *Fausto appetente die,* 29 June 1921

[7] Second Vatican Council, *Lumen gentium,* 67

[8] cf Bl. Paul VI, Encyclical *Christi Matri,* 15 September 1966; Apostolic Exhortation *Marialis cultus,* 2 February 1974

of the Lord into heaven, by way of his Passion and Death.

The first five *Joyful Mysteries* cover the hidden life of Jesus and Mary. Contemplating them will teach us to sanctify the realities of ordinary life. The following five *Sorrowful Mysteries* lead us to reflect on and to re-live the events of the Passion. They teach us to sanctify suffering, sickness and the Cross that are present in the life of every man and woman. In the five *Glorious Mysteries,* we meditate on the triumphs of the Lord and of his Mother. They fill us with joy and hope as we bring to mind the glory God has reserved for us if we are faithful.

In his Apostolic Letter in 2002, *Rosarium Virginis Mariae*, Pope St John Paul II indicated that, in order to highlight the Christological content of this Marian devotion, five new mysteries, the "mysteries of light", should be added to the fifteen traditional mysteries. Each of these mysteries is *a revelation of the Kingdom now present in the very person of Jesus.* The Baptism in the Jordan is first of all a mystery of light. Here, as Christ descends into the waters, the voice of the Father declares him the beloved Son. Another is the first of the signs, given at Cana, when Christ changes water into wine and opens the hearts of the disciples to faith, thanks to the intervention of Mary, the first among believers. Then comes the preaching by which Jesus proclaims the coming of the Kingdom of God, calls to conversion and forgives the sins of all who draw near to him. The mystery of light *par excellence* is the Transfiguration on Mount Tabor. The Godhead shines forth from the face of Christ as the Father commands the astonished Apostles to prepare to experience with him the agony of the Passion. A final mystery of light is the institution of the Eucharist.

By reflecting on these mysteries we go to Jesus through Mary. We rejoice with Christ as we ponder his being made Man like us. We suffer patiently with him, and anticipate his glory. To ponder these truths with piety, we need to direct our prayer to the heart of her who was closest to Christ on earth. In this way, we can *become privy to favourable meditation on the mysteries of the life of the Lord. The never-ending wealth of truth contained in these mysteries open before our mind's eye.*[9] To pray the Holy Rosary thus, *considering the mysteries, repeating the Our Father and Hail Mary, with the praises of the Blessed Trinity and constant invocation to the Mother of God, is a continuous act of faith, hope and love, of adoration and reparation.*[10]

During the time of St Dominic, people greeted the Virgin with the invocation of *rose,* the symbol of beauty and joy. Images of her were already adorned with crowns of roses in representation of the rosary beads. Singing to Mary as the *garden of roses* (*Rosarium* in medieval Latin) was common throughout Christendom. The present term *Rosary* has its origin in this custom.[11] Let us not forget that each *Hail Mary* is like a rose we offer our Mother in heaven. May we not allow them to pass lifelessly from our lips, due to lack of interest or inattentiveness. In the face of the obstacles we encounter, let us not neglect this *powerful weapon.* Let us draw close to Our Lady through this devotion, when we feel the weight of our weakness most: *Immaculate Virgin, I know very well that I am only a miserable wretch, and all I do is increase each day the number of my sins.' You told me the other day that was how you spoke to Our Mother... And I was confident in advising you, with assurance, to pray the Holy Rosary. Blessed be that monotony of Hail Mary's which purifies the monotony of your sins!*[12]

---

[9] *idem,* Apostolic Exhortation, *Marialis Cultus,* quoted, 46

[10] St. J. Escrivá, *op cit,* p.9

[11] *The American Heritage Dictionary of the English Dictionary,* Boston 1969

[12] St. J. Escrivá, *Furrow,* 475

14 AUGUST

14. VIGIL OF THE ASSUMPTION OF THE BLESSED VIRGIN MARY

14.1 The Blessed Virgin, Our Lady, Ark of the New Covenant.

Glorious things are spoken of you, O Mary, who today were exalted above the choirs of Angels and into eternal triumph with Christ.[1]

The *First Reading* of the Mass on the Vigil of this Solemnity is the Old Testament account that narrates the translation of the Ark of the Covenant to its definitive resting place.[2] David convened all Israel, ordered the priests to purify themselves, and named singers and dancers, so that the procession would have the greatest possible solemnity and adornment. With boundless joy the Ark was moved to the city of David, and placed in the duly prepared Tabernacle. Its final repose lay in the perpetual dwelling place God himself had chosen on Mount Sion.[3]

The Ark was the sign of the presence of God in the midst of his People. Inside, his Word was kept, inscribed on the *the two tablets of the Law.*[4] This passage is mentioned today because Mary is the *Ark of the New Covenant.* In her womb the Son of God, the Word made flesh, dwelt for nine months.[5] With her Assumption into heaven she found her final abode in the heart of the

---

[1] *Entrance Antiphon*
[2] cf *First Reading*: 1 Chron 15:3-4; 15-16; 16:1-2
[3] *Responsorial Psalm*: Ps 131:14
[4] Deut 9:15
[5] cf C. Pozo, *Mary in Scripture and in the faith of the Church*, Madrid 1985

Blessed Trinity. *Mary was brought up to heaven amidst acclamations of joy and praise. She went directly into God's presence, and there took her throne in glory above all the angels and saints.*[6]

The Ark of the Old Testament was built with precious materials, and adorned with gold in its interior. In the case of Mary, God bestowed on her untold gifts. Her external beauty was a reflection of the plenitude of grace within.[7] Thus, she was the new dwelling-place of God in the world.

Let us not forget today that where the Ark was, was a place of privilege for the Jews, since God heard their prayers there: *My Name shall be there* we read in the *Book of Kings.*[8] Mary, the *Ark of the New Covenant,* is special too, because she joins her voice to ours, so that God listens to our pleas which are all the more efficacious. Recourse to Our Lady is the best way to beseech God. She herself intercedes for us from above, and redirects our petitions if they are not altogether perfectly well-intentioned. *Taken up to heaven, she does not lay aside this salvific duty... by her constant intercession continues to bring us the gifts of eternal salvation,* the Second Vatican Council has reaffirmed.[9]

Our Mother went up to heaven, body and soul. Tell her often that we, her children, refuse to be separated from her. She will hear you![10] Mother of ours, you who are so close to God the Father, God the Son, and God the Holy Spirit, don't let us go from your hand...don't let me go, or them, my Mother. What great security devotion to the most Holy Virgin gives us all the time! She will always listen, no matter what circumstances we are in.

---

[6] St Amadeus of Lausanne, *Eight Marian Homilies,* Buenos Aires
[7] cf Bl. Paul VI, *Address,* 17 May 1975
[8] 1 Kings 8:29
[9] Second Vatican Council, *Lumen gentium,* 62
[10] St. J. Escrivá, *Furrow,* 898

14.2 The hope of heaven.

According to an ancient Jewish tradition, when Jerusalem was destroyed by the armies of Babylon the prophet Jeremiah brought the Ark away and hid it in a secret place. No one has seen it since. Only St John tells us, as we are reminded in the reading from this morning's Mass, he saw it in heaven, a clear allusion to the most holy body of Our Lady: *The sanctuary of God in heaven opened, and the Ark of the Covenant could be seen inside it.*[11] No one can tell for sure when, from where, or in what way the Blessed Virgin left the earth, but we know where she is. When Elias was taken up to heaven, the sons of the prophets of Jericho asked Eliseus if they could go out to look for him. They said to him: *'It may be that the spirit of the Lord has transported him to the top of a hill or has left him in a crevice in the valleys'.* Eliseus consented to their wish grudgingly. When they returned from the fruitless search, he reproached them: *'Didn't I tell you not to go?'* (2 Kings 2:16-18). The same situation arises concerning the body of the most Holy Virgin. Nowhere in Christendom will we ever hear a rumour of her whereabouts. So many churches throughout the world enthusiastically affirm that they possess the relics of this or that saint. Who can say for sure if St John the Baptist lies in Amiens or in Rome? No such claim will ever be made regarding Our Lady. And if anyone were still hoping to find so priceless a treasure, we know that the Holy Father declared an end to all investigation of the sort some time ago. We know where her body is: It is in heaven.

Naturally, we already knew it before.[12] Pope Pius XII defined the Assumption as a dogma of the Faith on November 1, 1950, in these words: *With the course of her*

---

[11] *First Reading*, Rev 11:19
[12] R.A. Knox, *Feasts of the Liturgical Year*

earthly life brought to completion, the Immaculate Mother of God, the ever Virgin Mary, was taken body and soul into celestial glory.[13] Since the beginnings of Christianity, the faithful have been convinced, Mary did not undergo corruption in the tomb, but was taken to heaven body and soul. An ancient Father of the Church writes: I*t was fitting for the one who preserved her virginity in giving birth to be conserved from any corruption after death. It was appropriate for her who had taken the Creator made Child into her womb, to dwell in the divine abode. It was right that she who saw her Son receive, heart and soul on the cross, what she had been freed from in giving birth, should contemplate him seated at the right hand of the Father. It was truly just for the Mother of God to possess the honour due her Son, and to be esteemed as Mother and Handmaid of God by all creatures.*[14]

The Assumption of Mary fills us with joy, and encourages us along the way still remaining before we reach heaven. She gives us the courage and energy to reach the sanctity we are called to by our vocation. Furthermore, it is necessary that we struggle to be good daughters and sons of God, *to make an effort to keep our souls clean through frequent sacramental confession and the reception of the Eucharist. In this way we will reach heaven, not in the same way as the most Holy Virgin, since due to sin our bodies will experience corruption. Nevertheless, if we die in God's grace, our soul will go to heaven, perhaps by way of Purgatory first so that we might put on the wedding garment indispensable for entering the heavenly banquet where we will see God 'sicuti est,' 'as He is' (1 John 3:2).*

---

[13] Pius XII, Apostolic Constitution, *Munificentissimus Deus,* 1 November 1950

[14] St John Damascene, *Second Homily on the Dormition of the Blessed Virgin Mary,* 11, 14

Later on, at the final resurrection of the dead, our bodies will also rise, and be reunited with our glorified souls, and we will then receive the eternal reward.[15] We will then join Jesus and his most holy Mother in endless joy.

14.3 Being faithful is worth while.

Seeing the happy conclusion of the Virgin's life, we understand the joy of being faithful each day. We realize that t*he struggle to say 'yes' to the Lord is worth while. In our pagan environment, we have the divine vocation to sanctify ourselves and to sanctify others. It is worth everything, to reject firmly anything that can separate us from God, and to respond positively to whatever draws us close to him. The Lord will help us, since He does not ask the impossible. Since He demands that we be saints, in spite of our undeniable wretchedness and the difficulties we encounter, He will grant us his grace. Therefore, 'possumus! ... we can!' (Mark 10:39). We can be saints, despite our defects and sins, since God is good and all-powerful, and we have the Mother of God herself, whom Jesus cannot refuse, as our own.*

Let us then be filled with hope and confidence. In spite of our shortcomings, we 'can' be saints, if we struggle one day after another, if we purify our souls in the Sacrament of Penance, and if we frequently receive the living bread that has come down from heaven (John 6:41), the Body and Blood, Soul and Divinity of Our Lord Jesus Christ, truly present in the Sacred Eucharist.

And when the moment to render an account of our soul to God comes, we shall not fear death. Dying will be like moving to a new home for us. It will come when God wants. It will be a liberation, the beginning of Life with a

---

[15] A. del Portillo, *Homily at the Shrine of Our Lady of the Angels of Torreciudad*, 15 August 1989

capital 'L'. 'Vita mutatur, non tollitur', 'Life is changed, but it does not end for us' (Preface I for the Deceased). For we will begin to live in a new way, closely united to the most Holy Virgin, to eternally adore the most Blessed Trinity, Father, Son, and Holy Spirit. This then is the prize awaiting us.[16] In the meantime, Our Mother helps us from heaven each day in our troubles and difficulties. May we not neglect to seek her patronage, in particular on her great feast days.

---

[16] *ibid*

15 AUGUST

15. THE ASSUMPTION OF
THE BLESSED VIRGIN MARY

Solemnity

Since the fifth century the Church has held implicitly the belief in the Assumption of the Blessed Mother, body and soul, into heaven. It can be deduced from the Liturgy, from pious documents and the writings of the Fathers and the Doctors of the Church. The dogma was promulgated by Pius XII on November 1, 1950.

15.1 Mary is taken into heaven body and soul. Consideration of the Fourth Glorious Mystery of the Holy Rosary.

I will put enmity between you and the woman, and between your seed and her seed.[1] Thus appears the Virgin Mary associated with Christ the Redeemer in the fight against and triumph over Satan. This is the message of the first book of Sacred Scripture, the divine plan Providence prepared from all eternity to save us. In the last book we find the admirable scene: *A great sign appeared in heaven: a woman clothed with the sun, and the moon beneath her feet, and on her head a crown of twelve stars.*[2] The Virgin Mary enters, body and soul, into heaven after finishing her life among us. The Mother of God arrives to be crowned Queen of the Universe. *So will the king desire your beauty,*[3] we proclaim in the *Responsorial Psalm* of the

---

[1] Gen 3:15
[2] *Entrance Antiphon*: Rev 12:1
[3] *Responsorial Psalm*: Ps 44:12

Mass today.

The Apostle John was surely a witness of Mary's passage to heaven, since the Lord had entrusted her to him, and he would not have been absent at that time. In his Gospel, however, he says nothing concerning Our Lady's last moments on earth. He who spoke of Jesus' death on Golgotha with so much clarity and force, is silent when it is a matter concerning the one he cared for as his own mother, the Mother of Jesus and of all men.[4] Witnessed firsthand, it must have been like a sweet dream: *Thou art she who, as it is written, appearest in beauty, and thy virginal body is all holy, all chaste, entirely the dwelling place of God, so that it is henceforth completely exempt from dissolution into dust. Though still human, it's life is changed into the heavenly life of incorruptibility, truly living and glorious, undamaged, and sharing in perfect life,*[5] an ancient writer relates. *At the end of her earthly life, she is taken up into heavenly glory, body and soul.*[6] There, her glorious Son Jesus awaits her, just as she contemplated him after the Resurrection. With divine power, God saw to the preservation of the integrity of Mary's body. He preserves her perfect unity and complete harmony, without permitting the least alteration. Our Lady wins *the supreme crown of her privileges, to be exempt from the corruption of the tomb. Overcoming death as her Son conquered it previously, she is raised body and soul to heavenly glory.*[7] The integral harmony of the Marian privileges points to it.

We often contemplate the Assumption of Our Lady in the Fourth Glorious Mystery of the Holy Rosary: *The mother of God has fallen asleep.. But Jesus wants to have*

---

[4] M.D. Philippe, *Mystery of Mary,* Madrid 1986
[5] St Germanus of Constantinople, *Homilies about the Virgin,* 1
[6] Pius XII, Apostolic Constitution, *Munificentissimus Deus,* 1 November 1950
[7] *ibid*

his Mother, body and soul, in heaven. And the heavenly court, arrayed in all its splendour, greets our Lady. You and I – children after all – take the train of Mary's magnificent blue cloak, and so we can watch the marvellous scene. The most blessed Trinity receives and showers honours on the Daughter, Mother and Spouse of God...And so great is the Lady's majesty that the Angels exclaim: Who is she?[8] We too, full of admiration, rejoice with the angels, and we congratulate her on her feast day. And we feel proud to be sons and daughters of so great a Lady.

Popular piety in Marian art frequently represents the Virgin in the midst of clouds *borne aloft by the angels.* St Thomas Aquinas sees, in these angelic interventions on behalf of those who have left the earth and are already on the way to heaven, a manifestation of the reverence the angels and all creatures render glorified bodies.[9] In the case of Our Lady, all that we can imagine is little, nothing, even, compared with the way it must have been in reality. St Teresa tells how she once had a vision of the glorified hand of Our Lord. Afterwards, the saint said, five hundred thousand suns reflecting in the clearest crystal were as a sad and dark night in comparison. How would the gaze of Christ be? One day, if we are faithful, we will contemplate Jesus and Mary, whom we have invoked so many times in this life.

15.2 The Blessed Mother intercedes from heaven and provides for her children.

For today the Virgin Mother of God was assumed into heaven as the beginning and image of your Church's coming to perfection, and a sign of sure hope and comfort

---

[8] St. J. Escrivá, *Holy Rosary*
[9] cf St Thomas, *Summa Theologiae,* Suppl., 84, 1

to your pilgrim people.[10]

Let us look at Our Lady, already taken up into heaven. *Just as a traveller, gazing out to contemplate a vast panorama, seeks some human figure in his surroundings to bring the distant objects into perspective, so do we look towards God with amazement, but can identify and welcome a purely human figure at the side of his throne. A ship has finished its passage, a destiny has been fulfilled, a human perfection has existed. Through her, his masterpiece, we see God's relations with humanity more clearly and with greater insight.*[11]

Our Lady's privileges are related to her Motherhood and, as such, with our redemption too. Taken into heaven, Mary is an image and forerunner of the Church, still on the way towards eternal life. From heaven, *she shines forth until the day of the Lord shall come, as a sure sign of hope and solace for the people of God during its sojourn on earth.*[12] By the mystery of the Assumption into heaven, *there were definitively accomplished in Mary all the effects of the one mediation of Christ the Redeemer of the world and Risen Lord... In the mystery of the Assumption is expressed the faith of the Church, according to which Mary 'is united by a close and indissoluble bond to Christ'.*[13] She is the assurance and proof that, as her children, we will one day be in our glorified bodies beside the glorious Christ. Our aspiration to eternal life gains impetus as we meditate on our heavenly Mother above. She sees and watches over us, with a look full of tenderness,[14] with more love the greater our need. *She also has the specifically motherly*

---

[10] *Roman Missal, Preface of the Assumption*
[11] R.A. Knox, *Sermon on the Feast of the Assumption of Our Lady,* 15 August 1954
[12] Second Vatican Council, *Lumen gentium,* 68
[13] John Paul II, Encyclical, *Redemptoris Mater,* 25 March 1987
[14] cf Bl. Paul VI, *Address,* 15 August 1963

role of mediatrix of mercy 'at the final coming'.[15]

She is our great advocate before God most High. Truly, life on earth is a *valley of tears,* we are called to make sacrifices and do endure suffering. Above all though, we are not in heaven yet. At the same time, the Lord gives us many joys, and we have the hope of heaven so that we may look ahead with optimism. Mary is one of our reasons for happiness. She is *our life, our sweetness, and our hope*: We feel the affection of our Mother in our lives as Christians. We tell her, *Turn, then, your eyes of mercy toward us....* Like her Son, she is full of mercy and compassion. She never withholds her helping hand from anyone who turns to her for help: *Remember O most gracious Virgin Mary, that never was it known that anyone who fled to your protection...*[16] May we make ever more of an effort to seek the intercession of the Blessed Virgin, Queen of heaven and earth. May we fly to her, *Refuge of sinners,* and say to her: *Show to us Jesus,* whom we are in need of above all else.

For those who look to Mary in every circumstance, with the simplicity and confidence of a child before his mother, there is great security and joy. A Father of the Church writes: *Just as the Virgin Mary was a most docile instrument in the hands of the Lord, I desire greatly to be subject to her service. Grant me this request Jesus, God and Son of man, Lord of all creation and Son of your Handmaid. Allow me to serve your Mother in such a way that You will acknowledge me as your servant. May she be my sovereign on earth, so that You may be my Lord for all eternity.*[17] We need to examine the quality of our daily dealings with her. *If you feel proud to be a Son of Our*

---

[15] John Paul II, *loc cit*
[16] Prayer of St Bernard
[17] St Ildephonsus of Toledo, *On the perpetual virginity of Holy Mary,* 12

Lady, ask yourself: How often do I express my devotion to the Virgin Mary during the day, from morning until night?[18] – the *Angelus*, the *Holy Rosary*, the *three Hail Mary's* before going to bed...

15.3 Our Lady's Assumption, hope of our own glorious resurrection.

Blessed is the womb of the Virgin Mary, which bore the Son of the eternal Father.[19]

The Assumption of Mary is a wonderful precursor of our own resurrection. It is made possible through Christ's rising from the dead. He will *refashion the body of our lowliness, and conform it to the body of his glory.*[20] St Paul also reminds us in the *Second Reading* of the Mass: *As death came through one man (through the sin of Adam), through the one man Christ has the resurrection also come. Through him, all things will be restored to life, but each one in its proper order. Christ as the first fruit, and then after the coming of Christ, those who belong to Christ. After that will come the end, when He delivers the kingdom to God the Father.*[21] The Apostle writes here of Christ's coming. *In the unique case of the Blessed Mother, shouldn't it be fulfilled 'immediately' when her earthly life ends? Life for all mankind ends in death. In the case of Mary, tradition more aptly refers to it as the 'dormition'.*

'Assumpta est Maria in caelum, gaudent Angeli! Et gaudet Ecclesia!' For us, the solemnity today is like a continuation of Easter, the Resurrection and Ascension of the Lord. It is, at the same time, a sign and source of hope for eternal life and the future resurrection.[22]

---

[18] St. J. Escrivá, *The Forge*, 433
[19] *Communion Antiphon for the Vigil Mass*: cf Luke 11:27
[20] Phil 3:21
[21] 1 Cor 15:20-26
[22] John Paul II, *Address*, 15 August 1980

Today on the Solemnity, our petitions are full of confidence. *Our Advocate rose up to heaven, so she will arrange for our salvation as Mother of the Judge, the Mother of Mercy.*[23] She continually strengthens our hope. *We are still pilgrims, but our Mother has gone before us, and is already pointing to the reward of our efforts. She reminds us that it is possible to reach it, and that if we are faithful, we will in fact do so. The most Holy Virgin is not only our example: She is also 'Help of Christians'. In light of our petition – 'Monstra te esse matrem.' 'Show us that you are our Mother' (Liturgical Hymn 'Ave Maris Stella') – she could not, nor would she ever, deprive her children of her motherly care.*

'Cor Maria Dulcissimum, iter para tutum.' 'Most Sweet Heart of Mary, prepare a safe way for your own'. Guide our steps on earth with strength and security in our path on earth. Become for us the path we are to follow, since you know the way and the quick and most direct passage-ways that lead through love of you to the love of Jesus Christ.[24]

---

[23] St Bernard, *Homily on the Assumption of the Blessed Virgin Mary*, 1
[24] St. J. Escrivá, *Christ is passing by*, 177-178

21 AUGUST

16. SAINT PIUS X

Memorial

Pius X was born in 1835 in the small town of Riese in northern Italy. As a child, he experienced the privations of a large and poor family of ten children. His father was the mayor of the community.

Pius X excelled in continuous service to the Church first as a parish priest, then as Archbishop of Venice, and finally as Roman Pontiff. He exercised holy intransigence in keeping the faith pure from doctrinal error. He reformed the Sacred Liturgy and promoted the custom of the frequent reception of Holy Communion. The motto of his Pontificate was *Instaurare omnia in Christo*. He died on August 20, 1914.

16.1 The need to give doctrine through every possible means.

The Lord established for him a covenant of peace, and made him the prince, that he might have the dignity of the priesthood for ever.[1]

The years of the Pontificate of Pius X were particularly difficult, due to the internal upheavals and transformations in many nations and the consequent serious impact they had on the Christian faithful. Fundamentally, the gale-force winds that tore through the Church at this time were ideological and doctrinal in nature. Attempts to reconcile the Faith with a philosophy whose principles were diametrically opposed to it brought numerous widely-diffused errors in its wake. These ideologies attacked the very foundations

---

[1] *Entrance Antiphon*: cf Sir 45:30

of Catholic doctrine and led directly to its denial.[2]

St Pius X made the motto of his Pontificate a reality – *to restore all things in Christ*[3] – through his deep concern to stem the tide of the many evils that threatened the faithful.[4] He frequently insisted on the damage ignorance of the Faith produces. He used to say: *It is useless to expect a person without formation to fulfil his Christian duties.* Time and again he pointed out the need to teach the *catechism.* From his uneasiness concerning the lack of Christian formation there was produced the *Catechism of St Pius X,* which has done so much good in the Church. His vehement desire to give doctrine in a world starving for the want of it, is reflected throughout his entire magisterium. Even as Pope he did not want to abandon the teaching of the *Catechism,* the traditional means of disseminating good doctrine. Until 1911 he customarily taught it in St Damascene Court in the Vatican. On Sundays he used to invite the faithful from a Roman parish to celebrate Mass with him.

Many of the errors St Pius X fought against are uncritically accepted in our own day. In countries evangelized almost twenty centuries ago great numbers of people are ignorant of the most elementary truths of the Faith. Many are defenceless and with the complicity of their own passions allow themselves to be taken in by the erroneous opinions of a few.[5] The call of St Pius X to conserve and spread good doctrine is still a fully current and vital issue. In whatever way possible, it is especially urgent to make known the teachings of the Church on the meaning of life, on the end of man and his eternal destiny, on marriage, on

---

[2] cf R. Garcia de Haro, *Theological history of Modernism,* Pamplona 1972
[3] St Pius X, Apostolic Letter, *Bene nostis,* 14 February 1905
[4] cf *idem,* Decree, *Lamentabili,* 3 July 1907; Encyclical, *Pascendi,* 8 September 1905
[5] cf John Paul II, Apostolic Exhortation, *Christifideles laici,* 30 December 1988, 34

generosity in the number of children, on the right and duty of parents to choose the education their children receive, on the social doctrine of the Church, on love for the Pope and his teachings and on the evil of abortion. We should do all we can – family catechism, the diffusion of good books, daily conversations concerning faith and morals... Moreover, may we never forget as St John Paul II reminded us, that *faith is strengthened by sharing it.*[6]

16.2 Serenity and good humour in the face of difficulties.

St Pius X stands out for great firmness in confronting an adverse environment. At the same time he was profoundly humble and simple. In the *First Reading* of the Mass, the words of St Paul to the Thessalonians are quoted.[7] The Holy Pontiff could himself have written them: *We had courage in our God to declare to you the gospel of God in the face of great opposition.* Nevertheless, like St Paul, St Pius X remained serene, cheerful, and in good humour in the midst of difficulties, since his life was strongly rooted in prayer.

A soldier of the Swiss Guard recalled how one night it was his turn to be on guard duty on the patio outside the Pope's bedroom. With lance on shoulder he paced from one side of the esplanade to the other. His steps resounded on the stone pavement. At some time during the night the window opened and the Pope appeared: *My son, what are you doing there?* The young man explained his charge as best he could. St Pius X, benevolent, recommended: *Better yet, go and rest. Then we can both get some sleep.*[8]

The Pope was renowned for performing miracles. One day his former parishioners went to the Vatican to pay him

---

[6] cf *idem,* Encyclical, *Redemptoris missio,* 7 December 1990, 2

[7] 1 Thess 2:2-8

[8] cf J.M. Javierre, *Pius X,* Barcelona 1961

a visit. With their customary simplicity and confidence, devoid of tact, they asked him: *Father Beppo (as they used to call him when he was a parish priest), is it true you can work miracles?* And the Pope, with simplicity and good humour responded: *Look, here in the Vatican, you have to turn your hand to a bit of everything.*[9] Nevertheless, a Brazilian bishop, hearing of the Pontiff's great reputation for sanctity, went to Rome during the first month of 1914 to implore the cure of his mother, then very ill with leprosy. Confronted with his persistence, the Pontiff exhorted him to beseech Our Lady and some other saint. But the insistent bishop begged him: *At least repeat the words of Our Lord to the leper 'Volo, mundare!' (I so desire, be cleansed). And the Pope, condescending, with a smile repeated: 'Volo, mundare!' When the bishop returned to his country he found his mother cured of her disease.*[10]

Amidst the grave responsibilities and harsh events that bore down on St Pius X, the Lord granted him the grace not to lose his simplicity and good humour. For us who have taken our faith in the middle of the world seriously, today we can ask the Lord for these two human virtues through the intercession of the Holy Pontiff. They will help us to keep up our awareness of our divine filiation, and to be serene and cheerful no matter what the difficulty.

16.3 Love for the Church and for the Pope.

St Pius X loved and served the Church with great fidelity. From the beginning of his Pontificate he effected a series of far-reaching reforms. In a particular way he gave special attention to priests, from whom he expected *everything*. He often said, in different ways, that the sanctity of the Christian people depends in large measure on the

---

[9] cf L. Ferrari, *Pius X: Dalle mie memorie*, Bicenza 1922
[10] G. Dal-Gal, *Pius X, the Pope Saint,* Madrid 1988

holiness of their priests. On the fiftieth anniversary of his own ordination he dedicated an exhortation to all clerics entitled: *On the kind of priests the Church needs.*[11] Above all, he asked for saintly priests, entirely given to their work for souls.

Many of the problems, needs and circumstances in evidence during the eleven years of his Pontificate are still relevant. Today can therefore be a good occasion to examine the quality of our love for the Church shown with deeds. In the midst of temporal cares, do we have a living consciousness of *being members of the Church, of a personal, irreplaceable, and non-transferable task entrusted to us for the good of all?*[12] We all have this need to give good doctrine, taking advantage of every occasion, or creating occasions, to help others find the way to reconciliation with God through sacramental confession, to pray each day and offer hours of work well-finished for the sanctity of priests, to generously help to sustain the Church and good works, to contribute to the diffusion of magisterial teachings, principally in matters that refer to social justice, public morality, education, and the family. *What joy to be able to say with all the fervour of my soul: I love my Mother, the holy Church!,*[13] with a love translated each day into specific actions.

Let us also examine our filial love for the Pope, a love which is for all Christians *a delightful passion, since in him we see Christ.*[14] May we consider, with Our Lord, whether we remember to pray every day for the person and intentions of the Roman Pontiff, *so that the Lord may watch over, strengthen , and sanctify him on earth.*

---

[11] St Pius X, Encyclical, *Haerentis animo,* 4 August 1908

[12] John Paul II, Apostolic Exhortation, *Christifideles laici,* 28

[13] St. J. Escrivá, *The Way,* 518

[14] *idem, In Love with the Church,* 13

At Mass we pray: *O God, who to safeguard the Catholic faith and to restore all things in Christ, filled Pope St Pius X with heavenly wisdom and apostolic fortitude, graciously grant that, following his teaching and example, we may gain an eternal prize.*[15]

---

[15] *Collect*

22 AUGUST

17. OUR LADY, QUEEN AND MOTHER

Memorial

Pius XII instituted this feast day in 1954 in response to the unanimous traditional belief in the Mother of the *King of Kings and Lord of Lords* as Queen. All graces come to us through the intercession of the Blessed Mother, the most accessible ruler of all. Her coronation as Queen of all Creation is intimately connected to her Assumption into heaven. We contemplate this wonderful scene in the Fifth Glorious Mystery of the Holy Rosary.

17.1 Mary is Queen of heaven and earth.

The Mother of Christ is glorified as 'Queen of the Universe'. She who called herself the 'handmaid of the Lord' at the Annunciation remained faithful to what this name expresses throughout her earthly life. In this she confirmed that she was a true 'disciple' of Christ, who strongly emphasized that his mission was one of service: The Son of Man 'came not to be served, but to serve, and to give his life as a ransom for many' (Matt 20:28). In this way Mary became the first of those who, 'serving Christ also in others, with humility and patience lead their brothers and sisters to that King to serve whom is to reign' (Lumen gentium, 36), and she fully achieves that 'state of royal freedom' proper to Christ's disciples: To serve Christ is to reign with Him... Her 'glory in serving' is completely compatible with her royal exaltation. Taken up into heaven, she does not cease her service for the sake of our salvation.[1]

---

[1] John Paul II, *Redemptoris Mater,* 25 March 1987

The dogma of the Assumption which we celebrated last week leads in a natural way to the feast we celebrate today, the Queenship of Mary. Our Lady departed for heaven to be crowned by the Blessed Trinity as Queen of all Creation: *The Immaculate Virgin, preserved free from all guilt of original sin, on the completion of her earthly sojourn, was taken up body and soul into heavenly glory, and exalted by the Lord as Queen of the universe, that she might be the more fully conformed to her Son, the 'Lord of Lords' (Rev 19:16), and the conqueror of sin and death.*[2] This truth has been affirmed since antiquity by the piety of the faithful, and taught by the Magisterium of the Church.[3] St Ephraim puts these beautiful words on the lips of Mary: *Let heaven hold me in its embrace, for I am more honoured than heaven, since heaven was only your throne, not your Mother. Of course, how much more worthy of honour and veneration than his throne is the Mother of the king!*[4]

It has been quite popular to bestow Queenship on Mary through the custom of canonically crowning her images, with the express approval of the Popes.[5] Since the first centuries Christian art has represented Mary as Queen and Empress, surrounded by angels and seated on a royal throne, with all the accoutrements of such majesty. Sometimes, she is shown being crowned by her Son. The faithful have long had recourse to her as Queen through popular prayers like the *Salve Regina,* the *Ave Regina Caelorum,* and the *Regina Coeli.*

Frequently we have sought her protection, reminding her of this beautiful royal epithet. We have pondered it in the Fifth Glorious Mystery of the Holy Rosary. Today, in

---

[2] Second Vatican Council, *Lumen gentium,* 59
[3] cf Pius XII, Encyclical, *Ad caeli Reginam,* 11 October 1954
[4] St Ephraim, *Hymn about the Blessed Virgin Mary*
[5] J. Ibaez-F. Mendoza, *Mother of the Redeemer,* Madrid 1988

our prayer and throughout the day, we will do so in a special way: *You are all Fair, and without blemish. You are a garden enclosed, my sister, my Bride, an enclosed garden, a sealed fountain. 'Veni: coronaberis...Come: You shall be crowned' (Song of Songs 4:7, 12:8).*

If you and I had been able, we too would have made her Queen and Lady of all creation.

A great sign appeared in heaven: A woman with a crown of twelve stars upon her head, adorned with the sun, and with the moon at her feet (Rev 12:1). Mary, Virgin without stain, has made up for the fall of Eve: And she has crushed the head of hell's serpent with her immaculate heel. Daughter of God, Mother of God, Spouse of God... The Father, the Son and the Holy Spirit crown her as the rightful Empress of the Universe. And the angels pay her homage as her subjects... and the patriarchs and prophets and Apostles... and the martyrs and confessors and virgins and all the saints... and all sinners, and you and I.[6]

17.2 The royal titles of Our Lady.

We read in the Gospel of the Mass today: *And behold, you will conceive in your womb and bear a son, and you shall call his name Jesus. He will be great, and will be called the Son of the Most High. And the Lord God will give him the throne of his father David, and He will reign over the house of Jacob for ever. Of his kingdom there will be no end.*[7]

The sovereign royalty of Mary is intimately connected to her Son's. Jesus Christ is King since total, proper and absolute power belong to him, as much in the natural order as in the supernatural. The royalty of Mary is entire as well: it stems from her Son. The terms *Queen* and *Lady*

---

[6] St. J. Escrivá, *Holy Rosary*
[7] Luke 1:31-33

with reference to the Virgin are not metaphors. By means of them, we designate a true pre-eminence and an authentic dignity and power in heaven and on earth. As Mother of the King, Mary is truly and properly Queen. She is the apex of creation, and effectively the first entirely human person of the universe. *Almighty God placed her far above all the angels and all the saints, and so filled her with every heavenly grace, taken from His own divine treasury, that she was always free from all stain of sin, all beautiful and perfect, possessing such a fullness of innocence and holiness to be found nowhere outside of God, and which no one but God can comprehend.*[8]

Mary's entitlements to Queenship are her union with Christ as his Mother, just as the Angel Gabriel had announced, and her association with the redemptive work of her Son in the world. By the first title Mary is Queen Mother of a King who is God, and is thus raised above all other human creatures. Through the second, Mary is Queen as dispenser of the treasures and goods of the kingdom of God through her co-redemption.

When he instituted this feast day, Pius XII invited all Christians to draw near to *the throne of grace and mercy of our Queen and Mother, to ask her for help in adversity, light in obscurity, and relief in suffering.* He encouraged everyone to ask grace from the Holy Spirit, to make an effort to hate sin, to be free of its slavery, *so as to be able to render the Queen, who is so great a Mother, constant obedience, fragrant with filial devotion.*[9] *Adeamus ergo cum fiducia ad thronum gratiae, ut misericordiam consequamur... Let us therefore draw near with confidence to the throne of grace, that we may obtain mercy and find*

---

[8] Pius IX, Bull *Ineffabilis Deus,* 8 December 1854
[9] Pius XII, *loc cit*

grace in time of need.[10] This, her royal throne, is a symbol
of the authority of Christ. He wanted his Mother to be the
throne of grace, where we could easily encounter compassion, since he gave her to us as *our advocate of grace
and the Queen of all creation.*[11]

Today we contemplate the great celebration in heaven
as the Blessed Trinity greets Our Lady to take her to
heaven for all eternity. *It is indeed just, that the Father, the
Son, and the Holy Spirit should crown the Blessed Virgin,
Our Lady, as Queen and Mistress of all creation.*

*You have to make use of her power. With the daring of
a child, join in this celebration in Heaven. For myself,
since I have no precious stones or virtues to offer, I crown
the Mother of God and my Mother with my failings, once
they have been purified.*

She expects something from you too.[12] She is waiting,
and wants us to be united to the joy of the angels and
saints. We have a right to participate in such a big celebration, since she is our Mother.

17.3 The Queenship of Mary over heaven, earth, and purgatory.

*And a great sign appeared in heaven: A woman
clothed with the sun, with the moon at her feet and upon
her head a crown of twelve stars.*[13] Besides representing
the Church, this woman symbolizes Mary, the Mother of
Jesus.[14] On Calvary, He entrusted her to John, who took
care of her with so much refinement, contemplated her so
often, and later, in his old age, wrote of these visions when

---

[10] Heb 4:16
[11] *Roman Missal, Preface of the Blessed Virgin Mary, Queen of all Creation*
[12] St. J. Escrivá, *The Forge,* 285
[13] Rev 12:1
[14] St Pius X, Encyclical, *Ad Diem illum,* 2 February 1904

Mary was already exercising her sovereignty from heaven. The three features from the Apocalypse used to describe Mary are a symbol of her dignity: *clothed with the sun* means shining with grace as the Mother of God, *the moon at her feet* indicates her power over all created things, *the crown of twelve stars* is the expression of her Queenly dignity and of her rule over all the angels and saints.[15] In the Litany of Loreto following the Rosary, we call to mind each day that she is *Queen of angels, of patriarchs, of prophets, of apostles, of martyrs, of virgins, and of all saints.* She is also our Queen and Lady.

The rule of Mary is daily exercised over all the earth, as she generously distributes the grace and mercy of the Lord. Every day we seek her patronage and ask her protection. On Saturday many Christians visit one of her numerous shrines. They piously sing or pray the ancient prayer: *Hail, Holy Queen, Mother of mercy, hail, our life, our sweetness, and our hope...* Her rule extends in heaven over all the angels and the blessed, who increase their accidental glory *through the lights she communicates to them, the joy they have in her presence, and in the realization of all she does for the salvation of souls. She conveys the Will of Christ to the angels and saints for the sake of the spread of the kingdom.*[16]

The reign of Mary affects Purgatory too. Dante declares: *Hail, Holy Queen! singing on and on, close-hid till then beneath the valley's lee, on flowers and grass I there saw spirits strown.*[17] Our Mother constantly leads us to pray and offer suffrages for those who are still being purified, waiting to enter Heaven. She presents our prayers before God, and thereby increases their value. In the name

---

[15] cf L. Castan, *Mary's Beatitudes,* Madrid 1971

[16] R. Garrigou-Lagrange, *The Mother of the Saviour,* pp.236-237

[17] Dante Alighieri, *The Divine Comedy: Purgatory*, VII, 82-84

of her Son she applies his merits and her own to these souls. Our Mother is an ally of ours in helping the souls in Purgatory. If we have recourse to her often, she will move us to purify ourselves of our sins and faults in this life. She will grant us the grace of contemplating her immediately after death, without having to pass through the place of waiting and purification, since we will have already cleansed our soul of its errors and weaknesses here on earth.

O God, who made the mother of your Son to be our Mother and our Queen, graciously grant that, sustained by her intercession, we may attain in the heavenly kingdom the glory promised to your children.[18]

---

[18] *Roman Missal, Collect*

24 AUGUST

18. SAINT BARTHOLOMEW

Apostle

Feast

Bartholomew, sometimes referred to as Nathaniel in the Gospel, was one of the twelve Apostles. He was from Cana of Galilee. His friend the Apostle Philip brought him to the Lord in the region of Jordan. Jesus bestowed great praise on meeting him: *Behold a true Israelite in whom there is no guile.* He preached the Faith in Arabia and then in Armenia where he was martyred.

18.1 The encounter with Jesus.

Tradition identifies the Apostle Bartholomew with Nathanael, the friend of Philip, who conveyed his own joyful meeting with Jesus: *We have found him of whom Moses in the Law and also the Prophets wrote, Jesus the son of Joseph of Nazareth.*[1] Nathanael, like every good Israelite, knew that the Messiah would come from Bethlehem, the city of David.[2] Thus the prophet Michah had foretold: *And you, Bethlehem, Ephrathah, who are not least among the clans of Judah, for from you shall come forth one who is to be a ruler in Israel.*[3] Perhaps the town's small size is why Nathanael then answered in a rather scornful tone: *Can anything good come from Nazareth?* Without relying too much on his own explanations, Philip then invited his surprised listener to meet the Master personally: *Come and see,* he said to him. Philip knew as

---

[1] John 1:45
[2] cf St John Chrysostom, *Homilies on St John's Gospel*, 20, 1
[3] Mic 5:2

well as we do that Christ does not mislead anyone. Jesus himself *calls Nathanael through Philip, as he calls Peter through his brother Andrew. This is how divine Providence works – by calling and leading us through others. God does not want to work on his own: his Wisdom and Goodness include our participation in the creation and order of things.*[4] How many times shall we ourselves be instruments, so that our friends and family can receive the Lord's call? How many shall we have invited like Philip to *come and see*?

The sincere Nathanael accompanied Philip to Jesus... and he was astonished. The Master won his fidelity forever. On seeing him arrive with Philip, the Lord says to him: *Behold a true Israelite in whom there is no guile!* What great praise! Nathanael was surprised, and asked him: *How do you know me?* And the Lord responded in words that are mysterious for us, but were clear and enlightening for his guest: *Before Philip called you, when you were under the fig tree, I saw you.*

On hearing Jesus, Nathanael understood clearly. The words of the Lord reminded him of some intimate event: perhaps the confirmation of a resolution he was about to make. The encounter caused Nathanael to make a heartfelt explicit confession of faith in Jesus as the Messiah: *Rabbi, you are the Son of God, you are the King of Israel.* The Lord answered him: *Because I have told you I saw you under the fig tree, you believe? Greater things than this you will see.* Jesus then evoked a text of the prophet Daniel,[5] to give greater depth to the words he had just finished speaking to the new disciple: *Truly, truly, I say to you, you will see heaven opened up, and the angels of God rising and descending on the Son of Man.*

---

[4] O. Hophan, *The Apostles*
[5] Dan 7:13

18.2 Praise from the Lord. The virtue of sincerity.

In Jesus' praise for Nathanael we discover the predilection of Christ for the sincere person. The Master says of the new disciple, in him *there is no guile*: he is a man without pretence. He does not have *two tongues, one for saying the truth and another for telling lies*.[6] The same should be said of each one of us, since we are men and women of one piece who try to live the faith we profess with all its consequences. The lying person filled with duplicity, ever vacillating, always sounds like a broken bell: *You were reading in that dictionary the synonyms for insincere: 'two-faced, surreptitious, evasive, disingenuous, sly'. As you closed the book, you asked the Lord that nobody should ever be able to apply those adjectives to you, and you resolved to improve much more in this supernatural and human virtue of sincerity*.[7]

This virtue is fundamental for following Christ, since He is divine Truth and abhors all deceit.[8] Even his enemies recognized Christ's love for the truth: *Master – they told him on one occasion – we know you are truthful and teach the way of God in truth, and care not for any man; for you do not regard the person of men*.[9] He teaches us that our own ideas and thoughts have to be in accordance with the truth: *Let your speech be 'Yes, yes' or 'No, no' and – whatever is beyond these comes from evil*.[10] The devil, on the other hand, is the father of lies, since he always tries to lead men into sin, the greatest deception.[11] Jesus himself, who is always understanding and merciful with every human weakness, strictly condemns the hypocrisy of the

---

[6] St Augustine, *Commentary on St John's Gospel*, 78, 7, 16

[7] St. J. Escrivá, *Furrow*, 337

[8] cf John 14:6

[9] Matt 22:16

[10] Matt 5:37

[11] cf John 8:44

Pharisees. We can the more readily imagine the Lord's joy
in his encounter with Nathanael.

Truth will bring us authentic freedom. The Gospel
verse establishes a close relationship between truth and
freedom.[12] *Jesus Christ meets the man of every age, even
our own, with the same words: 'You will know the truth
and the truth shall make you free' (John 8:32). They
contain, simultaneously, a fundamental requirement and a
warning: An honest rapport with respect to the truth is a
condition for real freedom.*[13] May we never fear the truth,
though on occasion it may seem that being truthful will
bring some trouble which we could avoid with a lie. Only
good can come from the truth. Lying is never worth while
– not even for economic gain at the expense of a little
sacrifice of truth, or for freeing us from punishment, or
from having to undergo a rough time.

18.3 Sincerity with God in spiritual direction and in dealing with others. The virtue of simplicity.

We need to be truthful and sincere in our ordinary
relations with others. Without this virtue, living together
becomes difficult or even impossible.[14] *In a world
separated from truth, human existence becomes
increasingly clouded and darkened by error. Then, almost
imperceptibly, society begins to deceive itself by preferring
evil to good.*[15] We have to be particularly straightforward
with God, in order to approach him *without anonymity,* not
wanting to cover anything up, and with the joy and trust a
good son has in the presence of good parents.

This virtue is especially necessary in spiritual direct-

---

[12] cf Spanish Episcopal Conference, Pastoral Instruction, *The Truth
will make you free*
[13] John Paul II, *Redemptor hominis*, 12
[14] cf St Thomas, *The Ten Commandments*
[15] Spanish Episcopal Conference, *loc cit,* 37

ion: we need to learn to reveal the state of our soul to those who in the name of the Lord help us direct our steps toward heaven. In Confession, sincerity is so important that if a person does not recognize his guilt, he cannot receive grace. Nor is it only a matter of attitude towards another person, the confessor, but to God himself.

The opposite disposition – dissimulation, deceit, silence – would be as sterile, with respect to the benefits we receive, as for the one who *visiting a doctor to be cured, forgot whom he was consulting, and showed the healthy parts of his body while hiding the sick ones. God –* continues St Augustine – *is the one, not you personally, who can bandage your wounds. If you hide your sores with bandages, the doctor will not be able to cure you. It is necessary to let the doctor do the dressing, since he covers them with the right medicine. While wounds heal with the doctor's treatment, they fester with the inexpert intervention of the sick person. From whom do you suppose you are hiding them? From the one who knows all things.*[16] If we are sincere, our sins themselves will be an occasion to unite ourselves more intimately with God.

Closely related to sincerity is simplicity, another virtue we can admire in St Bartholomew, and a necessary one for seeking God. Opposed to this virtue is affectation in words and deeds, the wish to stand out, pedantry, an air of sufficiency, or boasting. These are shortcomings that make difficult following Christ closely united to him, and they pose serious impediments to helping others draw near to Jesus. The simple person does not get muddled or complicated. He sets out directly to please God in all circumstances, both in what appears good and in what seems bad. Alongside sincerity, naturalness and simplicity constitute *two marvellous human virtues which enable one*

---

[16] St Augustine, *Second Discourse on Psalm 31*

to receive the message of Christ. Conversely, all interior entanglements and complications, the twisting and turning inside and out of one's own problems, present a barrier to anyone who hears Our Lord's voice.[17]

Today, let us ask St Bartholomew to gain for us these two virtues that please the Lord so much, and are so necessary for prayer, friendship, dealings with others, and apostolate. Let us ask our Lady for the grace to go through life without subterfuge, and always with sincerity and simplicity: *'Tota pulchra es Maria, et macula originalis non est in te'... 'You are all fair, O Mary, without original sin!' In her, there is not the slightest shadow of duplicity. I pray daily to our Mother that we may be able to open our souls in spiritual direction, and that the light of grace may shine out from all our behaviour.*

Mary will obtain for us the courage to be sincere, if we ask her for it, so that we may come closer to the Most Blessed Trinity.[18] Today St Bartholomew will be our principal intercessor before Our Lady.

---

[17] St. J. Escrivá, *Friends of God*, 90
[18] *idem, Furrow*, 339

27 AUGUST

19. SAINT MONICA

Memorial

Monica was born of a Christian family in Tagaste, northern Africa in 331. At a very young age, she was given in marriage to a pagan gentleman named Patrick. She bore him several children including Augustine whose conversion she won through constant prayer and abundant tears. This saint is a great example of Christian motherhood. She died in Ostia, Italy, in 387.

19.1 St Monica's prayer for the conversion of her son Augustine.

The Gospel of today's Mass narrates Jesus' arrival in the city of Naim, in the company of his disciples and a large crowd of people. On entering, the Lord encountered a funeral procession, with a widow whose only son they were bringing to bury. *And the Lord, seeing her, had compassion, and said: 'Do not weep.' He went up and touched the stretcher, so the bearers stood still. Then he said, 'Young man, I say to thee, arise.' And the dead man sat up and began to speak. And He gave him to his mother.*[1] This miracle is wrought in souls again and again. Many who were dead to God have been restored to Life.

For many years, Augustine, the son of St Monica, lived outside of God's favour. He was dead to grace through sin. The saint whose feast we celebrate today is the irreproachable mother who through her example, tears, and prayers, obtained from the Lord the spiritual resurrection of

---

[1] Luke 7:12-17

one who would later become one of the greatest saints and doctors of the Church. Furthermore, St Monica's daily fidelity to God also won the conversion of her husband Patrick, who was a pagan. She exerted a profound influence on all those who formed part of the family circle. St Augustine summarizes the life of his mother in these words: *She looks after everyone as if she truly were the mother of all. She also serves everyone, as if she were the daughter of all.*[2]

St Monica constantly kept the conversion of her son in mind. She wept much, begged God insistently, and never stopped asking good and wise people to speak to her son and try to convince him to abandon his errors. One day St Ambrose, the bishop of Milan, whom she had already visited several times, took his leave from her in words that have been the consolation of so many mothers and fathers throughout the centuries: *Go away from me now. As you live, it is impossible that the son of such tears should perish.*[3] The example of St Monica remained engraved on the soul of St Augustine so that years later, perhaps recalling his mother, he exhorted: *Do everything in your power to obtain the salvation of those in your family.*[4]

The family is truly the appropriate place for children to receive, develop, and often recover the Faith. *How pleasing to the Lord to see the Christian family as truly a 'domestic church', a place of prayer and of the transmission of faith, of learning through the example of the older ones and of solid Christian attitudes preserved throughout life as a most sacred legacy. People said of St Monica that she was 'twice mother of St Augustine', since she not only gave him birth, but also won for him the Catholic faith and a*

---

[2] St Augustine, *Confessions*, 9, 9, 22
[3] *ibid*, 3, 12, 21
[4] *idem, Sermon* 94

Christian life. Thus, all Christian parents are called to be procreators of their children twice over – as far as their natural life is concerned, and with respect to their spiritual vitality in Christ.[5] They will receive a double reward from the Lord and twice the joy in heaven.

19.2 Transmitting the faith in the family. Family piety.

Prayer for one's children should never slacken. It is always effective, even if at times, as in the case of St Augustine, the fruit of the prayer is slow in coming. All prayer for the family is very pleasing to the Lord, especially when accompanied by our diligent efforts to lead an exemplary life. St Augustine says of his mother: *She strove to win him to you, speaking to him about you through her conduct, by which you made her beautiful, an object of reverent love, and a source of admiration to her husband.*[6] If we want to lead those around us to God, our example and joy need to come first. Complaints, bad moods and bitter zeal achieve little or nothing. Constancy, peace, cheerfulness and humble and persevering prayer to our Lord gain all things.

The Lord makes use of the prayer, example and the words of parents to forge the souls of their children. Together with an exemplary life, this being a continuous education in itself, parents have to teach their children practical ways of dealing with God, especially during the first years of their childhood, when they are barely beginning to utter their first words. Children should become accustomed to simple vocal prayers passed on from generation to generation, short, clearly comprehensible phrases, capable of planting in their hearts the first seeds of what will one day be solid piety. They should

---

[5] John Paul II, *Address*, 10 March 1989
[6] St Augustine, *Confessions*, 9, 9, 19

become familiar with ejaculatory prayers, words of
affection for Jesus, Mary and Joseph, and the invocation of
the Guardian Angels. Little by little, over the years, they
should learn to greet the images of the Lord and of Our
Lady with piety, to bless and give thanks at meals, to pray
before going to bed. Parents should never forget that,
above all, their sons and daughters are children of God.
They need to teach them to behave as such.

From this climate of joy, piety, and the practice of
many human virtues – industriousness, sobriety and
effective concern for those who suffer need – vocations
will spring up naturally, these being the greatest reward and
honour parents can receive on earth. For this very reason St
John Paul II exhorted parents to create a human and
supernatural tone for the encouragement of vocations. He
counsels: *Though the time is coming when you as fathers
and mothers will think your children could become
enthralled by the fascinations of the present age, do not
despair. They will always look to you, to see whether you
yourselves consider the call of Jesus Christ a restriction or
as an enriching encounter in your lifetime, as a joy and
source of strength in everyday affairs. More than anything,
don't stop praying. Think of St Monica whose worries and
prayers intensified when her son, Augustine, later to
become a bishop and a saint, strayed from the path of
Christ in the belief he had found freedom. There are so
many mothers today in the same situation as St Monica.
Nobody can thank them enough for what they have done
through prayer and sacrifice for the Church and the Kingdom of God. May God reward them for it. If the desired
renewal of the Church depends for the most part on its
priests, then it will also depend to a large degree on the
families and in particular on women and mothers.*[7] They

---

[7] John Paul II, *Address,* 4 May 1987

can do a great deal in the sight of God and for the rest of the family.

19.3 Prayer as a family.

If the prayer of St Monica as a mother was so pleasing to God, how much more will that of the entire family praying for the same ends be. *Family prayer*, St John Paul II wrote, *has its own characteristics. It is done in common, husband and wife together, parents and children united. The words of the Lord promising his presence among us can be applied to the members of the Christian family in a special way: 'I say to you further, if two of you shall agree on earth about anything at all for which they ask, it shall be done for them by my Father in heaven. For where two or three are gathered together for my sake, there am I in the midst of them' (Matt 18:19).*[8] Through common prayer, the members of the family are brought together with greater strength, among themselves, and with God.

The gist of family prayer is family life itself; joys and sorrows, hopes and disappointments, births and birthday celebrations, the wedding anniversary of the parents, departures, separations, homecomings, important and far-reaching decisions, the death of loved ones, etc. These moments mark God's loving intervention in the family's history. They should also be seen as suitable moments for thanksgiving, for petition, for trusting abandonment of the family into the hands of their common Father in heaven. The dignity and responsibility of the Christian family as the domestic Church can be achieved only with God's unceasing aid, which will surely be granted if it is humbly and trustingly petitioned for in prayer.[9]

---

[8] *idem*, Apostolic Exhortation, *Familiaris Consortio*, 22 November 1981, 59

[9] *ibid*

The centre of the Christian family should be the Lord. Therefore, whatever circumstance may be incomprehensible through a strictly earthbound outlook, it is understood to be permitted by God for the greater good of all. In this way, sickness or death, the birth of a physically impaired child or any other trial, is acknowledged with supernatural vision. These things should not lead to discouragement or bitterness, but to increased trust in the Lord, and to abandonment in the hands of the Father of all.

Today we ask St Monica for the constancy she had in prayer. May she help all families to preserve the treasure of family piety, though the habits now prevalent in many places may not be conducive to it. Such a situation should lead us to greater resolve that God be truly the centre of every home, beginning with our own. In this way family life will be a foretaste of heaven.

28 AUGUST

20. SAINT AUGUSTINE

Memorial

Augustine was born in Tagaste, northern Africa in 354. After a tumultuous youth, he converted at the age of 33 and was baptized in Milan by St Ambrose.

On returning to his homeland, he was chosen to be the Bishop of Hippo and developed a broad and deep apostolate through his preaching and his doctrinal writings in defence of the Faith. The head of his flock for thirty-four years, he was a model of service to all through a life of constant oral and written catechesis. He is one of the greatest Fathers of the Church. He died in 430.

20.1 Life should be a continual conversion.

St Augustine received a Christian education from his mother St Monica. Though there were years during which he lived far removed from true doctrine, as a consequence of her maternal solicitude he always kept in mind the memory of Christ, whose name, he says, *he drank from his mother's breast.*[1] When he returned to the Catholic faith after many years, he affirmed that he came back *to the religion imbued in him from childhood, that penetrated the very marrow of my being.*[2] In countless cases, primary education has been the firm foundation of the faith for many to return to, after living, perhaps, very tragically alienated from God.

Love for the truth, ever present in the soul of Augustine, is especially apparent in some of his classic

---

[1] St Augustine, *Confessions,* 3, 4, 8
[2] *idem, Against the Academics*, 2, 2, 5

works.[3] Yet despite this love, Augustine, early on, fell into serious doctrinal errors. Scholars point to three directions of his straying: *First, a mistaken account of the relationship between reason and faith, so that one need choose between the two of them; second, in the supposed contrast between Christ and the Church, with the consequent conviction that it is necessary to abandon the Church in order to adhere more fully to Christ; and third, the desire to free oneself from the consciousness of sin, not by means of its remission through the working of grace, but by means of the denial of the involvement of human responsibility in the sin itself.*[4]

After years of seeking the truth without finding it, through the grace his mother constantly implore, he became convinced that only in the Catholic Church was he to find truth and peace for his soul. He came to realize that faith and reason are mutually destined to help lead man to the knowledge of the truth, each in its own way.[5] He concluded that for faith to be sure, the divine authority of Christ found in Sacred Scripture and guaranteed by the Church was required.[6]

We too receive many graces in our intelligence, to see clearly and to learn revealed doctrine in depth. We have abundant assistance for our will also, to maintain a continual state of conversion, so as to be a little closer to Our Lord each day: *For a son of God, every day should be an occasion for renewal, knowing for sure that with the help of grace we will reach the end of the road, which is Love.*

That is why if you begin and begin again, you are doing well. If you have the will to win, if you struggle, then

---

[3] *idem, Confessions,* 3, 4, 7

[4] John Paul II, Apostolic Letter, *Agustinum hipponensem,* 28 August 1986

[5] St Augustine, *Against the Academics,* 3, 20, 43

[6] *idem, Confessions,* 6, 5, 7

*with God's help you will conquer. There will be no diffi-
culty that you cannot overcome.*[7] God will never withhold
his help. If we ever have the misfortune to separate
ourselves from him in a serious way, He will await our
return, as did the father of the prodigal son, and as Our
Lord awaited the return of St Augustine for so many years.

20.2 To begin and begin again.

Although Augustine saw the truth clearly, he still had
not reached the end of the road. He sought excuses to avoid
taking the final step. For him, this would involve a radical
surrender to God, the abjuring, through the predilection of
Christ, of a human love.[8] He well knew *he was not
prohibited from marrying, but he did not want to be a
Catholic Christian in any other way except by renouncing
the excellent ideal of family in order to dedicate himself
with 'all' his soul to the love and possession of Wisdom ...
He accused himself with great shame, 'Cannot you do what
these youths and maidens do?' (Conf. 8:11,27). A deep and
painful struggle ensued, which was brought to its close by
divine grace once again.*[9] He took the final step in the
summer of the year 386. Nine months later, on the evening
between April 24 and 25 of the following year, during the
Easter vigil, he received Baptism from St Ambrose.
Augustine relates the serene but radical decision that
completely changed his life: *We went* [St Augustine, his
friend Alypius, and his son Adeodatus] *to my mother and
told her the decision we had taken. She was overjoyed. We
recounted how it all happened, and she rejoiced all the
more and began to praise God 'because You, Lord, grant
more than we ask and understand' (Eph 3:20). She saw*

---

[7] St. J. Escrivá, *The Forge*, 344

[8] cf St Augustine, *Confessions*, 6, 15, 25

[9] John Paul II, *loc cit*

*that through her sighs and moving tears you had granted
more than she had asked for with respect to me. In fact,
you brought me so completely back to you that I no longer
sought wife or career in this world.*[10] Christ entirely filled
his heart.

St Augustine never forgot that memorable night: *We
received Baptism* – he recorded years later – *and all
uneasiness over our past life was dissipated. I could not
relish enough in those days your tremendous and profound
plans for the salvation of the human race.* He adds: *How
many tears I shed listening to your hymns and canticles
resonate sweetly in your Church.*[11]

The life of the Christian – our life – entails frequent
conversions. We often have need to *play the part of the
prodigal son,* to return to the house of our Father, who
always awaits our return. All the saints knew of profound
interior changes that drew them in a renewed, more
sincere, and humble way to God. In order to return to the
Lord, it is necessary to overcome our weaknesses and sins.
How St Augustine would recall his conversion, when years
later as a bishop he would preach to the faithful: *'I
acknowledge my guilt; my sin is always before me'. The
one who prays in this manner examines his own conscience
rather than that of other people. And he does so in a
profound way. Because he does not forgive himself, he can
humbly ask for forgiveness.*[12]

Confident of obtaining divine mercy, we should not
worry about always having to begin again. *All contrite, you
told me: How much wretchedness I see in myself! I am so
stupid and I am carting around such a weight of
concupiscence that it is as though I had never really done*

---

[10] St Augustine, *Confessions*, 8, 12, 30
[11] *ibid*, 9, 6, 14
[12] *idem*, Sermon 19

anything to get closer to God. Lord, here I am beginning, beginning, always just beginning! I will try, however, to push forward each day with all my heart.

May he bless those efforts of yours.[13]

20.3 The importance of little things that separate us from the Lord. The Blessed Virgin and conversion.

'Search for the Lord and your soul shall live.' May we go out to meet him, and may we continue to seek him after finding him. So that we may search for him, He withdraws from view that we may keep on looking, even after finding him. He is immeasurably bountiful. He satisfies our desires according to our own capacity to seek him.[14]

St Augustine's life was a continual seeking for God. Ours must grow in this way too. The more we find and possess him, the greater will be our capacity to continue growing in his love.

Conversion brings with it a renunciation of the state of sin – any disposition not in accord with the teachings of Christ and his Church – and a sincere turning to God. We should frequently ask Our Mother Mary to grant us the grace to give importance even to what seems small, but separates us from God, so as to uproot it and throw it far from us. The way of conversion always begins with faith. Moved by grace, the Christian looks on the infinite mercy of God and recognizes his own fault or his lack of correspondence with what God has been expecting from him. At the same time, a firmer hope and surer love are born within.

As we finish our prayer today, *may we not forget that to Jesus we always go, and to him we always return,*

---

[13] St. J. Escrivá, *The Forge,* 378

[14] St Augustine, Commentary on St John's Gospel, 61, 1

through Mary.[15] *Turn to Our Lady and ask her – as a token
of her love for you – for the gift of contrition. Ask that you
may be sorry, with a sorrow of Love, for all your sins, and
for the sins of all men and women throughout the ages.*

*And with the same disposition be bold enough to add:
'Mother, my life, my hope, lead me by the hand. If there is
anything in me displeasing to my Father God, grant that I
may see it, so that between the two of us we may uproot it.'*

*Do not be afraid to continue, saying to her: 'O
clement, O loving, O sweet Virgin Mary, pray for me, that
by fulfilling the most lovable Will of your Son, I may be
worthy to obtain and enjoy what Our Lord Jesus has
promised'.*[16] May we not forget that Our Lord patiently
expects our coming back to him again and again. He calls
us to a life of fuller faith and dedication. May our arrival in
His presence not be delayed.

---

[15] St. J. Escrivá, *The Way*, 495
[16] *idem, The Forge*, 161

29 AUGUST

21. THE MARTYRDOM OF
ST JOHN THE BAPTIST

Memorial

St John the Baptist is the only saint who is honoured by the Church on both the occasion of his birth and of his death. Christ's Precursor teaches every one of us by his example of heroic fortitude to fulfil God's Will in our lives no matter what the obstacles may be.

21.1 The fortitude of St John the Baptist.

I spoke, O Lord, of your decrees before kings, and was not confounded; I pondered your commands and loved them greatly.[1] The Church celebrates the birth of St John the Baptist on June 24.

Today, she commemorates his *dies natalis,* the day of his death. *King* Herod, as St Mark calls him, ordered his execution. Herod is one of the most pitiful individuals in the Gospel. He ruled during Christ's years of preaching and his manifestation as the awaited Messiah, and had even met the Saviour's precursor. *Behold the Lamb of God* the Baptist told some of his own disciples. Herod also used to enjoy hearing him speak.[2] He could have met Christ, whom he longed to see in person, but he committed the enormous injustice of beheading the one entrusted with the mission of pointing him out. Immoral habits and evil passions led him to the awful crime. Moreover, they prevented him from perceiving Truth. When he finally did meet Christ face to face he blasphemously proposed the Lord of heaven and

---

[1] *Entrance Antiphon:* Ps 118:46-47
[2] Mark 6:17-20

earth entertain him and his friends with a miracle.[3]

St John the Baptist preached what specific individuals needed to hear, given their particular circumstances in society. He spoke to common townspeople, publicans, soldiers,[4] Pharisees and Saducees,[5] and even to Herod himself. Through his humble and austere example of integrity, he affirmed his testimony concerning the arrival of the Messiah.[6] The Baptist told Herod: *It is not lawful for you to have your brother's wife.*[7] He had no fear of the great and powerful, nor did he give importance to their threats. He bore in his heart God's counsel to the prophet Jeremiah which we recall in the *First Reading* of the Mass today: *Brace yourself for action. Stand up and tell them all I command you. Do not be dismayed at their presence, or in their presence I will make you dismayed. I, for my part, will make you into a fortified city, a pillar of iron, and a wall of bronze to confront the whole land: The kings of Judah, its princes, its priests and the country people will fight against you, but shall not overcome you, for I am with you to deliver you.*[8]

The Lord asks for our fortitude in everyday things. He wants our exemplary life and words to be a simple witness of our love for Christ and for his Church without our ever giving in to fear or human respect.

21.2 The Baptist's martyrdom.

St Mark narrates how *Herod had taken John and bound him in prison because of Herodias, his brother Phillip's wife, whom he had married.*[9] She hated the Baptist, since

---

[3] Luke 23:6-9
[4] Luke 3:10-14
[5] Matt 3:7-12
[6] John 1:29; 36-37
[7] Mark 6:18
[8] Jer 1:17-19
[9] Mark 6:17 ff

he had reproached the tetrarch for the notorious scandal of their illegitimate union. She therefore sought occasion to kill him. But, *Herod liked to hear him speak. Knowing that John was a just and holy man, he feared and protected him.* Her opportunity arose, however, when the king gave a banquet on his birthday and invited the foremost men of the region. The daughter of Herodias danced in the sight of all and pleased Herod and his guests. The king swore to her: *Ask me for whatever you wish, and I will give it to you, even though it be half my kingdom.* Prompted by her mother, the girl demanded the head of John the Baptist. *Grieved as he was, the king was unwilling to displease her because of his oath and the guests.* The disciples of the Baptist later took away his body and laid it in a tomb. Many of them would now become faithful followers of Christ.

John the Baptist was completely dedicated to the Lord. He put all his energy into preparing Christ's first disciples for the Master's arrival. In the end, he surrendered his very life. St Bede comments: *There is no doubt St John suffered prison and chains as a forerunner of our Redeemer. Though Herod did not demand that he deny Christ, he did try to oblige the Baptist to remain silent about the truth. We can therefore affirm the precursor did suffer martyrdom.*

Since death was ever near at hand through the inescapable necessity of nature, the martyrs considered it a blessing to embrace it for acknowledging Christ's name in return for the reward of eternal life. Hence, the Apostle Paul rightly says of them: 'You have been granted the privilege not only to believe in Christ but also to suffer for his sake.' He tells us why it is Christ's gift that his chosen ones should suffer for him: 'The sufferings of the present life are not worthy to be compared to the glory that is to be revealed in us'. [10]

Throughout the centuries, close followers of Christ

---

[10] *Liturgy of the Hours,* 2nd Reading, St Bede the Venerable, *Sermon 23*

have rejoiced in suffering persecutions, tribulations and unexpected difficulties for the faith. Many have imitated the example of the Apostles: *After being lashed, they were enjoined not to speak in the name of Jesus, and then released. They departed from the Sanhedrin, rejoicing over being deemed worthy to endure trial for the name of Christ.*[11] Far from being intimidated, *not for a single day did they cease teaching and preaching the Good News of Jesus as the Christ.*[12] They must have recalled the Lord's counsel as recorded by St Matthew: *Blessed are you when men reproach you and persecute you and speaking falsely say all manner of evil against you for my sake. Rejoice and be glad, because your reward in heaven is great. For so did men persecute the prophets who were before you.*[13]

Are we going to become disheartened or complain, if at some point we have to suffer for being faithful to the call we have received from Our Lord?

21.3 Joyfully bearing the difficulties we encounter.

The history of the Church shows that all who follow closely in the footsteps of Christ experience difficult moments and encounter the Cross. To ascend Calvary and co-redeem with Jesus there are no easy and comfortable routes. Even in the early Church, St Peter writes a letter to all Christians imbued with consolation in the midst of suffering. It was not a matter of the bloody persecutions that would come later, but of the distressing circumstances many would experience for living in accordance with their faith. For some, adversity would come through the family: Slaves had to put up with injustices from their masters[14] and

---

[11] Acts 5:40-41
[12] Acts 5:42
[13] Matt 5:11-12
[14] cf 1 Pet 2:18-25

women with the intolerance of their husbands.[15] For others, calumnies, discrimination or similar affronts arose.

St Peter reminds the faithful that the difficulties they encounter are not meaningless. They should contribute toward one's personal purification. God's judgement, not man's, is what counts. In imitation of Jesus Christ, we should keep in mind that during adversity we can draw down many graces for our persecutors, including faith, as has so often occurred in the past. He calls these individuals blessed and encourages them to bear their sufferings with joy. He also invites them to consider that through Baptism, the Christian is incorporated into Christ and participates in the Easter mystery. In the midst of suffering, each one of us can share in the Passion, Death, *and* Resurrection of Jesus who gives fruition to our daily Cross.[16]

Since the time of St John the Baptist countless souls have given their lives in fidelity to Christ. *Jesus awakened enthusiasm among his followers. Immediate contact with Him infused confidence. These benefits established a certain tone of living faith among the first Christians, which lent their lives solidity and strength. These attributes are still preserved in the community of the faithful. Christianity has yielded rich and magnificent fruits since its inception. Christ enjoys the testimony of a nearly two-thousand-year history. In spite of all external opposition and even hidden resistance, the Faith has penetrated the inner recesses of hearts and has had an enormous impact on the world. The Church today is a haven for every noble and sacred value. It has passed the test of time Gamaliel spoke of with astounding success (Acts 5:28) If it were a mere fabrication of men, it would have fallen into ruin long ago.*[17] We can

---

[15] cf 1 Pet 3:1-3

[16] cf The Navarre Bible, *The Epistles*, pp. 116-117

[17] A. Lang, *Fundamental Theology*, Madrid 1966

see the strength of faith and the love of Christ at work in ourselves and in millions who profess Him, despite what at times seems overwhelming opposition.

Most likely the Lord will not ask for our bloody martyrdom as a witness to the Faith. If he should though, we would gladly correspond with the grace. Our normal duty, however, will be our constant cheerfulness in confronting a pagan environment, since calumny, sarcasm or scorn may come our way. Our joy will then abound on earth and be doubled in heaven.

We need always to see problems in a positive light. *Let obstacles only make you bigger. The grace of Our Lord will not be lacking. 'Through the very midst of the mountains, the waters shall pass.' You will pass through mountains!*[18] *But we need faith, a keen and living faith. A faith like Peter's. When we have it – Our Lord has said so – we will move mountains, humanly insuperable obstacles that rise up against our apostolic undertakings.*[19]

Moreover, God's consolation will never be lacking. If at some point, following the path of Jesus is more trying, we shall seek refuge in the Blessed Mother, the *Help of Christians*. She will provide us protection and the shelter of her cloak.

---

[18] cf St. J. Escrivá, *The Way*, 12
[19] *ibid*, 489

8 SEPTEMBER

22. THE BIRTHDAY OF OUR LADY

Feast

Initially in the Eastern Church and subsequently in the Universal Church, the faithful have celebrated the birthday of our Blessed Mother from the earliest centuries of Christianity. This special Feast of the Mother of God and our mother is an occasion of great joy because Mary's arrival is a sign that the Redemption is drawing near. On this day, many peoples and nations honour Our Lady as their Patroness.

22.1 Joy over the birth of Our Lady.

Let us celebrate with joy the nativity of the Blessed Virgin Mary, for from her arose the sun of justice, Christ our God.[1]

Ever since the ancient inception of this feast the liturgical texts invite us to rejoice today with uplifted hearts.[2] This makes sense. We exult on the Blessed Mother's birthday just as family, friends and neighbours delight in the birth of a newborn child. Besides, so happy an event is a foreshadowing of the coming of the Messiah yet to be born. As the dawn before sunrise, Mary is the *Morning Star* who precedes the Saviour, the *Sun of Justice,* into the history of the human race.[3] An ancient writer observes: *The most significant deed of God's coming to dwell among men certainly required a joyful prelude to introduce for us the great gift of salvation. The present festival, the birth of the Mother of God, is this prelude. The*

---

[1] *Entrance Antiphon*
[2] cf J. Pascher, *The Liturgical Year,* Madrid 1965
[3] cf John Paul II, Encyclical, *Redemptoris Mater,* 3

*final act is the foreordained union of the Word with flesh ...
Therefore, let all creation sing and dance and unite to
make worthy contribution to the celebration of this day. Let
there be one common festival for saints in heaven and men
on earth. Let everything, mundane things and those above,
join in festive celebration.*[4]

The Liturgy of the Mass calls the newborn Virgin the
fulfilment of God's design in calling all men to everlasting
life.[5] From all eternity, the Blessed Trinity predestines
Mary to be the Mother of the Son. God adorns her with all
graces for this purpose. *She is the most beautiful fully
human soul ever created, second only to the Incarnation of
the Word.*[6] God gives each person the necessary strength
for a specific mission in the world.[7] Given Mary's exalted
vocation, her grace from the time of her conception
surpasses that bestowed on all the angels and saints
together. Her tremendous participation in the divine nature
was proportional to the singular dignity to which God
called her from all eternity.[8] St Bernard deduces: *Mary's
sanctity and beauty were so superlative that it was fitting
God be her Son and she His Mother.*[9] St Bonaventure
affirms: *God could have made a greater world, but he
could not have made a mother more perfect than the
Mother of God.*[10]

May we too remember that we have received a
personal call to sanctity from God to fulfil a specific
mission in the world. Besides the joy of contemplating the

---

[4] *Liturgy of the Hours, Second Reading*: St Andrew of Crete, 1
[5] Rom 8:28-30
[6] St Alphonsus Liguori, *The Glories of Mary*, II, 2
[7] cf St Thomas, *Summa Theologiae*, 3, q27, a5
[8] cf *ibid*, 3, q7, a10
[9] cf St Bernard, *Sermon 4 on the Assumption of the Blessed Virgin
Mary*, 5
[10] St Bonaventure, *Speculum*, 8

plenitude of Our Lady's grace we should not forget that God gives unfailingly to each person sufficient grace to bring a specific mission in the world to completion.

We may also consider how reasonable it is to celebrate our own birthday, since God explicitly wanted us to be born and called us to never-ending happiness and love.

22.2 Mary's birth leads us to have deep respect for every human being.

May your Church exult, O Lord, for you have renewed her with these sacred mysteries, as she rejoices in the Nativity of the Blessed Virgin Mary which was the hope and the daybreak of salvation.[11]

How old is Our Lady? As with God, time no longer has any significance for her. She has reached the fulness of age, the eternal youth born of participation in the constantly fresh vigour of the divine nature. As St Augustine teaches: *The Almighty is younger than all,*[12] precisely because He is immutable. Perhaps we have seen for ourselves the joy and interior youth of a holy person. We are amazed how strength of heart surges with boundless energy from a body that perhaps bears the weight of many years. The greater the personal union with God, the deeper such a habitual disposition can be. As the creature most closely united to Christ, Mary is certainly the youngest of all. When we seek God directly, when we turn *ad Deum qui laetificat iuventutem meam,* to the one who rejuvenates us each day and fills us with joy,[13] youth and maturity coalesce in us too.

From the time of her adolescence, the Blessed Virgin enjoyed full spiritual maturity in proportion to her age.

---

[11] *Roman Missal, Prayer after Communion*
[12] St Augustine, *Homily on Genesis,* 9,26,48
[13] Ps 42:4

Now in heaven, in the plenitude of her initial grace and that merited through union with the work of her Son, she keeps watch over us and lends her ear to our praise and petition. Today, she listens to the thanksgiving we offer to God for creating her. She looks on us and understands our life since, after God, she is the one who knows most about our weariness and struggles.[14]

Most parents believe their newborn infant is the most special child in the world. Saints Joachim and Anne must have thought so when Mary was born too. They certainly were not mistaken. All generations will call her blessed: *Little did her parents realize how great was the fruit of their chaste love. And they never grasped it in their lifetime. Who indeed can predict what is to become of a new-born babe? No one knows for sure.*[15] The future of every child is mysterious: Each one is entrusted by the Creator with a specific task to carry out in the world.

Today's feast should induce us to revere the life of every human being. Parents cooperate in the act of procreation, and God infuses a unique immortal soul at the moment of conception. *On the birthday of the Mother of God, the great joy we feel and celebrate bears with it a serious responsibility. We should be glad to learn when a child comes into being in a mother's womb, and rejoice when it enters the world. Even when the arrival of a new-born implies hardship, entails renunciations, or presents restrictions and burdens, the child should always be accepted and feel safe in the love of its parents.*[16] Every human being is called to become aware of our divine filiation, to give God glory, and ultimately to enjoy everlasting happiness.

---

[14] cf A. Orozco, *About Mary,* Madrid 1975
[15] *ibid*, p.9
[16] John Paul II, *Address,* 8 November 1985

God the Father rejoiced infinitely when a human creature full of grace was born, destined to become the Mother of the Eternal Son. The woman was free from original sin and most chaste. Although God granted Joachim and Anne special joy as a participation in the grace poured out on their daughter now born into the world like all others, what would they have felt if they had had an inkling of her vocation? More to the point, how much we should appreciate the immeasurable efficacy of our own passage through life, if we remain faithful to the grace we receive to enable us to carry out the mission granted us through the eternal Providence of God.

22.3 The value of ordinary things.

Nothing spectacular accompanied Mary's birth. The Gospels make no mention of it. She was born in a city of Galilee, probably in Nazareth itself. No extraordinary revelation took place. The world continued giving importance to other events which would soon fade and vanish from all memory. What is most important in the eyes of God often passes unnoticed by men, who commonly seek extraordinary things in order to carry on their existence. Only in heaven was there rejoicing on Mary's birthday. And a great celebration it must have been.

The Blessed Virgin spent many years of her life in obscurity. All Israel awaited the handmaid foretold in Sacred Scripture[17] without realizing her actual presence among men. Judging from appearances she hardly differed at all from others in the small town. She had free will and was capable of love, but she loved with an intensity hard for us to appreciate. Moreover, her desires were always in keeping with the love of God.

The Blessed Mother was intelligent. She placed her

---

[17] cf Gen 3:15; *Is* 7:14

mind at the service of the mysteries she gradually grew to understand more deeply. Our Lady could learn, like other girls, to sew and to cook. Moreover, she would have been able to grasp the perfect relationship between the wonders she witnessed and the prophecies referring to the Redeemer. We know she could remember and make use of specific incidents, passing from one event to another in her mind's eye. *She pondered all these things in her heart.*[18] The most Blessed Virgin must have had a vivid imagination to spur her on to a life of initiatives and simple genius in serving others. She must have known how to make life more pleasant for others, especially when sickness or misfortune would arise. Mary, moreover would have rejoiced in carrying out her mundane duties. For the most part, they would be unnoticed, but she was well aware that God lovingly contemplated her while she carried out those countless daily tasks.

By reflecting on her daily life we are led to realise that we do our ordinary work in the presence of God. We will serve others without fanfare, finish our work well, and avoid looking out for our entitlements and privileges all the time. By imitating Our Lady, we learn to understand the value of little things done every day out of love. We approach with a supernatural spirit ordinary acts that normally do not stand out at all. It takes only a minute to put some household furnishing in order. Updating information on a computer is soon over and done with. Making up the bed of a sick person is a brief task. Finding the exact citations for the lesson we are preparing takes just a little more time ... Such small tasks, done with affection to please God, draw down divine mercy on us and on our friends. They can be occasions we frequently renew for increasing sanctifying grace in our soul. Mary is the

---

[18] Luke 2:51

finished example of fidelity in the ongoing process of our sanctification *which consists in making the whole of our life into a fit offering to the Lord.*[19]

Many people throughout the world fervently celebrate our Blessed Mother's birthday. St Peter Damian teaches: *Just as Solomon and the chosen people celebrated the dedication of the Temple with great and solemn sacrifice, so should we be filled with joy at the birth of Mary. Her womb was a most holy temple. There, God received his human nature and thus entered visibly into the world of men.*[20] May we shower Our Lady with the details of affection that should be second nature to her children.

---

[19] John Paul II, *Address,* 12 October 1979
[20] St Peter Damian, *Sermon 45,* 4

14 SEPTEMBER

23. THE EXALTATION
OF THE HOLY CROSS

Feast

Devotion to the Holy Cross dates back to the earliest days of Christianity. The feast itself has been celebrated since the fourth century. Today the Church commemorates the recovery of the True Cross by the Emperor Heraclius following his victory over the Persians.

The texts of the Mass and of the *Liturgy of the Hours* proclaim the Holy Cross as the instrument of our salvation. For inasmuch as our first parents sinned beneath the shadow of a tree, God has deigned to accomplish our redemption on the wood of the Cross.

23.1 The origin of the feast day.

Through the Passion of Our Lord the Cross became a throne of glory, not a gallows of infamy. *How radiant is that precious cross which brought us our salvation. Through the cross we are victorious. With the cross we shall reign. By the cross all evil is destroyed, Alleluia.*[1]

The feast we celebrate today has its origin in the first centuries of Christianity. According to ancient testimony this commemoration began the day the Cross of Our Lord was found.[2] It developed quickly in the Eastern Church and soon spread throughout all Christendom. In Rome a solemn procession from the Basilica of St Mary Major to that of St John Lateran took place to venerate the Holy Cross before

---

[1] *Liturgy of the Hours: Lauds prayer*
[2] cf Egeria, *Journey,* Madrid 1980

Mass.[3]

At the beginning of the seventh century the Persians ransacked Jerusalem. They destroyed many churches and took possession of the sacred relics. A few years later the Emperor Heraclius recovered them. According to pious tradition, the splendidly-dressed monarch, in full regalia, personally wanted to carry the Holy Cross to its original place on Calvary. The weight became increasingly unbearable as he walked on the Via Dolorosa. The Bishop of Jerusalem, Zecariah, explained to him that to carry the Cross he must imitate the poverty of Christ, who bore it free of every earthly attachment. Heraclius immediately divested himself of the imperial garments and put on humble pilgrim's clothes. He was then able to carry the Holy Cross, unshod, to the summit of Golgotha.[4]

Most probably as children, we learned to make the sign of the Cross on our forehead, lips and heart as an external sign of our profession of faith. The Church makes use of the Cross on its altars during worship for the Liturgy and has its place outside on sacred buildings too. As a *tree of the most savoury fruit* it is a powerful weapon for warding off all kinds of evil, and especially for instilling fear in the spiritual foes of our salvation: *Lord, through the sign of the Holy Cross free us from our enemies,* we pray each day before blessing ourselves.

A Father of the Church teaches: *The Cross is a shield against the devil as well as a trophy of victory. It is the promise that we will not be overcome by the Angel of Death (Exod 9:12). The Cross is God's instrument to lift up those who have fallen and to support those still on their feet fighting. It is a crutch for the crippled and a guide for the wayward. It is our constant goal as we advance, the*

---

[3] cf A. G. Martimort, *The Church in prayer,* Barcelona 1987
[4] cf P. Croisset, *Christians,* Madrid 1846, VII

*very wellspring of our body and soul. It drives away all
evils, annihilates sin and draws down for us abundant
goods. This is indeed the seed of the Resurrection and the
tree of eternal life.*[5] During Mass we pray: *O God, who
willed that your Only Begotten Son should undergo the
Cross to save the human race, grant, we pray, that we who
have known his mystery on earth, may merit the grace of
his redemption in heaven.*[6]

The Cross is present in our lives in different ways. It
may be manifest through sickness, poverty, tiredness, pain,
scorn, or loneliness. Today in our prayer we can examine
our habitual disposition on coming face to face with the
Cross. Though hard to bear at times, the encounter with it
can become a source of purification, Life, and joy if it is
embraced with love. Embracing the Cross should lead us
never to complain when confronting difficulties, and even
to thank God for the failures, suffering, and setbacks that
purify us. Such adversities should be additional occasions
for drawing us closer to God.

23.2 The Lord blesses those he loves with the Cross.

The *First Reading* of the Mass describes the Lord's
punishment of the people of Israel for murmuring against
Moses and Yahweh when they encounter obstacles in the
desert.[7] God sends snakes that wreak havoc on the
Israelites. When they finally repent the Lord tells Moses:
*Make a fiery serpent and put it on a stand. If anyone is
bitten and looks at it he shall live. So Moses fashioned a
bronze serpent which he put on a stand. If anyone was
bitten the person looked at the bronze figure and lived.* The
bronze snake is a symbol of Christ on the Cross, since all

---

[5] St John Damascene, *De fide ortodoxa*, IV, 11
[6] *Roman Missal, Collect*
[7] Num 21:4-9

who gaze on it with faith achieve salvation.

The Lord explains further in his conversation with Nicodemus: *The Son of Man must be lifted up as Moses lifted up the serpent in the desert, so that everyone who believes in him may have eternal life.*[8] From that moment on, the path of holiness passes through the Cross. Incomprehensible realities such as pain, poverty, failure and voluntary mortification take on significance in its shadow. Moreover, the Cross is a sign of the special predilection of God who sometimes blesses us with it when he wants to bestow great graces. May we joyfully embrace the encounter, and thus be supernaturally effective, because God's love alone is capable of satisfying the human heart. Herein lies sanctity. Let us always bear the cross with love. *Are you suffering some great tribulation? Do you have setbacks? Say very slowly, as if savouring the words, this powerful and manly prayer: 'May the most just and most lovable will of God be done, be fulfilled, be praised, and eternally exalted above all things. Amen. Amen.' I assure you that you'll find peace.*[9]

23.3 The fruit of the Cross.

Cross, most faithful, you are the noblest tree of all. No other tree can compare with your leaves, your flower and your fruit.[10]

Love for the Cross produces abundant fruit in the soul. In the first place it brings us to discover Jesus immediately. He comes out to meet us and bears on his own shoulders the most burdensome part of any trial we experience. Our suffering, in union with the Master's, is no longer an evil that oppresses us. It becomes a means of union with God. *If*

---

[8] John 3:14-15
[9] St. J. Escrivá, *The Way,* 691
[10] Hymn, *Crux fidelis*

you are suffering, unite your sorrow to his sorrow: unite
your Mass to His. The world will probably not understand
this advice, but do not be disturbed. It is enough that Jesus,
Mary and the saints know what is going on. Live in union
with them, then, and let your blood flow for the benefit of
all mankind ... just as He did.[11]

The Cross of every day is a great opportunity for purification, detachment and even for an increase in grace.[12] St
Paul frequently reminds Christians that tribulation is
always brief and endurable. The prize for suffering out of
love for Christ is eternal and satisfying. Therefore, the
Apostle rejoices in his tribulations. He even glories in
them, considering himself blessed to be able to unite his
own suffering to the sacrifice of Jesus Christ. In this way
he helps bring the Lord's Passion to completion for the
good of the Church and of souls.[13]

The only real tragedy is to stray from Christ. All other
sufferings pass. Every one of them can become a real
source of peace and joy for us. *Is it not true that as soon as*
you cease to be afraid of the Cross, of what people call the
cross, when you set your will to accept the Will of God,
then you find happiness, and all your worries, all your
sufferings, physical or moral, pass away? Truly the Cross
of Jesus is gentle and lovable. There, sorrows cease to
count; there is only the joy of of knowing that we are co-
redeemers with Him.[14]

Moreover, our constant recourse to and friendship with
the Master teach us to bear difficulties that crop up with a
firm and youthful spirit. We need never complain or give
in to sadness. As happens in the lives of the saints,

---

[11] C. Lubich, *Meditations,* Madrid 1989
[12] cf A. Tanquerey, *The divinization of suffering*, Madrid 1955
[13] cf Rom 7:18; Gal 2:19-20; 6;14; etc.
[14] St. J. Escrivá, *The Way of the Cross*, 11

adversity will become a stimulus for us. We shall accept it with cheerful spirit, as one more obstacle to be overcome, enabling us to be more identified with Christ.

Joy and optimism during rough moments is not a fruit of temperament or of age. It is born of a deep interior life and the frequent consideration of our divine filiation. Our serene perspective on passing events will create a positive tone in our family, while we are at work, and in all our social relations. This equanimity will then be an occasion for others to draw closer to the Lord.

We finish our time of prayer with Our Lady: *'Cor Mariae perdolentis, miserere nobis'. Invoke the Heart of Mary. Have the purpose and determination of uniting yourself to her sorrow in reparation for your sins and the sins of all men. Pray to her – for every soul – that her sorrow may increase in us our aversion from sin, and that we may be able to love the physical or moral suffering of each day as a means of expiation.*[15]

[15] *idem, Furrow*, 258

15 September

24. OUR LADY OF SORROWS

Memorial

Today's feast follows immediately upon the Triumph of the Cross. The Church reminds us of the special union that Mary shared in the Sacrifice of her Son on Calvary. The Christian faithful have long meditated upon this momentous scene as it is recorded by the four Evangelists.

During the fourteenth century a *Sequence* for the Mass, *Stabat Mater Dolorosa,* came into popular use in some countries. In 1814, Pope Pius VII extended the devotion to the whole Church. In 1912, St Pius X decreed that the feast would be celebrated on September 15. The Blessed Virgin exemplifies for us the co-redemptive meaning of our own pains and sufferings.

24.1 The suffering of Mary is united to Christ's suffering.

> *O sweet Mother, font of love,*
> *Touch my spirit from above,*
> *Make my heart with yours accord.*
> *Make me feel as you have felt,*
> *Make my soul to glow and melt,*
> *With the love of Christ, my Lord.*[1]

Jesus wanted to associate his Mother with the work of redemption and make her a participant in his supreme sacrifice. As we celebrate the co-redemptive suffering of Mary today the Church invites us to offer our many little difficulties and voluntary mortifications for the salvation of souls. Through union with the Lord's work of redemption

---

[1] *Sequence of the Mass*, Hymn, *Stabat Mater*

Mary underwent the torments of any good mother who sees her son in the throes of death, but in addition her pain had the salvific quality of Christ's own Passion. She who is full of grace and the most pure *handmaid of the Lord* offers up all of her actions in intimate union with her Son. Their value, therefore, is virtually without limit.

We will never entirely comprehend Mary's immense love for Jesus which is the cause of her great suffering. The Liturgy applies the words of the prophet Jeremiah to the sorrowful Virgin as to Christ himself: *All you who pass by the way, look and see, was there ever a sorrow to compare with my sorrow.*[2] The anguish of Our Lady is greater on account of her eminent holiness. Her love for her Son allows her to endure His sufferings as though they were her own: 'When the soldiers strike the body of Christ, it is as if Mary is subjected to every blow. When they pierce his head with thorns, Our Lady feels their sharp penetration. When the same men offer Him gall and vinegar, the Blessed Mother tastes all the bitterness. As they spread His body on the cross, Mary is torn from within.[3] The more a person loves, the more he or she identifies with the pain of the beloved. *A brother's death is more upsetting than a pet's. A son's dying is more trying than a friend's. To get a grasp of Mary's grief at the crucifixion we need somehow to appreciate the great extent of her love for her Son.*[4]

Christ's agony is greatest in Gethsemane. On account of his profound sensitivity to the malice of sin, that night also meant untold moral suffering. Sin is an offence against God, a wicked affront to His infinite holiness and the cause of the Passion. It is much more serious than a mere transgression. The Virgin realized this more than any other

---

[2] Lam 1:12
[3] A. Tanquerey, *The divinization of suffering*, p.108
[4] St Alphonsus Liguori, *The Glories of Mary*, 2,9

creature. On account of her own awareness of the
enormous evil of sin, Mary was plunged in bitter grief on
beholding its horrible consequences for her Son. *Every one
of us contributes in some way toward increasing the
suffering of Christ. For this reasons, we should rejoice to
be able to meditate slowly on sin's impact on the loving
Hearts of Jesus and Mary. We will then accept our share in
their suffering and make reparation gladly.*[5]

24.2 The co-redemption of Our Lady.

The Lord wanted to show us through Mary and
Joseph, the creatures he most loved, the close relationship
happiness and redemptive efficacy have with the Cross.
Even though Our Lady's entire life leads up to Calvary at
her Son's side, there is a special moment when her
participation in the sufferings of Jesus the Messiah is
revealed with particular clarity. We remember how Mary
comes with Joseph to the temple to offer sacrifice for a
legal impurity that did not oblige her and to entrust her Son
to the Most High. In the immolation of her Son Mary
glimpses the grandeur of his final redemptive act. God also
wants to reveal to her the depth of his sacrifice to come and
her own particular role in it. Moved by the Holy Spirit, the
just man Simeon tells Mary: *Behold, this child is destined
for the fall and rise of many in Israel and for a sign that
shall be contradicted. And your own soul a sword shall
pierce, that the thoughts of many hearts may be revealed.*[6]

These prophetic words to Mary clearly announce that
her life will be intimately associated with the redemptive
work of her Son. John Paul II comments: *Simeon's words
seem like a 'Second Annunciation' to Mary for they tell her
of the historical circumstances in which the Son is to*

---

[5] A. Tanquerey, *op cit,* p.110
[6] Luke 2:34-35

*accomplish his mission, namely in misunderstanding and
sorrow ...They also reveal that she will have to live her
obedience of faith in suffering at the Saviour's side and
that her motherhood will be mysterious and sorrowful.*[7]

Even though the Blessed Virgin had perhaps already
moved into a modest home in Bethlehem with the Child
Jesus and Joseph, the Lord does not spare his own mother
the confusion of a precipitous flight into Egypt. She was
probably happy in her life centred upon Jesus when called
upon to gather the family's modest belongings and
undertake the hasty journey. Neither does God spare her
exile in a strange land where she would have to begin
family life anew. Once established in Nazareth again, Mary
is suddenly disconcerted over the disappearance of the
twelve-year-old Jesus who has been missing in Jerusalem
for several days. We see again here how God permits the
Blessed Mother to undergo such unsettling trials.

During the Lord's public ministry Mary hears false
rumours and calumnies regarding her Son. She is surely
aware of the various plots of the Jews against Jesus. Closer
to the consummation of his redemptive mission, reports
arrive, one by one, concerning the events taking place
during the night of the Passion. She hears the shouts calling
for his death the next morning, and experiences his
abandonment by the disciples, in union with him. Our Lady
meets her Son on the slope leading up to Calvary. Who can
comprehend the agony engulfing the Blessed Virgin's heart
at this juncture? She stands there and sees how they nail
him to the Cross. Horrible insults and the prolonged
torment of the crucifixion follow.

> *O, how sad and sore distressed*
> *Was that Mother highly blessed*
> *Of the sole begotten One.*

---

[7] John Paul II, Encyclical, *Redemptoris Mater,* 25 March 1987

> *Christ above in torments hangs,*
> *She beneath beholds the pangs*
> *Of her dying, glorious Son.*[8]

As we consider the active role our own sins play in the sorrow of our Mother, we ask her today to help us share in her suffering through profound contrition for all sin. With her help may we be more generous in making reparation for our own offences against God and the ones committed in the world every day.

24.3 Sanctifying our sufferings through recourse to the Blessed Virgin, *Comforter of the Afflicted.*

Today's feast is an occasion for us to accept all the adversity we encounter as personal purification, and to co-redeem with Christ. Mary our Mother teaches us not to complain in the midst of trials as we know she never would. She encourages us to unite our sufferings to the sacrifice of her Son, and so offer them as spiritual gifts for the benefit of our family, the Church, and all humanity.

The suffering we have at hand to sanctify often consists in small daily reverses. Extended periods of waiting, sudden changes of plans, and projects that do not turn out as we expected are all common examples. At times setbacks come in the form of reduced circumstances. Perhaps at a given moment we even lack necessities such as a job to support our family. Practising the virtue of detachment well during such moments will be a great means for us to imitate and unite ourselves to Christ. Mary is there when her Son is stripped even of his tunic. She well knew this garment he wore, since she had sewn it with her own hands. With her as our model we will find consolation and the energy to strive forward with peace and serenity.

---

[8] *Sequence of the Mass*, Hymn, *Stabat Mater*

Sickness may knock at our door. In such an event we will ask for the grace to welcome the illness as a *divine caress* and we will give thanks for the gift of health we did not entirely appreciate before. In whatever form sickness assails us, even if it should involve psychological disturbance, it can be the touchstone of our love for God, an occasion for renewing our confidence in Him and for growing more rapidly in the theological virtues. We can grow in *faith,* because we can learn to better perceive the provident hand of our Father God at work both in sickness and in health. Our *hope* can be strengthened, since we entrust ourselves more into the Lord's hands when we are most in need. *Charity* has a chance to grow too, because we can offer our situation with exemplary joy because we realize that God permits it for our greater good.

The particular circumstances are frequently the most trying dimension of sickness. Perhaps its unexpected duration, our own helplessness or the dependence on others it engenders is the most difficult part of all. Maybe the distress due to solitude or the impossibility of fulfilling our duties of state is most taxing. A priest, for example, may not be able to continue his works of apostolate. A religious may be unable to follow the rule. The mother of a family might be prevented from looking after her children. Any of these situations, or a combination of them, would go against our nature and would be hard to bear. But despite any such sufferings, after using all the necessary means for recovering our health we must join the saints in saying: *Lord, I accept all of these circumstances, whatever you want, whenever and however you so desire.*[9] We ask Jesus for an increase of love, and tell him slowly and with complete abandonment as we have perhaps so often told him in a variety of situations: *Is this what you want Lord?*

---

[9] A. Tanquerey, *op cit,* p.168

... Then it is what I want too.[10]

A mother always understands her children and consoles them in their troubles, and Mary is our spiritual Mother. When our responsibilities become too heavy for our limited strength we have recourse to her and implore from her help and relief. *She continues to be the loving consoler in the many physical and moral sufferings that afflict and torment humanity. She knows our sorrows well, because she too suffered from the time of Bethlehem until Calvary: 'And a sword will pierce your own soul too' (Luke 2:35). From Jesus on the Cross she has the specific mission only and always to love us in order to save us. Mary consoles us above all by pointing out to us Christ Crucified and paradise. O Consoling Mother, comfort us all, make us understand that the secret of happiness lies in goodness and in always faithfully following your Son Jesus.*[11] He always knows the best way for each one of us to follow Him.

---

[10] cf St. J. Escrivá, *The Way*, 762
[11] John Paul II, *Address*, 13 April 1980

21 SEPTEMBER

25. ST MATTHEW

Apostle and Evangelist
Feast

St Matthew the Apostle was born in Capharnaum. He was working as a tax collector when Our Lord called him to be one of the Twelve Apostles. Tradition unanimously recognizes him as the author of the first Gospel, originally written in Aramaic, but soon translated into Greek. This Evangelist was martyred in Persia.

25.1 St Matthew's correspondence to the Lord and our own vocation.

The Evangelists Matthew, Mark, and Luke narrate Matthew's call by Our Lord immediately after the cure of the paralytic in Capharnaum. A day or so after the miracle Jesus sets out for the seashore followed by a great crowd.[1] The place he is coming from is a small seaport city that borders the land of Perea on the other side of the Jordan. On the way he passes a booth for collecting taxes on interregional trade.

Matthew is a publican in Herod's service. Though not a court official he has purchased the right to collect taxes. The office is not highly esteemed and is even scorned by many. It is an attractive post, however, due to its great potential for acquiring wealth. A tax collector seems to have enjoyed high social status, since Matthew *made Jesus a great feast in his house; and there was a large company of tax collectors and others sitting at table with them.*[2]

---

[1] Mark 2:13
[2] Luke 5:29

The Lord invited him to become a disciple of his as he crossed in front of the taxation booth. Matthew *arose and followed him.*[3] His response is quick and generous. He had probably met the Master on other occasions and was looking forward to this momentous occasion. He does not hesitate to leave everything and follow Jesus at the first indication. God alone knows why the Lord chooses Matthew and only the Apostle could tell us what he perceived in Jesus to leave his collection tables immediately and follow him. St John Chrysostom suggests: *We see by the prompt and complete obedience of Matthew, who left all his worldly possessions in an instant, that the Lord had called him at just the right moment.*[4]

The time and place the Lord selects to ask for complete dedication are foreseen by Divine Providence and for this reason are the most opportune. At times Christ calls someone in the prime of youth. For such a person then is the best time to respond. For others Christ manifests their vocation during adulthood. He makes use of colleagues at work, family ties or other social dealings to reveal his purposes. Along with the tremendous grace of seeing our vocation God grants the strength to respond quickly and to be faithful to the end. If a person says 'No' to the Lord with the idea of saying 'Yes' at a time perceived to be more suitable, it can happen that another such occasion never comes up. Furthermore, the Lord may not lovingly knock a second time. All resistance to grace hardens the heart.[5] St Augustine describes very succinctly the urgency with which we should respond to God's gift, to his passing close by where we are on the road of life: *Timeo Jesus praetereuntem et non redeuntem, 'I fear Jesus may pass by*

---

[3] Matt 9:9
[4] St John Chrysostom, *Homilies on the Gospel of St Matthew*, 30,1
[5] cf F. Suarez, *Mary of Nazareth,* pp.49-50

and not come back'.[6]

Jesus Christ draws very near to each one of us – no matter what our age or circumstances – and his gaze meets ours in a unique way. He invites us to follow him closely. In the majority of cases he leaves us in the heart of society, our work and our family. *Think about what the Holy Spirit says, and let yourself be filled with awe and gratitude: 'Elegit nos ante mundi constitutionem' – he chose us before the foundation of the world, 'ut essemus sancti, in conspectu eius!' – that we might be holy in his presence.*

To be holy is not easy, but it isn't difficult either. To be holy is to be a good Christian, to resemble Christ. The more closely a person resembles Christ, the more Christian he is; the more he belongs to Christ, the holier he is.

And what means do we have? The same means the early faithful had, when they saw Jesus directly or caught a glimpse of him in the accounts the Apostles and Evangelists gave of him.[7]

25.2 The joy of our vocation.

To celebrate and give thanks for his vocation, St Matthew gives a great banquet and invites his friends. Many of them are considered *sinners*. This gesture reflects the new Apostle's gratitude for his vocation. Such a grace is a tremendous gift for which it is always necessary to be grateful.

We need to appreciate the wonderful results God will bring about through our vocation. If we were only to consider the renunciation every invitation to follow God entails, sadness could well ensue as in the case of the rich young man who did not want to leave his wealth.[8] He

---

[6] *The Navarre Bible,* note to Luke 18:35-43
[7] St. J. Escrivá, *The Forge,* 10
[8] cf Luke 18:18

thought only about what he would be giving up. He did not comprehend the marvel of living with God and being his instrument for accomplishing great things in the world. *Perhaps yesterday you were one of those people whose ideals have gone sour, who were defrauded in their human ambitions. Today, now that God has entered into your life – thank you, my God! – you laugh and sing and carry your smile, your love and happiness wherever you go.*[9]

The life of a person called to follow Christ, as we have all been, cannot be like that of the older brother in the parable of the Prodigal Son. He faithfully remains on his father's estate, works well, and does not spend beyond his father's means. However, he lacks joy and charity toward his younger brother, who has just repented. He is the living image of the just man who does not fully understand that to enjoy God's presence and friendship is itself a continual celebration. Serving God is a reward in its own right since to serve the Lord is to reign with Him. He wants us to work in his service with gladness, not begrudgingly, *for God loves a cheerful giver.*[10] There are always plenty of reasons to rejoice, to give thanks and be happy when we are dedicated to the Lord and respond positively to his call.

St Matthew becomes an exceptional witness to the life and death of Christ. He is chosen to be one of the *Twelve* and to follow the Lord everywhere. He listens to the Master's words, contemplates his mission, and is among his intimates at the Last Supper. He is present at the institution of the Eucharist, personally hears the Lord's proclamation of the Greatest Commandment, and accompanies the Saviour in the Garden of Olives. There with the other disciples he begins a calvary of anguish for abandoning Jesus. A little later he savours the joy of the Resurrection. Before the

---

[9] St. J. Escrivá, *Furrow,* 81
[10] 2 Cor 9:7

Ascension, he is among those who accept the command to bring the Good News to the utmost parts of the earth. Together with the Blessed Mother and the others he receives the gift of the Holy Spirit on Pentecost.

While writing his Gospel the Apostle undoubtedly relishes the memory of so many occasions in close contact with Jesus, since his life at the Lord's side is worth while. How different all of it would have been if he had remained passively at the tax collector's booth. We know that our life is precious if we live it in union with Christ and correspond with his grace more faithfully with each passing day. We too will be effective witnesses of the Lord if we respond with promptitude and joy.

25.3 Our essentially apostolic vocation.

Many of Matthew's friends and acquaintances attend the banquet to which he invites the Lord. Some are publicans and others are the Scribes and Pharisees who murmur among themselves and ask the disciples: *Why do you eat and drink with publicans and sinners?*[11] St Jerome playfully comments in a marginal note that it must have been quite a gathering of sinners!

Jesus attends the celebration in Matthew's home. He is probably glad to come and will take advantage of the opportunity to gain the affection of the new disciple's friends. Jesus responds to the criticism of the Pharisees with a wise and simple saying: *Those who are well have no need for a physician, but those who are sick.*[12] Many of the guests feel welcomed by our Lord. In time they will be baptized and become faithful Christians.

The Lord teaches us, through example, to be open to all souls. In this way we can help win over many people to

---

[11] Luke 5:30
[12] Matt 9:12

the faith. *The dialogue of salvation is not based on the personal merits of those with whom it is carried out or on the results that may or may not come about. Our Lord teaches: 'It is not the healthy who need a physician ...' The dialogue concerning salvation is open to everyone without distinction. Similarly, our own conversations should be potentially universal and capable of embracing all ...*[13] We cannot remain indifferent to anyone. The greater a person's need, the more should be our own apostolic effort to use the human and supernatural means to help spread the vision of faith. Let's examine in our prayer the quality of our social dealings. Do we treat others with human warmth and affection and are we courteously refined even with those who seem furthest removed from the faith?

You are right. 'The peaks', you wrote me, 'dominate the country for miles around, and yet there is not a single plain to be seen', just one mountain after another. At times, the landscape seems to level out, but then the mist rises and reveals another range that had been hidden.'

So it is, so it must be, with the horizon of your apostolate. The world has to be crossed. But there are no roads made for you. You yourselves will make the way through the mountains, beating it out by your own footsteps.[14]

---

[13] Bl. Paul VI, Encyclical, *Ecclesiam suam,* 6 August 1964, 74,76
[14] St. J. Escrivá, *The Way,* 928

24 September

26. OUR LADY OF RANSOM

Memorial

A pious tradition holds that one night Our Lady appeared to King James I of Aragon, to St Raymond of Penafort and to St Peter Nolasco to ask them to establish the Order of Ransomers whose purpose would be to ransom captives from the Moors. Today's feast commemorates the event. Our Lady of Ransom is the Patroness of Barcelona, Spain. Innocent XII extended the celebration to the entire Church in the seventeenth century.

26.1 Mary as intercessor for the persecuted and those bound by sin.

My soul magnifies the Lord, since in keeping with his mercy as promised our fathers he watches over his servant Israel.[1]

The most holy Virgin is venerated under the title *Our Lady of Ransom* in many parts of Aragon and Catalonia (in Spain) and in Latin America. Under this invocation, a religious order was born to save Christians held captive by the Moors. *The symbols and images of Our Lady of Ransom – broken chains and open cell doors – remind us of her role as our liberator. She opens her arms in an offer of the freedom won for us by her Son the Redeemer.*[2] Nowadays the Order's principal endeavours are directed primarily toward freeing souls from the chains of sin, an enslavement worse than any prison. Today we can pray in a special way for our brothers and sisters who are somehow marginalized

---

[1] *Entrance Antiphon*: Luke 1:46; 54-55
[2] A. Vazquez, *Our Lady of Ransom,* Madrid 1988

on account of their faith. The unbloody persecution
Catholics have experienced since the beginning of the
Church is still common even in countries with a long
Christian tradition.

In a sense the Passion of Christ continues into the present
day. The Redeemer still passes through our streets and
squares carrying the cross, and continues to suffer through
his members, the baptized. Of course, *He does not weep in
heaven where he enjoys eternal happiness with the Father
in wondrous light, but here on earth where he lives on and
endures contradiction and adversity. The tears of God roll
steadily down the divine face of Jesus. Jesus himself weeps
in each person who suffers. If we do not help stem the flow
of these tears we cannot truly say that we love him.*[3]

We cannot remain indifferent and impassive as mere
spectators in the face of the crying needs of those around
us. Our compassion for the sick and needy should be
continually renewed and refined, especially with people
who are prisoners of sin, the worst slavery of all. Above all
we can depend on the Communion of Saints to pray for
them and for all those who suffer persecution as well, that
they may be strong and bear testimony to Christ.

The *First Reading* of the Mass describes Judith, the
woman who courageously freed the chosen People from
the siege of Holofernes. The inhabitants sing out, filled
with joy: *You are the exaltation of Jerusalem, the great
glory of Israel, the pride of our nation! You have done all
this good for Israel with your might ...*[4] The Church applies
this Old Testament song of jubilation to Our Lady of
Ransom, the 'new Judith', who with her *Fiat* cooperates in
a unique way to bring about our salvation. *Mary is the
faithful Mother who stands fearlessly beside the cross as*

---

[3] W. van Straaten, *Where God Weeps*, pp.7-8
[4] Jud 15:8-10; 16:13-14

her Son sheds his blood for our salvation and reconciles all things to himself in peace.[5] We approach Our Lady of Ransom as a powerful intercessor to move our friends, relatives and colleagues to draw closer to her Son, especially through the Sacrament of Penance. She will bring relief and renewed strength to those who in any way suffer persecution for being loyal to the faith. We also ask her help for the special family intentions so close to our heart, since Our Mother in heaven has always excelled in generosity by granting us the graces we need.

26.2 She reserves many graces for us.

In the Gospel of the Mass we read about the occasion the Lord gave us his Mother as our own: *When Jesus, therefore, saw his mother and the disciple whom he loved standing by, he said to his Mother, 'Woman, behold thy son.' Then he said to the disciple, 'Behold, thy Mother'. And from that hour the disciple took her into his home.*[6] He gave us Mary as a most loving Mother.[7] *She always watches over her children with motherly affection so we may be rescued from all dangers and anxiety. Thus set free from the chains of oppression we can attain to perfect liberty of body and soul.*[8] She keeps many benefits in store for us and showers them down on each one of her children. Our first instinct should be to seek the patronage of our Mother in heaven when we are in trouble or in need. This is especially important if the devil introduces a complication into our soul that creates an obstacle in our path to God or separates us from others. Our Lady is *the Help of Christians*, as we pray in the *Litany*. She is our rescue and

---

[5] *Preface,* Mass of the Blessed Virgin Mary, *Queen of Peace*
[6] John 19:26-27
[7] *Mother most Lovable, Prayer after Communion*
[8] cf *Preface of the Mass*

haven in the midst of the adverse winds and gales that can arise during the long voyage of life.

We Christians seek our Our Lady's intercession in a thousand and one different ways. We visit her shrines, have recourse to her while out on the street, seek her protection in the face of temptation, and converse with her intimately while saying the Rosary. One of the most ancient testimonies of filial devotion to the Blessed Virgin is the prayer we have so often repeated: *Sub tuum praesidium confugimus ..., We place ourselves under your protection, Holy Mother of God. Despise not our petitions, but in your mercy hear and answer us. Save us from all dangers, O ever glorious and blessed Virgin.*[9] With the *Memorare* we can pray daily for the one in our family who happens to be most in need.

We can tell her in the words inscribed by a Catalan poet in the recess behind a wayside image of Our Lady: 'Virgin and Mother, our consolation, show us the sure path. I am a man, but your son. You are the star and I am the pilgrim.'

26.3 To count always on her divine Motherhood.

Woman, behold your son. By accepting John as her own son Mary shows her unparalleled love as Mother. On this note St John Paul II prayed: *And through that man He entrusted every person to you. At the moment of the Annunciation you consecrated the whole plan of your life in those simple words: 'Behold the handmaid of the Lord. Be it done unto me according to your Word (Luke 1:38)'. You embrace and draw close to everyone. You seek everyone out with motherly care ... In a wonderful way you are always found in the mystery of Christ, your only Son. You are always present whenever His brothers and sisters are present, wherever the Church is present.*[10] Your hands

---

[9] A. G. Hamman, *Prayers of the early Christians*, Madrid 1956
[10] John Paul II, *Address*, 27 January 1979

are laden with graces for us, and you are ever ready to shower them down on your children.

St John accepts Mary as his Mother. Until she is taken up into heaven, body and soul, he watches over her with great tenderness: *From that very hour the disciple received her into his home. Spiritual writers have seen in these words of the Gospel a direct invitation to all Christians to bring Mary into their lives. Mary certainly wants us to invoke her and to approach her confidently. She wants us to appeal to her as our Mother, asking her 'Show us you are our Mother.'*[11] The Blessed Virgin has never failed to hear us.

May we never forget that the presence of the Blessed Virgin in the Church is always *a motherly presence.*[12] She tends to make the way easier. She prevents our straying from the right path in great and small matters alike as our short-sightedness sometimes inclines us to do. Where would we be without her motherly vigilance? Let us make an effort to petition her frequently as faithful daughters and sons.

Our Lady is always vigilant where her children are concerned. The Catalan poet continues his poem saying: *Why, Most Holy Virgin, do you look at us with eyes so wide open? Create in our soul a holy fear. May the miracles of the past be repeated today, and may you free us from every sin and from vile cowardice.*

---

[11] St. J. Escrivá, *Christ is passing by*, 140

[12] cf John Paul II, Encyclical, *Redemptoris Mater*, 25 March 1987, 24

27. ST MICHAEL THE ARCHANGEL

Feast

The liturgy for today celebrates the feast of the three archangels who have been venerated throughout the history of the Church. Michael (from the Hebrew *Who is like God?*) is the archangel who defends the friends of God against Satan and all his evil angels. Gabriel, (*the Power of God*), is chosen by the Creator to announce to Mary the mystery of the Incarnation. Raphael, (*the Medicine of God*), is the archangel who takes care of Tobias on his journey.

27.1 The mission of the Archangels.

We read the words of Jesus in the Gospel of the Mass: *Amen, amen, I say to you, you shall see heaven opened and the angels of God ascending and descending upon the Son of Man.*[1] The angels continually praise God. According to the plan established by Divine Providence *they play a part in the Almighty's dominion over creation as 'mighty doers of his word' (Ps 102). The Creator entrusts special care and concern for each person to a guardian angel in particular. In a special way the guardian angels influence those who play a special role in our salvation, like priests for example. They present our petitions and prayers to God for our benefit.*[2] Their mission as ambassadors of God extends to entire nations as well.[3] Men call on the angels and the archangels every day and at every hour, within the Mass, to praise the glory of God throughout the entire world.

---

[1] John 1:51
[2] John Paul II, *Address*, 30 July 1986
[3] cf *ibid*

Today's feast is a special opportunity to consider that the Church honours three archangels in the Liturgy by name. The first is *Michael the Archangel* (Dan 10:13-20; Rev 12:7; Jude 9). The etymology of the word is a synthesis of the essential disposition of these good spirits. 'Mica-El' signifies: *Who is like God?* The second is *Gabriel,* who is connected above all with the mystery of the Incarnation of the Son of God (Luke 1:19,26). The term means *Power of God* or *My power is God.* The third is *Raphael,* whose name means *God heals.*[4] By meditating on his mission to Tobias we better understand the verse in *Hebrews* concerning the purely spiritual beings we honour today: *Are they not all ministering spirits sent for service for the sake of those who shall inherit salvation?*[5]

Their proximity to our everyday life moves us to pray in the words of the Liturgy: *O God, who dispose in marvellous order ministries both angelic and human, graciously grant that our life on earth may be defended by those who watch over us as they minister perpetually to you in heaven.*[6] We receive countless deeds of assistance from the Archangels, and from our Guardian Angels whose feast day we will celebrate in a few days. The existence of angels is frequently a tangible proof of God our Father's loving concern for us his children.

Do we frequently seek their intercession in the midst of our daily work? Do we feel secure in their company throughout the day, especially in the midst of tribulation or when we are about to lose the serenity and peace proper to the sons and daughters of God?

---

[4] cf *ibid*, General Audience, 6 August 1986
[5] Heb 1:14
[6] *Collect*

27.2 The Archangel St Michael helps us fight the devil.

In the *First Reading* of the Mass today we read: *Now war broke out in heaven, when Michael with his angels attacked the dragon. The dragon fought back with his angels, but they were defeated and driven out of heaven. The great dragon, the primeval serpent known as the devil or Satan who had deceived all the world, was hurled down to the earth and his angels were hurled down with him.*[7] The Fathers of the Church interpret these words of the Apocalypse as a testimony of the battle between Michael and the devil when the angelic spirits were put to the test. They also understand the fight Satan sustains against the Church throughout the centuries. The ongoing battle will reach a final conclusion at the end of time.[8] According to Jewish tradition some Church Fathers corroborate that the devil is an angelic creature who became God's enemy by not accepting the dignity granted mankind by the Incarnation.[9] The devil and his followers were ejected from heaven, and ever since have never ceased tempting men and women so that through sinning they might be deprived of glory.

St Michael appears in the Old Testament. He defends the chosen people on God's behalf.[10] St John Paul II reminded us: *The continuous struggle against the devil that characterizes Michael the Archangel is still going on since the devil who seeks to take advantage of every situation, is still living and operative in the world.*[11] *There are periods in which the existence of evil among men becomes singularly apparent. We have the impression today that people do not want to see the problem. Everything possible*

---

[7] Rev 12:7-9
[8] cf St Gregory the Great, *Moralia,* 31,12
[9] cf *The Navarre Bible,* note to Rev 12:7-9
[10] Dan 10:13;12:1
[11] John Paul II, *Address,* 24 May 1987

is done to remove from public awareness the existence of the 'cunning attacks of the devil', who 'holds dominion over the underworld' as spoken of in Ephesians. Nevertheless, there are historical periods when the profound truth of this revelation of faith is expressed with greater force and is almost tangibly perceived.[12]

Given that the devil's activity in society is occasionally *expressed with great force and is almost tangibly perceived*, the Church therefore invokes St Michael as a protector in adversity and against his ploys: *Send Michael, the prince of the heavenly hosts, to the aid of your people. May he defend them against Satan and his angels on the day of battle.*[13] Their plots are real and threatening, since they try to extinguish the life of Christ in souls. Their manoeuvres would be terrible if we did not count on divine grace, the help of the good angels, and the help of our Blessed Mother from heaven.

We are also reminded on today's feast: *At the beginning of Creation came the first adoration of the Almighty on the part of angelic beings of the spiritual calibre of 'Who like God', Michael, and his angels (Rev 12:7). While the Apocalypse makes us aware of the most exulted affirmation of the Creator's majesty in Michael's complete love of God, it leads us to realize the fulness of hatred which broke out in rebellion against Christ.*[14] The impact of Satan is still prevalent in the world today in countless ways. When loving service to God and others is falling off and more keenly felt in our surroundings, it should be a reminder for us Christians to love and serve Him even more, with all our being, and without expecting anything in return. *Serviam! Lord, I shall serve you*, we can tell him

---

[12] *ibid, Address*, 3 May 1987
[13] *Liturgy of the Hours, Lauds prayer*
[14] John Paul II, *Address*, 29 September 1983

many times throughout the day in the intimacy of our hearts. May we take advantage of the feast day today to say: *Jesus, I have no other ambition than to serve you.*

27.3 Petitioning the Holy Archangel for his continual protection of the Church.

Christ is the true conqueror of sin, death and the devil. With Him and in Him we always achieve victory since he helps us through the angels and the saints. Referring to the final events of his life on earth Jesus says: *Now is the judgement of the world, now will the prince of the world be cast out. And I, if I be lifted up from the earth, will draw all things to myself.*[15] When the disciples report that the devils are subject to them in His name the Lord exclaims: *I saw Satan fall as a bolt of lightning from heaven.*[16]

Nevertheless, the triumph of Christ over the devil will not take place until the end of the world. Therefore after exhorting the first Christians to have full confidence in God, St Peter tells them: *Cast all your anxieties upon Him, because he cares for you.* He also rouses them to vigilance: *Be sober and be watchful. Your adversary the devil prowls around like a roaring lion seeking some one to devour.*[17] St Cyprian appropriately comments: *He encircles each one of us like an enemy besieging a fortress examining the walls to find a weak spot at which to launch an attack.*[18] Perhaps St Peter recalls the following words of the Master as he writes his counsel to the early Christians: *Simon, Simon, behold Satan has desired to have you that he may sift you as wheat. But I have prayed for you that your faith may not fail.*[19]

---

[15] John 12:31-33
[16] Luke 10:18
[17] 1 Pet 5:7-8
[18] St Cyprian, *De zelo et livore*, 2
[19] cf Luke 22:31-32

Perhaps the greatest triumph of Satan and his followers in our own day is that many have either forgotten about them or question their existence. They may say belief in angels was held only during less culturally advanced periods of history. Let us not forget though: Their mysterious action in the life of the world and their influence on people is real and effective. May we frequently seek the protection of St Michael the Archangel to triumph over every evil.

During the previously mentioned discourse St John Paul II repeatedly came back to an ancient prayer made through the intercession of the angelic warrior: *St Michael, Archangel, defend us in battle and be our safeguard against the wickedness and snares of the devil. May God rebuke him, we humbly pray. And do you O prince of the heavenly host, by the power of God thrust into hell Satan and all the evil spirits who prowl about the world for the ruin of souls. Amen.*[20]

---

[20] *Prayer to St Michael*

28. ST GABRIEL THE ARCHANGEL

Feast

God chose St Gabriel to announce to the Most Blessed Virgin the mystery of the Incarnation of the Son of God. St Bernard says: *Among all the angels only Gabriel was found worthy to declare God's plans to her and accept her 'Fiat'.* The angel's greeting is so simple and charged with meaning. 'Hail Mary, full of grace' has become the most familiar and long-standing prayer of the Christian people. Gabriel is linked to the Messianic messages and his presence in Sacred Scripture points to the fulness of time. Earlier, he had been sent to Daniel, to presage the period of Christ's birth, and to Zachary, to foretell the birth of John the Baptist.

Since the first centuries of Christianity St Gabriel has been honoured in the Liturgy. In the ninth century his name appears in the list of saints for 24 March, associated with the feast of the Annunciation. In 1921, Benedict XV declared St Gabriel's a feast for the universal church. Currently, the celebration occurs together with the feast of the Archangels Michael and Raphael on September 29.

28.1 St Gabriel, the Power of God.

The Archangel Gabriel appears to men to communicate the divine message. His name signifies both *Servant of God* and *God has shown his Strength.* He is always present as the bearer of good news.[1] Above all he is entrusted by the Creator to deliver the most joyful message of all – the Incarnation of the Son of God.

In the Old Testament the prophet Daniel has already

---

[1] cf J. Dheilly, *Biblical Dictionary,* Barcelona 1970

announced the time for the coming of the Messiah.[2]
Gabriel is sent by God to make known to Mary the ineffable mystery to take place in her most pure womb.[3]
*Since it was a message of such transcendence, the
Almighty chooses for the mission an Archangel, an angel
of the highest calibre. His name signifies 'Strength of God'
because he would presage Christ, who, despite his humble
appearance, would inspire awe even in the Principalities
and Powers. It is natural for such an exalted figure to
foretell the coming of the Lord of hosts and the hero of
battles.*[4] The Archangel's words are repeated countless
times each day in everlasting praise of the Blessed Mother:
*Hail Mary, full of grace, the Lord is with thee. Blessed are
thou amongst women ...* as we often tell her in the intimacy
of our prayer.

28.2 The Archangel foretells the child to be born. The value of each infant.

St Gabriel prefigures the birth of St John the Baptist
too. He states: *Do not be afraid, Zachary, for your petition
has been heard. Your wife Elizabeth shall bear you a son
and you shall call his name John.*[5] He also provides the
surprised father with three more reasons for joy over the
miraculous birth of the Precursor. God will grant him
extraordinary grace and sanctity. He will be an instrument
for the salvation of many souls. And his entire life will be
consecrated to preparing the arrival of the awaited
Messiah.[6]

We know Gabriel through his appearance when children

---

[2] cf Dan 8:15-26; 9:20-27
[3] Luke 1:26-38
[4] *Liturgy of the Hours*, Second Reading: *St Gregory the Great, Homilies on the Gospels*, 34,8-9
[5] Luke 1:13
[6] cf Luke 1:14-17

are to be born. In a mysterious supernatural way he expedites the marvellous work of the Holy Spirit in the womb of Mary. Previously in the case of John the Baptist, he tells Zachary before taking his leave: *I am Gabriel who stand in the presence of God. I have been sent to speak to you and to bring you this good news.*[7] News of a birth to come is always good tidings. We know that God directly intervenes in the creation of each person by bestowing an immortal soul. *You shall have joy and gladness and many will rejoice at his birth,* the Archangel proclaims.[8] St Ambrose aptly comments: *Through this text parents are reminded of their duty to give thanks to God and the saints are invited to rejoice over the birth of their children. For the Lord has greatly blessed us with this awesome capability of propagating the species and our own families.*[9] The Holy Family of Nazareth and the family of Zachary and Elizabeth set off in a new direction from the moment Gabriel makes his message known. The Archangel can be a great intercessor before God for many married couples who desire children or who are already blessed with offspring.

Each baby who comes into the world has a divine purpose. Parents, therefore, collaborate with God as administrators of the sources of life. The gift of procreation is granted them in order that they may have many children who will know, love, and serve the Lord and reach eternal life. In the face of aggressive propaganda in favour of population control mothers and fathers have more need than ever to be responsible before God in their parenthood. He frequently asks them to have a large family in keeping with personal and family circumstances.

---

[7] Luke 1:19-20
[8] Luke 1:14
[9] St Ambrose, in Catena Aurea, V, p.22; cf T*reatise on the Gospel of St Luke, in loc*

St John Paul II pointed out: *To maintain a joyful family requires a great deal from both the parents and the children. Each member of the family has to become, in a special way, the servant of the others and share their burdens (Gal 6:2; Phil 2:2). Each one must show concern, not only for his or her own life, but also for the lives of the other members of the family, for their needs, their hopes, their ideals. Decisions about the number of children and the sacrifices to be made for them must not be taken only with a view to adding to comfort and preserving a peaceful existence. Reflecting upon this matter before God, with the graces drawn from the sacrament and guided by the teaching of the Church, parents will remind themselves that it is certainly less serious to deny their children certain comforts or material advantages than to deprive them of the presence of brothers and sisters who could help them to grow in their humanity and to realize the beauty of every stage of life in all its variety.*[10]

As with other aspects of our fidelity to God the Lord rewards our generosity even in this life. We experience the fruit of knowing and striving to fulfil the Will of God. We must never forget that *matrimony is a great and marvellous divine path on earth. As in all human participation in divine things on earth, there are concrete manifestations of correspondence to grace which are generosity, dedication, and service.*[11]

28.3 Children are a reason for rejoicing.

There is no greater delight in a family than the arrival of a new child. No gift of God is superior. This is the joyful doctrine of the Church we need to transmit to the whole world.

---

[10] John Paul II, *Address,* 7 October 1979
[11] cf *Conversations with Monsignor Escrivá,* 93

The words of the Archangel Gabriel are always fulfilled when a child is born: *You shall have joy and gladness and many will rejoice at his birth.* St John Paul II frequently insisted on the idea that Christian civilization is a life-enhancing and life-valuing society: *Human life is precious because it is the gift of a God whose love is infinite. When God gives life, it is forever. Life is also precious because it is the expression and fruit of love ... The great danger for family life in a society that values pleasure, comfort and independence lies in the fact that people may close their hearts and become selfish.*[12] They may prefer a little more material comfort to the joy of bringing more children into the world and educating them to be good citizens and sons and daughters of God. *Each child that God grants is a wonderful blessing from him. Do not fear having children.*[13]

We ask the Archangel Gabriel, who informed the Blessed Virgin of the coming of Life itself into the world, to gain us the fortitude to do apostolate in favour of life, generosity and joy. The Pope points out: *When the sacredness of life before birth is attacked we shall affirm that no one has the authority to destroy unborn life. When a baby is described as a burden or looked upon only as a means of satisfying an emotional need, we will stand up and insist that every child is a unique and unrepeatable gift of God with the right to a loving and united family. When the institution of marriage is abandoned to human selfishness or reduced to a temporary and conditional arrangement that can easily be prescinded, we will stand up and affirm the indissolubility of the marriage bond. When the value of the family is threatened because of social and economic pressures, we will reaffirm that the family is*

---

[12] John Paul II, *loc cit*

[13] cf St. J. Escrivá, *The Forge*, 691

necessary not only for the private good of every person, but also for the common good of every society, nation and state. When freedom is used to dominate the weak, to squander natural resources and energy, or to deny basic necessities to people, we will insist on the demands of justice and social love. When the sick, the aged or the dying are abandoned in loneliness, we will reiterate time and again that they are worthy of love, care and respect.[14]

The Lord has wanted us to be apostles of all that is positive, good, and noble in the world by *drowning evil in an abundance of good.*[15] Like St Gabriel, may we too be bearers of good news for the family and the world from our place in society. Many are bent on spreading evil. May we put even more effort into radiating goodness, beginning with our own family. *In national life there are two things which are really essential: the laws concerning marriage and the laws having to do with education. In these areas God's children have to stand firm and fight with toughness and fairness for the sake of all mankind.*[16]

[14] John Paul II, *loc cit*
[15] Rom 12:21
[16] St. J. Escrivá, *op cit,* 104

29. ST RAPHAEL THE ARCHANGEL

Feast

Scripture identifies St Raphael as *one of the seven spirits who stand before God.* Raphael means the *medicine of God* in Hebrew. God sent him to take care of Tobias on his journey. He also comforted Sarah in her adversity.

The Church has long invoked Raphael as the Patron for Travellers. He is most especially the intercessor for travelling along the way of life. The feast of St Raphael is found in liturgical texts in the Middle Ages. Devotion to him was extended to the universal Church by Benedict XV in 1921. Currently, the feast is celebrated together with the Archangels Michael and Gabriel on September 29.

29.1 St Raphael the Archangel in Sacred Scripture.

I give thee thanks, O Lord, with my whole heart; in the sight of the angels I will sing your praises, my God.[1]

We know St Raphael the Archangel principally through the history of Tobias *which is significant for the account of the Creator's confiding to the angels the little children of God who are always in need of vigilance, care, and protection.*[2] Sacred Scripture narrates how the young Tobias prepared to set out on a journey. He first went in search of someone to accompany him, and found Raphael, who was an angel.[3] At the beginning of the trek he didn't know his companion well, but repeatedly had occasion to experience his protection on the road. Raphael led the

---

[1] *Responsorial Psalm*: Ps 137:1
[2] John Paul II, *Address,* 6 August 1986
[3] Tob 5:4

young man happily to his relative Raguel, whose daughter, Sarah, Tobias would marry. The helpful fellow-traveller exorcised the bride-to-be of an evil spirit and later cured Tobias' father of his blindness. Today, therefore, St Raphael is venerated as the patron of both travellers and of the sick.[4] On the way back, the Archangel revealed his identity: *I am Raphael, one of the seven angels who present the prayers of the just before the majesty of the Holy One.*[5]

Life itself is a long journey that ends in God. To reach the end of the road safely, we need help, protection and advice, since there are many possibilities of straying or getting perilously detained on the road. We want to avoid losing precious time. God points out to each one of us the personal vocation that leads to Him. It is important not to go astray on the road since it is a matter of knowing and following the Will of God. For this reason, though, we can all entrust ourselves to the patronage of St Raphael, the archangel who is a special guide for those who still need to find out what God expects of them in life.

For some, the path will be the road of matrimony. This state in life is a way to holiness. Parents cooperate with God in bringing children into the world. They educate and make sacrifices for them so that they may grow to become good children of God. *Do you laugh because I tell you that you have a vocation to marriage? Well, you have just that, a vocation. Commend yourself to St Raphael that he may keep you pure, as he did Tobias, until the end of the way.*[6]

For others, God has plans of particular predilection: *How frankly you laughed when I advised you to put your youthful years under the protection of St Raphael so that he'll lead you, as he did young Tobias, to a holy marriage,*

---

[4] cf B. Baur, *The Light of the World*, Barcelona 1959
[5] Tob 12:15
[6] St. J. Escrivá, *The Way*, 27

*with a girl who is good and pretty – and rich, I added
jokingly.*

*And then how thoughtful you became, when I went on
to advise you to put yourself under the patronage of that
youthful Apostle John, in case God were to ask more of
you.*[7] He may ask for complete availability.

29.2 Personal vocation.

*I will give him a white stone, with a new name written
on it which no one knows except the one who receives it.*[8]
St John makes reference here to the custom of showing a
stone stamped in the right way as an entrance ticket to
verify payment and gain admittance to a banquet. On a
deeper level it refers to one's vocation and the unique
personal relationship with God such a grace brings with it.

God invites each person to voluntarily participate in
the divine plan of salvation. He is always the one who
issues the call and has the best design in mind: *You have
not chosen me, but I have chosen you.*[9] Something similar
happens when a film director wants to select the cast for
his production. *He is seated at a desk strewn with dozens of
photographs of actresses that their agents have given to
him. After a while he picks one up, pauses and says to his
secretary: 'Yes, this is the kind of woman we need. Call
and set up an appointment with immediately.'*

Through this crude example we can get some idea of
the purpose of our existence. From all eternity God
planned the universe in its entirety and selected the
protagonists who would perform in the production until the
end of time. He saw the picture, as it were, of every soul he
would create. When he arrived at your picture it is as if He

---

[7] *ibid*, 360
[8] Rev 2:17
[9] John 15:16

stopped and said: *This is a soul that speaks to my heart. I need this one to carry out a unique and personal role in my plans and then enjoy my presence for all eternity.*[10] God loved us, called us to life, and then to dedication towards the fulfilment of His plan, so that we might reach the plenitude of happiness. St John Paul II pointed out: *In fact, from eternity God has thought of us and has loved us as unique individuals. Every one of us he has called by name as the Good Shepherd 'calls his sheep by name' (John 10:3).*[11]

Vocation is the divine plan for our life. It is a road to travel that leads to God, who awaits us at the end of it. It is important to find this path since finding it will show the role God wants us to play in His salvific design. *When we really choose to do 'what God wants', we renounce 'what we ourselves want'. This is not to say that God's Will and my will have to be always in conflict. In most cases to do God's will is most appealing. There will be times, however, when God's Will and our will are not in perfect harmony. So inasmuch as such conflict will probably arise from time to time, we have to be disposed to identify our will with his Will. This is the ultimate test of whether we love God. It is certainly the best way to correspond to his love.*[12]

Today let us ask St Raphael the Archangel to guide us amid the many decisions we have to make in our life. May we always seek the Will of our Father God. May we also pray for our friends, especially the youngest among them, so that they too may find their path to the Lord. Let's make an effort to accompany them in their difficulties, in a discreet and simple way, like a good friend – as the

---

[10] L.J. Trese, *God has need of you*, pp.17-18
[11] John Paul II, Apostolic Exhortation, *Christifideles laici*, 30 December 1988, 58
[12] L.J. Trese, *op cit*, p.19

Archangel did with Tobias. May our advice and firm friendship never be lacking for them. May we always remember that the most divine task is to cooperate with God in the salvation of souls.

29.3 To help others find the path of vocation.

One of the most noble duties of our existence is to encourage others to imitate Our Lord. We ourselves want to go directly to Him. On the way, though, we frequently find that others vacillate, doubt, or don't know the best route to take. God provides us with light for the benefit of these others: *You are the light of the world,* the Master has said to all who follow him.[13] The closer we draw to Christ, the more light we shall have to lead others by. When we Christians enjoy true friendship with the Lord, *we are children of God, bearers of the only flame that can light up the paths of the earth for souls, of the only brightness which can never be darkened, dimmed or overshadowed.*

The Lord uses us as torches, to make that light shine out. Much depends on us; if we respond, many people will remain in darkness no longer, but will walk instead along paths that lead to eternal life.[14] What a great joy to be the occasion for a friend to find his vocation or to reassure someone who has already set out on the way.

What we read in Tobias happens very often: *He went to look for someone to accompany him.* Our friends have to find us readily available to travel with them along the divine path. Friendship is the ordinary means God uses to draw many people to Him or for them to discover their call to follow Christ more closely. For this reason, those virtues which are at the basis of friendly dealings with others are so important – good example, cheerfulness, cordiality,

---

[13] Matt 5:14
[14] St. J. Escrivá, *The Forge,* 1

optimism, understanding, and selflessness.

Sacred Scripture refers to friendship with the highest praise: *A faithful friend is a sturdy shelter: He that has found one has found a treasure. There is nothing so precious as a faithful friend and no scales can measure his excellence.*[15] The same must be capable of being said of each one of us. Have we been the *faithful friend* of untold value for others because our affection always leads them to draw closer to God? In many cases others will then see and follow their vocation, the one God has called them to follow from all eternity.

Cor Mariae dulcissimum iter para tutum. May the most sweet heart of Mary prepare for them and for us a sure path.

---

[15] Sir 6:14-15

2 OCTOBER

30. THE GUARDIAN ANGELS

Memorial

Devotion to the Guardian Angels goes back to the beginnings of Christianity. Pope Clement X proclaimed the feast a universal celebration in the seventeenth century. The Guardian Angels serve as the messengers of God. The Almighty has allocated a Guardian Angel to each one of us for our protection and for the good of our apostolate.

30.1 The existence of the guardian angels.

Angels of the Lord, bless the Lord, praise and exalt him above all for ever.[1]

The Angels often appear in Sacred Scripture as ordinary ministers of God. They are the most perfect creatures of Creation with one exception. They can grasp reality beyond the capacity of our human intelligence, and they contemplate God face to face as glorified beings.

At the most important junctures in human history angels have served as ambassadors of God to point out the way for us, or otherwise convey the divine Will. They act as messengers of the Most High to illuminate, exhort, intercede, punish, and preserve us from danger. At times they appear in corporeal form. *Angel* meaning *messenger* expresses their role as intermediaries between God and men.[2] The chosen people have always venerated them and shown them respect. Sacred Scripture has this to say of them: *Are they not all ministering spirits, sent for service,*

---

[1] *Entrance Antiphon*: Dan 3:58
[2] cf John Paul II, *Address, 30 July 1986*

for the sake of those who shall inherit salvation?[3]

Faith in the mission of the angels to protect individual persons is what made Israel exclaim when he blesses his grandchildren, the sons of Joseph: *May the angel who redeemed me from all evil bless them.*[4] The *First Reading* of the Mass recalls the Lord's words to Moses. Today we can imagine them addressed to each one of us: *Behold, I send an angel before you, to guard you on the way and to bring you to the place which I have prepared.*[5] When the Prophet Elijah awoke to find himself surrounded by menacing Syrian forces, he said to his frightened servant: *Fear not, for those who are with us are more than those who are with them.* Then Elijah prayed and said, *O Lord, I pray thee, open his eyes that he may see.* So the Lord opened the eyes of the young man and he saw; and behold the mountain was full of horses and chariots of fire round about Elijah.[6]

What security the presence of the Guardian Angels lends us before God! They console and illuminate us. They battle in our favour against unseen forces. At the climax of that conflict, *when the battle became fierce, there appeared to the enemy from heaven five resplendent men on horses with golden bridles, and they were leading the Jews. Surrounding Maccabeus and protecting him with their own armour and weapons they kept him from being wounded. And they showered arrows and thunderbolts upon the enemy, so that, confused and blinded, they were thrown into disorder and cut to pieces.*[7] The holy angels intervene daily on our behalf in many different ways. How lovingly manifest is God's provident vigilance over us is shown through the protection afforded us by these spiritual companions.

---

[3] Heb 1:14
[4] Gen 48:16
[5] Ex 23:20-23
[6] 2 Kings 6:16-17
[7] 2 Mach 10:29-30

May we seek their help in our ordinary ascetical struggle as
God's children, and may we constantly call on them to help
set our hearts on fire with Love of God.

30.2 The continuous service of the Guardian Angels.

*In the presence of the Angels I will praise you my
God.*[8] The life and teaching of Christ is filled with
reference to the presence of ministering angels. Gabriel
announces to Mary she is going to be the Mother of the
Saviour. An angel enlightens and reassures St Joseph and
the shepherds in Bethlehem. The purely spiritual servants
of God witness the Flight from Egypt, the Temptations of
the Lord in the desert, his sufferings in Gethsemane, and
the Resurrection and Ascension. They constantly watch
over the Church and each one of its members as the *Acts of
the Apostles*[9] and ancient Tradition testify. *Truly, truly, I
say to you, you will see heaven opened and the angels of
God ascending and descending upon the Son of man.*[10]

Many saints and holy people enjoyed friendship with
their Guardian Angel, whose intercession they frequently
besought.[11] St Josemaría Escrivá had a special devotion to
the Guardian Angels. Precisely on this Feast the Lord let
him clearly *see* the founding of Opus Dei. Through this
institution the universal call to holiness would resound
throughout the world. People from all walks of life would
seek God in the midst of their everyday life and daily tasks.
St Josemaria dealt with his own Guardian Angel and
customarily greeted the angel of the person to whom he
was speaking.[12] He called him 'a great accomplice' in the
apostolate, and asked him for material favours too. During

---

[8] *Communion Antiphon*
[9] Acts 5:19-20
[10] John 1:51
[11] cf G. Huber, *My angel will go before you*, p.33 ff
[12] A. Vazquez de Prada, *The Founder of Opus Dei,* Madrid 1983

one particular period he called his constant companion *my watchkeeper,* because he had entrusted him with getting his watch going when it stopped, since he didn't have enough money to have it repaired.[13] He set aside Tuesday as a day on which to put more effort into communicating with his Guardian Angel.[14]

Once during a time of intense anticlerical persecution in Madrid a would-be aggressor stood menacingly in St Josemaria's path with the obvious intention of doing him harm. Someone suddenly stood between them and drove off the assailant. It all happened in an instant. The protector came up after the incident and whispered to him: 'Mangy donkey, Mangy donkey', the expression Blessed Josemaria used to refer to himself in the intimacy of his soul. Only his confessor knew about this. Peace and joy filled his heart as he recognized the intervention of his Angel.[15] *You seemed amazed because your guardian angel has done so many obvious favours for you. But you shouldn't be: That's why Our Lord has placed him at your side.*[16] Today can be a great day to reaffirm the devotion to our Guardian Angel since we are in so much need of him. Using the words of the Mass we can pray: *O God, who in your unfathomable providence are pleased to send your holy Angels to guard us, hear our supplication as we cry to you, that we may always be defended by their protection and rejoice eternally in their company.*[17]

30.3 The Guardian Angels, our very good friends.

St Bernard comments on the following words of Scripture in a reading from the Liturgy of the Hours for

---

[13] *ibid.*
[14] *ibid.*
[15] cf *ibid.*
[16] St. J. Escrivá, *The Way,* 565
[17] *Collect*

today: *He has given his angels orders to watch over you in all your ways. He says: These words should fill you with respect, inspire devotion and instil confidence because of their protection. The angels are at your side, with you, and present on your behalf. They are there to protect you and to serve you. But even if it is God who has given them this charge we should nonetheless be grateful to them too for the great love with which they obey and come to help us in our great need.*[18]

On their hands they will bear you up lest you dash your foot against a stone.[19] They sustain us in their care as if we were a precious treasure entrusted them by God. Just as older children help to watch over the younger ones as they grow up, the angels will keep us safe until we enter happily into the home of our Father. Only then will the celestial host we so depend on for many favours have fulfilled their mission.

We have to deal with our Guardian Angels in a familiar way, while at the same time recognizing their superior nature and grace. Though less palpable in their presence than human friends are, their efficacy for our benefit is far greater. Their counsel and suggestions come from God, and penetrate more deeply than any human voice. To reiterate, their capacity for hearing and understanding us is much superior even to that of our most faithful human friend, since their attendance at our side is continuous; they can enter more deeply into our intentions, desires and petitions than can any human being, since angels can reach our imagination directly without recourse to the comprehension of words. They are able to incite images, provoke memories, and make impressions in order to give us

---

[18] *Liturgy of the Hours, Second Reading*, St Bernard, *Sermon 12 on the Psalm 'Qui Habitat'* 3:6-8
[19] Ps 90:12

direction. How many times will they have helped us to keep on going as they did Elijah, who was so tired while being hunted down by Jezebel that he prepared to die under a bush on the way. Like Elijah's angel, ours will draw near to us and help us understand: *Arise and eat, else the journey will be too great for you.*[20]

If we get used to dealing with our most intimate, faithful and generous friend, we will never feel lonely.[21] The Guardian Angel unites his prayer to our own and presents it before God.[22] First, however, it is necessary for us to speak, at least mentally, since these spiritual entities cannot penetrate our understanding as the Almighty can. At this point our own angel will be able to deduce from our personal interior dispositions more than we ourselves are capable of doing. *We have no right to claim that the Angels should obey us – but we can be absolutely sure that the Holy Angels hear us always.*[23] This is sufficient.

Our Guardian Angel will accompany us to the end of the way. If we are faithful to grace we will join the angels and saints in contemplating the Blessed Mother, *Queen of Angels,* whom everyone will praise for all eternity.

---

[20] 1 Kings 19:7
[21] cf A. Tanquerey, *The Spiritual Life,* 187
[22] cf Origen, *Contra Celso,* 5,4
[23] St. J. Escrivá, *The Forge,* 339

4 OCTOBER

31. ST FRANCIS OF ASSISI

Memorial

Born in 1182 of a noble Catholic family in Assisi, Italy, Francis was a tireless preacher of the virtue of poverty and of God's boundless love for men. He founded the Franciscan religious order and together with St Clare also established the Poor Clares. He organized the Third Order of Franciscans for lay men and women. The saint died in the year 1226.

31.1 The poverty of St Francis and the practice of this virtue for the ordinary Christian.

At a time when excessive splendour together with political and social power were common among clerics, God wanted the poor life of Francis to act as a new leaven in a society then sliding further away from spiritual values because of its attachment to material goods. Dante hails the saint as a *sun born into the world.*[1] God used his existence to proclaim to everyone the certainty that true hope lies in God alone.

One day while praying in the dilapidated Church of St Damian, Francis heard these words: *Go and repair my house now in ruins.* Taking this divine locution literally, he put all his energy into fixing up the broken-down chapel. He later committed himself to restoring others, and soon came to understand that poverty as an expression of his entire life would be a tremendous good for the Church. He

---

[1] Dante Alighieri, *The Divine Comedy, Paradise,* XI, 5,47

used to call the virtue *Dear Lady,*[2] as the medieval knights
used to refer to their heart's love, and as Catholics are wont
to address the Mother of God.

Francis realised that the restoration of Christianity
would come about through detachment from material
goods since poverty well-lived according to one's own
state in life permits us to put our hope in God alone. One
day in February 1209 when the saint heard these words of
the Gospel, *Don't take gold, nor silver, nor purse...* he was
moved to make a stirring gesture in order to show that
nothing in the world is good if it is preferred to God. He
removed his fine clothes and leather belt, put on a rough
woollen garment, wrapped a thick rope around his waist
and, trusting in Providence, set out on the road.

Poverty is a virtue the Lord asks of everyone –
religious, priests, mothers of families, lawyers, and
students. It is evident, though, that the lay faithful as
stewards of Creation and in affirmation of the whole gamut
of noble human realities should practise this virtue in a
way different from the followers of St Francis. By vocation
the religious give a public and official testimony of their
consecration to God. Yet *all* Christians are called to practise
the virtue of poverty just as everyone is called to live the
virtues of temperance, obedience, humility, industriousness
etc., in accord with their particular vocation.

The virtue of poverty for the ordinary Christian is
*based on detachment from material goods, confidence in
God, sobriety and the willingness to share with others.*[3]
Just as a traveller must know the right road before setting
out on a journey if he is to make progress, the laity need to

---

[2] cf St Francis of Assisi, *Testament of Siena,* in *Biographical Writings,*
Madrid 1985
[3] S.C.D.F., *Instruction on Christian Freedom and Liberation,* 22
March 1986, 66

learn to reconcile *two aspects of this virtue which at first
seem contradictory; 'true poverty', which is obvious and
made up of definite things. This poverty should be an
expression of faith in God and a sign that the heart is not
satisfied with created things and aspires to the Creator,
that it wants to be filled with love of God so as to be able to
give this same love to everyone.*[4] On the other hand, the
secular condition – living in the middle of the world –
requires the Christian *'to be one more among his fellow
men', sharing their way of life, their joys and happiness;
working with them, loving the world and all the good
things that exist in it; using all created things to solve the
problems of human life and to establish a spiritual and
material environment which will foster personal and social
development.*[5]

The following considerations can help us practise the
virtue of poverty the Lord expects from us with ever-
increasing refinement. Do I practise detachment from
material goods in the midst of everyday life through
concrete deeds? Do I love the sacrifices poverty entails?
Can I say 'I am truly poor in spirit' because my heart is
reserved for God and other people even though I may be
responsible for abundant material resources? *Detach
yourself from the goods of this world. Love and practise
poverty of spirit: Be content with what is sufficient for
leading a simple and temperate life. Otherwise, you'll
never be an apostle.*[6]

31.2 The special need of the virtue of poverty today and some ways to practise it.

The Lord makes his words resound in every age: *You

---

[4] cf *Conversations with Monsignor Escrivá*, 111
[5] *ibid.*
[6] St. J. Escrivá, *The Way,* 631

cannot serve God and mammon.[7] It is impossible to please God, to take to him all the ways of the earth, if at the same time we are not open to making renunciations in the possession and enjoyment of material goods. This counsel of Our Lord is particularly important in our own day. It may sound strange when the desire for comfort and selfish gain is so widespread. Many in society aspire to possess and spend more, and to maximise life's pleasures as if this were the purpose of human existence.

'Real poverty' is shown in many ways. In the first place we enjoy created goods as gifts of God without considering them necessary for our health or rest. We can always do without them given some good will. *It is important to make demands on ourselves in daily life. In this way we will not invent false problems or create needs really prompted by conceit, capriciousness, or a lazy and comfort-loving approach to life. We should stride towards God at a steady pace without carrying any deadweight or impedimenta that might hinder our progress.*[8] We can fall into 'creating needs' for ourselves, with respect to anything we use, including the equipment and implements of our profession, sports equipment, articles of clothing etc.

St Augustine advises the Christians of his time: *Be satisfied with what is sufficient. Any more than that is burdensome and does not bring relief. It will weigh you down and not support you.*[9] This Doctor of the Church knew well the struggles of the human heart. Truly, Christian poverty is not compatible with the possession of superfluous goods or with anxious longing for imagined necessities. Disordered desires for material goods are already an indication of lukewarmness and a lack of love of God.

---

[7] Luke 16:13
[8] St. J. Escrivá, *Friends of God,* 125
[9] St Augustine, *Sermon 85,* 6

The virtue of poverty is shown in our finishing our professional work well and in taking care of the things we wear, our home and its furnishings, and the tools we use whether or not they belong to us. It shows clearly when we avoid inessential expenses even though our company pays them. It is also manifest if we truly never *consider anything our own*,[10] and if we choose what is least attractive for ourselves provided our choice passes unnoticed.[11] In family life we can discover many opportunities for putting the virtue of poverty into practice. We live the virtue well by accepting the shortage of material means with peace and calm and by avoiding capricious personal expense, vanity, luxury, and laziness. We are poor in spirit when we are consciously temperate in food and drink and always generous with others.

One day St Francis had a great cross set up for his friars in the abbey chapel. While putting it up he said to them: 'This should be your book of meditation.' The poor man from Assisi well understood the relative worth of earthly goods. He knew where the true riches in life lie. Today, when society is so thoroughly impregnated with materialistic values, there is a need for Christians to love poverty with particular decisiveness.

31.3 The benefits of having limited material means.

Many fruits derive from the virtue of poverty. In the first place the soul is better disposed to receive supernatural graces. A person's heart expands so as to be sincerely concerned about other people.

Let us ask the Lord today through the intercession of St Francis for the grace to understand and practise Christian poverty more deeply. May we learn to live the

---

[10] cf St. J. Escrivá, *The Forge*, 524
[11] cf *ibid.*, *The Way*, 635

virtue to its ultimate consequences and practise it in a way God rewards even in this life. Jesus grants the detached soul special joy even in the absence of necessities. *There are many who feel unhappy, just because they have too much of everything. Christians, if they really behave as God's children, will suffer discomfort, heat, tiredness, cold... But they will never lack joy, because that – all that – is ordained or permitted by him who is the source of true happiness.*[12]

True poverty of spirit disposes us to be available for Christ. Just as the Lord himself taught, complete dedication is the supreme form of freedom. It constantly opens us to doing God's will in charity, without holding anything back for ourselves. In order to love God we need to *want to be poor* when everything around us seems to lead us to *want to be rich*.[13] Poverty, like any other virtue, is a positive affirmation. It disposes us to live in accord with the divine will by using material goods as a means to reach heaven. We thus help make the world more just and human.

The virtue of poverty is a consequence of faith. In Sacred Scripture it is the state of the person who has unconditionally placed his life in the Lord's hands and therefore turns the reins of control over to him without seeking any other security. Consequently, rectitude of intention is essential for effectively resolving to be poor in spirit. A person must not place his confidence in impermanent goods though he may happen to possess them.

Many Christians are tempted by the attractions of the modern cult of consumerism. When life is given over to the accumulation of material wealth, money itself becomes a god. Such idolatry as St Paul warned the first Christians

---

[12] *ibid.*, Furrow, 82
[13] Spanish Episcopal Conference, Pastoral Instruction, *The Truth will make us free,* 20 November 1990, 18

against should never even be named among them. This tendency causes people to forget the immense treasure of God's love, the only real good that can truly fill the human heart. We should have the firm intention of serving only one master, since no one can serve two.[14] In a society dominated by an excessive desire for riches and comfort, our temperate life will act as a leaven to bring souls back to God just as the life of Francis did in his time.

As we finish our time of prayer we petition God through the intercession of the saint from Assisi to help us form a new leaven in the midst of society. At the tomb where the remains of the Franciscan founder lie, St John Paul II prayed: *You who drew your age close to Christ, help us draw our own turbulent and critical times to him. People are eagerly awaiting our example, perhaps without even realizing it. As we approach the year 2000, might not now be the opportune time to begin to prepare a new Advent in our world?*[15] The Blessed Virgin, Our Mother, will show us, through her life of dedication, how we too can be protagonists in the struggle to bring about the new age of Christ now dawning.

---

[14] cf Matt 6:24
[15] John Paul II, *Address,* 5 November 1978

THANKSGIVING DAY

32. DAY OF THANKSGIVING AND PETITION

Memorial

Today the Church invites the faithful to give thanks for the many blessings God our Father has bestowed on us. We also ask the Lord to grant us generously the material and spiritual favours we need.

32.1 Prayer in imitation of Christ.

You have crowned the year with your bounty, the hope of all the ends of the earth.[1]

The *Temporals* are days the Church sets aside for thanksgiving and petition to God. They traditionally occur after the harvest is taken up. For many it is an annual occasion to rest and a favourable time for asking the Lord's help to begin our normal work activities and the interior life afresh.[2]

We have a great deal to be thankful for, and still stand in great need. Expressing gratitude and asking for specific graces are two ways we can daily pray to God Our Father. In the first place we need to recognize the gifts the Lord has given us. *We will not learn how to love if we are not grateful.*[3] The *First Reading* of the Mass further reminds us of the importance of gratitude to God for all his blessings: *Be careful not to forget the Lord your God. Do not neglect his commandments and decrees and statutes, I enjoin on you today. When you have eaten your fill, built and lived in fine*

---

[1] *Communion Antiphon*: cf Ps 64:11,6
[2] cf J.A. Abad–M. Arrido Bonano, *Introduction to the Church's Liturgy,* Madrid 1988
[3] St Teresa, *Life,* 10,3

*houses, increased your herds and flocks, your silver and gold
and your property, may you not become haughty of heart and
unmindful of the Lord your God who brought you out of the
land of slavery in Egypt, guided you through the vast and
terrible desert, with its serpents and scorpions and parched
ground, and brought forth water for you from the flinty rock.*[4]

We find Christ in the gospel constantly giving thanks
to God. And He is our Model. When raising Lazarus from
the dead Jesus exclaims: *Father, I give you thanks that you
have heard me.*[5] On the occasion of another miracle, *Jesus
took the loaves and, after giving thanks, distributed them
and the fishes to those who were reclining.*[6] At the
institution of the Holy Eucharist the Lord *gave thanks*
before blessing the bread and wine.[7]

St John Paul II affirmed: I*n the truest sense we can say
that the prayer of the Lord and his entire earthly existence
become a revelation of the fundamental truth: 'Every good
and perfect gift is from above, coming down from the
Father of Lights' (James 1:17). Thanksgiving is the source
of all blessings from on high. 'Gratias agamus Domino
Deo nostro, Let us give thanks to the Lord our God,' is the
invitation the Church places at the centre of the
Eucharistic liturgy.*[8] Nothing is more appropriate than to
give thanks to the Lord each day of our lives. We cannot
forget: *The best way of showing our gratitude to God is by
becoming passionately aware that we are his children.*[9]
Today we especially recall our divine filiation as we give
God thanks and praise.

---

[4] *First Reading*: Deut 8:11-15
[5] John 11:41
[6] John 6:11
[7] Luke 22:17
[8] John Paul II, *Address,* 29 July 1987
[9] St. J. Escrivá, *The Forge,* 333

32.2 There is a great deal to be thankful for.

Our entire life is a gift we have received from God through no merit of our own. For this reason our habitual disposition of thanksgiving to God should overflow in acts of thanksgiving throughout the day. We are reminded in the *Preface* of the Mass: *Father, all-powerful and ever-living God, we do well always and everywhere to give you thanks through Jesus Christ our Lord.* We can recall St Paul's principal reproach to the pagans as well. Having known God, *they did not honour him as God or give thanks to him.*[10]

We need to be continually thankful to the Lord for the benefits we have received during the past year. Some we are aware of, but, perhaps even more valuable benefits have come to us without our recognition of them. These graces include rescue from dangers of body and soul, the making of new friends who will play a part in our salvation, and even apparent setbacks like sickness or professional failure. We should enjoy great peace, since we should know that God will draw abundant fruit from circumstances and events that present themselves as unwelcome and are seemingly counterproductive. We later understand these very occasions to be divine caresses. *These veiled 'graces' are like the wood God showed Moses. When he threw it into the sea, the salt water was changed to fresh (Ex 15:25).*[11]

The Founder of Opus Dei used to recommend giving thanks to the Lord *pro universis beneficiis ... etiam ignotis,* for all his benefits including those we are unaware of.[12] Perhaps *one of our greatest embarrassments at the Last*

---

[10] Rom 1:21

[11] J. Tissot, *The Interior Life*, p.154

[12] cf S. Bernal, Monsignor Josemaría Escrivá: *A Profile of the Founder of Opus Dei*, p.151

Judgment will come from knowing the enormous number of divine gifts we did not appreciate as such. There may also be our unwarranted resentment at what seemed to be indifference to our prayers. At least then, though, we will finally but with shame offer thanks since we will know the Lord had the goodness not to answer our many foolish requests. It is possible that if he had granted our misguided petitions we would have had heard the same reprimand the rich man heard: Remember son, in your lifetime you received many good things (Luke 16:25).[13]

How surprised many will be to learn that with more supernatural outlook they could have understood the Providence of God at work in the midst of both good and apparently ill fortune. Furthermore, our present gratitude is a foretaste of heaven and purgatory. *After death we will thank God for the times of tribulation He permitted us to undergo during our life. We will perceive in every occasion of suffering the tender affection of a Father who wants his children to be purified and to arrive all the more quickly at his side in glory. In the end we will thank him, above all because He will have granted us 'spatium verae poenitentiae', the opportunity for true and fruitful penance.*[14] May we thank the Lord *always and everywhere,* but especially during Mass, which is the supreme act of thanksgiving. In today's liturgy we pray: *We offer you, Father, this sacrifice of praise and thanksgiving for the gifts you have granted us. Help us to recognize them as the benefits we have received from you through no merit of our own.*[15]

[13] J.M. Pero-Sanz, *The Sixth Hour,* Madrid 1978
[14] *ibid.,* 275
[15] *Prayer over the Offerings*

32.3 Asking with confidence and entrusting our requests to the Blessed Virgin.

Since we are in need of a great deal of assistance in order to advance, we join constant petition to our continual thanksgiving. Although the Lord grants us many graces without our asking for them, he permits other graces to come to us in proportion to the fervour of our prayer. Since we do not know the measure of petition his unfathomable Providence expects from us, it is necessary to keep praying with intensity: *We must always pray and not lose heart.*[16] In the Gospel of today's Mass the Lord grants us the full assurance that everything we ask for that is in our best interests will *always* be granted. God himself gives his word: *Ask and it shall given, seek and you shall find, knock and it shall be opened to you. For everyone who asks receives, and he who seeks finds, and for him who knocks it shall be opened.*[17]

There is another reason to persevere in prayer: the more we petition Christ the more our friendship with God matures. In human affairs, when it is necessary to ask a powerful person a favour we seek a bond of union and an opportune moment, perhaps when the one approached is in a good mood, before making our request. With the Lord, however, we find him ever ready to hear us. *What man is there among you who, if his son asks for a loaf, will hand him a stone, or if he asks for a fish will hand him a serpent? Therefore if you, evil as you are, know how to give good things to your children, how much more will your Father in heaven give good things to those who ask him?* We have every reason to approach Our Father God with confidence, no matter at what hour of the day. Nothing should be able to diminish our faith in God's almighty power.

---

[16] Luke 18:1
[17] Matt 7:7-11

What can we request? *Who has nothing to ask for?*
Lord, that sickness... Lord, this moodiness... Lord, that
humiliation I don't know how to bear for love of you. We
desire good things, including happiness and joy, for people
at home. Besides, there is the lot of those who hunger and
thirst for bread and justice and which weighs down our
hearts. Furthermore, we can remember individuals who
experience the bitterness of loneliness. At the end of their
days they receive no affectionate glance or any helping
gesture. The greatest misfortune we want to remedy
through our petition, however, since it makes us suffer
most, is sin. Here there is a flight from God and the danger
of souls being lost for all eternity.[18]

The Church constantly points out that our prayers will
reach God's presence more quickly through the mediation
of Mary, the Mother of God and our Mother. For this
reason she perennially recommends the Rosary for
efficacious prayer of petition, and does so in a special way
during the month of October. Pope Pius XI advises: *Don't*
forget to give importance to spreading devotion to the
Rosary. It is very dear to the Blessed Virgin and is so
highly recommended by the Roman Pontiffs. It is a fine way
for the faithful to fulfil the command of the Divine Master:
'Ask and you will receive, seek and you shall find, knock
and it shall be opened to you'.[19] May we not overlook this
advice.

---

[18] St. J. Escrivá, *In Love with the Church*, 47
[19] Pius XI, Encyclical, *In gravescentibus malis,* 29 September 1937

7 OCTOBER

33. OUR LADY OF THE ROSARY

Memorial

This feast day was instituted by Pope Pius V in thanksgiving for the Blessed Virgin Mary's assistance in the Christian victory over the Turks at Lepanto on October 7, 1571. The Pontiff foretold that the Rosary would win that battle in 1569. Clement XI extended the feast to the universal Church in 1716.

33.1 The Rosary is a *powerful weapon* in the apostolate.

And when he came to her he said: Hail Mary, full of grace, the Lord is with thee.[1] The angel greeted Our Lady in this way which is now so familiar to us since we have often repeated the very same words to her.

In the Middle Ages Christians greeted the Virgin Mary with the invocation *Mystical Rose,* the symbol of love and joy. As an expression of this affection her images were adorned with crowns or bouquets of roses called *Rosarium* in medieval Latin as they still are today. Whoever was unable to recite the one hundred and fifty Psalms of the *Liturgy of the Hours* each day would pray as many Hail Marys instead. The faithful used stones strung together by the decade or knots on a rope to keep count of each invocation. At the same time they would meditate on a particular aspect of Our Lord's or Our Lady's life.

The Hail Mary has long been amongst the richest prayers of the Church. Popes and Councils have frequently recommended it. The wording itself would acquire its final form with the addition of the petition for a happy death:

---

[1] Luke 1:28

Pray for us sinners now and at the hour of our death. We beseech the Virgin's help in each situation *now,* and at the climactic moment of our definitive meeting with Christ.

The mysteries focus on the central events in the life of Jesus and Mary. In a sense they are a summary of the liturgical year and of the whole Gospel. The prayers of the Litany that ensue are a song of love for the Blessed Mother. They are Marian praises, petitions for her help and manifestations of joy and exaltation before her virtue and power.

St Pius V attributed the Victory of Lepanto to the intercession of the Blessed Mother, since a grave threat to the Faith soon came to an end when Rome and the Christian world invoked her patronage through the Rosary. Today's feast recalls the wonderful event. On the occasion of its institution, the petition to Our Lady *Help of Christians* was added to the Litany. From that moment on the Roman Pontiffs would encourage devotion to the Blessed Virgin with renewed fervour as *public and universal prayer, for the ordinary and extraordinary needs of the universal Church and the nations of the entire world.*[2]

The Church devotes the month of October to the Rosary in order to honour our Blessed Mother in a special way. Our love for this devotion should be constantly renewed. How is our contemplation of the various mysteries going? Do holy ambitions, such as the Christians had who prayed for victory at Lepanto, enter into our stream of praise and petition during the Rosary? Given our great need for help and our concern for the spiritual growth of our families, Our Lady's presence is crucial. There are always the needs of the friends we do apostolate with to remember too. We need to bring constantly to mind: *Today as in other times the Rosary must be a powerful weapon to enable us to win*

---

[2] John XXIII, Apostolic Letter *Il religioso convegno,* 29 September 1961

in our interior struggle and to help all souls.[3]

33.2 Contemplating the mysteries of the Rosary.

The name *Rosary* comes from the group of prayers to the Virgin we gather like so many roses for her.[4] St Bernard, the great champion of the Blessed Mother, gives the term a different sense by referring to each day of her life as either a snow-coloured or a crimson rose. *White roses and red ones; the white of serenity and of purity, the red of suffering and of love. Have we often tried to unravel the content of her life, day by day, while passing the beads through our hands?*[5] This is what it means to contemplate the lives of Jesus and of Mary while the decades successively unfurl before our mind and heart.

In one way or another we always accompany the Blessed Virgin in the consideration of these mysteries so that the Rosary involves much more than the repetition of the Hail Mary. We divide the scenes into three groups – Joyful, Sorrowful, and Glorious – and so meditate on different aspects of the great mysteries of salvation including the Incarnation, the Redemption, and Resurrection.[6] We make an effort to pray with love, perhaps adding a petition to each decade or every invocation so as to avoid routine. With attentive and thoughtful devotion we *contemplate* the mysteries. Pondering each one helps us foster true piety since each consideration gradually reveals to us the habitual dispositions of Christ and his Blessed Mother, in the presence of God the Father, with whom we can identify in our own behaviour. We rejoice as the events leading to our salvation unfold, and suffer compassionately

---

[3] St. J. Escrivá, *Holy Rosary,* p.7

[4] cf J. Corominas, *Etymological Dictionary* , Madrid 1987

[5] J.M. Escartin, *Meditation on the Rosary,* Madrid 1971

[6] cf R. Garrigou-Lagrange, *The Mother of the Saviour,* p.252

with the Holy Family during their many trials. We look ahead with sure hope towards the final radiance and glorious victory of the risen Christ.[7] To contemplate better the various aspects of the Holy Family's life, we can *pause for a few seconds – three or four – in silent meditation to consider each mystery of the Rosary before reciting the Our Father and the Hail Marys of that decade.*[8] In this way we can involve ourselves in the particular scene as one more person and imagine the manner of the daily activities of Jesus, Mary, and Joseph.

Through reflection on the lessons of the various scenes the Rosary becomes *a conversation with Mary, leading to intimacy with her Son.*[9] In the midst of our everyday concerns we can gain a keen familiarity with the truths of faith and at the same time practise recollection while at work or at our leisure. We thus become increasingly more cheerful and refine our relations with those around us. The life of Jesus and Mary becomes the love of our life as we learn to perceive their ordinary greatness in a deeper way. How true are the poet's verses:

> *You who tire and are slow to pray,*
> *Because the same words we always say,*
> *Have little understanding what it is to be,*
> *In love forever as I and she.*[10]

33.3 The Litany of Loreto.

After contemplating the lives of Jesus and Our Lady during the recitation of the Our Fathers and Hail Marys, we finish the Rosary with the Litany of Loreto. The compilation of invocations bursts forth with vivid praise in

---

[7] cf Bl. Paul VI, Encyclical, *Marialis cultus,* 2 February 1974, 46
[8] St. J. Escrivá, *op. cit.,* p.254
[9] R. Garrigou-Lagrange, *op. cit.,* p.254
[10] cf A. Royo Marin, *The Virgin Mary,* Madrid 1968

all the splendour of the images expressed in these phrases. The form of the particular praises and petitions varies according to country, family and personal piety.

The origin of the Litany of Loreto goes back to the first centuries of Christianity. Then it consisted of short dialogue prayers between the celebrant and the faithful. They focused above all on beseeching divine mercy, and were said at Mass and during processions. At first they were directed to Our Lord, but soon invocations to the Blessed Virgin and other saints developed as well. The original praises of the Marian Litany stem from popular expressions of loving admiration which accrued over time. Many come from the writings of the Eastern Fathers of the Church. Round about the year 1500 at the shrine of Loreto, Christians began to sing them in solemn worship. The devotion soon spread throughout the world.

Each invocation is an ejaculatory prayer we affectionately address to Our Lady. Every one of them reflects a particular dimension of the Blessed Mother's magnificent soul. The phrases are ordered according to the principal Marian truths. These include her divine maternity, her perpetual virginity and mediation, her universal Queenship and her universal example of Christian living. When we beseech the *Holy Mother of God* we are explicitly calling on her most intimate relationship to God. When we praise her as the *Virgin of Virgins* we lovingly recognize her full dedication to the Father's plan of salvation. As we invoke the *Mother of Christ* we emphasize her key role in the mission of Christ the Mediator, Saviour and King. By praising her as Queen and Mediatrix we exult in the Lord's Kingship over all creation.

The initial phrases of the Litany suggest her attributes in broad strokes and the rest develop and expound upon these. The Virgin our Mother is the *Holy Mother of God.*

This is the greatest title we can address her with since it is the basis for all the others. As the *Mother of Christ,* she is rightly praised as the *Mother of our Creator* and the *Mother of our Saviour.* She is consequently the *Mother of the Church* and the *Mother of Divine Grace.* We shower her with other loving reminders of her special qualities that follow naturally from these first ones – *Mother most Pure, Mother most Chaste, Mother Inviolate, Mother Undefiled, Mother most Amiable,* and *Mother most Admirable.* Then we sing forth other notes of the harmonious chord of Mary's most intimate union with God. These have to do with her perpetual virginity. She is *Virgin most Prudent, Virgin most Venerable, Virgin most Renowned, Virgin most Powerful, Virgin most Merciful,* and *Virgin most Faithful.*

After invoking our Mother as a perfect example of all virtue, we continue to exalt her with further admiring salutations. We call on her as the *Mirror of Justice, Seat of Wisdom, Cause of our Joy, Spiritual Vessel, Vessel of Honour, Singular Vessel of Devotion, Mystical Rose, Tower of David, Tower of Ivory,* and *House of Gold.*

The Mother of God continually exceeds her duty in our service as mediator between God and men through Christ.[11] Three different symbols represent her universal mediation. She is the new *Ark of the Covenant* and the *Gate of Heaven* since through her we reach God. We also beseech her as the *Morning Star* who always helps us find our way in life. We often ask her intercession as the *Health of the Sick,* the *Refuge of Sinners,* the *Comforter of the Afflicted,* and the *Help of Christians.*

Finally, Mary is Queen of heaven and of earth because she is the Mother of the universal Sovereign. In the broad spectrum of Christ's heavenly kingdom there are angels, saints, and holy souls who are striving for sanctity now in

---

[11] cf John Paul II, Encyclical *Redemptoris Mater,* 25 March 1987, 38

this life as wayfarers. We petition each one of them through our Mother as the Queen who stands at the summit of all creation. She is *Queen of Angels, Queen of Patriarchs, Queen of Prophets, Queen of Apostles, Queen of Martyrs, Queen of Confessors, Queen of Virgins and Queen of all Saints.* The Litany of Loreto concludes with four further expressions of Queenship. We hail Mary, *Queen conceived without Original Sin, Queen assumed into Heaven, Queen of the most Holy Rosary,* and *Queen of Peace.*

By pausing slowly to consider each one of these praises we can marvel at the gifts God has bestowed on Our Lady. We are filled with awe before the countless divine graces she is adorned with. How fortunate we are to have such a Mother constantly at our side. At times we can use each individual invocation of the Litany as an ejaculatory prayer to remind her frequently of our love for her and of our desire for her protection.

12 OCTOBER

34. OUR LADY OF THE PILLAR

Feast (in Spain)

Christians everywhere have long rendered Our Lady homage under this invocation. According to pious tradition the Blessed Virgin Mary appeared in Saragossa above a column or pillar. On the site of the apparition the faithful built a church and later a basilica.

Pius XII extended the feast from Spain to the nations of South America. The shrine is one of the main pilgrimage centres of the Ibero-American world.

34.1 Devotion to the Virgin of the Pillar.

All generations will call me blessed, for he who is mighty has done great things for me.[1]

According to an ancient and venerated tradition, the Virgin Mary appeared in the company of angels to the Apostle James in Saragossa. The celestial host brought a pillar as a symbol of Our Lady's presence. The Blessed Mother comforted the Apostle of Spain during the apparition by promising her maternal assistance in the evangelization of the country entrusted to him.

Our Lady of the Pillar is now honoured as *the symbol of firm faith* throughout the world.[2] She is the strong foundation of our fidelity.[3] Furthermore we go *ad Iesum per Mariam, to Jesus through Mary* for our firm support in all our apostolic endeavours. *Countless Christians grow in faith in Christ, the Son of God, through devotion to Mary,*

---

[1] *Communion Antiphon*: Luke 1:48
[2] John Paul II, *Address*, 6 November 1982
[3] cf *ibid.*, Encyclical *Redemptoris Mater*, 25 March 1987, 27

the Mother of the Son. They are sustained through the one who is our sure guide to salvation since she conserves and strengthens our faith.[4]

People of many nations celebrate today's feast. As we contemplate such widespread devotion to the Virgin Mary we can appreciate her as the prophetic fulfilment of Sacred Scripture: *I took root in an honourable people. In the portion allotted by God, I have his inheritance. My abode is in the full assembly of saints. I was exalted like a cedar tree in Libanus, a cypress on mount Sion, a palm in Cades, a rosebush in Jericho, a fair olive tree in the plains and a plain olive tree in the street. I gave a sweet smell like cinnamon, aromatical unction, the best myrrh, storax, galbanum, onyx, aloes, and uncut frankincense. My aroma is the purest balm.*[5] True devotion to the Blessed Mother has sprung up throughout the world, and love for her continues to spread to all people as a sweet fragrance.

Today is an excellent occasion to petition her for an increase of faith. The greater the difficulties we may have in our daily effort to improve and do apostolate, the more graces we will receive from Our Lady so our example will be all the stronger and efficacious. With her at our side we will always be victorious. We ask her to make us firm pillars of faith so that our family and friends may lean on us for support. *Father, all-powerful and ever-living God, you grant heavenly aid to those who call on her with the invocation 'Pillar'. Through her intercession grant us fortitude in faith, security in hope, and constancy in love.*[6]

---

[4] *ibid., Address,* 6 November 1982
[5] Sir 24:13-15
[6] *Entrance Antiphon*

34.2 Counting on Mary's help to prepare the way for our personal apostolate.

You precede the chosen people in the desert like the cloud that guided and sustained them both day and night.[7]

In *Exodus,* Yahweh goes before the chosen people by day in the form of a column-shaped cloud to guide them. At night he looms overhead as a pillar of fire to light up the path.[8] The inspired writer of *Wisdom* recalls as well: *Therefore, they received a burning pillar of fire for a guide on the unfamiliar path, a sun that did not burn them during their glorious pilgrimage.*[9]

From the time of the Church's inception, the Virgin Mary has cast light on the way for the evangelization of the world. She goes ahead now to illuminate the personal apostolate we carry out as ordinary Christians at home, at work, and in all our surroundings. With this in mind, when we propose to draw a relative or friend closer to God we first commend the person to Our Lady. She shows us the way to proceed and removes any and all obstacles. Perhaps each one of us has experienced the powerful help of our Lady. *Yes, our guide is a strong column. She accompanies the New Israel, the Church, in its pilgrimage towards the Promised Land through Christ Our Lord. In this way, Our Lady of the Pillar is a 'flaming torch' and the 'throne of glory'. She affirms the faith of a people who never tire of asking her in the Salve Regina: 'Show unto us the blessed fruit of your womb Jesus'.*[10]

Whether evangelization began in some places many centuries or only a few years ago, the kingdom will not be complete until the end of time. Sustaining such effort and

---

[7] Wis 18:3; Exod 13:21-22
[8] cf Exod 13:21
[9] Wis 18:3
[10] John Paul II, *Address,* 15 November 1987

pushing on with the task is now in our hands. In order to participate effectively in this divine adventure we need to have our hearts engaged, and increasingly make an effort to understand others better. The further from Christ a person is, the greater the charity we need to practise with them, without ever compromising our personal conduct or the teachings of the Church.

Calling on Our Lady's help is an excellent beginning for all apostolate. May we ask her guidance to set goals as we propose to carry out the apostolic mission we receive in our Baptism. Let us especially seek her help each day during October, the month of the Rosary. We can resolve to visit one of her shrines and perhaps offer up some small sacrifice in doing so. She will accept this sign of affection with a smile and will return it tenfold in keeping with her greatness.

Mary is our Model in the evangelization we as Christians are called to carry out with naturalness and simplicity. Let us contemplate her very normal life on earth so as to learn from her. We can imagine her friendly charity, the spirit of service she shows in Cana, and her *haste* to help her cousin Saint Elizabeth. We might especially focus on her habitual smile which made her ordinary social relations so attractive. This must be our way too.

34.3 Practising faith and charity in doing apostolate.

In today's Mass we ask the Lord through the intercession of Our Lady of the Pillar to grant us *to be strong in faith and generous in love.*[11]

Faith is the greatest gift we have received. We need to protect it as a treasure from all that can be harmful, including unsuitable reading, television programmes

---

[11] *Prayer over the Offerings*

detrimental to a Christian outlook, and inappropriate public spectacles. Our Lady can help us be vigilant over ourselves and for the sake of others, so that we may never give in to a way of life contrary to the faith we have received. We need ever more firmly to practise fortitude in preserving the teachings of the Church. We cannot let a permissive environment be intolerant of Christian principles that are not open to compromise. Saint Peter exhorts the first Christians in the relativistic society of his own day: *Be resistant and steadfast in the Faith.*[12] Each of us is called to give upright example in matters of faith and morals even if it means conspicuous difference from the majority. Our integrity can help others who later may come to appreciate faith in Jesus Christ as a result of our behaviour.

When the moral tone in society is low, our faith needs to be strong and accompanied by *loving generosity with others.* We should continue to learn how to have a good rapport with everyone, including those who do not understand us. Our heart should continue to expand to include others who hold different social or political views from our own. Whether we are dealing with highly educated individuals or with people who are barely literate, we need to have a friendly disposition which comes from dealing with God intimately in daily prayer. Such an attitude of affection is perfectly compatible with great fortitude in speaking out in support of the teachings of the Church.

Given that the spread of Christianity throughout the world has come about under the patronage of the Virgin Mary, the new evangelization of the nations is taking place under her watchful vigilance as well. As the column that guided and sustained the Chosen People on their way in the desert, the Blessed Mother leads us along the sure path to

---

[12] cf 1 Pet 5:9

Jesus, who is our Promised Land: *She always does so as many of her images depict. There she appears with her Son in her arms like Our Lady of the Pillar. She never ceases to point out to us Christ, who is the Way, the Truth and the Life.*[13]

St Josemaría Escrivá described his own love for the Blessed Virgin of Saragossa: *God wants us to draw close to Our Lady of the Pillar so that we may be comforted by her understanding, her affection and her power. She will increase our faith, assure our hope and help us to be more fervent in our loving concern to serve all souls. May we dedicate ourselves to others with renewed energy as we sanctify our work and our everyday activities. In a word, may we convert every aspect of our life into an occasion for dealing with God.*[14]

Let us draw near to Our Lady of the Pillar on her feast, and ask her to guide us always and be our strength and security throughout our entire life.

---

[13] John Paul II, *Address,* 6 November 1982
[14] St. J. Escrivá, *Memories of Our Lady of the Pillar*, p.47

15 October

35. ST TERESA OF AVILA

Doctor of the Church
Memorial

St Teresa of Avila was born in Spain on March 28, 1515 and joined the Carmelite Order at the age of eighteen. In response to the extraordinary graces she received from the Lord, she undertook the reform of her Order with the assistance of St John of the Cross. In carrying out her work, she met all sorts of setbacks with noble spirit and had to overcome many obstacles in our Lord's service. Her writings are a sure guide for reaching union with God. She died in Avila on October 4, 1582. Blessed Paul VI declared her a Doctor of the Church on September 17, 1970.

35.1 The need for prayer and its primary importance in Christian life.

St Teresa was certain that through prayer we can achieve all God asks of us including what seems impossible through our own effort alone. Several times throughout her life she heard the Lord's words: *What is it you fear?* Though she was old, sick and tired, God gave her strength to carry out her resolutions by way of her constant union with him. After prayer the foundress could return to her work and apostolate ready to overcome any obstacle.

One day after communion when her body was offering resistance to setting up even more new convents she heard Jesus from within say: *What is it you fear? When have I failed to help you? I am the same now as before. Don't hold back from setting up those two foundations,* he told her, referring to the new convents to be set up in Burgos and Palencia. St Teresa exclaimed: *Almighty God, how different are your words from those of men.* She continues in the same vein: *I was then so determined and encouraged that the whole world could not stand in the way.*[1]

Years later she wrote of what must have been a difficult foundation in Palencia: *All is going so smoothly I don't know how long it can go on like this.*[2] In another letter she went on to say: *Each day it is more obvious how right it was to establish a foundation here.*[3] She would say the same about the new one in the other city too: *In Burgos there are so many who want to join it is a pity not to have enough room.*[4] All her confidence from God filled her with joy and cheerfulness in spite of the difficulties of the situation: *For me to go to Burgos with so many ailments when it was so cold outside did not seem at all feasible.*[5] However, the Lord never left her on her own.

Through prayer we gain energy to carry out whatever the Lord asks of us. This is as true for the priest or the mother of a family as it is for the religious or the student. The devil therefore makes a concerted effort to get us to omit our daily prayer or do it in a perfunctory way. *The tempter knows that the soul who perseveres in prayer, and who through the goodness of God advances in his service after every fall, is lost to him.*[6] Souls who have always been close to the Lord speak to us of the primary importance of prayer in Christian life. The Curé d'Ars taught: *It is not surprising the devil does everything in his power to get us to lessen the time of our personal dialogue with the Lord or*

---

[1] St Teresa, *Foundations,* 29,6
[2] *ibid., Letter,* 348,3
[3] *ibid., Letter,* 354,4
[4] *ibid., Letter,* 145,8
[5] *ibid., Foundations,* 29,11
[6] *ibid., Life,* 19,2

to do it poorly.[7]

Prayer is the foundation of faithful perseverance in the Lord's service. St Teresa teaches: *A person who does not stop going forward will eventually arrive, though perhaps late... There is no greater cause of straying from the path of faithful perseverance than letting up in prayer.*[8] Therefore we have to prepare carefully for prayer beforehand, and bring to it the clear realization that we pray in the presence of the living and glorious Christ. He sees and hears us with the same affection as he had for those who drew near him during his life on earth. How wonderfully well the day goes when we take care of our daily conversation with God with calm and attention. How joyful we should be to enjoy the presence of Christ. *Look at that senseless set of reasons the enemy gives you for abandoning your prayer. 'I have no time' – when you are constantly wasting it. 'This is not for me.' 'My heart is dry ...' Prayer is not a question of what you say or feel, but of love. And you love when you try hard to say something to the Lord, even though you might not actually say anything.*[9]

Let us make the resolution never to slacken in our devotion to prayer. May we always dedicate the best possible time and place to it, in front of the tabernacle as often as we possibly can.

35.2 Dealing with the most Sacred Humanity of Jesus.

Our prayer will be easier if together with the decisive effort not to give in to voluntary distractions we try to have dealings with the most Sacred Humanity of Jesus, an inexhaustible source of Love. This practice will greatly

---

[7] St Jean Vianney, The Curé d'Ars, *Homily on Prayer*
[8] St Teresa, *Life,* 19,5
[9] St. J. Escrivá, *Furrow,* 464

facilitate our fulfilling the divine Will.

St Teresa tells us of the capital impact on her soul of a passing occurrence. It left an indelible impression on her. She wrote: *Going into the oratory one day I saw an image some workers had brought in to be put into storage. It depicted the wounded Christ and was so true a rendering of the unspeakable horror of what took place for our sake that it moved me to visualize him that way from that moment on. I felt so ungrateful for those wounds that my heart seemed to split in half within me. I threw myself down near him weeping bitter tears and begged him to strengthen me once and for all so that I might not offend him again.*[10] This great outpouring was not provoked by sentimentality, but by contrite love for Christ, who loves us so much He suffers for us as a most convincing proof of his love. How natural it is for St Teresa to long to behold an image of the One dearest to her. She later added: *How deprived are they who have no conception of the look of Our Lord. It would seem their love were small since if it were not they would long to see his face. Even here on earth it makes us happy to see whoever it is we love a great deal.*[11] We cannot let our relationship with Jesus be distant and impersonal.

It is often helpful to make use of our imagination in order to represent Jesus at different moments during his life. He is born in Bethlehem. The Christ child is subject to Mary and Joseph. Later the young worker Jesus learns his trade. We can remember Mary being hard pressed during the flight into Egypt and her pain at the summit of Calvary. Sometimes we may draw near the group of disciples to whom Jesus is explaining a parable. We can join him too, on his long journeys from city to city and from town to town. We might decide to simply remain at his side and

[10] St Teresa, *Life,* 9,1
[11] *ibid.,* 9,6

enter the house of his close friends from Bethany. There we can contemplate the affection those close friends must have shown him. No matter what particular occasion we consider, Jesus is our closest friend, one we can always rely on. In front of the Tabernacle we can continually learn to refine our dealings with the Lord.

We pray so that we may encounter the living Christ, who is awaiting us. *Teresa had no time for books that proposed contemplation as a nebulous immersion in the divinity (Life 22,1) or as 'not thinking about anything' (Interior Castle 4,3,6). She perceived the danger of self-absorption and of getting separated from Jesus, the 'source of all that is good' (Life 22,4). Thus, her loud cry: 'To go off from Christ? I couldn't bear it' (Life 22,1). This exclamation is valid in our own day in the face of certain methods of prayer that are not inspired by the Gospel. These approaches tend to do without Christ in favour of a mental emptiness far removed from Christianity.*[12]

Many of our difficulties in prayer disappear when we pause to consider that we are in the presence of God. We need to focus our attention on the preparatory prayer we may be in the habit of saying: *My Lord and my God, I firmly believe that you are here, that you see me, that you hear me. I adore you with profound reverence...* If we realize that He is as much at *our* side as He was with the ones who heard him in Nazareth or Bethany, we are already praying. We look at him and he looks at us. Perhaps we formulate a petition. At times we may identify with a particular reading or pause at a given point to make a resolution to improve somehow in our ordinary life. Perhaps we see a way to attend to our family better. We could smile more though we are tired or when we are frustrated in trying to resolve certain challenging problems.

---

[12] John Paul II, *Address,* 1 November 1982

Maybe we need to struggle to work with more intensity
and greater presence of God. Maybe we could arrange to
speak with a friend about going to confession. Given our
effort and the grace of God we will share the experience
encountered by Teresa and by all those who try to pray
well. She confides: *I would habitually finish my prayer
with consolation and renewed energy.*[13]

35.3 Difficulties in mental prayer.

The most serious difficulty that militates against
perseverance in our daily prayer is discouragement. We
should not get disheartened if in spite of every effort we
still experience distractions, or the time spent seems
fruitless. Prayer requires work on our part. St Teresa relates
her own struggles: *For many years I kept wishing the time
would be over. I had more in mind the clock striking twelve
than other good things. Often I would have preferred some
serious penance to becoming recollected in prayer.*[14]

As many spiritual authors point out, if we try to reject
distracting thoughts and are firmly decided to seek more
the Lord of consolation, than the consolation of the Lord
our prayer will always be fruitful. Besides, it will often be
beneficial for us not to have sensible consolations. This
way we seek Jesus with greater rectitude of intention and
thus unite ourselves more intimately to him. At times the
aridity we experience is not a trial sent or permitted by God
so much as a lack of real interest on our part in speaking to
him. We may not have prepared sufficiently well beforehand, or perhaps we are lacking the necessary generosity to
control our imagination. We need continually to relearn
how to focus our attention with real generosity.

For whoever is seriously trying to pray well, the time

---

[13] St Teresa, *Life,* 29,4
[14] *ibid.,* 8,3

will come when prayer seems like wandering in the desert, because in spite of all our efforts, nothing is 'felt'. These trials are not spared anyone who takes prayer seriously. We should be aware that the experience is common to all Christians who pray. We should not immediately identify this fairly common experience with 'the dark night of the soul' described in mystical theology. In any case, however, we should make a firm effort to continue praying during such periods though it seems 'artificial'. The exact opposite is in fact the case. Precisely at this juncture prayer represents a true expression of our fidelity to God. We want to remain in his presence despite not having any sensible consolations. When this moment arrives the time has come for proving that our love for God is real.[15]

Now as in the day of St Teresa *there is great necessity for prayer, since there are so many needs.*[16] The Church, society, families and the health of all souls, including our own, stand to profit from it. Prayer allows us to make progress in the face of every difficulty. It unites us to Jesus, who awaits us each day in our work, in our family duties and in a particular way during the time of prayer we dedicate to him alone.

---

[15] S.C.D.F., *Letter on Christian meditation*, 15 October 1989
[16] cf St Teresa, *Letter,* 184,6

18 OCTOBER

36. ST LUKE

Feast

St Luke the Evangelist was born of a noble pagan family in Antioch. He was a doctor who converted to the faith in the year 40 and later accompanied St Paul on his Second Apostolic Journey. He was also at the side of the Apostle of the Gentiles towards the end of his life. This author of the third Gospel and of the *Acts of the Apostles* gives us the most informative account of Christ's infancy and provides us with a masterful portrayal of the truth of divine mercy.

36.1 The Gospel of St Luke and striving for perfection in our work.

How beautiful upon the mountains are the feet of him who brings glad tidings of peace.[1] We should thank St Luke today for *bringing good tidings* to mankind because he was a faithful instrument in the hands of the Holy Spirit. Moved by the grace of divine inspiration he passed on to us a remarkable Gospel account as well as the history of primitive Christianity which we have in the *Acts of the Apostles*.

As in all work done well, the inspired writing of Sacred Scripture required human effort. The help of God does not supplant human talent. Luke himself refers to the diligence involved in the task: *After following up all things carefully from the very first* he made *an orderly account.*[2] He indicates too, that the information is in keeping with the testimony of those *who were eyewitness from the beginning.*[3] The task of composition meant assiduously interviewing

---

[1] *Entrance Antiphon*: Is 52:7
[2] cf Luke 1:3
[3] Luke 1:2

firsthand observers, most probably Our Lady herself, the
Apostles and the protagonists of the miracles who were
still alive. St Jerome observes of his finely wrought style
that it is a reflection of the reliability of his sources.[4]

Thanks to Luke's attentive correspondence with the
grace of the Holy Spirit, today we can read an account of
Jesus' infancy and the series of superb parables that he
alone recounts. We recall the parable of the prodigal son,
the one of the good Samaritan, the other about the
negligent administrator, and of course the episode of poor
Lazarus and the rich man. Also unique to his Gospel is the
wonderful account of the two travellers to Emmaus. It is
exquisitely crafted down to the last detail.

St Luke describes the divine mercy shown to those
most in need of it as no other Evangelist does. He stresses
Christ's love for sinners to show that Jesus came to *save
those who were lost*.[5] He also relates to us the Lord's
forgiving of the woman taken in adultery,[6] his stay in the
home of Zachaeus of ill repute,[7] and the gaze of Jesus that
works a transformation in Peter after his denials.[8] He tells
us about Christ's promise of salvation to the repentant
thief,[9] and of our Saviour's prayer for those who crucify
and insult him on Calvary.[10]

The role of women in society, seldom considered in
the first century of Christianity, plays an important part in
St Luke's Gospel. Jesus makes a concerted effort to restore
to them their dignity, and this Evangelist alone describes

---

[4] cf St Jerome, *Letter,* 20,4
[5] Luke 19:10
[6] Luke 7:36-50
[7] Luke 19:1-10
[8] Luke 22:61
[9] Luke 23:42
[10] Luke 23:34

several such figures, including the widow of Naim,[11] the woman who bathed Christ's feet as a sign of her fervent repentance,[12] and the Galileans who put their goods at Jesus' disposal to follow and serve him.[13] Then there are his friends, the two sisters from Bethany,[14] the stooped woman whom he cured,[15] and the group of weeping women from Jerusalem who show Christ compassion while he carries the Cross.[16]

We have a great deal for which to thank St Luke. The man who was to become Pope John Paul I penned an imaginary letter of esteem to this particular gospel writer: *You are the only one who offers us a moving account of the birth and infancy of Christ which we can savour every Christmas. There is one verse that stands out above all the others: 'Wrapped in swaddling clothes, he was laid in a manger.' This single phrase has given rise to crib scenes throughout the world and to thousands of beautiful paintings.*[17] These artistic creations are one more invitation for us to contemplate the life of the Holy Family in Bethlehem and share in their daily life in Nazareth.

Today we pause to consider the human perfection required and the effort involved in our own work. It may not stand out in a startling way so as to be admired by all, but all our tasks well-done for God are of lasting value. This is the precious gift we always have at hand to offer our Lord. Work carried out without interest or attention to detail is not worthy of the name, because it cannot be pleasing to God or of service to others. Let us pause to consider how we carry out the responsibilities that we

---

[11] Luke 7:11-17
[12] Luke 7:36-50
[13] Luke 8:1-3
[14] Luke 10:38-42
[15] Luke 13:10-17
[16] Luke 23:27-32
[17] A. Luciani, *Illustrissimi*, pp.234-235

should offer up every day for the glory of the Creator.

36.2 The Evangelist's message. The painter of the Virgin.

We find fundamental teachings of the Lord in St
Luke's Gospel. He succinctly points out the importance of
humility, sincerity, poverty, the acceptance of the daily
Cross and the need for thanksgivings. Our love for God
moves us to give thanks to Luke for the exquisite delicacy
of his soul which is shown in his refined work. From the
days of antiquity, Christians have called him *the painter of
the Virgin.*[18] Some sketches and paintings of our Blessed
Lady are attributed to him.

The Gospel of St Luke is a fundamental source of
knowledge for devotion to our Lady, and has inspired Christian art for centuries. No person in the history of the Gospel
except for Jesus himself is described with as much affection
as our Mother Mary. Under the inspiration of the Holy
Spirit the Evangelist writes to us about the gifts bestowed
on the Blessed Virgin. She is *full of grace* and the Lord is
with her. As Mother of Jesus she conceives by the power
of the Holy Spirit without losing her virginity and is
intimately united to the redemptive mystery of the Cross.
All generations shall call her blessed, since the Almighty
has done great things for her. Rightly does a local woman
full of fervent enthusiasm praise the Mother of Jesus.[19]

Our Lady's faithful correspondence to her vocation is
continually apparent. She humbly receives the announcement from the Archangel about her dignity as the Mother
of God by wholeheartedly accepting the divine plan. She
immediately hastens to help others. Twice does Luke show
us that *she pondered all these things in her heart.*[20] The

---

[18] Eusebius, *Ecclesiastical History*, II:43
[19] cf *The Navarre Bible,* Pamplona 1983, pp.706-707
[20] Luke 2:19,51

Virgin herself would have shared with St Luke her most intimate memories of life with our Lord.

36.3 Reading the Holy Gospel with reverence.

We honour the legacy of St Luke by contemplating the noble and uplifting description he gives us of the Saviour. Let us ask him for the joy and apostolic fervour of our first brothers in the faith as we read and meditate on the *Acts of the Apostles,* the renowned *Gospel of the Holy Spirit.*

In keeping with an ancient Christian custom, when someone was troubled or puzzled the person concerned would open the Gospel at random and read the first verse he happened upon. The individual did not often resolve the particular problem at hand but would always find peace and serenity in this encounter with Jesus. *As many as touched him were saved,*[21] the Evangelist comments on a certain occasion. Jesus continues to impart to us something of his courage and strength each time we enter into contact with him through the inspired Word.

St Luke's writings teach us to have constant recourse to the Lord. We need frequently to seek out his mercy and treat him as our faithful Friend who lays down his life for us. The Evangelist permits us to penetrate deeply into the mystery of Jesus today when so many confused ideas circulate about Christ the Son of God, the *cornerstone* of every human life. He is the most significant phenomenon to confront humanity throughout twenty centuries. The words of divine inspiration have the power to bring us into contact with the Person of the Saviour as no other spiritual reading can. We can therefore turn to the Holy Gospel to learn *the surpassing worth of knowing Christ Jesus,*[22] as St Paul tells the Philippians, since *to be ignorant of the*

---

[21] cf Mark 6:56
[22] Phil 3:8

Scripture is to be ignorant of Christ.[23]

The Gospel should be the Christian's favourite book since it is indispensable for knowing Christ. We contemplate its scenes and grow to understand all that is revealed to us there from memory. *When you open the Holy Gospel, think that what is written there – the words and deeds of Christ – is something that you should not only know, but live. Everything, every point that is told there, has been gathered, detail by detail, for you to make it come alive in the individual circumstances of your life. You too, like the Apostles, will burn to ask, full of love, 'Lord, what would you have me do?' And in your soul you will hear the conclusive answer, 'the Will of God!' Take up the Gospel every day then, and read it and live it as a definite rule. This is what the saints have done.*[24]

St Luke often meditated on the deeds he recounts. He can teach us to love the Holy Gospel as the first generations of Christians did. In Sacred Scripture we will find *food for our soul, since the Gospel is the clear and perennial source of the spiritual life.*[25]

---

[23] St Jerome, *Commentary on the Prophet Isaiah*, Prologue, PL 24:17
[24] St. J. Escrivá, *The Forge,* 754
[25] Second Vatican Council, *Dei Verbum,* 21

28 OCTOBER

37. STS SIMON AND JUDE

Apostles
Feast

Simon was also called *the Zealot* perhaps for belonging to the party of the Jewish enthusiasts for the Law. He was originally from Cana of Galilee. Judas, also called Thaddeus, meaning *the courageous one,* is remembered in ecclesiastical tradition as the author of the Epistle that bears his name. They reportedly preached the doctrine of Christ in Egypt, Mesopotamia and Persia and were both martyred for the Faith.

37.1 The Apostles seek no personal glory.

The Lord *had no need for anyone to bear witness concerning him.*[1] Nevertheless he wanted to choose the Apostles to be his companions during his life and to provide the continuity of his work following his death. In early Christian art we often find Christ surrounded by *the Twelve* who formed an inseparable company around him. These disciples belonged neither to the influential class of Israel nor to the priestly caste of Jerusalem. They were not philosophers but simple people. *It is a constant marvel to see how these men spread a message radically opposed in its essence to the common wisdom of their age. Currently, the practice of Christianity still runs contrary to popular thought and we are confronted with the same challenge.*[2]

The Gospel frequently alludes to Jesus' suffering

---

[1] John 2:25
[2] O. Hophan, *The Apostles,* p.16

because of the disciples' incomprehension. He addresses those He most confides in: *Do you not yet perceive nor understand? Is your heart still blinded? Though you have eyes do you still not see, and though you have ears do you still not hear?*[3] *They were not educated, nor were they even very bright, judging from their reaction to the supernatural. When even the most elementary examples and comparisons are beyond their grasp they turn to the Master and ask: 'Explain the parable to us.' When Jesus uses the metaphor of 'the leaven of the Pharisees' they think he's reproaching them for not buying bread (Matt 16:67)... So ordinary were the disciples Christ chose that they remain unchanged until the Holy Spirit fills them and they grow into pillars of the Church. Nevertheless, they remain the everyday sort of men, complete with defects and shortcomings. Often they are more eager to say than to do. Despite their undeniable weaknesses Jesus calls them to be fishers of men and co-redeemers. These simple men are to be dispensers of the grace of God.*[4]

The Apostles the Lord chooses are very different from one another. Nonetheless, they share the one Faith and the same message. It should therefore not be surprising that little is known about most of them. For each of them, giving testimony to Jesus and passing on the doctrine they received from him was what was most important, not receiving personal acclaim. In a manner of speaking, they would consider themselves *the envelope* of a letter from God, since their sole mission was to transmit the inheritance they had received. St Josemaría Escrivá occasionally used this metaphor to highlight the Christian virtue of humility. Christ's closest followers had only one desire, and that was to be faithful instruments of the Lord. *The*

---

[3] Mark 8:17
[4] St. J. Escrivá, *Christ is passing by*, 2

letter containing the divine message was important to them, not *the envelope* it came in.

Today, as a result, we have precious little information about the two great Apostles Simon and Jude. We know Simon was expressly chosen by the Lord to be one of *the Twelve*. We further know that Jude was the relative of Christ who asked him a question at the Last Supper: *Lord, how is it that you will manifest yourself to us and not to the world?*[5] We have no clue as to where their bodies are buried, nor do we know precisely the lands they evangelized. They had no concern to have their personal talents stand out, particularly their apostolic victories and the sufferings they endured for the sake of the Master's kingdom. On the contrary, they tried to pass unnoticed and simply be useful in spreading the message of Christ. In this way they found the deepest meaning of their lives. Despite modest human abilities for the mission Christ entrusted to them, the Apostles became the glory of God in the world.

We too can rejoice in carrying out God's Will by quietly fulfilling the work and mission the Lord has entrusted to us in our life, no matter how modest our tasks may seem. *I advise you not to look for praise, even when you deserve it. It is better to pass unnoticed, and to let the most beautiful and noble aspects of our actions, of our lives, remain hidden. What a great thing it is to become little! 'Deo omnis gloria!' – all the glory to God!*[6]

Then we will be efficacious, since when one works wholly and exclusively for the glory of God, one does everything with naturalness, like someone who is in a hurry and will not be delayed by 'making a great show of things'. In this way one does not lose the unique and incomparable

---

[5] John 14:22
[6] St. J. Escrivá, *The Forge*, 1051

company of the Lord.[7] Like someone in a hurry we too have to go from one task to the next without pausing unnecessarily over personal considerations.

37.2 The faith of the Apostles and our faith.

The Apostles were witnesses of the life and teachings of Jesus. They transmitted what they heard and the deeds they saw with diligent fidelity. They were not bent on spreading their personal theories nor did they merely propagate human solutions gleaned from their own experience. St John writes: *For we were not following fictitious myths when we made known to you the power and coming of Our Lord Jesus Christ but we were eyewitnesses of his grandeur.*[8] He insists: *I write of what was from the beginning, what we have heard with our ears and seen with our eyes. We have looked upon the Word of Life and touched it with our own hands. Thus we announce it to to you.*[9]

The doctrine of the Twelve is the foundation of the Christian faith. It is not the free interpretation of each one, nor does it derive from the authority of wise men. St Luke confirms that all the events he relates are *from the ones who from the beginning were eyewitnesses and ministers of the Word.*[10] We know furthermore that in the first Christian community *all persevered in the teaching of the Apostles.*[11]

The voice of the Apostles is the clear light of Jesus' teachings. It will resound throughout time until the end of the world. Their heart and lips overflow with veneration and respect for the words of Jesus and his Person. Their love leads Peter and John to exclaim in the face of the

---

[7] *ibid., Furrow,* 555
[8] 2 Pet 1:16
[9] 1 John 1:1
[10] Luke 1:1-3
[11] Acts 2:42

Sanhedrin's threats: *We cannot but speak of what we have seen and heard.*[12]

The faith has come down to us over the generations by means of the Magisterium of the Church through the continual assistance of the Holy Spirit. Growth in our understanding of these truths continues even today. In a sense we can compare our ever-deepening penetration of these truths to the development of a seed into a great tree. The Church, however, is always the channel though which we receive the teachings of Christ and a participation in his grace.[13] We need to make this doctrine known through catechism and personal apostolate just as priests do through their preaching. Many centuries separate us from the two Apostles we remember in a special way today. Nevertheless the Light and the Life of Christ they preached in the world continues to reach us. *The Lord's light has not lessened. The first Twelve passed the light on to their disciples, as these did to theirs, and so on for centuries until the deposit of faith reached our own day. This light has faithfully passed through many generations.*

For us, for the flock that draws near for nourishing sustenance now, God has provided teachers, pastors and priests. Through them He works the marvel of our salvation and takes care of us with divine affection. From him all the stars of the sky derive their splendour just as all the seas sing to him and all the heavens praise him.[14]

37.3 Love for Jesus in order to follow Him closely.

Like the other Apostles, Simon and Jude had the good fortune to learn from the lips of the Master the doctrine they would later teach. They shared their joys and sorrows

---

[12] Acts 4:20
[13] cf St Athanasius, *Letter to Serapion,* 28
[14] O. Hophan, *op. cit.,* pp.46-47

with him. How envious, in the good sense, we can be of them! The two learned many things in the intimacy of their conversation with the Lord: *What you hear whispered, preach it on the housetops.*[15] Surely they would absorb every detail of each miracle. Every tear and smile of the Lord would be important, since they would thereafter be *witnesses* to him in the world.

The Twelve considered intimate union with the Master essential for being an Apostle. When they are preparing to complete their number after the defection of Judas, they set forth one indispensable condition: *Out of the men who have been in our company since the Lord Jesus moved among us one must become a witness with us of his resurrection.*[16] All these men had accompanied Jesus from the beginning, even during the trials of the apostolate. Throughout tiring journeys under the sun and while they were at rest, the Lord calmly teaches them the mysteries of the kingdom. They share in Christ's joy when people respond well to his preaching. They participate in his suffering too on encountering the lack of generosity of some who set out to follow the Master.

They trusted Jesus as they would a father or a friend. They knew him for his noble bearing, his gentle tone of voice, and even his way of breaking bread. When his profound eyes rested on them and his voice resounded in their ears they would feel inundated by light and moved by joy. They would blush when He reprimanded them. When He needed to correct them, their faces, worn by years and toil, would fall downward, like those of little children caught in wrongdoing. Time and again towards the end of his earthly life they were in awe when He would speak to them of his coming Passion. They remained close to him

---

[15] Matt 10:27
[16] Acts 1:21

since they wanted to learn his doctrine, but above all because they loved him.[17]

Today let us ask the Holy Apostles Simon and Jude to help us know and love the Master more each day, and to follow him as the centre of our lives.

---

1 NOVEMBER

38. THE FEAST OF ALL SAINTS

Solemnity

We remember in a special way that sanctity is accessible to everyone in their various jobs and situations, and that to help us reach this goal we ought to put into practice the dogma of the Communion of Saints. The Church invites us to raise our hearts and minds to the immense multitude of men and women from all walks of life who followed Christ here on earth and are already enjoying his presence in Heaven. This feast has been celebrated since the eighth century.

38.1 Sanctification through ordinary life.

Let us all rejoice in the Lord, as we celebrate the feast day in honour of all the Saints, at whose festival the Angels rejoice and praise the Son of God.[1]

As we recall today with particular attention, Blessed John Paul II pointed out that a wealth of Christian truth is at the core of the Liturgy, in a special way on the Feast of All Saints. Here lies the fount of all holiness, God himself. Herein we practise the Communion of Saints through Christ in a particular way. The supernatural last end of universal redemption is signified in the Mass. It is the source of sanctity for all those who strive to practise the Beatitudes as described by Our Lord. From the Mass comes an indestructible hope in future glory and here we find the key to the relationship between suffering and salvation. The Roman Pontiff emphasizes: *As we pray in the 'Entrance antiphon', the fundamental dimension of the*

---

[1] *Entrance Antiphon*

feast we celebrate today is joy: 'Let us rejoice in the Lord and keep festival in honour of all the saints.' The experience is similar to what we savour in a large family where we are very much at home.[2] Included in this *large family* are the saints in heaven and those striving for sanctity on earth as well.

Our Mother the Church invites us today to bring to mind in a special way those who have experienced difficulties and temptations similar to our own during life, yet in the end triumphed over them. There is a *great multitude, which no man could number, out of all nations and tribes and tongues* as the *First Reading* of the Mass relates.[3] *They are sealed on the forehead as the servants of God.*[4] The Church recognizes many saints of every age and condition today. We remember them each year and also have recourse to them as intercessors for our various needs. The seal they receive and their white robes washed in the blood of the Lamb are symbols of Baptism. This sacrament of initiation involves incorporation into Christ, this life of grace being later renewed and increased through the other Sacraments, especially Penance and the Eucharist. Our good works also contribute to heightening this participation in the divine nature during our present life.

Today we rejoice and ask the help of the countless multitude who have reached heaven after cheerfully passing through life sowing affection and joy almost without realizing it. Perhaps while living among us they worked at a job similar to our own. Since their working backgrounds varied so greatly there may be office workers, manual workers, university professors, businessmen, secretaries etc. among them. Without doubt they must have

---

[2] John Paul II, *Homily,* 1 November 1980
[3] Rev 7:9
[4] cf Rev 7:3-9

had to confront difficulties similar to our own and had to begin again and again many times, as we make an effort to do each day.

The Church does not mention the entire multitude of saints by name in the Canon of the Mass. Through the light of faith though we understand that they form *a magnificent panorama of lay men and women who through the activity of each day's task were tireless workers in the Lord's vineyard. After passing unnoticed and perhaps being misunderstood by the high and mighty they were lovingly greeted by God our Father. They were humble yet great labourers for the growth of the kingdom of God in history.*[5] In sum, they are the ones who knew *how with the help of God to conserve and perfect during their life the sanctification they received in Baptism.*[6]

Throughout our life we are all called to the fullness of Love. A struggle against our passions and inordinate tendencies is necessary. We have to make a constant effort to improve, since *sanctity does not depend on one's state in life – single, married, widower, or priest – but on our personal correspondence with the grace God grants each one of us.*[7] The Church reminds everyone that both the worker who takes up his trade or profession each morning and the mother of a family committed to the daily running of the home should sanctify themselves by faithfully fulfilling their daily duties.[8]

It is consoling to realize that people with whom we had dealings a short time ago are now contemplating *the face of God.* We continue to be united to them by profound

---

[5] John Paul II, Apostolic Exhortation, *Christifideles laici,* 30 December 1988

[6] Second Vatican Council, *Lumen gentium,* 40

[7] St. J. Escrivá, *In Love with the Church,* p.67

[8] cf John Paul II, Apostolic Exhortation, *Christifideles laici,* 30 December 1988

friendship and affection through the Communion of Saints. They lend us assistance from heaven and we remember them with joy and seek their intercession as well. Today we make St Teresa's prayer to the Blessed in heaven our own. She too will be among those to hear our prayer: *O holy ones who knew how to prepare so delightful an inheritance, help us now that you are so near the fount of all holiness. Draw water for those of us who are perishing from thirst.*[9]

38.2 The universal call to holiness.

On this Solemnity we pray in the Preface of the Mass: *Today by your gift we celebrate the festival of your city, the heavenly Jerusalem, our mother, where the great array of our brothers and sisters already give you eternal praise. Towards her, we eagerly hasten as pilgrims advancing by faith, rejoicing in the glory bestowed upon those exalted members of the Church.*[10] We, the faithful, are the pilgrim Church on our way to heaven. While we make progress towards heaven we need to gather up the treasure of good works we will one day present before God. We hear the Lord's invitation clearly: *If anyone will come after me...*

Each one of us is called to the fullness of Christian life through our professional occupation. God wants us all to encounter him in our work by carrying it out with human perfection and supernatural outlook. We long for the presence of the Lord whom we will one day see face to face. Therefore we offer up all our activities to God, practise charity in our dealings with others and are generous in bringing the work entrusted to us to completion. By dealing with our Father God as a friend we can continually refine our contemplative spirit in the midst of the ordinary

[9] St Teresa, *Exclamations of the Soul to God*, 13:4
[10] *Roman Missal, Preface of the Mass*

everyday actions of our life. We can repeat certain duties many times a day in union with the Lord. *To love God and serve him it is not necessary to do extraordinary things. Of every man without exception Christ asks he 'be perfect as his Father in heaven is perfect' (Matt 5:48). For the great majority of men, to be a saint means sanctifying our work, sanctifying ourselves in our work and sanctifying others through all the circumstances of that work. In this way, we find God on all the pathways of our life.*[11]

What else did the vast host of glorified souls do – mothers, intellectuals, and manual workers – to win heaven? This question is of absolute importance since we, too, desire to abide with God forever in heaven. Those who persevere in union with Christ make an effort to sanctify the small realities of every day that Our Lord looks upon with affection. If at a given moment our fidelity is lacking, we rectify accordingly and once again set out on the right path. This is our way on earth.

Winning heaven is the challenge we face with the grace of God each day. Happily it always involves the task in hand and is effected precisely among the persons God has wanted to place at our side. We need to realize fully that our generous and holy resolve to improve constantly has an important impact on others. If through God's grace and the help of others we do reach heaven, we will not enter into eternal glory alone, but will draw many others there with us.

38.3 Christ is the measure and model of holiness.

Many of those who now contemplate the face of God in heaven perhaps did not have the opportunity during their time on earth to carry out great deeds. However, they did fulfil their modest daily duties as best they could. On

---

[11] *Conversations with Monsignor Escrivá*, 55

occasion they made mistakes – giving in to impatience, laziness or pride – and perhaps even sinned gravely. Nevertheless they repented right away and took advantage of the sacrament of Confession to begin anew. The Blessed in heaven had big hearts and led fruitful lives since they knew how to sacrifice themselves for Christ. We too are very much in need of the Lord's great mercy during our journey to heaven. Jesus – we need constantly to recall – keeps us going day after day. It is a tremendous good for us to pause frequently to consider him and the graces we have received, especially during moments of temptation or discouragement.

The Blessed in their lives never consider themselves saints. On the contrary, they are convinced of their great need for divine mercy. To a greater or lesser degree everyone experiences sickness, tribulation or *low-energy periods* in which everything entails a particular effort. Failure may come our way, but we have our successes as well. Perhaps at times the saints were moved to tears, but they knew and put into practice those words of Our Lord which the Mass brings to our attention today: *Come to me all you who labour and are heavy burdened and I will give you rest.*[12] The Blessed always lean on Christ for support. They often visit him in the Tabernacle to draw renewed energy from his presence there. The personalities of the Blessed vary enormously, but in this life they had in common one distinguishing feature: They lived charitably with those around them. The Lord said: *In this will everyone know you are my disciples, if you have love for one another.*[13] This is the common denominator of the saints who presently enjoy the vision of God.

A countless multitude of friends awaits us in heaven.

---

[12] *Alleluia* of the Mass: Matt 11:28
[13] John 13:34-35

The light of their example shines down on us, and makes it easier, sometimes, to see what we ought to do. They can help us with their prayers, strong prayers, wise prayers, when ours are so feeble and so blind. When you look out on a November evening, and see the sky all studded with stars, think of those innumerable saints in heaven, all ready to help you.[14] They will fill us with joy in the midst of any trials we need to undergo. Our Blessed Mother awaits us in heaven too. She will offer us her hand and take us into the presence of her Son and of our faithful departed loved ones who even now watch over us.

---

[14] R.A. Knox, *Sermon*, 1 November 1950

2 NOVEMBER

39. THE COMMEMORATION OF ALL SOULS

Today we dedicate our prayers in suffrage for the souls in Purgatory, still being purified of the remains of sin. Our ties with deceased relatives and friends do not end with their death. Priests can celebrate Mass three times on this day for their benefit, and all the faithful can gain special indulgences to expedite their entrance into heaven.

39.1 Purgatory is a place of purification.

During the month of November the Church invites us to pray more insistently and offer suffrages for the souls in Purgatory. St John Paul II encouraged us: *We feel bound by charity to offer those brothers and sisters who have experienced the fragility proper to human existence the help of our vigilant prayer. May whatever residue of human weakness still remaining in them to delay their happy encounter with God be definitively wiped out.*[1]

To enter into eternal life it is necessary that we be purified of all sin. A soul stained by venial faults cannot enter the dwelling place of God; *nor the one who practises abomination or falsehood, but only those who are written in the book of life of the Lamb.*[2] St Catherine of Genoa writes: *No one is barred from heaven. Whoever wants to enter heaven may do so because God is all-merciful. Our Lord will welcome us into glory with his arms wide open. The Almighty is so pure, however, that if a person is conscious of the least trace of imperfection and at the same*

---

[1] John Paul II, *Address,* 2 November 1982
[2] cf Rev 21:27

time understands that Purgatory is ordained to do away with such impediments, the soul enters this place of purification glad to accept so great a mercy of God. The worst suffering of these suffering souls is to have sinned against divine Goodness and not to have been purified in this life.[3] This waiting room of heaven is not a lesser hell, but a place of preparation where souls are duly cleansed of the remains of sin before entering heaven.

The inclination to sin we acquire through original sin is increased by personal sin. If one has not sufficiently expiated any specific offences against God during the course of our present life, there is further need for reparation to be accomplished. In the first place, evil dispositions may remain rooted in our soul at the hour of our death. There is, too, the temporal punishment left over from sins forgiven in confession. Furthermore, lack of love and refinement in dealing with our Lord can also defer our union with him. If our transgressions are not eliminated by a constant and generous purification in this life, we will perceive these faults with absolute clarity at the moment of death. Together with a strong desire to be united to God we will possess a tremendous yearning to be free of our evil inclinations. Purgatory at this time is the only possibility of achieving this purification.

In Purgatory the soul experiences very intense suffering due to a kind of flame *more painful than anything a man can suffer in this life.*[4] There is great joy too, though, since heaven comes afterwards. The soul in Purgatory has already won the last battle and is awaiting a more or less imminent encounter with God. The soul in Purgatory can be compared to an adventurer at the edge of the desert. The sun is relentless, the heat suffocating and water is not

---

[3] cf St Catherine of Genoa, *Treatise on Purgatory,* 12
[4] St Augustine, *Commentary on the Psalms*, 37:3

readily available. On the horizon lies the distant mountain where his treasure lies. In between stretches a vast expanse. He sets out to cross the torrid plain prepared to travel the long distance on foot. On the far off peak fresh breezes blow. There rest and refreshment awaits him. Meanwhile, the asphyxiating heat makes him stumble and fall again and again. The soul in Purgatory differs from the adventurer in that he knows most assuredly that he will eventually arrive at the summit of his distant mountain. No matter how suffocating the torrid heat may be, it cannot definitively separate him from God.[5]

We can help the Holy Souls in Purgatory pass more quickly over the great divide that separates them from God by making reparation for sin. We can thus also shorten our own passage through this waiting room of heaven. If we are generous in our spirit of penance, in the offering of our sufferings and in our love for the sacrament of Confession, with the help of grace we may enter straight away into heaven. This is the case with the saints whose living example we can accept as an open invitation to spur us on. Their example stimulates our own desire to help make up for the effects of personal sin in the lives of countless souls.

39.2 Close union with the souls in Purgatory through suffrages.

We can greatly help the souls in Purgatory to enter heaven. *We know our union with the brethren who have died in the grace and faith of Christ is not in the least weakened or interrupted by their death. On the contrary it is strengthened by our conveying spiritual goods for their benefit.*[6] According to the perpetual faith of the Church, we

---

[5] cf W. Macken, *Purgatory*
[6] Second Vatican Council, *Lumen gentium,* 49

can be more united than ever before to those who precede
us into eternal life.

The *Second Reading* of the Mass recalls Judas
Maccabeus, who took up a collection and sent one
thousand drachmas of silver to Jerusalem to offer a
sacrifice for the sins of those who died in battle: *He
thought well and religiously concerning the resurrection.
For if he had not hoped that they who were slain should
rise again, to pray for the dead would have been in vain.*
The sacred author adds: *It is therefore a holy and
wholesome thought to pray for the dead that they may be
loosed from their sins.*[7] The Church continues to offer
suffrages and prayers for the faithful departed as a
perennial custom. St Isidore of Seville already affirms this
practice as taught by the Apostles themselves.[8]

The infinite value of the Mass makes it the most
important prayer we have to offer up for the Holy Souls in
Purgatory.[9] We can also offer our prayers for their benefit,
especially the Rosary, our work, the sufferings of life and
all kinds of difficulties we experience, as well as the
indulgences we merit for them during our earthly
existence.[10] Offering these suffrages is the best way we can
show our love for those who have gone before us and await
their definitive encounter with God. We should remember
our parents with particular devotion, and pray especially
for our relatives and friends.

*Through the Communion of Saints our great allies in
Purgatory can help us too. The holy souls in Purgatory.
Out of charity, out of justice, and out of excusable
selfishness (they have such power with God!) remember*

---

[7] *Roman Missal, Second Reading,* All Souls' Day: 2 Mach 12:43-44
[8] cf St Isidore of Seville, *On Ecclesiastical Offices,* 1
[9] cf Council of Trent, *Session 25*
[10] cf Bl. Paul VI, Apostolic Constitution, *Sacrarum indulgentiarum
recognitio,* 1 January 1967

them often in your sacrifices and in your prayers. May you be able to say when you speak of them, 'My good friends, the souls in Purgatory.'[11]

39.3 Personal purification on earth, and the desire to bypass Purgatory.

St Teresa encourages us to make an effort to do penance during our present life: *How sweet will death be for the person who has fully repented of all personal sins and can leap over Purgatory.*[12]

While being purified, the holy souls cannot earn merit for good works. Their task is more trying and painful than any other we will face in the present life. They suffer all the agonies of the man dying in the desert. Nevertheless, their travail does not help them grow in charity. Such is in fact the case when we accept earthly sufferings out of love for God. In Purgatory rebellion is no longer possible. Even if they would have to remain there until the end of time, the Holy Souls would do so gladly, so fervent is their desire for purification.

Besides contributing to shortening their time of purification, we can merit for them and at the same time more quickly purify our own inordinate tendencies. Pain, sickness and suffering are all excellent means permitted by the Lord – they can be a grace – to make reparation for personal sin. While we are awaiting the eternal contemplation of God our passage through life should be a time for purification. Through penance our soul is rejuvenated and disposed for Life with a capital 'L'. *Do not ever forget that after death you are going to be welcomed by Love itself. Within the love of God you will find implicit all the noble human loves on earth as well. Our Lord has*

---

[11] St. J. Escrivá, *The Way*, 571
[12] St Teresa, *Way of Perfection*, 40:9

*arranged for us to spend this brief day of our earthly
existence working, and like his only-begotten Son, 'doing
good'. Meanwhile we have to be on our guard and alert to
the call St Ignatius of Antioch felt within his soul as the
hour of his martyrdom approached: 'Draw close to your
Father. Come to him who is so desirous of your
company.'*[13]

Our intention of reaching heaven without passing
through Purgatory can be immensely fruitful. We need to
have an effective desire so that with the help of grace we
can achieve the necessary purification during this life. Our
Blessed Mother Mary, *Refuge of sinners,* will obtain the
grace for us to act accordingly. May we be filled with a
holy determination to convert our life into *spatium verae
poenitentiae, a time for true penance,* in reparation for our
unworthy thoughts, words, and deeds.

---

[13] St. J. Escrivá, *Friends of God,* 221

9 NOVEMBER

40. THE DEDICATION OF THE LATERAN BASILICA

Feast

The basilica of St John Lateran was one of the first churches built by Christians following the early persecutions. It was raised in Rome under the Emperor Constantine and is the first Western church to have the invocation of the Saviour. The Lateran Basilica was consecrated by Pope Sylvester on this day in the year 324.

Originally celebrated only in Rome, the feast became universal in the Roman Rite as a sign of unity with the Holy See. This church continues to be the Cathedral of the Roman Pontiff to this day. The basilica is called *'Mater Ecclesiae Romae Urbis et Orbis'*, Mother of all the churches in Rome and of the world. Its long history evokes memories of the many thousands of people who have received Baptism within its ancient walls.

40.1 Churches are a symbol of the presence of God among us.

Each year the Jewish people commemorate the feast of the *Dedication*[1] in memory of the purification and re-establishment of worship in the Temple of Jerusalem following the victories of Judas Maccabeus over the King of Antioch.[2] The celebration was a week-long event throughout Judaea. It was called the *Festival of Lights* since it was the custom for people to place lanterns, as a symbol of the Law, in their windows at home to commemorate the

---

[1] John 10:22
[2] cf 1 Mac 4:36-59; 2 Mac 1:1 ss; 10:1-8

anniversary. Families would increase the number of lights with each passing day of the Feast.[3] The reason for the custom was to recall the time when the pagan temples were converted into places of worship. Similarly, every year the whole Roman rite recalls the dedication of the Lateran Basilica. It is the oldest and most dignified of all the Western churches. Besides this universal Feast, *on some other day, each diocese celebrates the dedication of its Cathedral. Every individual church remembers its own consecration in a special way too.*[4]

Among the Jews the temple was considered a place of the special presence of Yahweh. God already made his presence known in the *Tent of Meeting* in the desert. There Moses spoke with the Lord *as to a friend.* The cloud in the shape of a column came to him as a sign of the Almighty's presence. It descended and paused at the entrance to the sanctuary.[5] Here *his Name would be present,* his infinite and ineffable Being, to hear and to attend to his faithful ones.

When Solomon had finished the construction of the Temple of Jerusalem he prayed the following words on the feast of the dedication: *Is it true God can dwell upon the earth? For if heaven cannot contain you, how much less can this house which I have built. Listen to the prayer of your servant and his supplications, O Lord my God. Hear the hymn and the prayer your servant offers you this day. May your eyes be upon this house night and day. Whatever people shall pray for in this place, you will hear them from your abode in heaven. When you hear their petition show them your mercy.*[6] We, too, go to our churches to encounter God. He awaits us there with his real presence in our

---

[3] cf 2 Mac 1:18

[4] A.G. Martimort, *The Church in Prayer,* Madrid 1987

[5] Ex 33: 7-11

[6] 1 Kings 8:27-30

Tabernacles.

St John Paul II taught: *Any church is your house, and the house of God. Value it as the place where we encounter our common Father.*[7] The church building is a sign of the Church-assembly. The congregation is formed by *living stones* – men and women consecrated to God by their Baptism.[8] *The church building is the place where the Christian community gathers together to hear the word of God, to offer up prayers of petition and praise, and, in a principal way, to celebrate the Sacred Mystery of our Faith. The Blessed Sacrament of the Eucharist, a unique image of the Church, is reserved here. The altar is surrounded by people made holy by participating in the sacrifice of the Lord and nourished by the celestial banquet. The august Sacrament is a sign of Christ, who is priest, host and the altar of his own sacrifice.*[9]

Let us approach our churches with a great spirit of reverence since there is no place more worthy of respect than the house of God. What great devotion these buildings should inspire in us, since the sacrifice of heaven and earth, the Blood of God made Man, is offered up there.[10] Let us visit them with the confidence of a person on his way to greet his best friend, Jesus Christ. He gave his life for each one of us out of love, and eagerly awaits us every day. In our churches we also encounter the house we share in common with our brothers and sisters in the Faith.

40.2 Jesus Christ is truly present in our churches.

Churches are places where the members of Christ congregate to pray together. We find Jesus there too, since

---

[7] John Paul II, *Homily,* 3 November 1982
[8] cf *Ritual for the Dedication of Churches and Altars*, Presentation, 26 October 1978
[9] cf *Decree,* 29 May 1977
[10] Anonymous, *The Holy Mass,* Madrid 1975

where two or more are gathered in his name, there He is in the midst of them.[11] Above all, our Lord is truly and substantially present in the Eucharist. He is present both in his Divinity and in his most holy Humanity, with his Body and Soul, and He sees us and hears us. There Christ nurtures us from the Tabernacle as he used to care one by one for those who came to him *from all cities and villages.*[12] We can present him with our deepest desires to love him more and more with each passing day, and entrust to him our preoccupations, our difficulties and our weaknesses. We should cultivate a profound reverence for our churches and oratories since the Lord awaits us there.

Truly the world would be considerably different if Christ had not wanted to remain with us. In front of the tabernacle we can draw strength for our interior struggle and leave all our worries in his hands. On how many occasions have we returned to the hustle and bustle of ordinary life with renewed hope! We cannot forget that the Sacrifice of infinite value which the Lord offered on Calvary is renewed each day in our churches so as to draw down upon us from heaven innumerable graces of divine mercy.

It would be a lack of courtesy to withhold our vigilant attention from a distinguished guest staying in our home. We need to be equally conscious of the fact that Jesus in the Blessed Sacrament is our Guest here on earth, and that He is as eager for our attention as He is to help us in in all our needs. Let us examine ourselves today to see if we immediately greet Our Lord in the Tabernacle when we enter a church. Do we behave in God's house as good daughters and sons? Are our genuflexions before Jesus in the Blessed Sacrament true acts of faith? Is our heart stirred within us when we pass near a church where Christ

---

[11] cf Matt 18:20
[12] cf Mark 6:32

is sacramentally present? *As you make your usual way through the city streets, aren't you happy when you discover another tabernacle?*[13] We can then continue our work with renewed joy and peace.

40.3 Divine grace makes us living temples of God.

The true temple of the New Covenant is no longer made by human hands. From now on, the holy Humanity of Jesus is the new Temple of God. Christ said: *Destroy this Temple and in three days I will raise it up.* The Evangelist explains: *He was speaking of the Temple of his Body.*[14] If the Body of Jesus is the new Temple of God, so is the Church the Body of Christ and we are members of his Mystical Body. As the *cornerstone* and foundation of his Church, the Lord supports the new building constructed from each one of the baptized built upon him. *In the same way now as then, he is rejected, disregarded and given up for dead. But the Father has made the Son the solid and firm-set base of the new building forever through Christ's glorious resurrection. The Mystical Body is as strong as the degree to which the members adhere to their Head, and the measure to which they 'grow' in him toward 'the fullness of Christ'. In and through the Church, 'the dwelling place of God in the Spirit', the Lord is glorified by virtue of the spiritual sacrifices of the 'holy priesthood' of the faithful (1 Pet 2:5). The Lord's kingdom is thus established in the world.*[15] St Paul also frequently reminds the first Christians: *Do you not know that you are the temple of God and that the Spirit of God dwells in you?*[16]

We should often bring to mind that the most Holy

---

[13] St. J. Escrivá, *The Way,* 270
[14] John 2:20-21
[15] John Paul II, *op. cit.*
[16] 1 Cor 3:16

Trinity *inhabits the souls of the just in a singular way. By means of the grace of God, Christ dwells in each one of us as in a temple.*[17] Meditation on this marvellous reality will help us to be more conscious of the transcendent importance of living in God's grace. We need to have a deep horror of offending the Lord, because *sin destroys Christ's temple* and deprives our souls of friendship with God. Through the indwelling of the Holy Spirit we enjoy in anticipation the beatific vision. *This admirable union differs only in condition from the one God grants the blessed in heaven.*[18] God's presence in our soul in this life is an invitation to increase constantly the intensity of our personal closeness to the Lord. He is the one we are called to seek out in the depths of our soul at every moment.

---

[17] Leo XIII, Encyclical, *Divinum illud munus,* 9 May 1897
[18] *ibid.,* 11

21 NOVEMBER

41. THE PRESENTATION OF THE BLESSED VIRGIN MARY

Memorial

Today we recall the consecration of the church in Jerusalem dedicated to the Presentation of the Blessed Virgin. It was built to commemorate the commitment Our Lady made to the Lord when she was moved by the grace of the Holy Spirit during her childhood to dedicate herself completely to God. Through the grace of her Immaculate Conception Mary enjoys the greatest participation in life of grace of any creature. This feast has been celebrated in the Western world since the fourteenth century.

41.1 Mary's dedication and the significance of the feast day.

We know very little about Our Lady's life until the moment the Archangel appears to her to announce that she has been chosen by God to become the Mother of the Eternal Son. Mary's existence on earth up to that decisive moment must have been wholly unique, however, since she was full of grace from the first moment of her Immaculate Conception. Throughout her life God watched over her with a singular predilection and an unrepeatable love. At the same time, Our Lady was a normal child, who grew up like all the other children in her neighbourhood. She was the delight of her contemporaries in all the circumstances and events of her everyday life in an ordinary town.

St Luke is notably diligent in examining all the sources that can offer personal information concerning the people he describes. In the case of Mary's childhood, however, he omits any mention of specific facts. Our Lady most probably never mentioned anything about her earliest years, since there would be very little in them of extraordinary interest. The most important events of her life happen in the intimacy of her soul, in the context of a continual dialogue with God the Father. At the Annunciation, the Almighty calmly awaits her correspondence for the Incarnation of the Son of God to occur. *O most holy Mother, why do you remain silent about the years of your childhood? The apocryphal gospels relate pious lies that are really deceitful images of your true nature. They falsely inform us that you lived day and night in the Temple, where the angels brought you meals and conversed with you. Such fabrications represent you to us as far removed from our daily experience.*[1] In reality, the course of Our Lady's everyday life very much resembled the ordinary tasks and duties of our own daily lives.

The feast we celebrate today does not have its origin in the Gospel, but in ancient tradition. The Church, however, does not accept the fictitious narrative that supposes Our Lady to have lived in the Temple under a vow of virginity from the time she was a young maiden. But the essential basis of today's feast is firm – the personal oblation that the Blessed Mother made to the Lord during her early youth. She was moved by the Holy Spirit to consecrate her life to God, who filled her with grace from the first moment of her conception.[2] Mary's complete dedication was efficacious, and continued to grow as her life went on. Her example moves us not to withhold anything in our own life of dedication to the Lord.

Today we celebrate the complete surrender the Blessed Virgin makes to God's plans for the salvation of mankind.

---

[1] S. Munoz, *The Gospel of Mary,* Madrid 1973
[2] Paul VI, Apostolic Exhortation, *Marialis cultus,* 2 February 1974, 8

In the light of her total commitment, which implies the state of virginity, Our Lady will later say to the Archangel Gabriel: *I know not man.*[3] In this way she tactfully reveals an entire history of fidelity to God that takes place deep within her soul. Mary already personifies the fulfilment of the New Testament affirmation of virginity's superiority of state over marriage. Its higher vocation in no way lessens the sanctity of marriage, which Christ himself raised to the dignity of a sacrament.[4]

Let us ask Our Lady's help today in living our own dedication to the full, in whatever state God has placed us, in accordance with the specific vocation we have received from the Lord. *Talk with Our Lady and tell her trustingly, 'O Mary, in order to live the ideal which God has set in my heart I need to fly very high – ever so high.'*

It is not sufficient to detach yourself, with God's help, from the things of this world, recognizing them as the merest clay. More is needed: even if you were to put the whole universe in a pile under your feet to get closer to heaven ... it wouldn't suffice!

You have to fly, without the support of anything here on earth, relying on the voice and the inspiration of the Spirit. And you will tell me: 'But my wings are stained and smeared with the clinging mud of many years.'

And I repeat: 'Turn to Our Lady.' 'Mary,' you should say to her again, 'I can hardly get off the ground. The earth draws me like an accursed magnet. Mary, you can make my soul take off on that glorious and definitive flight which has as its destination the very heart of God.'

Trust in her, for she is listening to you.[5]

---

[3] Luke 1:34
[4] Second Vatican Council, *Gaudium et spes,* 48
[5] J. Escriva, *The Forge,* 994

41.2 Our full dedication and correspondence with grace.

The intimate relationship which the Blessed Virgin has with the Lord far surpasses that of all of God's creatures. She is the one who receives the maximum donation of divine love, since she is truly full of grace.[6] Mary never denies Our Lord anything. Her correspondence with the graces and motions of the Holy Spirit is always complete. Mary stands out among all other human beings throughout history as exemplar for our imitation. From her we can learn to give ourselves generously in service to the Lord. Like her, we strive to make the most of our talents, in the state and vocation to which God has called us, in the specific task with which we have been entrusted in the world. St Ambrose points to the Mother of God as our model: *Mary lives in such a way that her life itself is a lesson for everyone.* He concludes: *Represent before your mind's eye the virginal life of the Blessed Virgin, in whom is reflected, as in a mirror, the lustre, purity and energy of virtue itself.*[7]

Only in Our Lord does the virtue of charity not admit the possibility of any increase, since He enjoys the absolute fruition of divine strength from even before the Incarnation.[8] Furthermore, the Second Council of Constantinople teaches that it is false to say Jesus Christ made progress in virtue through good works.[9] Mary, on the contrary, grows increasingly in holiness during the course of her earthly life. Our Blessed Mother corresponds in a consistent way with the motions of God, and thus grows continually in sanctity. From the beginning of her life she is filled with the fullness of God's supernatural gifts. Her

---

[6] cf *Prayer over the Offerings*
[7] St Ambrose, *On Virgins,* II, 2
[8] R. Garrigou-Lagrange, *The Mother of the Saviour,* p. 100
[9] Second Council of Constantinople, Dz 224

plenitude of divine life progressively expands to the degree in which she is quick in corresponding with the promptings of the Holy Spirit. Mary's union with God intensifies as the great events of her life unfold the Incarnation of her Son, her Co-redemption with him on Calvary and her Assumption into Heaven.

The lives of all the saints develop incrementally in similar fashion. The closer they draw to the Lord, the more docile they become to the graces they receive and the more surely they advance in union with Jesus. *Uniformly accelerated movement is a symbol of the spiritual development of the virtue of charity in someone who avoids backsliding. The more steadily a person makes progress in union with Jesus, the stronger becomes the attraction of the soul toward him.*[10] Since Christ calls each one of us to the fullness of holiness, no matter what our particular state or circumstances in life may be, it is God's will that our own lives unfold in similar fashion.

As we correspond with the graces the Lord grants us with increasing faithfulness, the joys and sorrows of life will turn into so many more occasions for our greater union with Christ. Moments of triumph and of trial alike, provide everyday opportunities for showing the Lord our love for him. The Blessed Virgin's example invites us to cast aside all earthly attachments in our struggle to please Jesus. May nothing remain in our hearts that does not entirely lead us to give glory to God: *Lord, take away my pride; crush my self-love, my desire to affirm myself and impose myself on others. Make the foundation of my personality my identification with you.*[11] May I live a little more closely to you with each passing day. Give me that never-ending thirst of the saints to grow more and more in your love.

---

[10] *ibid.*, 103
[11] J. Escriva, *Christ is passing by*, 31

41.3 Renewing our dedication through following the example of the Blessed Virgin.

Our Lady was moved by a special grace of the Holy Spirit to commit her entire life to God. Perhaps she made the decision just as she reached the age of reason, a milestone in any life, and a moment that must have been particularly significant for a person as full of grace as Mary was. Maybe the Blessed Virgin never made a formal declaration of her commitment to God, but was simply accustomed from the beginning of her life to living her dedication in a natural way. St Alphonsus Liguori affirms: *The child Mary is well aware that complete oblations alone are acceptable before the Most High. In conformity with the divine precept, hearts that are divided do not please him: 'You shall love the Lord your God with your whole heart, your whole soul, and with your whole strength (Deut 6:5).' From the beginning of her life, the Blessed Mother strives to love God with all her strength and is entirely given over to his service.*[12] Mary was always the handmaid of the Lord. Her surrender continued to blossom and reached a renewed fullness through the circumstances and events of her life.

Today is a good opportunity – as every day is – to renew our own dedication to the Lord, in the midst of our daily duties, in the specific situation in which God has placed us. Every advance in our union with God necessarily entails more frequent recourse to the Holy Spirit, who is the Divine Guest of our soul. Our Lady's docility to the Holy Spirit, as we have seen, grows throughout her life. To petition a similar grace from God, St Josemaria Escriva composed the following prayer for personal devotion: *Come, Holy Spirit, enlighten my understanding to know your commandments. Strengthen my*

---

[12] St Alphonsus Liguori, *The Glories of Mary*, II, 3

heart against the snares of the enemy. Inflame my will ... I hear your voice and do not want to harden my heart and resist saying: "Later ... tomorrow. 'Nunc coepi' ... Now I begin!" Now, since tomorrow may never come.

Oh Spirit of Truth and Wisdom, Spirit of Understanding and Counsel, Spirit of Joy and Peace, I fully accept whatever you desire for me, in the way and at the time that you do, simply because you so want it.[13]

Let us ask Our Lady today that there may be many who, as our Mother Mary did from the time of her youth, follow the inspirations of the Holy Spirit and give their lives entirely over to the Lord's service.

---

[13] J. Escriva, *Postulation Articles for his Beatification and Canonisation, Historical Records of the Founder,* 20172, p.145

30 NOVEMBER

SAINT ANDREW

Apostle
Feast

Andrew was a native of Bethsaida and a fisherman like his brother Simon, whom he introduced to the Lord. He was a disciple of John the Baptist and one of the first to become a follower of Jesus. He pointed out to Jesus the boy who had the few loaves and fishes so that Our Lord could work the miracle of their multiplication. St Andrew preached the Gospel in Greece and died a martyr on an inverted cross.

42.1 Andrew's first encounter with Christ.

They came and saw where He was staying; and they stayed with him that day. It was about the tenth hour.[1] The Gospel informs us that Andrew and John are the first Apostles to follow Jesus. Soon after Our Saviour begins his public ministry – *the following day* – he meets John the Baptist and two of his disciples. Seeing the Lord as He passes by, the Precursor says: *Behold the Lamb of God.*[2]

Christ then calls the ones who are the first to be closely associated with his Person and mission and they respond immediately: *Jesus turns around, and seeing the two following him, says to them: 'What is it you seek?' They say, 'Rabbi (which interpreted means Master), where dwellest thou?' He says to them, 'Come and see'.* How friendly our Lord's invitation to them must have been. *Now Andrew, the brother of Simon Peter, was one of the two*

---

[1] John 1:39
[2] John 1:37

who heard John the Baptist and followed him. That day Jesus speaks to them with divine wisdom and human charm, and they remain committed to Our Lord for good. After many years have passed, St John records the exact time of their encounter in his Gospel. *It was about the tenth hour,* about four o'clock in the afternoon. He never forgets the moment when Jesus says to him: *What do you seek?* Andrew will also always remember that decisive day. Neither of the Apostles ever forgets his crucial encounter with Jesus.

To accept God's call and live as one of the Lord's intimate friends is the greatest grace a person can receive in this life. The joyful day we accept the clear invitation to follow the Master is an occasion we will always treasure in our heart. The grace of vocation is always an unmerited gift. The more divinely inspired it is, the more highly we should esteem it, since our calling illuminates the whole panorama of the future for us and gives meaning to our life. The call of vocation is often a gradual realization we come to understand in the peace and calm of our prayer. At times, however, as in the case of St Paul, his invitation is manifested in a fashion as clear as a flash of lightning which tears open the darkness that clouds our perspective. The Master may also simply put his hand on one's shoulder and say: *You are mine! Follow me!* The person in question is then filled with joy and *goes and sells all that he has and buys that field*[3] where his treasure lies. Like a collector of fine pearls,[4] the soul concerned discovers *the pearl of great price* among the many gifts of life.[5]

Jesus encourages the first disciples: *Come and see,* He says to them. In their personal dealings with the Lord,

---

[3] Matt 13:44

[4] Matt 13:45

[5] J.L.R. Sanchez, *The Gospel of St John,* Madrid 1987

Andrew and John learn what is not immediately apparent to them through his words alone.[6] Through frequent prayer, we too can grow to perceive the many invitations He addresses to us. We will then have greater intimacy with Christ and thus be able to follow him more closely. While we are speaking to him now, we might ask ourselves if we are striving to be attentive to the promptings of his voice. Do we respond fully to what Christ asks of us, since he has wanted to depend on our support? Let us remember that the Lord is always present in the world, just as He was twenty centuries ago. Now more than ever Jesus is seeking men and women to collaborate in this divine venture for the salvation of souls. Responding positively to his invitation is immensely worthwhile, since it entails cooperating in an enterprise of eternal significance.

42.2 The apostolate of friendship.

Andrew told his brother Simon: We have found the Messiah (the Christ), and he brought him to Jesus.[7] The meeting with Jesus leaves Andrew overjoyed. His newfound happiness is a tremendous grace he yearns to share with others immediately. It is as if he were incapable of keeping so great a blessing to himself. The first one to meet Andrew after his definitive encounter with the Lord is his brother Simon. St John Chrysostom comments: *After Andrew spends the entire day with Jesus, he does not keep the treasure for his personal benefit, but hastens to share it with his brothers.*[8] Andrew's enthusiasm over this discovery when he speaks to Peter must have been remarkable: *We have found the Messiah!,* he exclaims.

---

[6] St Thomas, *Commentary on St John, in loc.*
[7] *Communion Antiphon*: John 1:41-42
[8] *Liturgy of the Hours*, Second Reading: St John Chrysostom, *Homilies on St John's Gospel*, 19, 1

In the particular tone of voice proper to someone who is completely convinced, Andrew encourages his brother, perhaps tired after a day's work, to visit the Master who is at that moment awaiting him. We read in the Gospel of today's Mass that *he led him to Jesus*. In imitation of Andrew, we too can lead our relatives, friends and acquaintances to Christ by speaking to them of the Lord with confident conviction. This personal testimony is appropriate for the man or woman who *is filled with joy over the salvation Jesus offers. So wonderful is the news that the individual in question hastens to spread it to others. It is a proof of sincere fraternal charity.*[9] Anyone who truly finds Christ, in a manner encounters him for all his closest relatives, friends and colleagues.

Perhaps at a particular juncture in our life Christ revealed himself to us and we have been dealing intimately with him for many years since then: *Like Andrew, we too, through the grace of God, have had an encounter with the Saviour and so understand more clearly the meaning of the hope we are called to share with others.*[10] The Lord often makes use of the bonds of blood and friendship to call other souls to his service. Family and social ties can often be the occasion for the hearts of our relatives and friends to go out more fully to Jesus. At times He is prevented from entering their lives because of prejudice, fear, ignorance, mental reserve or laziness. When friendship is authentic, however, no great effort is needed to speak of Christ, since sincere confidence follows naturally in its wake. Friends interchange points of view and insights with ease. It would be unnatural for us to refrain from speaking about Christ, since He is the greatest discovery we have made in our life, and is the motivating force behind all our actions.

---

[9] *ibid.*
[10] John Paul II, *Address,* 30 November 1982

Through the grace of God ordinary friendship can be a Divine channel for a profound personal apostolate. Backing up our cheerful words of hope for those we deal with every day, many will be able to discover the very same Jesus who is ever at our side. St Peter, as perhaps we ourselves have done, found him through his being reflected in a person with whom he had regular contact. *One day perhaps an ordinary Christian, just like you, opened your eyes to horizons both deep and new, yet as old as the Gospel. He suggested to you the prospect of following Christ earnestly, seriously, of becoming an apostle of apostles. Perhaps you lost your balance then and didn't recover it. Your complacency wasn't quite replaced by true peace until you freely said 'yes' to God, because you wanted to, which is the most supernatural of reasons. And in its wake came a strong, constant joy, which disappears only when you abandon him.*[11] We have found this joy in following in the footsteps of the Master, and because of it desire many others to share in our happiness.

42.3 The call of vocation. Detachment and promptness in following the Lord.

A little later, *as He was walking by the Sea of Galilee, He saw two brothers, Simon, who was called Peter, and his brother Andrew, casting a net into the sea, for they were fishermen. And He said to them, 'Come and follow me, and I will make you fishers of men.' And at once they left the nets, and followed him.*[12] This call is the culmination of their first encounter with the Master. Like the other disciples after him, Andrew responds at once. Each of them practises heroic detachment from his material possessions so that he can follow in the footsteps of the Master without

---

[11] St. J. Escrivá, *Christ is passing by*, 1
[12] Matt 4:18-20

hindrance.

St Gregory the Great comments on the definitive call of these fishermen. He concludes that the kingdom of heaven *is all the more valuable the greater the extent of the earthly riches we forgo for the sake of the kingdom.*[13] Our surrender to Jesus, whose life intermingles with our own, must be total. Peter and Andrew leave a great deal behind them, *given that both lose the desire for their possessions.*[14] The Lord wants to depend on men and women who are pure of heart, people with big hearts not tied to earthly goods. Each Christian is called to live this spirit of dedication in accordance with his or her personal vocation. There is no room for anything in our life that does not serve completely for giving God glory. When we have recourse to the Master who is so close to us every day, what could we possibly hold back for ourselves alone?

In one way or another, Christ enters into our lives too. The virtue of detachment helps us to stay at Jesus' side as he goes forward on his mission at a fast and steady pace. It is not possible for us to keep up with him if we have too much baggage. We cannot be left behind on account of a few material possessions that are not worth our excessive concern for them. At times, Jesus issues a personal call at an early age. At others, one's vocation becomes clear in the course of one's mature years, when we have only a short distance to go before we arrive in his presence. Such variety in the time the Lord chooses to call each of us is shown in the parable concerning the labourers who go out to work at different times of the day.[15] Whichever our own case may be, we are called to respond with the joy the Evangelists express when they recall the circumstances of

---

[13] St Gregory the Great, *Sermons of the Gospels,* I,5,2
[14] *ibid*
[15] Matt 20:1

their own definitive vocation. Jesus is the same now as then: He is the one who invites us to accompany him on our way.

Tradition recalls how St Andrew died praising the cross of his crucifixion, since it was the means for at last drawing him finally close to the Master: *Hail, O Cross! Receive the disciple of him who hung from thee – my Master, Christ! O good Cross, so long desired and now awaiting my thirsty heart. In tranquil joy and exultant security I come to thee! Thou hast received the beauty and loveliness of the members of the Lord; do thou now receive me and take me from men and join me again to my Master, so that He who by thee redeemed me, may by thee also receive me.*[16] Whatever is most difficult for us to offer Jesus will be easy if we join our own sacrifice to the loving oblation of Christ.

---

[16] *The Passion Prayer of St Andrew*

IMMACULATE CONCEPTION NOVENA

DAY 1 – 30 NOVEMBER

43. MORNING STAR

Mary constantly showers down graces and favours on the faithful, and so has won the prerogative *all-powerful intercessor*. Through the inspiration of the Holy Spirit, Christians know that they can reach God through his Mother. She is our shortcut – the most direct path to God for us. Our love for her is shown in our continually coming up with new ways of expressing affection for her. We begin the Novena leading to the Solemnity of the Immaculate Conception by trying to offer Our Lady something special each day.

43.1 Mary is prefigured in the Old Testament.

A bright light appears in the darkness and announces to fallen creation that the *Light* is soon to arrive. The birth of the Virgin is the first sign that the Redemption of mankind is drawing near. *Our Lady's appearance is the first ray of dawn that shines forth in the world. She rises over the horizon and is forerunner to the brilliant splendour of salvation that will enter the world through Jesus Christ. Her arrival is tantamount to the blossoming of the most beautiful flower that has ever sprung up in the garden of Humanity, befouled as it is by the stain of sin. She is the most pure, innocent and perfect creature ever to dwell on the face of the earth. She is the most worthy of being called 'the image of God', the name God gives man in the act of creation. Mary restores to mankind a semblance of humanity as it was before the fall.*[1] Never have the angels beheld so beautiful a creature, nor will anyone ever match her perfection.

The Blessed Virgin Mary is prefigured throughout the Old Testament from the very first pages of Revelation. After the Almighty proclaims the coming of the Redemption following the fall of our first parents, God says to the serpent: *I will place enmity between you and the woman, between her seed and your seed: He shall crush your head, and you shall lie in wait for his heel.*[2] On the literal plane, the woman is Eve who is tempted and falls. On a deeper level though, the woman represents Mary, the new Eve, who will give birth to Christ, the absolute conqueror of the devil, who is symbolized by the serpent. Satan himself is powerless before her grandeur. The Blessed Virgin confronts the greatest enmity conceivable on earth: she personifies the glory of grace in the face of the devil and the degradation wrought by sin, the wilful separation from God. The prophet Isaiah announces that Mary is to be the Virgin Mother of the Messiah.[3] St Matthew explicitly refers to the fulfilment of this prophecy through Our Lady.[4]

The Church also applies to our Blessed Mother the praise the people of Israel grant to their heroine Judith, who saved her people. *You are the pride of Jerusalem, the glory of Israel, and the honour of our nation. By your hand was all this done on behalf of Israel. May God be pleased by this deed. Blessed be you through the all-powerful Lord forever!*[5] These words of praise can readily be applied to Mary. She cooperates in freeing us from an enemy greater than that Holofernes whose head Judith cut off, since she

---

[1] Bl. Paul VI, *Address,* 8 September 1964
[2] Gen 3:15
[3] Is 7:14
[4] Matt 1:22-23
[5] Jud 15:9-10

collaborates in winning for us freedom from the complete and final impoverishment that is the result of sin.[6]

The Church points to other passages from Sacred Scripture that prefigure Our Lady. For the most part they refer on the literal level to Divine wisdom. Nevertheless, within the depth of the salvific plan reflected in the inspired Word of God from all eternity, these verses also suggest the image of Our Lady. *The depths had not yet formed, and I was already conceived, neither had the fountains of waters as yet sprung out.*[7] The Old Testament also anticipates the purest love that is to reign in her most sacred Heart: *I am the Mother of fair love, and of fear, and of knowledge and of holy hope. In me is all grace of the way and of the truth , in me is all hope of life and of virtue...He who hears me shall not be confounded, and they that work by me shall not sin.*[8] The *Song of Songs* foresees her Immaculate Conception: *You are all fair, my love, and there is no stain in you.*[9] Ecclesiasticus prophetically announces: *In me is found all grace of the way and of the truth, in me lies all hope of life and of virtue.*[10] How wise the Church is to put these words on our Mother's lips, so that we may never forget them. She is our safety and we know that her love for us never fails. Her refuge is ever open for our protection. Her hand is ready to stretch forth to grasp our own at every moment.[11] May we seek her help and consolation during these days when we are preparing to celebrate her Immaculate Conception.

---

[6] C. Pozo, *Mary in Scripture and in the Faith of the Church*

[7] Prov 8:24

[8] Eccl 24:24-30

[9] Cant 4:7

[10] Eccl 24:25

[11] J. Escriva, *Friends of God,* 279

43.2 Our Lady illuminates our way and guides us through life.

In the same way that Mary is present at the very dawn of the Redemption and from the very first book of Sacred Scripture, she is also found at the origin of our conversion to Christ, of our personal sanctity and salvation. Christ reaches us through her. All spiritual benefits come to us by way of Mary. We will receive as many graces as we need from her and she will continue to pour them down on us for our benefit.

The Blessed Virgin makes it easy for us to begin over and over again. She frees us from innumerable temptations that we could not have overcome by ourselves. She offers us all that *she ponders in her heart,*[12] all that refers specifically to Jesus, *towards whom she draws us by the hand.*[13] Mary is the foremost sign of hope for humanity. In her, every man and woman finds direction for the future, since she is the light that illuminates our path. She guides us along the way of life. *She does not shine for herself, or from herself, but she is the reflection of her and our Redeemer, and she glorifies him. When she appears in darkness, we know that He is close at hand.*[14]

Whenever sailors are disoriented at sea or in need of confirming the course of their ship, they take their bearings based on the brightest star they can see. We approach Mary when we feel lost or are in need of rectifying our own conduct so as to advance more directly in the way Our Lord is encouraging us. The Blessed Virgin is *our glowing star when we are on the sea of life.*[15] The Liturgy calls her our *sure hope of salvation* who *shines forth in the midst of*

---

[12] Luke 2:51
[13] John Paul II, *Address,* 20 October 1979
[14] St J .H. Newman, *Mystical Rose*
[15] John Paul II, *Address,* 4 June 1979

the difficulties of life.[16] She can help us in the face of those inexplicable storms in life that may rise up on account of our not knowing how to be as close to God as we could be. St Bernard advises us: *Don't take your eyes off the splendour of the brightly-glowing Star Mary if you do not want to be overcome by the squalls.*[17]

A special radiance issues from Mary which lightens the way so that we may most profitably follow the urgings of Our Lord in the midst of the different tasks and challenges of our life. Through the intercession of Mary we can discover the marvellous path in the service of God to which we are called. She sheds light on our specific vocation in a particular way. Whenever we beseech her with an upright intention, we will always discover the best way of fulfilling God's Will. Mary's special capacity for helping us to perceive our calling has its origin in the fulness of grace that is hers from the very first moment of her Immaculate Conception.

St Thomas points out that she pours forth her grace on all men. He affirms: *It is wonderful for a saint to possess grace enough for the salvation of many other souls. Mary, however, is the greatest saint, who has sufficient grace to save every other person in the world through her most intimate corredemptive union with her Son.*[18] Theologians distinguish the absolute fullness of grace proper to Christ, sufficient fullness, found in the angels, and superabundant fullness, which is the privilege of our Blessed Mother. She pours out on her children all the grace she holds. St Thomas says: *The Mother of God is full of grace to a degree that surpasses even that of the angels. Therefore, rightly is she called 'Mary' which means 'illuminated one'.*

---

[16] *Liturgy of the Hours,* Hymn of Lauds on August 15
[17] St Bernard, *Homily on the Blessed Virgin Mary,* 2
[18] St Thomas, *On the Hail Mary* in *Catechetical writings,* p.182

It also signifies 'illuminator of others', with respect to the whole world.[19]

Today, on the first day of the Novena to the Immaculate Heart of Mary, we make the resolution always to ask her help whenever our soul is in darkness, whenever it is necessary to readjust our direction in life, or whenever we need to make an important decision. Since we will continually need to make new beginnings in our spiritual struggle, we strive always to have recourse to her, so that she can point out to us the road we need to take in order to continue to be faithful to our vocation. We ask her to help us to advance along our path of holiness with human elegance and supernatural perspective.

43.3 Our Lady, Star of the Sea.

Our Lady is *blessed among women*, since she is free from all attraction to sin and the evil remains it leaves in the soul: *She alone dispels the darkness, brings down all blessings, and opens the door of Paradise for us. For this reason, the name 'Mary' which signifies 'Star of the Sea', most appropriately belongs to her. Just as the brightest star in the sky guides sailors toward a safe haven, Mary leads Christians to glory.*[20] The Liturgy of the Church also honours her in this way: *'Ave, maris stella!...Hail, Star of the sea!', Mother of God in the highest...*[21]

On this first day of the Novena to our Blessed Mother in heaven, we can make the firm resolution, which would so gratify her, to have recourse to her intercession for all of the many needs we have. A Father of the Church gives the following advice:

If the winds of temptation blow, if you stumble when

---

[19] *ibid.*
[20] *ibid.*, p.185
[21] Hymn, *Ave Maris Stella*

confronted by temptation; look to the star of the sea by calling out to Mary. If the waves of pride, ambition or envy tug at your heart, call on Mary as well. If anger, avarice or impurity imperil the course of your soul's journey, look to Mary.

If you are disturbed by the memory of your sins, confused with the ugliness of your conscience, fearful in the face of judgment, or you begin to sink into the bottomless pit of sadness or into the abyss of despair, think of Mary. In every danger, moment of anguish or doubt, invoke Mary. May her name be ever on your lips and engraved on your heart too. Never stray from the example of her virtue, so that you may always gain her help as an intercessor.

You will not soon swerve from the path if you follow her, nor will you soon despair if you beseech her. You will never be lost if you think about her. With her taking you by the hand, you will not stay down in the case of a fall. With her protection, you will have nothing at all to fear. You will not lose strength, for she is your guide. You will reach a safe haven happily, if you count on her as your most intimate helper.[22] In every moment of the day, she will guide us on a sure path... *Cor Mariae Dulcissimum, iter para tutum.*

---

[22] St Bernard, *loc. cit.*

IMMACULATE CONCEPTION NOVENA

DAY 2 – 1 DECEMBER

44. HOUSE OF GOLD

44.1 Through the gifts of the Holy Spirit God dwells in the Blessed Mother.

You are the temple of God, and God's spirit dwells in you.[1] In the *Litany of Loreto* we call upon Mary, *House of Gold,* the abode of greatest conceivable splendour. When a family turns a house into a home by taking up residence there, the place reflects the individual qualities of the people. They accentuate the beauty of the dwelling place. Just like the Holy Spirit dwelling in Our Lady, the home and its inhabitants make up a particular unity, in much the same way as the body and its garments do. The foremost Tabernacle in the Old Testament, later to be the Temple, is the *House of God,* where the meeting of Yahweh and his people takes place. When Solomon makes the decision to build the Temple, the Prophets specify that the best available materials are to be used – abundant cedar wood on the inside and clad with gold on the outside. The most highly skilled craftsmen are to work on its construction.

Before God made known his coming into the world in the fullness of time, He prepared Mary as the suitable creature within whom He would dwell for nine months, from the moment of his Incarnation until his birth in Bethlehem. Evidence of God's power and love show forth

---

[1] *Communion Antiphon,* Mass of the Blessed Virgin, *Temple of the Lord*

in his creation. Mary is the *House of Gold,* the new *Temple of God,* and is adorned with so great a beauty that no greater perfection is possible. The grace of her Immaculate Conception, including all the graces and gifts God ever bestowed on her soul, are directed towards the fulfilment of her divine Maternity.[2]

The Archangel Gabriel is full of veneration for Mary when he greets her, since he is aware of the extent of her participation in grace and virtue, and the degree of her exceptional union with God. The initial grace God bestows on the Blessed Virgin disposes her for divine Motherhood. God's gift of supernatural life to her exceeds that of all the Apostles, Martyrs, Confessors and Virgins combined. It reaches far beyond the experience of anyone who has ever lived, or ever will live, until the end of time. God dwells in Our Lady more than in all the angels and saints, since the foundation of the world, taken together.[3] Truly God has prepared a human vessel in keeping with the dignity of his eternal Son.

When we say that Mary has an *almost infinite dignity,* we mean that among all God's creatures she is the one who enjoys the most intimate relationship with the Blessed Trinity. Her absolute honour is the highest possible and her majesty is in every way unique. She is the firstborn and most highly favoured daughter of the Father, as she has often been called throughout the history of the Church, and as has been reiterated by the Second Vatican Council,[4] Our Lady's blood relationship with Jesus Christ, the Son of God, leads her to a singular relationship with him, since we can truly say that Mary is the Temple and Tabernacle of

---

[2] St Thomas, *Summa Theologiae,* 3, q27, a5
[3] R. Garrigou-Lagrange, *The Mother of the Saviour,* p.411
[4] Second Vatican Council, *Lumen gentium,* 53

the Holy Spirit.[5] What joy it gives us to recall during the Novena that we have a Mother who is so close to God, so pure and beautiful, and so closely in touch with our own daily experience. *How men like to be reminded of their relationship with distinguished figures in literature, in politics, in the armed forces, in the Church!... Sing to Mary Immaculate, reminding her: Hail Mary, Daughter of God the Father! Hail Mary, Mother of God the Son! Hail Mary, Spouse of God the Holy Spirit!*

Greater than you – no one, but God![6]

44.2 The gifts of Understanding, Knowledge and Wisdom in Our Lady.

The soul of Mary is uniquely adorned with the gifts of the Holy Spirit. These precious attributes are the most valuable jewels with which God can beautify a person. God grants them to the Mother of his eternal Son to an eminent degree.

Mary enjoys the *gift of Understanding* to a greater extent than any other creature in the entire history of humanity. Through vibrant faith rooted in the authority of God, who reveals to her his Will, she knows her blessed virginity is most pleasing in the sight of God. Her contemplative gaze plumbs the utmost depths of meaning contained in Sacred Scripture. She immediately understands that the angel's greeting to her has to do with the coming of the Messiah. She knows that the most Blessed Trinity has chosen her to become the Mother of the so long-awaited Saviour. She receives confirmation on various occasions, as her life unfolds, concerning her role in the fulfilment of the divine promise of salvation for humanity. She also fully understands the ramifications of her voca-

---

[5] John Paul II, Encyclical, *Redemptoris Mater,* 9
[6] St. J. Escrivá, *The Way,* 496

tion: *Mary will have to live her obedience of faith in the midst of contradiction, at the side of the suffering Saviour; her motherhood will be mysterious and sorrowful.*[7]

The *gift of Understanding* is closely linked to purity of heart. In the same way, this supernatural virtue is associated with the blessedness of the clean of heart who *shall see God.*[8] The *most pure* soul of Mary was especially enlightened to see the loving Will of God behind every happening and event in her life. No one is more aware than she is of what the Lord expects in the life of every person. For this reason, she is our best ally in all our petitions to God.

The *gift of Knowledge* further enlarges Mary's immense panorama of faith. Through ordinary daily realities the Blessed Mother perceives *signs of God in the world.* Because she consciously evaluates all the circumstances of life with respect to the truths of the Redemption, Our Lady can appreciate every moment of her existence as a means of drawing closer to the Creator. By the grace of God she encounters so many invitations to see the loving hand of God in every event of daily life.[9] Mary is more sensitive than anyone else to the immense evil of sin. Her suffering for the sins of all mankind is therefore all the more acute. Through a compassion the likes of which humanity will never again know, Our Lady is efficaciously united to the suffering of her Son as He dies on the Cross: *She cooperates in a singular way in the work of the Saviour in restoring supernatural life to souls.*[10]

In the life of our Blessed Mother, the *gift of Wisdom* perfectly complements the virtue of charity. She is led to savour in her heart the truths of revelation with an

---

[7] John Paul II, Encyclical, *Redemptoris Mater,* 16
[8] Matt 5:8
[9] J. Polo, *Mary and the Blessed Trinity*, Madrid
[10] Second Vatican Council, *Lumen gentium,* 61

experiential knowledge that leads to a profound understanding of the mysteries concerning the mission of her
Son the Redeemer. Our Lady understands, contemplates,
and loves. Her loving wisdom infinitely exceeds the penetration of the most profound theological minds. Through
her abundant meditation she gains deep insights into the
actual workings of God in the course of her life. Her whole
existence is permeated by spiritual light and warmth.

Through our insistent petition during these days of the
Novena, we will obtain for ourselves a share in these same
gifts. *Among the gifts of the Holy Spirit, I would say that
there is one which we all need in a special way: It is the
gift of wisdom. It makes us know God and rejoice in his
presence, thereby placing us in a perspective from which
we can judge accurately the situations and the events of
this life.*[11]

44.3 The gifts of Counsel, Piety, Fortitude and Fear of the Lord.

For Our Lady the *gift of Counsel* enhances her practice
of the virtue of prudence. She consistently acts with ease,
in accordance with the commandments of God.[12] This
grace brings her to discover quickly the divine Will in the
ordinary circumstances of life. Our Lady abandons herself
with docility into the hands of God, and so carries out the
tasks the Lord entrusts to her in the mundane details of
service which each day brings with it.

In the Gospel we see how the Blessed Virgin was
continually moved by the impulse of the Holy Spirit.
Though she lived the greater part of her earthly life in the
quiet of Nazareth, *she goes in haste* when her cousin

---

[11] St. J. Escrivá, *Christ is passing by*, 133
[12] J. Polo, *op. cit.,* p.39

Elizabeth is in need.[13] She occupies a modest place in the Gospel, but she is present to offer her support when the disciples need her after the Passion of Our Lord. She later prayerfully accompanies them as they await the coming of the Holy Spirit. Mary stands at the foot of the Cross, but she does not go the tomb with the other holy women. She knows in her heart that they will not find the most beloved Body of her Son there. She knows Christ has risen.

Our Lady was fully devoted to the small duties of a housewife. At the wedding in Cana, she realized before anyone else did that they had run out of wine. Her deeply contemplative life leads her to be sensitive even to the most minute needs of those around her. She is the *Mater boni consilii ... Mother of Good Counsel,* who helps us discover and correspond to the will of God in the hundred and one little incidents of each day.

Through the *gift of Piety* a filial relationship with God profoundly pervaded all her dealings with Jesus. It affected her way of praying and her basic attitude in every prayer of petition. Her way of facing up to the many different and sometimes trying events of her life stemmed from this intimate interior disposition. Mary was constantly aware of her divine filiation. Her deep conviction continued to grow throughout her mortal life too. As the Mother of God, she is keenly aware of her maternal role in the service of all humanity. Both realities are permeated by her exquisitely refined piety. She will continue to love us since we are her children, and mothers are always closest to those of their offspring who are most in need.

God expended his divine grace most abundantly on Our Lady, since her exceptional docility led to a wholly unique correspondence with the divine gifts. To a heroic degree, she lived fidelity in both the small duties of each

---

[13] Luke 1:39

day as well as in the midst of the great trials of her life. God disposed her to lead on earth a simple life, comparable to that of other women of her epoch and region, but she underwent the most grievous sorrow any creature could ever be called upon to suffer. Only the suffering of her Son, the *Man of Sorrows* presaged by the Prophet Isaiah, exceeded it.[14] She received the *gift of Fortitude* to the utmost degree and could therefore bear with patience the many daily contradictions and changes of plans she had to endure. She confronted difficulties in silence, but with integrity and courage. Through her fortitude she could remain at the foot of the Cross.[15] Christian piety reveres her attitude of strength in the face of suffering, and invokes her as *Queen of Martyrs* and *Comforter of the Afflicted*.

Let us also remember that the Holy Spirit has adorned Mary with the gift of the *Fear of the Lord*. For her this entails a filial veneration of the greatest intimacy with her Creator and Redeemer. She constantly holds a profound attitude of adoration before the infinite greatness of God, who has bestowed on her every gift of grace. She therefore refers to herself as the *Handmaid of the Lord*. At the same time, she very well knows she is the Mother of Jesus, the Mother of God, and our Mother as well.

---

[14] Is 53:3
[15] John 19:25

IMMACULATE CONCEPTION NOVENA

DAY 3 – 2 DECEMBER

45. HANDMAID OF THE LORD

45.1 The vocation of Mary.

My soul magnifies the Lord, and my spirit rejoices in God my Saviour; because He has regarded the lowliness of his handmaid.[1] Prior to Our Lady's positive response, when the fulness of time had come, *the angel Gabriel was sent from God to a town of Galilee called Nazareth.*[2] This exceptional envoy visits the most beloved creature of God to convey the special news. The Archangel tells her: *Do not be afraid, Mary, for you have found favour with God.*[3]

As a consequence of Mary's meditation on Sacred Scripture she knows well the passages that refer to the Messiah. The Blessed Virgin is familiar with the various allusions that refer to him, and she joins to this knowledge an extraordinary interior sensitivity to whatever has to do with the Will of God. Through a particular grace, Our Lady learns that she is going to be the Mother of the Redeemer about whom the Prophets of the Old Testament spoke. She is the fulfilment of Isaiah's prophecy concerning a virgin,[4] since she is to conceive and give birth to *Emmanuel,* which means *God with us.*

---

[1] *Entrance Antiphon,* Mass of the Blessed Virgin Mary, *Handmaid of the Lord*
[2] Luke 1:26
[3] Luke 1:30-33
[4] Is 7:14

During her youth Our Lady was moved by an influence of the Holy Spirit and consecrated her entire being entirely to the Lord. Her later correspondence with grace is a reaffirmation of her commitment to fulfilling the divine Will in her life: *Behold the handmaid of the Lord. Be it done unto me according to your word.*[5] *It can be said that this consent to motherhood is above all a result of her total self-giving to God in virginity... And to the very end of her life she lives her motherly sharing in the life of Jesus Christ, her Son, in a way that matches her vocation to virginity.*[6]

From the moment Our Lady gives her consent, the Word of God, the Second Person of the Blessed Trinity, takes on flesh in her most pure womb. This event is the most momentous since the Creation of the world. And it happens in a small unknown town. Mary understands the plans of God regarding her vocation. She is aware of the reason for the many graces she receives from the Holy Spirit through the Lord, and how it comes about that she is so responsive to these inspirations. The same holds true of every vocation. *All the minute incidents that go to make up the framework of our existence take on new interest and meaning. With the declaration of the Angel, the whole of reality takes on a completely supernatural explanation. It is as if, all of a sudden, we were to be placed at the centre of the universe, beyond the dimensions of time and space.*[7]

Mary, the adolescent girl, does not hesitate at the prospect of assuming the incomparable dignity of becoming the Mother of God, since she is humble and confides in the Almighty, to whom she has dedicated herself completely. *The Blessed Virgin Mary is the Teacher*

---

[5] Luke 1:38
[6] John Paul II, Encyclical, *Redemptoris Mater,* 39
[7] F. Suarez, Mary of Nazareth, p.29

of unlimited self-giving. Ask of this good Mother that her answer, with the generosity it shows, may with the strength of love and affection gain strength in your soul. 'Ecce ancilla Domini... Behold the handmaid of the Lord'.[8] We can tell Jesus in the intimacy of our prayer: Lord, count on me for whatever you want. I do not want to put any limits on your grace or on whatever you are asking of me each and every day. Don't stop making demands ... and continue to grant me the continual support of your strength.

45.2 God calls each one of us.

The radical reality of being the Mother of God presupposes, from the very first moment, complete openness to the Person, mission and work of Christ.[9] On this third day of the Novena of the Immaculate Conception, let us learn from Our Lady how we can always be available for and be open to the plans of God through our complete dedication to the call we have received. May we be able to say at the end of a truly great life: Lord, I've always made an effort to fulfil your Will. My only objective has always been to please you.

Our specific vocation is God's greatest gift to us. It is the reason for our being created, and is therefore our sure way to happiness. From all eternity the Lord provides each one of us with all the graces necessary for us to correspond with his Will. From the moment the Almighty directly creates each unique and immortal soul, and bestows on this new person a body as well through the cooperation of the parents, He wants something that will have importance in his sight from this gift of life. The greatness of man consists in discerning this Will of God and in carrying it out. Each person is called to collaborate in the order of

---

[8] St. J. Escrivá, *Furrow,* 33
[9] John Paul II, *loc. cit.*

Creation and to forward the divine plan of Redemption. To discern our vocation is to find the pearl of great price.[10] When we spend our entire existence in carrying out our calling, we come to comprehend the deepest meaning of our being and possess the fullness of life. God calls a few to the religious life or to the priesthood. *But he wants the vast majority to stay right where they are, in all earthly occupations in which they work: in the factory, the laboratory, the farm, the trades, the streets of the big cities and the trails of the mountains... There they should behave in such a way that people should be able to recognize the Master in his disciples.*[11]

By contemplating the vocation of Mary we can better understand how the Lord's call to each one of us always proceeds from his grace: *You have not chosen me, but I have chosen you.*[12] Frequently the words of Sacred Scripture are fulfilled to the letter: *My ways are not your ways...*[13] The call of Our Lord does not always coincide with personal inclinations and preferences, since these tend not to stem from a supernatural perspective. The plans our imagination conjures up seldom have anything to do with Our Lord's greater and more perfect designs. Moreover, vocation is not merely the culmination of a life of ardent piety, although normally a prayerful disposition of loving vigilance is necessary in order for us to understand what God is quietly trying to show us. The specific call we receive does not belong to the order of *feeling,* but to that of *being.* It is objective, since God has prepared it from all eternity. The words St Paul addresses to the Ephesians, on which we have meditated so often, are fulfilled to the letter

---

[10] Matt 13:44-46

[11] St. J. Escrivá, *Christ is passing by*, 105

[12] John 15:16

[13] Is 55:8

in each man and woman: *Elegit nos in ipso ante mundi constitutionem ... The Lord has chosen us before the constitution of the world to be holy in his sight.*[14]

God usually seeks out and grants his grace to ordinary people in order to carry out his plan of redemption. The point St Thomas Aquinas makes about the Blessed Virgin is applicable to every Christian: *God prepares whomsoever he desires for a specific mission. He also grants the particular person the necessary graces to carry out the task they are entrusted with.*[15] We should frequently remember, especially if at some point our responsibilities begin to weigh down on us: Since I have a vocation for this particular task, God will grant me the grace to bring it to completion if I do all that I can.

The Lord can prepare a given person's vocation from the time of childhood. Frequently the Lord makes use of personal friends as instruments to make a vocation known. He can also make it known in a sudden or unexpected way, as in the case of St Paul while travelling on the road to Damascus.[16] One experiences an interior motion, *like a two-edged sword.* For most people, discovering their calling involves a combination of manifestations. Certainly God often relies on other people to prepare or make known a definitive calling. When parents fulfil well their task as educators in the Faith, they help to cultivate, perhaps unwittingly, the seed of vocation that God sows in the soul. To be an instrument of God as a parent is an enormous privilege, and the Lord will never withhold the assistance of his grace in carrying out well so crucial a role.

When someone truly desires to gain insight into his or her personal vocation, prayer and sincerity in spiritual

---

[14] Eph 1:4
[15] St Thomas, *Summa Theologiae*, 2, q27, a4
[16] Acts 9:3

direction are the most important means of discovering God's Will. Through consistent recourse to both of these means we can be virtually sure of not erring in the matter. *Do you want to be daring in a holy way so that God may act through you? Have recourse to Mary, and she will accompany you along the path of humility, so that, when faced with what to the human mind is impossible, you may be able to respond with a 'fiat!' – be it done!, which unites the earth to Heaven.*[17] Daring is necessary when first responding to the invitation of God, and throughout life as well, since we are called each day and every hour of our existence. If we ever encounter *insurmountable obstacles*, they will fade from our path if we are humble and count on the grace of God as our Blessed Mother Mary did.

45.3 Discerning the Will of God.

The Blessed Virgin gives us a perfect example of how to fulfil the Will of God by our complete availability. How unfortunate it would be if, in one way or another, we were to try to exercise our own caprice in the matter. We can best cooperate with the Lord through our complete dedication when we allow him free rein in our life. *It is difficult for God to manifest his Will to us without our wholehearted desire to serve him in all things. However, the Lord acts in our life only to the extent that we allow him to do so. He always respects our human freedom and never imposes himself.*[18]

Our Lady's life shows clearly that in order for us to hear the Lord's call in all the circumstances of our existence we need to carry out our acts of piety with sincerity and great refinement. In this way we will ponder things in our heart as Mary did during her life. We will see

---

[17] St. J. Escrivá, *Furrow*, 124
[18] M.D. Philippe, *Mystery of Mary*, pp.86-87

the events of our life from the point of view of Jesus and consistently broaden the horizon of our ideals. Together with prayer, spiritual direction is a great help in our understanding what God continues to ask from us. Detachment from our personal preferences in order to adhere to what God is asking from us is important, even if at times the acquisition of this virtue seems arduous.

Our Lady's response to her vocation is a summary of her total response to God's loving invitations throughout her life: *Ecce ancilla Domini.* She has no desire other than that of fulfilling the Will of God. Today we can entrust our own unconditional 'Yes' to Our Lady, even though at times our complete response requires renewed generosity on our part. She will present our gift of self at the throne of her Son.

3 DECEMBER

46. ST FRANCIS XAVIER

Memorial

St Francis was born in the castle of Xavier, Spain on the 7th of August 1506. He studied in Paris, where he met St Ignatius of Loyola. He was one of the first members of the Society of Jesus. After being ordained priest in Rome in 1537 he was primarily occupied with carrying out works of charity. In 1541 he left for the Orient and for ten years worked tirelessly to evangelize India and Japan, where many were converted to the Faith. He died in China in 1552.

46.1 The apostolic zeal of St Francis Xavier.

What does it profit a man to gain the whole world and forfeit his soul?[1] These words of Jesus sank deeply into the heart of St Francis Xavier and lead him to a radical change of life.

What can all the treasures of life be worth if we let what is most essential in it pass us by? What good can success and applause, triumphs and rewards, be if at the end of it all we do not find a welcome by Jesus, who will be awaiting us? Our whole life would then have been a waste, our most precious time would amount to nothing, and the sum total of all our efforts would add up to the most devastating kind of failure. Francis Xavier appreciated the value of his own immortal soul, and that of others, ever since Christ became the true centre of his life. Since then, zeal for souls became *a dominant passion* for him.[2] In his own heart he experienced a pressing concern

---

[1] Mark 8:36
[2] John Paul II, *Address,* 6 November 1982

for souls. Furthermore, he was ready to give his very life to Christ in order to win their salvation.[3]

The apostolic zeal that burned in the heart of St Francis caused him to write the following words while carrying out the evangelization of the Far East: ...*deprived of priests, the natives barely realize that they are Christians. There is no one to celebrate Mass for them and no one to teach them the Creed or the Our Father... Therefore, since arriving here, I haven't had a moment's rest. I spend my time going from village to village, baptizing the children who have not yet received the sacrament. So far, I've purified an enormous number of children who, as they say, did not even know their right hand from their left. These little ones won't allow me to pray the breviary until I've taught them some prayer.*[4]

Francis Xavier pondered – as we do today – the vast panorama of people who have no one to speak to them about God. The words of the Lord continue to be relevant today: *The harvest indeed is great and the labourers are few.*[5] This saint was moved by a tremendous zeal for the salvation of souls when he wrote: *Many around here are not Christians simply because no one is available to teach them how to practise their faith. I have often had the desire to visit the universities of Europe, especially the one in Paris, and shout like a madman so as to provoke those who have more knowledge than charity: How many souls may be excluded from heaven on account of their negligence!* If men and women were to apply the same fervour they apply to their studies to the salvation of souls, all of us would be able to account for the talents God entrusts to us. Many

---

[3] F. Zubillaga, *Letters and Writings of St Francis Xavier*, Madrid 1953
[4] *Liturgy of the Hours, From the Letters of St Francis Xavier to St Ignatius*
[5] Matt 9:37

would be moved, through meditation on supernatural reality, to leave off their strictly human ambitions and listen to the voice of God within. He is calling them to complete dedication to the Will of God. Many are in conditions that would enable them to say: *Lord, here I am; what would you have me do? Send me wherever you want, even to India.*[6]

Our own hearts may be inflamed with this same ardent concern for souls. Ordinarily, the Lord wants us to practise this virtue right in the midst of our everyday circumstances – in our family, at work and with our friends and acquaintances. *A missionary. You dream of being a missionary. You vibrate like a Xavier, longing to conquer an empire for Christ – Japan, China, India, Russia; the peoples of North Europe, or of America, or Africa, or Australia!*

Foster that fire in your heart, that hunger for souls. But don't forget that you're more of a missionary when you are simply obeying. Geographically far away from those apostolic fields, you work both here and there. Don't you feel your arm tired – like Xavier's – after administering Baptism to so many?[7] We can still encounter many people in our daily circumstances – at the university, in business and within any social milieu – who are still living far removed from the warmth and glory of the Faith.

46.2 Winning new apostles for Christ.

And He said to them, 'Go into the whole world and preach the gospel to every creature.'[8] Every Christian needs to feel urged by our Lord to fulfil Christ's command with courage and daring in the ordinary circumstances of his or

---

[6] *Liturgy of the Hours, loc. cit.*
[7] St. J. Escrivá, *The Way,* 315
[8] Mark 6:15

her life. As John Paul II reminds us: *We Christians are called to be apostolically daring, with our confidence firmly placed in the Holy Spirit.*[9]

As we look around us we realize that there are many people who still do not yet know Christ. Many who are baptized live as though Christ had not redeemed them, as if He were not truly present in our midst every day. Many go about their lives like those who drew down the compassion of Jesus, crowds who *were bewildered and dejected, like sheep without a shepherd.*[10] They go on and on, without any specific aim in life, disoriented, and wasting their precious time, since they seem to have no sense of direction. Like the Lord, we too are filled with compassion for those people. Though at times they seem – humanly speaking – happy and successful, they fail in the worst way possible because they do not behave as, nor are they even aware of being, children of God on a journey to the eternal Home of their Father. We cannot let the eternal salvation of anyone be at risk due to our lack of apostolic spirit.

We are called to share our faith and zeal for souls with others. These souls in their turn can become messengers of the *Good News* that Christ has left us. In the thousand and one different details of our everyday life, we need to echo John Paul II's words when he spoke in Xavier, the birthplace of the saint whose feast we celebrate today: *Christ needs you and calls you to help a great many of your brothers and sisters to be saved and fulfil their humanity. Live your life according to upright and noble ideals. Do not give in to the temptations of hedonism, to the hate and violence that degrade humanity. Open your heart to Christ, to his law and his love, without putting conditions on your availability, and fearing to make a*

---

[9] John Paul II, Encyclical, *Redemptoris missio,* 30
[10] Matt 9:36

lasting commitment, because love and friendship have no limits since they are everlasting.[11] If we are ever unable to convince our relatives and friends to take part in this divine adventure, the most joyful undertaking of all, let us consider how Ignatius won over the young student Xavier for the work of the Lord: *Reasons?... What reasons could the poor Ignatius have given to the wise Xavier?*[12] Surely they must have been few and shabby for bringing about so profound a change in the soul of his friend. Prayer brought about the conversion. We are all called to be daring, to confide always in Our Lord's grace, in the help of the Blessed Virgin and of the Holy Guardian Angels in spreading the Faith.

Let us ask the Lord to *kindle in us that fire of charity with which Saint Francis Xavier burned for the salvation of souls...*[13] Let us also not fail to have recourse to the Blessed Virgin, so that we may draw many others with us to Christ, and so that these in their turn might become apostles of the Lord.

46.3 Apostolic efficacy in our life.

Like many saints, St Francis Xavier used to ask those he wrote to for *the help of their prayers,*[14] since effective apostolate is always founded on personal prayer and sacrifice and on the petition of others. We need to always keep in mind, especially if our situation impedes our carrying out a direct apostolate, that our prayer, our work well-done, and our sufferings, are always efficacious in this regard.

Like St Francis, St Thérèse of Lisieux lived an intense

---

[11] John Paul II, *Address, supra cit.*

[12] St. J. Escrivá, *op. cit.,* 798

[13] *Prayer after Communion*

[14] John Paul II, *Address, supra cit.*

apostolic life as an intercessor for the missions, despite the fact that she never left the convent. Her concern for the salvation of souls, including those farthest off from the Faith, was always vigorous. She experienced the words of Christ from the Cross – *I thirst* – in her heart. She burned inwardly with prayer, through her effective desire to win grace for souls in the most far-flung regions of the globe. She writes: *I so desire, my Love, to travel the length and breadth of the earth, preaching your name and planting the hope of your glorious Cross in pagan territory. Furthermore, one mission alone would not be enough for me. I would want to spread your Gospel throughout the world all at once, including the most distant islands. I would want to be a missionary, not just for a few years, but from the time of the world's creation until the con-summation of the world itself.*[15] At the end of her life, when taking a short walk while she was gravely ill, a sister nun saw her fatigue and recommended that she rest. Teresa responded to her concern: *Do you know what gives me strength? I am walking for the benefit of a missionary. I believe there is one working far away, on the verge of collapse on account of his apostolic undertakings. To lessen his fatigue, I offer my own to God.*[16] The Little Flower's intentions, together with her prayer and sacrifice, effective-ly stretched to the utmost ends of the earth.

Our zeal for souls should be vitally active at every moment. Not even sickness, old age or isolation can be an excuse for us. Through the *Communion of Saints* we are able to strengthen other souls around the world. This efficacy depends on the extent of our love for God. In a word, our entire life, up to our last breath on earth, can be a means of helping to prompt souls towards everlasting life.

---

[15] St Thérèse of Lisieux, *Autobiography of a Soul*
[16] *ibid.,* XII,9

This was precisely the case in the life of St Francis. He died somewhere off the coast of China while offering every moment of his suffering in petition to Our Lord to bring the *Good News* of Christ to those far-off lands. No prayer, no sacrifice of ours offered with love, is ever lost. By the mercy of God, every act of ours can be supernaturally fruitful, in a mysterious but real way. One day in heaven we will see the results of our efforts and they will fill us with overflowing happiness.

IMMACULATE CONCEPTION NOVENA

DAY 4 – 3 DECEMBER

47. CAUSE OF OUR JOY

47.1 Mary brings authentic joy into the world.

Lord our God, you were pleased to bring joy into the world through the Incarnation of your Son. Grant that we who honour his Mother, the cause of our joy, may always walk in the way of your commandments with our hearts set on true and lasting joy in you.[1] Authentic happiness has its origin in God. All of Our Lord's gifts come to us with this particular savour. When the Almighty created the world out of nothing, the whole stupendous act was a celebration, particularly when man was created in the image and likeness of God. The Creation account in Genesis concludes with a similar expression of glorious satisfaction: *God saw all that He made and it was very good.*[2] Our first parents enjoyed everything in existence and exulted in the fullness of love, rendering praise and thanksgiving to God for it. Before the Fall they had no experience whatsoever of sadness. Along with the first sin, though, a catastrophic consequence for man came about. A certain solemn gravity took the place of the serene and delightful joy which man originally enjoyed as a gift from God. Misery crept into the depths of the human heart. With the Immaculate Conception, the first new spark of authentic joy came

---

[1] *Prayer over the Offerings,* Mass of the Blessed Virgin Mary, Cause of our Joy

[2] Gen 1:31

silently into the world.

Many in heaven rejoiced over Mary's birth, so great was the joy this wonderful event brought to the world. The Most Blessed Trinity looked down on creation with satisfaction because the Mother of God had entered into it. With her *Fiat,* from the very first moment, her personal and irrevocably committed assent to God's plan of Redemption, the Blessed Virgin's heart was inundated with a joy from the Holy Trinity that overflows for the benefit of all humanity. *When God desires to raise someone to the utmost heights of divine love, the Lord first fills the person concerned with joy.*[3] He proceeded in this way with the Blessed Virgin. Her joy is redoubled primarily because she is *full of grace,* as no other creature has ever before been or ever will be again. Then, from the moment of her consent to the angel's message, the Son of God takes on flesh in her most pure body.

As has been the case throughout history, Christ continues to bring men and women this same authentic joy today. The announcement of the Saviour's birth in Bethlehem is made with the following significant words: *Do not be afraid, for behold, I bring you good news of great joy which shall be to all the people; for today in the town of David a Saviour has been born to you, who is Christ the Lord.*[4] Christ is our principal reason for happiness. He removes every trace of sadness from our hearts. Our Lady is truly the *Cause of our joy,* since her co-operation in the economy of salvation makes it possible for Christ to enter into us. Every day she makes it possible for us to experience his presence and continues to offer her Son to the Father for our sake. All our interior life is directed toward union with Jesus by way of Mary. We

---

[3] M.D. Philippe, *Mystery of Mary,* p.134
[4] Luke 2:10-11

must never forget that our most profound joy lies in union with Jesus, especially when suffering and contradictions of all sorts surround us. Only losing intimacy with the Lord would be reason for true sorrow. *The living experience of Christ and of our union with him is our true reason for hope. Our friendship with the Lord gives zest to our life. We enjoy life with upright rectitude and are not obliged to censure our joy in any way so as to make it compatible with our faith.*[5]

47.2 Mary teaches us how to bring joy to others.

The Blessed Virgin brings joy to the hearts of everyone she meets on the path of her life. *And it came to pass, when Elizabeth heard the greeting of Mary, that the babe in her womb leapt for joy. And Elizabeth was filled with the Holy Spirit...*[6] Mary bears the Son of God physically within her. Mere proximity to her is the cause of such great rejoicing that even the unborn John the Baptist in his mother's womb expresses his joy. *He cannot restrain his joy when the Lord is present* – St John Chrysostom writes – *nor can he bear to wait for the normal interval of time to elapse. He tries to leap out from within the confines of the maternal womb in testimony to the Saviour whose own arrival is imminent.*[7]

The Blessed Virgin can show us how to be the cause of joy for others in our family life, at our place of work and in all our social contacts, our most casual encounters with acquaintances, our interviews and business trips. The brief duration of our meeting with neighbours does not matter.

Our cheerfulness comes to bear in our cordiality in

---

[5] L. Giussani, *Utopia and the Present* in *30 Days,* August-September 1990, p.9
[6] Luke 1:41
[7] St John Chrysostom, *Homily preserved by Metaphrastus*

dealing with others, especially in the midst of adverse circumstances, as when traffic is slow or when we use public transport. In the same way that many different-sized containers can be filled from the same tap, the variety of people who have occasion to deal with us in the course of the day should leave our company with increased peace and joy. Small containers are filled to overbrimming, and larger ones as well. Some receptacles are dirty and the water cleans them... In any case, whoever has occasion to visit us when we are sick, or out of sheer neighbourliness, can and will be moved to return to his task with renewed happiness.

Normally, water comes to a tap from a larger reservoir. Our own original source of joy is God, to whom the Blessed Virgin leads us. When a tap does not run, the water gets stagnant and can become polluted. The same occurs with someone who ceases to be a cause of peace for others. Most probably, such a person's relationship with the Lord is inhibited. *You are unhappy? Think: There must be an obstacle between God and you. You will seldom be wrong.*[8] Once we discover the reason for our discontent, Our Lady will help us to remedy whatever it is that has to be set straight.

St Thomas teaches: *Authentic joy is born of love.*[9] The power of affection is so great that we forget about our own happiness in order to make the people we love happy. Whenever we aim to please God, even if our undertakings are wearisome, the tasks before us will never be bitter, but sweet.[10] Having recourse to Jesus prevents us from giving importance to minor differences of opinion or to the kind of petty antipathies that arise on occasion. We will then

---

[8] St. J. Escrivá, *The Way,* 662
[9] St Thomas, *Summa Theologiae,* 2, q2,a 28
[10] St Teresa, *Foundations,* 5,10

reach the heart of people who are often longing for a smile, a friendly word or a cordial answer.

On this fourth day of the Novena in honour of the Immaculate Conception we can examine the quality of our joy. Can others find God through our cheerful disposition? Are we uplifting – do we bear *charm not harm* for those with whom we come into contact every day? Today we can offer Our Lady a firm and sincere resolution: *May we make the way lovable and easier for others, since life brings enough bitterness with it already.*[11] Our cordiality is a way of imitating the Blessed Virgin, who smiles on us from heaven as we brighten up the way of holiness for our fellow men. She encourages us to discover her Son in others. On certain days, making the way pleasant for those around us is easy. But on others, forgetting about our personal concerns in order to become engaged with the preoccupations of our friends and acquaintances may require a little more of an effort because of our tiredness or our concern over an issue of pressing importance. On these occasions Our Lady will grant us her special assistance from heaven.

47.3 Casting all sadness far from us.

Whoever lived near to Our Lady during her life would somehow have participated in the immense joy and ineffable peace that filled her soul. Every aspect of her bearing reflected *the richness and beauty with which God exalted her. God kept her free from all sin. The love of God, the Holy Spirit, dwelt in her in a continuous fashion. Other invocations from the Litany allude to the direct result of her most intimate relationship with the Holy Trinity: 'Mother most amiable, Mother most admirable, Virgin most prudent, Virgin most powerful, Virgin most*

---

[11] St. J. Escrivá, *Furrow,* 63

faithful...' Our joy is constantly renewed with her help, when we keep her before our eyes and look to her with reverence and affection. Even if a tiny bit of her grandeur were to take root in our soul and beautify it, how great would our joy be![12] We can easily imagine why those who knew her looked forward to being with her. Neighbours, relatives and friends often must have come to her house. No one would ever have heard a complaint or even the hint of a pessimistic tone issue from her lips. Her only concern would have been to serve other people and help make life more pleasant for them. Though there are sufferings and even tears at times, one who has this interior joy, who is truly happy, constantly turns towards others and is a positive stimulus for them.

Gloom and despondency, on the contrary, darken the atmosphere. *As a moth affects a garment, and a worm the wood, so the sadness of man consumes the heart.*[13] It damages friendship and family life and shows through in everything. Such a state is a predisposition for sin. Therefore it is important to struggle against it immediately, because it threatens to weigh us down and take away our peace: *Have pity on your own soul, pleasing God, and contain yourself; gather up your heart into his holiness, and drive sadness far away from you. For sadness has killed many, and there is no profit in it.*[14] To be happy and serve those around us we need to forget about ourselves and not become excessively concerned about personal matters which are seldom very important. Complete confidence in God is also a necessary condition. Whoever worries too much about his personal affairs will not easily find the genuine happiness which causes us to be united to

---

[12] F.M. Moschner, *Mystical Rose,* Madrid 1957, p.180
[13] Prov 25:20
[14] Eccl 30:24-25

God and to other people. Our joy will then provide one more opportunity for others to encounter the Lord.

Prayer prepares us to be open to the grace of God. With this powerful source of help we can accept any of the difficulties we experience. Whatever is bothering us we leave in God's hands. Our personal conversation with Christ brings us to be more generous in serving God and others. It helps us to make a good Confession if lukewarmness and sin, the real cause of our sadness and ill-humour, begin to take root in our soul.

We finish our prayer by seeking out the help of the Blessed Virgin: *'Causa nostrae laetitiae... Cause of our joy, pray for us.' Teach us how to resolve in our own lives the paradox of Christian joy which is born and flourishes in suffering, renunciation and union with your crucified Son. May our cheerfulness always be true and complete, so that we are able to share our joy with those we meet every day.*[15] On this fourth day of the Novena let us offer our Mother in heaven the firm resolution to reject sadness in all its forms, and to make every effort to be the cause of peace and joy for the people we meet every day.

---

[15] John Paul II, *Address,* 31 May 1979

IMMACULATE CONCEPTION NOVENA

DAY 5 – 4 DECEMBER

48. MYSTICAL ROSE

48.1 Having Jesus abide at our side always through a life of prayer.

But Mary kept in mind all these things, pondering them in her heart.[1] *And his mother kept all these things carefully in her heart.*[2] Twice the Evangelist refers to Mary's contemplative perspective on the events that will lead up to the Redemption. The first occasion is on Christmas Eve when the Holy Family is in Bethlehem. The second situation arises in Nazareth on their return from Jerusalem. St Luke repeats his report after Mary and Joseph find the child Jesus teaching in the temple. Such insistence seems to be in response to Our Lady's constant meditation. Most probably she herself would have been the one who disclosed to the Apostles her interior disposition just after Jesus' ascension into heaven.

The Blessed Mother treasures in her heart the events she is privileged to witness. She ponders the great and small happenings of her ordinary life in the light of faith. Her considerations, full of affection, colour her entire attitude toward the various occurrences of her life as they unfold. Mary gives us a supreme example of interior recollection. Her insistent prayer rises to heaven like the

---

[1] Luke 2:19
[2] Luke 2:51

sweet perfume of the rose. *Our Lady's praise and petition goes up in a constant stream to God. It advances with the same fresh vigour as during her very first days in Our Lord's service, because her love is ever vibrant and virginal. The fragrant aroma of her prayer is stirred by the breeze of our petition and even by the stormy winds that blow throughout the world. She joins our thanksgiving and petition to her own, and presents it to the Father through Jesus Christ her Son.*[3]

When Mary looks or smiles at Jesus, or even so much as thinks about him, she is speaking to God. This is truly what it means to pray.[4] As a wayfarer on earth, Our Lady carried out all her actions with the express desire of pleasing her Son. Our own daily meditation leads us to identify ourselves fully with Jesus and approach even the relatively unimportant details of each day with supernatural perspective. At the wedding feast with her relatives and close friends in Cana of Galilee, she shows how we can petition Our Lord with delicate tact. *She was his mother. She had seen him sleeping in her arms, but nevertheless she did not venture here to tell him what He should do. She merely pointed out the problem to him and left the rest to his own judgment, convinced that whatever solution He offered, no matter what He decided to do, would be the best possible; she left the matter entirely to him, leaving him completely free to do his own Will without any feeling of obligation. Why? She knew that whatever He chose to do, it would be the most perfect thing that could be done, and the problem would be solved in the best possible way. She did not tie his hands, so to speak, or force him to take one line of action, determining a certain mode of proceeding for him; she trusted in his wisdom, in his*

---

[3] F.M. Moschner, *Mystical Rose*, p.201
[4] cf St J. H. Newman, *Mystical Rose*

superior knowledge, in his wider and deeper vision of things, a vision that took in aspects and circumstances perhaps unknown to her. She did not even ask whether He would think it fitting to intervene or not: She merely pointed out the problem and left it in his hands. The fact is that faith 'puts God under an obligation' more than the most skilful and forceful arguments.[5] Mary teaches us to remain at the foot of the cross in silent prayer during difficult moments of our life. The last we hear of Mary in the Gospel is when she is praying with the Apostles for the coming of the Holy Spirit.[6]

Our Lord himself learned from his Mother many prayers that had been passed down from generation to generation among the people of Israel. We too may recall prayers that we learned from our own mothers. Our Lady's example encourages us to deepen our prayer. *In brief fashion, the Gospel points out to us the way that we can best understand our Blessed Mother's example: 'Mary treasured up all these sayings, and reflected on them in her heart.' Let us try to imitate her in talking to Our Lord. We can converse about everything that happens to us, even the most insignificant incidents, like two people in love. We can never forget that we have to weigh circumstances and events, consider their value, and see them with the eyes of faith, in order to discover in them the Will of God.*[7]

48.2 Learning how to pray.

The incense of our prayer must rise up constantly to God Our Father. Time and again we ask Our Lady, who is already in heaven, body and soul, to petition Jesus for us: *Recordare, Virgo Mater Dei ... in conspectu Domini, ut*

---

[5] F. Suarez, *Mary of Nazareth*, p.209
[6] Acts 1:14
[7] St. J. Escrivá, *Friends of God*, 285

loquaris pro nobis bona... Remember O Blessed Virgin Mother of God...when you are in the presence of the Lord, to intercede before him on our behalf.[8] From her place in heaven Mary encourages us to give importance to our personal dialogue with Jesus every day, since it is our means for gaining the spiritual energy we need to grow in his love. In our mental prayer we ask the Lord's help with special recollection, offer him thanks and express our love and ask his help in confronting the challenges we face in our lives. This intimate conversation should continue to improve throughout our lives. Vocal prayer, too, is another efficacious means of raising our mind and our heart to the Lord and his Blessed Mother. We can take advantage of the prayers that we learned as children. Many generations of Christians have nourished their conversation with God in this way.

Prayer strengthens us against temptation. The Lord addresses the same words to us as he did to the disciples in Gethsemane: *Why do you sleep? Rise up and pray, that you may not enter into temptation.*[9] We need to pray always, but there are times when we must intensify our prayer by making an effort to focus our loving attention more fervently, as when family or work-related difficulties loom large or when we are assailed by temptation. Through the union established with the Lord when we pray well, we remain vigilant in the face of adversity. This personal dialogue also helps us to work better, to fulfil our duties to our family and society with more generosity, and to treat others with more consideration and courtesy.

The Blessed Virgin shows us how to ponder the truths of the Faith in our heart. We also come to perceive the events of our life in the light of God's presence. Apparent

---

[8] *Graduale Romanum*, 1979, p.422
[9] Luke 22:46

disaster and success, the birth of a child and the death of a loved one, the difficulties that arise at work and in family life and the experiences of our friendship, all these will take on their deepest meaning before our contemplative gaze. Like Mary our model, we can habitually seek the Lord in the intimacy of our soul in grace. *Be joyful and gladdened in your interior recollection with him, for you have him so close to you. Desire him there, adore him there. Do not go in pursuit of him outside yourself. You will only become distracted and wearied thereby, and you shall not find him, or enjoy him more securely, or sooner, or more intimately, than by seeking him within you.*[10] No other person in the world knew how to deal as intimately with the Lord as his Mother did. St Joseph came next in the exquisiteness of his refinement. He must have spent long hours contemplating and speaking to Jesus with simplicity and devotion concerning the ordinary business of every day. If we faithfully seek Mary's intercession in the course of our daily conversation with God we will immediately experience her efficacious help.

48.3 Vocal prayers and the Rosary.

In our mental prayer we speak to the Lord in a personal way. We come to understand the content of Sacred Scripture better and to perceive with greater clarity what He expects from us. *There is a growth of insight into the realities and words that are being used in such communication. This comes about in various ways. It comes through the contemplation and study of believers who ponder these things in their own hearts (cf. Luke 2:19,51).*[11]

Vocal prayer is also most pleasing to God when carried out in a meditative fashion. The Blessed Virgin in

---

[10] St John of the Cross, *Spiritual Canticle*, 1, 8
[11] Second Vatican Council, *Dei Verbum*, 8

all probability recited the Psalms and the other Old Testament verses common in the Hebrew tradition.[12] Through ejaculatory prayers we can stoke the fires of our contemplative life as we begin and finish off our work, when we are on the move from place to place, or even whenever we have occasion to go up or down stairs. Little by little, our whole life can be converted into a continual praise of God.

To stir up our prayer we can use short invocations gleaned from our reading and meditation on Sacred Scripture. Phrases from the *Our Father* and the *Hail Mary* can also be helpful. Many Christians have recourse to the words which various personalities from the Gospel have used to ask Our Lord's healing for a variety of needs. Some such quotations, for example, serve for us too to implore God's mercy and forgiveness. Some we may have learned in childhood, while others are born of our own spontaneous love and devotion. St Josemaría Escrivá confides: *Spontaneous prayers are made up of simple, ardent phrases addressed to God and to his Mother, who is our Mother as well. I still renew, morning and evening, and not just occasionally, but habitually, the offering I learned from my parents: 'O my Lady, my Mother! I offer myself entirely to you, and in proof of my filial love I consecrate to you this day my eyes, my ears, my tongue, my heart...' Is this not, in some way, a beginning of contemplation, an evident expression of trusting self-abandonment?*[13] For many Christians the *Memorare* continues to recall for them the heartfelt candour of the first occasion when they prayed it. We cannot afford to lose our ardent devotion for these simple prayers. Moreover, we fulfil a duty of charity by teaching them to

---

[12] F.M. Willam, *Life of Mary,* p.160
[13] St. J. Escrivá, *Friends of God,* 296

others. In a special way during this Novena we can make more of an effort to pray the Rosary well. It is the prayer the Church has so often highly recommended.

When Pius IX was on his deathbed and one of the prelates attending him asked what was on his mind during these climactic hours of his life, the Pope answered: *Actually, I'm contemplating the fifteen mysteries of the Rosary depicted on the walls of this room. If you only knew how encouraging they are to me. Considering them is most comforting. Meditating on the Joyful Mysteries, I forget about my pain. Considering the different phases of the Passion I am greatly heartened, since I tread the path of suffering in the company of Christ who went before me. When I bring the Glorious Mysteries to mind, I am filled with joy. It is very clear to me that all my pain is being converted into glory. What great solace the Rosary has been on my deathbed!* Speaking again in confidence to those surrounding him at that moment he said: *The Rosary is like an abridged version of the Gospel. It provides 'rivers of peace' to those who say it well. By far, it is the richest devotion and the one most abundant in graces. It certainly is the most pleasing to the heart of Mary. Remember me, my sons, by this final testimony I am giving to you now.*[14]

Let us make the resolution today to cherish more carefully our daily time of meditation and recite our customary vocal prayers, especially the Rosary, with increased affection and devotion. By always making an effort to pray well we will win many graces for those we long to help, by drawing them closer to Our Lord.

---

[14] H. Marin, Pontifical Doctrine Vol 4: *Marian Documents*, Madrid 1954

IMMACULATE CONCEPTION NOVENA

DAY 6 – 5 DECEMBER

49. MOTHER MOST AMIABLE

49.1 Jesus gives us his Mother to be our own.

When Our Lady consents to become the Mother of the Saviour, the first-born among many brethren, she becomes the Mother of all men. Moreover, Mary's spiritual maternity is superior to any purely human motherhood.[1] By giving birth to Jesus, the Head of the Church, she spiritually engenders each of us as members in the Mystical Body of Christ. Jesus is the source of all spiritual life, *having cooperated by charity that faithful might be born in the Church, who are members of the Head.*[2]

Next to the Lord, when he is nailed to the Cross, stands Mary, John the beloved disciple and some holy women. At this climactic moment the Lord speaks to the Blessed Virgin with words that have particular meaning for each one of us. He says to her: *'Woman, behold thy son'. Then He says to the disciple, 'Behold thy mother'.*[3] In union with his own suffering for the redemption of mankind, He offers up to the Father the suffering of his Mother as well. It is moving to see Jesus forgetful of his own sufferings and loneliness during the anguish of the Passion. His oblation is for the sake of all of humanity, for both the virtuous and those hardened by sin. The immense

---

[1] R. Garrigou-Lagrange, *The Mother of the Saviour,* p.219
[2] Second Vatican Council, *Lumen gentium,* 53
[3] John 19:27

love he shows for Mary, whom he does not want to leave on her own, still moves us today. There, next to Mary, John personifies every single one of us. Christ gave us his Mother to be our own. He addresses each one of us directly: *'Behold your Mother.' Treat her well for me, and seek her intercession in all your needs. Be sure to take advantage of this most precious legacy I am leaving you.*

Mary is united intimately to Jesus while he is consummating his redemptive mission. She thus cooperates in his sacrifice, and in our salvation. Her spiritual motherhood is confirmed by Christ from the Cross.[4] *'Behold your son.' This is a second Nativity. Mary gives birth, without pain, to her only-begotten Son in the stable of Bethlehem. Now though, she gives birth to her second son, John, amidst the sufferings of the Cross. Now she suffers the pangs of birth for the millions of other spiritual children who will call her 'Mother' over the centuries. Now we understand why the Evangelist calls Christ Mary's 'first-born son'. It is not because she has other sons of the flesh, but because she is to engender spiritual progeny through the love of her heart.*[5] She is united to the sacrifice of her Son through a redemptive suffering that is most fruitful. We well understand that the motherhood of Mary is of a higher order than any earthly motherhood. Our Lady engenders us into the order of grace and eternal life.

Behold your son. These words of Jesus to his Mother provoke an increase in charity on her part. They also lead to a deep filial love in St John, a reverence which is full of respect for the Mother of God. We can learn from the youthful apostle's example of confidence in the Mother of God how to deepen our devotion to Mary. On this fifth day of the Novena we can consider our own personal

---

[4] John Paul II, Encyclical, *Redemptoris missio,* 23
[5] F.J. Sheen, *From the Cross*

relationship with her. Do we approach her trustingly as St John would? Do we often remember that she is at our side? Do we seek her intercession frequently, saying with all our heart: *Mother, O Mother of mine...*?

49.2 Mother most amiable and most merciful.

Motherhood inherently entails care and vigilance for the children. Similarly, our Blessed Mother offers her spiritual protection to all without exception. She intercedes, and obtains the opportune graces of which all of us are in need. Just as Jesus is the Good Shepherd who calls his sheep *by name*,[6] Mary loves each of us in a special way. Every person is unique to her, and she distinguishes us personally from all others and knows us by our name. Her maternal concern extends to our overall well-being, both of body and soul, but her keenest interest has to do with *restoring supernatural life to our souls*.[7] She leads us to sanctity and to a more perfect identification with her Son. In this way, Our Lady is an excellent collaborator in the mission of the Holy Spirit, who bestows on us supernatural life and grants us the grace to persevere in it.

Mary is not a Mother to all men in the same way. She is an excellent Mother to those already in heaven who are already confirmed in grace. She is also mother to every Christian who is in the state of grace, since they are supernaturally alive. Finally, Mary is Mother to all those who have strayed from the path of God through committing mortal sin. She continually showers down the fruit of her charity on all her children, so that they can draw towards a more intimate friendship with her Son. In this way, Mary is our greatest help in the apostolate. She is even Mother to those who are not baptized, since they are

---

[6] John 10:3
[7] Second Vatican Council, *Lumen gentium,* 61

intended for salvation: *God desires all men to be saved and to come to the knowledge of the truth.*[8]

The Blessed Virgin is a most excellent Mother. She always has a smile and a friendly gesture to greet us. Her look inspires us with confidence, since she is ever disposed to understand the vacillations of our heart. We can abandon all matters of pressing concern to her intercession. Our Lady is supremely amiable and loved by all: *She is all things to all people. For the wise and the ignorant alike, she prepares the way through her most plentiful charity. Her mercy is open to us all: everyone can receive of her fullness. Those held captive by sin are freed, the sick gain healing, the afflicted receive consolation, and all sinners obtain pardon.*[9] Whenever we meet difficulties in our work or apostolate, run up against temptations of one sort or another, or lack material means, we should approach Mary for help with confidence, and say to her in the quiet of our heart: *Monstra te esse matrem... Show yourself to be our Mother.* We will always come out rewarded when we have had recourse to her intercession.

We approach Mary, Health of the Sick, in moments of weakness, with the guarantee of being heard. No experience, no matter how negative it seems, should discourage us, since we can always rely on our loving Mother. She is there to assist us in all our needs at every hour of the day, since she is most merciful. She hears our petitions with compassion and tenderness, and shortens the way, or at least makes it easier, for us to get back on track. If the struggles of our interior life or the other challenges our duties present become too taxing, we call on her with more energy than ever and she hurries to protect us: *Mother! Call her with a loud voice. She is listening to you;*

---

[8] J. Ibanez-F.Mendoza, *Mother of the Redeemer,* pp.237-238
[9] St Bernard, *Homily during the Octave of the Assumption,* 2

she sees you in danger, perhaps, and she – your holy mother Mary – offers you, along with the grace of her Son, the refuge of her arms, the tenderness of her embrace... and you will find yourself with added strength for the new battle.[10]

49.3 Learning to communicate more and better with our Mother.

And from that hour, the disciple took her into his home.[11] What a privilege for St John, and how cheerfully radiant Our Lady's presence must have made that dwelling. *Spiritual writers see in these words of the Gospel an invitation for all Christians to bring Mary into their lives. Mary certainly wants us to invoke her and to approach her confidently. We can appeal to her as her sons and daughters and ask her to 'show us you are our mother'.*[12] For this next day of the Novena let us make the resolution to contemplate Mary in the home of St John. We can visualize the young Apostle's tremendous respect in all his everyday dealings with her. How full of confidence the conversations between the two must have been. We can imagine her at our side by trying to contemplate her as the beloved disciple must have seen her each day. Let us approach Our Lady with complete filial confidence as St John before us assuredly did.

How easy it is to love Mary, since no more lovable creature ever existed! Mary is like *a smile from the Most High* bent upon us. There is no defect or imperfection in her. She is not far removed from our own experience, but very much attuned to our everyday life. She knows of our vacillations, our concerns and our needs. May we have no

---

[10] St. J. Escrivá, *The Way,* 516
[11] John 19:27
[12] St. J. Escrivá, *Christ is passing by,* 140

fear of going too far in our affection for her! We will never love her as does the Blessed Trinity, as God who loves her to the point of making her the Mother of Christ. We cannot overdo our love for Mary, since we know her whole life to be *an unmerited grace for us from the Heart of the dying Jesus.*[13]

The Lord wants each one of us to learn to love Our Lady more, and to show her the details of attentive care He himself would have regaled her with. We can strive to pray many short and spontaneous prayers and frequently glance at images of Our Lady to seek her help. We can say so much with a look! A loving thought of this kind can instantly heighten our attention, bringing us to be more keenly aware of the presence of God. We can make reparation for widespread negligence. We can seek out her help in the midst of our daily work by praying the *Angelus* and the *Rosary* with true piety... St Alphonsus Liguori affirms: *Among all the kinds of homage we can render Mary, the most pleasing to the Sacred Heart of our Mother is to implore with great frequency her maternal protection. We can ask her to aid us in all our specific necessities as when we give or receive advice, are in trouble or are experiencing trial or tribulation. Our good Mother will certainly free us from all danger, if we pray to her the antiphon 'Sub tuum praesidium... We fly to your patronage O Holy Mother of God...', or the 'Hail Mary'. We need only invoke her name. The demons tremble at its mere utterance.*[14] Like all mothers, Mary also finds special joy in coming to the help of those of her children who are most in need.

We are aware that *as we press on as wayfarers in this world, her merciful eyes and arms shall await us in heaven*

---

[13] Pius XII, Encyclical, *Haurietis aquas,* 15 May 1956, 21

[14] St Alphonsus Liguori, *The Glories of Mary,* III, 9

one day. We are called to enjoy indissoluble union with 'the fruit of her womb' Jesus. He won eternal glory for his Mother and for all of us who approach her for assistance.[15]

Sancta Maria, Mater amabilis, ora pro eis... Holy Mary, Mother most Amiable, pray for them... pray for me. Teach me to love you a little more each day.

[15] L.M. Herran, *Our Mother in Heaven,* Madrid 1988

6 DECEMBER

50. SAINT NICHOLAS OF BARI

Memorial

St Nicholas of Bari was born in Italy around the year 270. He was Bishop of Mira, in present-day Turkey, and died on January 6 between the years 345 and 352. After the transferral of the relics of St Nicholas to his homeland during the eleventh century, devotion to him developed rapidly in the Orient and later spread throughout the West. Many churches around the world are dedicated to him.

50.1 St Nicholas and all the saints are friends of God and our intercessors.

We read in the Old Testament that while God is about to destroy the cities of Sodom and Gomorrah in punishment for the sins of the inhabitants, Abraham intercedes: *'If there are fifty just men in the city, will you not spare the rest on account of them?'* Yahweh responds: *'If there are fifty just ones in the city of Sodom, I will spare them.* Full of confidence, Abraham insists: *And if forty? ... twenty? ... what if only ten are found? Yahweh answers: For the sake of the ten, I will not destroy the city.*[1] The Lord's response is always merciful. Moses also had confidence in the intercession of the friends of God: *Remember your servants Abraham, Isaac and Jacob.*[2] Similarly, we read of the deceased Jeremiah: *He is a lover of the nation, since he prays a great deal for the people and those of the holy city.*[3]

---

[1] Gen 18:24-32
[2] Ex 32:13
[3] 2 Mac 15:14

Intercession for the sake of others is a constant theme in Sacred Scripture. We see in the Gospel how a centurion sends a couple of elderly men who are friends of the Lord to intercede on his behalf: *And when they came to Jesus, they entreated him earnestly, saying to him, 'He is worthy that you should do this for him, for he loves our nation and has himself built us our synagogue'.*[4] Jesus heard favourably those Jews who were speaking up favourably for the Gentile... *He deserves this to be done for him...* Then we read how St Paul asks the Romans: *Now I exhort you, brethren, through our Lord Jesus Christ, and through the charity of the Spirit, that you help me by your prayers to God, that I may be delivered from the unbelievers in Judaea, and that the offering of my service may be acceptable to the saints in Jerusalem.*[5] St Jerome refers to the way in which even the deceased brethren intercede with God on our behalf: *If the Apostles and martyrs prayed for other people when they were still in their mortal bodies, how much more will they do so after they receive the crown of victory and triumph and heaven?*[6]

The Church has always believed that the saints already enjoy eternal beatitude and that the the souls in Purgatory are our great allies and intercessors. Through their merits they effectively reinforce our petition by presenting it to the Lord for us. In a word, the holiness they acquired throughout their lives continues to help us as we continue on our journey to heaven. St Nicholas, whose feast we celebrate today, while still in his youth was very generous with the fortune he had inherited from his wealthy parents. For this reason we honour him as an intercessor in all our material and financial needs.

---

[4] cf Luke 7:1-10

[5] Luke 7:1-10

[6] St Jerome, *Contra Vigilantium*, 1:6

The Founder of Opus Dei had great devotion to St Nicholas. Moments before Mass one day, while faced with some pressing financial concerns, St Josemaría Escrivá remembered to entrust to him these difficulties. There in the sacristy he made the following promise to the saint: *If you get me out of this predicament, I will name you an Intercessor.* Ascending the steps to the altar he immediately repented of the condition he had placed on his request and whispered a silent prayer: ... *and if you don't manage to get me out of it, I'll name you just the same.* He received the favour on that occasion and continued to seek the intercession of St Nicholas in the face of other financial difficulties.[7]

Family concerns, business affairs and apostolic endeavours often entail financial problems. Throughout the centuries many people have sought the intercession of St Nicholas in these matters. The Lord invited us in the *Our Father* to petition him for our material needs when he instructed us to pray: *Give us this day our daily bread.* Recourse to the mediation of the saints will strengthen our prayer of petition in this regard.

50.2 The need for human and material means.

While we are living out our mortal life we will need material means to sustain our family and set about the apostolic tasks that the Lord wants us to promote. Economic means are just that – *goods* – that become an impediment when we seek after them in such a way that we are not able properly to appreciate the supernatural means. St Leo the Great taught that God has left us material as well as spiritual goods,[8] so that we might make use of them for both the human and spiritual benefit of others.

---

[7] A. Vazquez de Prada, *The Founder of Opus Dei*
[8] St Leo the Great, *Sermons,* 10:1

Jesus himself teaches the disciples the importance of using the human means. Before their first apostolic mission he expressly tells them: *Do not take bag nor purse...* He leaves them without any material support at all, so that they clearly see that it is He himself who grants efficacy to their efforts. They fully comprehend that the cures, conversions and other miracles they are instrumental in carrying out are not due to their human qualities but to the power of God. Nevertheless, when on a later occasion they are about to set out, He adds to this first indication: *But now, let him who has a purse take it, and likewise a wallet.*[9] Although the supernatural means come first in all our apostolate, the Lord wants us to use the human and financial means within our reach as if the supernatural means did not exist. To fulfil his divine mission Jesus himself wanted to depend on human means – a few loaves of bread and fish, a little mud, or the modest support of those pious women who accompanied the Lord on his apostolic journeys.

Whenever our family or the apostolic works we collaborate in are in need, we should not hesitate to seek the help of the Lord. We must always recall that the first miracle, the one Our Lady instigates at the wedding in Cana, comes about in order to help a newly-wed couple save face, a matter of relatively scant importance. The Lord will not withhold his protection either, as long as we do all within our power like the good servants of Cana, who fill the water jugs *to the brim.*[10] They do all they can, humanly speaking, before the Lord works the miracle on the basis of their best efforts.

Whenever we find ourselves in straitened circumstances the following consideration can do much for our peace of mind: *My financial situation is as tight as it ever*

---

[9] Luke 22:36
[10] St Alphonsus Liguori, *Glories of Mary,* VI, 3, 5

has been. But I don't lose my peace. I'm quite sure that God, my Father, will settle the whole business once and for all.

I want, Lord, to abandon the care of all my affairs into your generous hands. Our Mother – your Mother – will have let you hear those words, now as in Cana: 'They have none!' I believe in you, I hope in you, I love you, Jesus. I want nothing for myself: it's for them.[11]

50.3 Generosity and detachment in the use of material goods. Seeking the patronage of St Nicholas in our material needs.

There will be times in our life in which the Lord encourages us in our generosity to contribute financial assistance – be it great or small – to sustain the Church or other good institutions which promote social justice. Possibly we will be called upon to help raise funds for these charitable works.

A great many pages from the New Testament make reference to the determination Christ's disciples showed in acquiring the necessary material goods they would need for the spread of the Gospel. We see how St Matthew enjoys considerable financial resources, and generously shares them with gratitude for all the Lord has done for him.[12] Then there is the group of women who follow Christ and *provide for the disciples out of their means.*[13] There are other disciples – wealthy ones like Joseph of Arimathea, for example, who gives up his own sepulchre and buys a fine linen cloth for the burial of Jesus.[14] We observe how Nicodemus purchases a large and expensive quantity of

---

[11] St. J. Escrivá, *The Forge,* 807
[12] Matt 9:9-10
[13] Luke 8:3
[14] Mark 15:46

myrrh and aloes to prepare the Lord's body for burial.[15]
Similarly, we can observe the heroic generosity of the first
Christians who *sell their possession and goods.*[16] *For those
who own lands or houses sell them, and bring the price of
what they sell and lay it at the feet of the Apostles.*[17]

St Paul organizes collections in Antioch, in Gaul, in
Macedonia and in Greece, to aid the faithful in Jerusalem.
He encourages good people to emulate the others in similar
acts of charity.[18] When the Apostle of the Gentiles writes
to the Corinthians, he thanks them for their generosity in
the collection they have taken up. He praises them for their
resolution to do good and says to them: *It is to your own
interest.*[19] St Thomas, commenting on these words,
emphasizes the benefit the donor draws from detachment
from the material goods he gives for the benefit of other
people: *A work of piety is more useful for the one who
practises it than for the one who receives it. The one who
does a good deed out of piety receives spiritual benefit,
while the one who receives merely the material good,
receives only temporal profit.*[20] Moreover, giving alms is
one of the principal means for healing the wounds in the
soul caused by sin.[21] The practice of this work of mercy
strongly attracts the grace of God.

Together with generosity and detachment from
material goods, we need to stimulate the practice of these
virtues in our dealings with friends. In this way we will
secure many blessings for them and their families. *Here is
an urgent task: To stir up the consciences of believers and*

---

[15] John 19:39
[16] Acts 2:45
[17] Acts 4:34-35
[18] 2 Cor 8:8
[19] 2 Cor 8:10
[20] St Thomas, *Commentary on the Second Letter to the Corinthians, in loc*
[21] *Roman Catechism*, IV, 14,23

non-believers, to gather together men of good will, who are willing to help and to provide the material instruments which are needed for the work with souls.[22] To finish our time of prayer well, it can be helpful to consider our own spirit of generosity and detachment from material goods: *Just ask yourselves, how much does it cost you – in financial terms as well – to be Christians?*[23] St Nicholas will be our ally in heaven so that we may be generous with God and with our brothers, in seeking out the financial means we need to carry out our apostolate. May we frequently invoke him to resolve our monetary difficulties. Now close to Our Lord, St Nicholas will continue to respond generously to those who have recourse to his intercession.

---

[22] St. J. Escrivá, *Furrow*, 24
[23] *idem, Friends of God*, 126

IMMACULATE CONCEPTION NOVENA

DAY 7 – 6 DECEMBER

51. REFUGE OF SINNERS

51.1 Mary's protection in the Sacrament of Penance.
I am the salvation of my people: When they call to me in time of trouble I will listen to their cry.[1] Ever since the age of the early Christians it has been a custom in the Church to depict Our Lady wrapped in a large cloak under which she offers refuge to people from every race and class. They all have in common an expression of profound peace on their faces. Popes and kings, businessmen and peasants, men and women from all walks of life find refuge beneath the protective shelter of her mantle.

Often in these pictures a few unfortunates are shown lying just outside the ambit of her protection. At times these pitiful creatures can be seen to have been wounded by some stray arrow or other. A lazy one, for example, may be here observed lounging complacently, with an arrow lodged in his limp and useless leg. A glutton, perhaps, may over there recline indulgently, with a plate in his hand and an arrow sticking out of his stomach.[2] In this way all these works of art are indicating that the souls concerned could have avoided their predicament by seeking refuge under Our Lady's patronage, for she is the *Refugium peccatorum ... Refuge of Sinners* for all

---

[1] *Entrance Antiphon*, Mass of the Blessed Virgin Mary, Mother of Reconciliation
[2] M. Trens, Mary: *Iconography of the Virgin in Spanish Art*, p.274

Christians. We strive always to appeal for her loving assistance, especially in moments of temptation or pressing difficulties. We also go to her for help, as if by instinct, when we have not been faithful, as the Lord expects, to his invitations to love, or to be more generous. Our Lady is our shortest way to Jesus, since she is always ready to facilitate our beginning again to live our contemplative life with her Son Jesus.

When considering the Incarnation of the Divine Word made flesh, the Fathers of the Church frequently affirm that the virginal womb of Mary is the locus of peace between God and all humanity. Through her most intimate relationship with Christ Our Lady exercises a unique spiritual motherhood, under God, for all men and women. Her maternal role consists above all in *cooperating by her obedience, faith, hope and burning charity in the work of the Saviour so as to win back supernatural life for souls.*[3] In this way Mary is a most important link in God's plan to free the world from sin: *She devotes herself totally as the handmaid of the Lord to the person and work of her Son, under him and with him, by the grace of almighty God, serving the mystery of the Redemption.*[4] She is most intimately associated with Christ's expiation for the sins of the world, since she perseveres faithfully alongside him as unique co-redemptrix in every moment of the Redemption that He toils to achieve during his earthly life. Her union with him is particularly evident on Calvary, where she offers herself with her Son to the Father. St John Paul II affirmed: *Mary is truly a cooperator with God in the work of reconciliation through her Divine motherhood.*[5]

Theologians have often taught that Our Lady is present

---

[3] Second Vatican Council, *Lumen gentium,* 61
[4] *ibid.,* 56
[5] John Paul II, Apostolic Exhortation, *Reconciliatio et poenitentia,* 56

in Sacramental Confession in a special way. Since the grace of the redemption is most appropriately applied to each one of us in this fountain of divine strength, it is logical that the Blessed Mother be closely concerned with it. *If anyone were to separate the co-redemption of Mary from the Sacrament of Penance he would be creating a division between Mary and Christ that never existed or can ever be admissible. Christ himself takes up into his own expiation all the reparatory cooperation of his Mother.*[6] Our Lady continues to play a pivotal role in our reception of the sacrament of Penance. Her motherly solicitude will help gain for each penitent who seeks her help the necessary dispositions of humility, sincerity and contrition in order to take the greatest possible advantage of so great a gift of Divine mercy. Moreover, she will be our most important ally in the apostolate of confession.

If at any time we are ashamed of the particular faults we commit, our Blessed Mother will be our first line of support. Little by little through her motherly intercession she will make the road of life easier for us to travel. When a child strays from the yard, what attentive mother would ever refuse to help the little one return to the safety of home? And so it is with Our Lady and us. *The Mother of God, who sought for her Son so anxiously when He was lost through no fault of her own, and experienced such great joy in finding him again, will help us retrace our steps and put right whatever may be necessary when because of our carelessness or our sins we have been unable to recognise Christ. With her help we will know the happiness of holding him in our arms once more, and telling him we will never lose him again.*[7] Holy Mary, *Refuge of Sinners* and our strength, grant us the grace to

---

[6] A. Bandera, *Our Lady and the Sacraments*, Madrid 1978
[7] St. J. Escrivá, *Friends of God,* 278

seek your help whenever we stray from the love of your Son, even in small ways. Help us to increase the contrition we have for our own personal sins and for the sins of others.

51.2 Mother most merciful.

Holy Mary, Mother of God, pray for us sinners ... The Lord desires our spiritual health and our ultimate salvation more than we ourselves do. He is all-powerful, our Father and the author of Love itself. In the sight of so splendid a Saviour, repentance for our sins is possible at any moment of the day. Jesus proclaims to one and all, including you and me: *I have not come to call the just, but sinners.*[8] During this Novena more than ever we are strengthened and sustained by the support of Mary, who calls each one of us to cast aside all selfish tendencies and pettiness. With Our Lady to help us we can avoid failures in loving God; we can refrain from passing judgment on others and put aside every inordinate attachment to material possessions. May we prepare to celebrate this feast day of Our Lady by welcoming with open arms the Lord's desire for our increased participation in the life of grace. May our purity of heart be increased more than ever.

An ancient tradition tells of Our Lord's appearing to St Jerome. It seems that Jesus asked him: *Jerome, what have you to offer me?* The Saint is said to have replied: *I can offer you my writings, Lord.* Christ indicated that this was not sufficient. *What can I offer you, then ... my life of mortification and penance?* The Lord again responded: *No, that is not enough either.* Jerome finally asked very pointedly: *Lord, what then is left for me to offer you?* Christ's immediate answer was: *You can offer me your sins, Jerome.*[9] It is frequently difficult for us to recognize our

---

[8] Matt 9:13
[9] cf F.J. Sheen, *From the Cross*, p.16

own sins and weaknesses for what they truly are, but with the help of Jesus, who continues to look upon us with affection, we can admit our faults, our weaknesses and omissions with courage and brutal sincerity if need be. Knowing that sin separates us from God and from our fellow men, we need to make an effort not to cover up anything or cushion the account of our personal sins with excuses. Such subterfuges only serve to impede the fervent contemplative life Our Lord desires for us in the midst of our daily duties. Jesus wants us to entrust our sins and their consequences to him so that he may relieve us of them. In exchange for our heartfelt contrition, Jesus offers us the peace and happiness of drinking from the source of eternal life.

St Alphonsus Liguori teaches concerning Mary that the principal duty the Lord entrusts to her is the dispensation of mercy. Our Lady constantly puts the weight of her privileges behind our attempts to improve our relationship with God.[10] The call Jesus addresses to sinners is perhaps as joyful for us as it is startling: *The Son of Man came to save what was lost.*[11] We know that many came to know the Lord through his continual practice of mercy with those around him: *The Son of Man came eating and drinking, and they say, 'Behold a glutton and a wine-drinker, a friend of publicans and sinners!'*[12] We further recall that, before the astonished gaze of many, Jesus freed the woman caught in adultery from her humiliating predicament with the simple words: *Go, and do not sin again.*[13] The Lord continues to deal with each person in the same way today, through the Sacrament of Penance.

Saint J. H. Newman recommends that we do not think

---

[10] St Alphonsus Liguori, *Glories of Mary,* VI,3,5
[11] Matt 11:18
[12] Matt 11:19
[13] John 8:11

of God as a severe and harsh taskmaster.[14] One who himself acts out of anger, with severity or harshness, or who is easily offended by others, is often led to perceive God in this light. Jesus, however, loves each one of us beyond our wildest imaginings. He seeks us out all the more earnestly the worse our situation may appear to us. Since God is forever kind and merciful, Our Lady's role is not to soften Divine justice, but to prepare our hearts to receive the countless graces the Lord has prepared for us. *Mary provides us with a mild yet powerful impetus towards helping us overcome the difficulties of making a good confession. Furthermore, she invites us to embrace the challenges we face so that we may transform these same difficulties into a means of purification for our own sins and those of others.*[15] May we grow in the custom of having recourse to her whenever we are preparing to receive the Sacrament of Penance.

Mary, you are our hope, so look on us with your eyes of compassion. Teach us constantly to approach Jesus whenever we fall. Help us to begin our struggle again without delay, through the confession of our faults and sins in the Sacrament of Penance, so that we may once again return to the strength of his grace, our sure source of peace.[16]

51.3 Mary is our refuge.

Sancta Maria, refugium nostrum et virtus ... Holy Mary, our refuge and our strength... The word *refuge* comes from the Latin *fugere,* to flee from something or someone. To seek refuge entails escaping from the cold, the dark of night or the approaching storm to warmth, or

---

[14] St J. H. Newman, *Sermon for the Fourth Sunday after the Epiphany*
[15] A. Bandera, *op. cit.,* pp.179-180
[16] John Paul II, *Prayer of Petition,* Mexico, January 1979

light, or shelter. In our refuge we find security in the midst of tumult, and defence from our enemies. When we call on Our Lady we find in her our best means of protection against every temptation to discouragement or the threat of loneliness. From the moment we begin to pray to her we see that our temptations vanish and recover the peace and optimism we have lost. In the face of more pressing difficulties, we seek refuge from the very first moment in the shelter of our Lady's cloak: *All the sins of your life seem to be rising up against you. Don't give up hope! On the contrary, call on your holy mother Mary, with the faith and abandonment of a child. She will bring peace to your soul.*[17]

We will always find refuge and protection with our Blessed Mother: *She takes away our fears, enkindles our faith, strengthens our hope and encourages us when we are beset by our weaknesses.*[18] Since we have an active appreciation of her motherly protection, we seek refuge with her and implore the pardon of God through her intercession. *Contemplating her spiritual beauty, we renew our effort to free ourselves from the hold of sin. Meditating on her words and example we will hasten to fulfil the commandments of her Son.*[19] O Mother of mine, *Refuge of sinners,* teach us all to recognize our sinfulness and our constant need for repentance. Bring us quickly back to the side of your Son when we stray from the path, so that there we may find our true place of rest.

---

[17] St. J. Escrivá, *The Way,* 498
[18] St Bernard, *Homily on the Blessed Virgin Mary,* 7
[19] *Preface of the Mass,* Mass of the Blessed Virgin Mary, Mother of Reconciliation

IMMACULATE CONCEPTION NOVENA

DAY 8 – 7 DECEMBER

52. GATE OF HEAVEN

52.1 We find Jesus through Mary.

> *Hail, O Star of ocean,*
> *God's own Mother blest,*
> *Ever sinless Virgin,*
> *Gate of heav'nly rest...[1]*

Just as we praise Our Lady in the ancient liturgical hymn in her honour, we often address Mary in the Litany of the Holy Rosary in the same way, under the invocation *Gate of heaven* since she is our way of access to the Lord. She is also the *Eastern gate of the Temple* that the Prophet speaks about, since through her the Sun of Justice, Jesus Christ, comes to us.[2] In a primary sense though, she is *the gate of heaven that we are confident of one day entering, where we will one day enjoy eternal happiness.[3]* It is important for us to realize more and more that we will always find Jesus by having recourse to Mary. Men and women today often seek in vain to please God, in a thousand and one indirect ways, including force of arms and speculative thinking. Many forget that Mary is the direct route for all of us to reach God. *She will lead us to the innermost sanctuary of heaven, and ultimately to ever-*

---

[1] Hymn, *Ave Maris Stella*
[2] Ez 44:1
[3] Benedict XIV, Apostolic Letter, *Gloriosae dominicae,* 27 September 1748

lasting life with God.[4]

Friar Leo was a Third Order Franciscan who was a close follower of St Francis during the saint's lifetime. After the beloved founder died, his pious disciple would regularly come and place herbs and flowers on his tomb. There he would meditate on the eternal truths. One day when the friar fell asleep in this place, he had a vision of the Day of Judgment. He saw an open window in heaven, and then Jesus, the most lovable Judge, appeared in the company of St Francis. The two let down a red ladder with steps so widely spread apart that it was impossible to climb up. Many people made an attempt to ascend, but few were capable of making any progress. After a while, a great clamour arose from below. Another window then opened where St Francis had appeared before. This time the Blessed Virgin was in their company, at the side of Jesus, and they let down another ladder. It was white this time, and the steps were considerably closer together. People began to make their way up with great jubilation, one after another. Whenever any one of them began to falter in upward progress, Our Lady would call him by his name and offer her encouragement. She would send an angel from among the cohort surrounding her to go and lend a hand to the one who was in difficulties. In the event, all of them who made an effort managed to get up the ladder, one after the other.[5]

This pious legend reflects an essential tenet of our faith: sanctity and salvation are easier of attainment with the help of the Blessed Virgin. Without her, everything is harder and sometimes even impossible, since God has wanted her to be the *dispenser of the treasures that Jesus won for us by his Passion and his Death on the Cross.*[6]

---

[4] F.M. Moschner, *Mystical Rose,* p. 240

[5] cf *Vita Fratris Leonis in Analecta Franciscana*, III, I

[6] St Pius X, Encyclical, *Ad Diem illum,* 2 February 1904

Our Lady is the Gate of heaven – *Ianua caeli* – and a powerful aid for us in reaching union with God. *Taken up to heaven, she does not lay aside the task she had on earth of cooperation in our salvation, but by her constant intercession continues to bring us the gifts that lead to eternal life. With her maternal charity she cares for the brethren of her Son who still pursue their journey here below beset by dangers and difficulties, until they are led to the happiness of their true home. For this reason the Blessed Virgin is invoked by the Church under the titles of Advocate, Auxiliatrix, Adjutrix, and Mediatrix.*[7] St Bernard tirelessly taught that by the Will of God the Blessed Virgin is our Mediatrix, since all graces come to us through her hands. Theologians affirm that we receive all graces through Our Lady, subordinate as she is to Christ, our one true Mediator.[8] Mary is constantly available to help in our salvation, and will grant us whatever we ask that is in our best interest. May we continue to renew our prayer of petition with increasing fervour during the course of this Novena. On the occasion of the great Solemnity we are preparing to celebrate, Our Lady will assuredly grant us the abundant divine blessings that we are at this time seeking through her intercession.

52.2 The intercession of Our Lady.

St Alphonsus Liguori affirms that Mary is the *Gate of heaven,* since in the way all benefits a king confers first pass through his palace gate, no grace comes down from heaven without first passing through the hands of Mary.[9] Even during her earthly life we see how Our Lady was the dispenser of Divine grace. Precisely through her the unborn

---

[7] Second Vatican Council, *Lumen gentium,* 62
[8] St Bernard, *Homily on the Blessed Virgin Mary* in *Summa Aurea*, VI, 996
[9] St Alphonsus Liguori, *The Glories of Mary*, I, 5, 7

Jesus blesses the Precursor from his Mother's womb on the occasion when Mary has gone in haste to visit her cousin Elizabeth. Jesus performs his first miracle by changing water into wine at the wedding feast in Cana of Galilee – at Mary's insistence. The disciples begin to put their faith wholly in Jesus from this very moment.[10] The Church in history and in the nations of the world began on that day of Pentecost – in the presence of Mary. *We know that the Mother of the Redeemer was present from the very beginning, since she was with the Apostles in the upper room 'imploring the gifts of the Holy Spirit with her prayers'.*[11]

It is impossible for the Lord to remain indifferent to Mary's pleas on our behalf. She is very well aware of all our needs, and she it is who distributes all the graces that we continue to receive through Christ's redemptive work. The efficacy of her intercession has increased in a manifold way since her Assumption into heaven, when she was raised in dignity above all the angels and archangels. St Bernard says that she provides us with the graces to renew the fervour of our devotion with each passing moment and throughout our life. To some she distributes more and to others less, in accordance with the Will of God and our own dispositions. From the source of the grace that springs forth from the heart of God, she grants to us the greatest degree of participation in the Divine life we are capable of receiving.[12] Only our own lack of good will can inhibit these graces from reaching down into the very depths of our soul.

Led by her immense charity, Our Lady is steadfast in interceding for us with God. She heightens the intensity of her petition when we remind her of our needs with unflagging persistence, as is our custom during the

---

[10] John 2:11
[11] John Paul II, Encyclical, *Redemptoris Mater*, 26
[12] St Bernard, *Homily on the Nativity of the Blessed Virgin Mary*, 3,5

Novena. We trustingly commend to her the difficult situations that perhaps are weighing us down, fully confident that no matter the outcome she knows what is best for us: 'Mother of mine ... you already see that I need this and that ... that this friend, this brother, this son of mine ... has strayed away from the house of the Father ...' Our Lady fulfils to the letter the words of Jesus in the Gospel: *For everyone who asks, receives; and he who seeks, finds; and to him who knocks, it shall be opened.*[13] Through her motherly protection she will gain for us the strength of God as often as we ask her for help. She cannot refrain from coming to the aid of any one of her children because of her great compassion for sinners and her role as the *Gate of heaven.*

52.3 Devotion to Our Lady, a sign of predestination.

Ianua caeli, ora pro eis ... ora pro me ... Gate of heaven, pray for them, pray for me. The epithet *Gate of heaven* is appropriate for Mary on account of her intimate union with her Son, and signifies her special participation in the fullness of power and mercy that derive from Christ Our Lord. More accurately though, Jesus himself is our way to glory, since through his Passion and Death he opened up the gates of heaven that were previously closed to humankind. We rightly call Mary the *Gate of heaven* because through her all-powerful intercession she procures for us the means we need to reach heaven, where God our Father himself awaits us.[14]

Since Jesus came to us through the Gate of heaven which is Mary, let us go quickly forward to greet her so that we may all the more swiftly find Jesus: *Mary is always the way that leads to Christ. Each encounter with her is*

---

[13] Matt 7:8
[14] I. Goma, *The Blessed Virgin*, II, pp.162-3

necessarily a meeting with the Lord himself. What else can constant recourse to Mary mean but a continual search for Christ our Saviour through her, with her, and in her?[15] As the Three Kings found him in Bethlehem, we find Jesus always *with Mary, his Mother.*[16] On account of the close relationship between Mother and Son, the Church has taught that devotion to the Blessed Virgin is a sign of predestination.[17] Mary looks after her children in order to expedite their journey along the path that leads to the house of God our Father. If at any point we ever stray from the true path, she will stretch out her hand to us – as all good mothers do with their children – so that we may begin the right way again immediately. Whenever we fall, she will be at our side to help us get up and set off again in the proper direction, so that we will be 'presentable' for her Son.

Mary's mediation is central to that of all the other saints. Not one of them could obtain the least benefit for us without her. Though her universal mediation is always subordinate to that of Jesus, the potency of her intercession is greater than all the influence of all the other saints combined. Through her deep identification with the Passion and Death of Christ, Our Lady merited to receive the graces she wins for us. Truly, only through her help shall we ever enter into the dwelling place of our heavenly Father.

We cannot even begin to imagine the great outpouring of grace which we receive for our souls, for those we are praying for and for the whole Church, through the small acts of love for God we offer through Our Lady each day of the Novena. *Mothers don't keep a record of their*

---

[15] Bl. Paul VI, Encyclical, *Mense Maio,* 29 April 1965

[16] Matt 2:11

[17] Pius XII, Encyclical, *Mediator Dei,* 20 February 1947

children's tokens of affection; nor do they weigh them up or measure them with meticulous calculation. A tiny gesture of affection is as sweet as honey to them, and they give themselves generously in return, bestowing much more than they receive. If good mothers on earth react in this way, just imagine what we can expect from our Holy Mother Mary.[18] May we always stay within the bounds of her loving vigilance, and may we not let a single day pass without our having recourse to her maternal protection.

---

[18] St. J. Escrivá, *Friends of God,* 280

8 DECEMBER

FEAST OF THE IMMACULATE CONCEPTION

53. THE IMMACULATE CONCEPTION OF THE BLESSED VIRGIN MARY

53.1 The Blessed Virgin and the mystery of Christ.

The Liturgy of the Solemnity we now celebrate puts the following words on the lips of Our Lady. They express the fulfilment of Isaiah's ancient prophecy: *I rejoice heartily in the Lord, in my God is the joy of my soul; for he has clothed me with a robe of salvation, and wrapped me in a mantle of justice, like a bride adorned with her jewels.*[1]

Today we want to shower upon Mary the highest praises any creature could be given. An early Father of the Church praises her above all creation on this magnificent occasion: *May all creation shout with joy, may heaven rejoice and may justice rain down in torrents from the clouds. Let the mountains exude sweet honey and the hills pour forth cataracts of jubilation. The Lord has shown mercy on his people. He has raised a powerful Saviour from the House of his servant David. The most pure and immaculate Virgin Mother arrives for the health and hope of all the peoples of the world.*[2]

Through a great desire to redeem the whole of humanity, the Holy Trinity chose Mary to be the Mother of

---

[1] *Entrance Antiphon*: Is 61:10
[2] St Andrew of Crete, *Homily on the birth of the Most Holy Mother of God*, 1

the Son of God made man. The Creator wanted Our Lady
to be joined indissolubly to both the human birth and the
salvific mission of the divine Word made flesh. In the
economy of salvation the Blessed Mother is eternally
united to Jesus. He alone is perfect God and perfect man,
the foreordained Mediator and Redeemer of the world.
*Mary was predestined from eternity to be the Mother of
God, by the decree of Divine providence which determined
the incarnation of the Word.*[3] From the first instance of her
natural existence Our Lady remains associated with her
Son in the Redemption of humanity through her unique and
exalted election by God. She is the woman referred to in
Genesis in the *First Reading* of today's Mass.[4] After the
first act of evil, the specific original sin, God said to the
serpent: *I will put enmity between you and the woman,
between your lineage and hers.* Mary is the new Eve from
which a new race, the Church, will be born.

By reason of her election as the Mother of the Saviour,
Our Lady receives more grace than all the angels and saints
combined. She thus occupies a unique place among the
sons and daughters of men because, after Christ, she
possesses the greatest dignity of any being in the whole of
creation. At the same time, she remains very close to us.[5]
In her unsurpassable excellence, she is a perfect type of the
Church on account of her faith, her charity and her perfect
union with Christ.[6] Moreover, she is an example for us in
our practice of all the virtues.[7] We need only look to our
Mother as the ideal we must strive to emulate. Coupled
with the grace of Christ, her intercessory power is so great
that the more devotion to her spreads, the more are believers

---

[3] Second Vatican Council, *Lumen gentium,* 61
[4] Gen 3:9-15; 20
[5] Second Vatican Council, *Lumen gentium,* 54
[6] *ibid.,* 63
[7] *ibid.,* 65

drawn into closer union with her Son and the Father.[8] Today, let us contemplate Mary, the most pure and exalted creature in the universe. We look up to her, *as on a Star that guides us, shining through the dark clouds of human uncertainty. The annual Solemnity of the Immaculate Conception shines bright from within the background of the Advent liturgy. We contemplate Our Lady in the divine economy of salvation as the 'Gate of heaven' through which the Redeemer comes into the world.*[9]

53.2 Her fulness of grace was received at the moment of her Immaculate Conception.

Hail Mary, full of grace, the Lord is with thee. Blessed art thou among women...[10] Through the merits of Christ and an extraordinary special grace, Mary is preserved from all stain of original sin from the very first moment of her conception. *God loved her with a unique predilection. He filled her with the greatest abundance of his celestial gifts and her participation in the divine nature exceeds that of all the angels and saints together. Her life reflects so great a fullness of innocence and sanctity that a more exalted creature cannot be conceived of, except by the Creator himself.*[11]

Our Lady's preservation from all stain of original sin is an absolutely unique privilege. According to theologians, the fullness of grace in Mary's case was the principal ground and characteristic of her human nature. Every aspect of her being shone with the splendour of that harmony with which God had originally wanted to endow all humanity. She was free from all actual sin and from

---

[8] *ibid.,* 65
[9] John Paul II, *Address,* 8 December 1982
[10] *Gospel of the Mass:* Luke 1:28
[11] Pius IX, Apostolic Letter, *Ineffabilis Deus,* 8 December 1854

even the slightest moral imperfection. She had no need to struggle against disordered passions, nor did she suffer interior temptations. Exempt from the consequences of concupiscence, she felt no attraction towards sin or to any of the allurements of the devil. Then, through the merits of Christ, Mary received the fullness of grace from the Redemption. We understand clearly that God prepared with infinite love the one who was to become the Mother of his Son: *How would we have acted if we could have chosen our own mother? I'm sure we would have chosen the one we have, adorning her with every possible grace. That is what Christ did. Being all-powerful, all-wise, Love itself (1 John 4:8), his power carried out his will.*[12]

Today in this great Solemnity we see a remarkably meaningful connexion with the Solemn feast of Christmas. For this reason the Church has wanted the one great celebration to follow chronologically close upon the other. *The first indication of spring while it is yet winter, when everything seems dead, is the appearance of green shoots. Similarly, in a world stained by sin and plagued by despair, the Immaculate Conception prefigures the restoration of man's innocence. We can sense the imminence of this development in much the same way as we do the appearance of a flower when at first all we see is the bud. It was still winter in the cold world around, but not in Joachim's tranquil home, where St Anne gave birth to a female child. Springtime was just beginning there.*[13] The hope of new life began the very same moment that Our Lady was conceived in the fullness of grace without the slightest disfigurement of original sin.

---

[12] St. J. Escrivá, *Christ is passing by*, 171
[13] R.A. Knox, *Feasts of the Liturgical Year*, p. 298

53.3 Having devotion to Our Lady in order to imitate her.

'Tota pulchra es, Maria ... You are all fair, Mary and there is no stain in you. The life of the Immaculate Mother of God will always be a worthy ideal for us all to imitate, because she is a model of sanctity in ordinary life, of the kind of holiness that is accessible to everyone in everyday circumstances. It is a quiet dedication that often passes unnoticed. To be able to follow her example well, we need frequently to seek out her protection. During these days of the Novena let us strengthen our relationship with Mary by our concerted efforts to intensify our striving to have recourse to her in everything we do. We cannot slacken in this renewed impetus, especially since we know that our Mother will desire us to always remain loyally at her side.

Today people of all ages and conditions continue to fulfil to the letter the ancient prophecy the Blessed Virgin herself made one day: *All generations will call me blessed.*[14] Poets, intellectuals, craftsmen, kings and warriors, mature men and women as well as children who have hardly learned to speak, all offer her their praise. This multitude includes those who work in the fields out in the countryside, and others who labour most of their lives in the offices of the city. Some spend a great deal of time on the high pastures of the mountains, and many others in long hours working at the factory bench. All these children of Mary get on with their lives with her help, in the midst of everyday joys and sorrows, and especially during those critical moments that are to be found in the lives of all of us. So many have died with the sweet name of Mary on their lips and lovingly held in their innermost thoughts. Thousands of voices in a multitude of languages have sung praises to the Mother of God. They have also quietly petitioned her to look on those sons or daughters of hers

---

[14] Luke 2:48

who are most in need of her mercy. Spurred on by the momentum of the Novena, we can strive to blend our voice with theirs as we continue to correspond with the various calls on our generosity that the Lord addresses to each one of us every day of our lives.

The Holy Spirit has taught countless generations of Christians throughout the ages that the truest path to the Heart of Jesus is through Mary. With this in mind we need to accustom ourselves to entrusting our needs with confidence to the Blessed Virgin, since she is 'the shortcut to God' for us. *Zealously conserve your tender and confident love for the Blessed Virgin* – the Holy Father encourages us – *and do not let it grow cold... Be faithful to the Marian practices of piety that are traditional in the Church* – the *'Angelus', special devotion to Our Lady during the month of May, and in particular, the Holy Rosary.*[15]

Mary is 'full of grace' and 'blessed among women'. She is resplendent with the love of God and she is our Mother. One way we can show her our affection and devotion is to carry a picture of her in our wallet or handbag. We might also keep an image of her at the office, in our car or in our bedroom. We naturally invoke her protection in all of these everyday places, probably without the sound of words. If we fulfil our resolution to have recourse to Mary more frequently during the day, beginning now, we will experience the fruit of entrusting our needs to her as described by one of the Fathers of the Church: *Our Lady is rest for those who work, consolation for those who mourn, and relief for those who are sick. She is a refuge for those caught in the storms of life, a fountain of compassion for sinners, a sweet relief for the sorrowful and a sure source of aid for those who pray.*[16]

---

[15] John Paul II, *Address*, 12 October 1980
[16] St John Damascene, *Homily on Our Lady's Dormition*

10 DECEMBER

54. OUR LADY OF LORETO

Memorial

The Holy House of Nazareth where Mary was born is still preserved in Loreto. In this sandstone and brick home that has been the site of many pilgrimages throughout the ages, the Blessed Virgin received from the angel the message concerning her Divine maternity. The image of Our Lady presently on display there replaces one from the sixteenth century that was destroyed during a fire in 1921.

54.1 The Holy House of Loreto.

Devotion to the Blessed Virgin under the invocation 'Our Lady of Loreto' *is linked to the house of the Holy Family in Nazareth. As the Gospel of the Mass reminds us today, Mary lived here after her betrothal to St Joseph.*[1] The holy Patriarch carefully prepared this home in order to provide the best possible place for Our Lady and the Child who was to come. From the beginning, though, this house was Mary's home. *Every home worthy of the name is above all a sanctuary created by the mother. She is the one to set it up in accordance with her particular personality.*[2]

God desires that *all children of the human family be born into the world within the protective warmth of a family. All children need to have a roof over their heads. Probably all the ancestors of Christ mentioned in today's Gospel came into the world with this privilege. As we know, though, the home in Nazareth was not the birthplace*

---

[1] John Paul II, *Address,* 8 September 1979
[2] *ibid.*

of the Son of Mary, the Son of God. Jesus was born far from home, in a stable at Bethlehem. He could not even go back to his own place in Nazareth on account of King Herod's edict that all infants in Bethlehem had to be slaughtered. St Joseph was obliged to flee with the Holy Family to Egypt. Only after Herod was dead did the Holy Patriarch dare to take Mary and the Child back to Nazareth. From the time of their return from exile, the Holy Family would have shared their daily life in this house, hidden for the most part from the world's view. Their home was the first church to be illuminated with the affection of Mary's maternity. In the midst of the ordinary work these most beloved creatures of God carried out, she most certainly must have lit up their home with a radiant cheerfulness that had its roots in the great mystery of the Incarnation, the mystery of her divine Son.[3]

Mutual care and respect permeated the life of the Holy Family. Their home was surely a model for all Christian homes, since it must have been clean and pleasant, complete with the kind of modest adornments that would have contributed towards the elevated human tone of sensibility and good taste. Each person would serve the other members of the family gladly. The tranquil order of their family life would have created an atmosphere in which Jesus and Joseph could find rest after a full day's work. We take good care that our own homes be decorous and orderly without ostentation or extravagance. Family life can thrive in a climate of mutual trust and affection. In such an atmosphere it is easy to carry on our daily affairs in the presence of God. By staying close to Our Lady's side we will continue to discover ways of practising charity with those we live with, and in this way turn the most mundane material concerns into occasions of expressing

---

[3] *ibid.*

our love for God with deeds.

54.2 The home of Nazareth, model of Christian homes.

The *Light of the world* dwelt in the house of the Holy Family in Nazareth. This reality must have suffused every deed carried out there and have been the background in all the human interaction of those three. The perfect naturalness of their dealings with each other would have made their home a byword in the neighbourhood for its wholesome cleanliness and neat condition. Everyone would contribute in some way towards the material maintenance of the home with Our Lady preparing the meals, mending clothes and eager to keep the house attractive through attention to many details. We can imagine the affection with which she must have served Jesus and St Joseph, since her love for God would bring her to have their needs constantly in mind. She would be aware of the hour they would be stopping for a break, and of the time at the end of the day when they would bring their work to completion. The Son of God grew in an environment of intimate family warmth, where each person served the others, until the time foreordained for him to begin preaching throughout the towns and villages of Galilee. He would always treasure the memory of that simple and pleasant home in Nazareth, that modestly cultivated, far from affluent but humanly attractive place in which He grew up.

The Mother of Jesus preserved in her heart those small ordinary events in the life of her Son which were the joy of her soul.[4] *We can't forget that Mary spent nearly every day of her life just like millions of other women who look after their families, bringing up their children and taking care of the house. Mary sanctifies the ordinary, everyday things –*

---

[4] Luke 2:51

what some people wrongly regard as unimportant and insignificant: everyday work, looking after those closest to you, visits to friends and relatives. What a blessed ordinariness, that can be so full of love of God![5]

God desires that all children be born and raised in a home that to a degree is similar to the home of the Holy Family where Our Lady as the mother was the heart of the home. Although women are called to carry out other important functions for the good of society, their dedication to the children and to the immediate concerns of the home are of fundamental importance. Here, above all, through a thousand and one details, mothers can effectively nurture their children. This task is the most significant commission each of them receives from the Lord. Christian couples should never forget *that the secret of married happiness lies in everyday things, not in daydreams. It lies in finding the hidden joy of coming home in the evening; in affectionate relations with their children; in everyday work in which the whole family cooperates; in good humour in the face of difficulties that should be met with a cheerful spirit; in making the best use of all the advances that civilization offers to help us bring up children, to make the house pleasant and life more simple.*[6]

The Holy Family provides us with a model of family life that we can strive to imitate. *Reflection on their life in Nazareth is the school where we begin to learn more about the life of Jesus. Through growing in our understanding of how things must have been in Our Lord's modest home, we can truly begin to understand the Gospel. Here we learn to notice, meditate on, and gradually penetrate the mysterious depths of the simple and charming life of the Son of God made man. Little by little we learn how to imitate the*

---

[5] St. J. Escrivá, *Christ is passing by*, 148
[6] St. J. Escrivá, *Conversations*, 91

Lord's hidden life.[7] Often in our mental prayer we can imagine ourselves as one more person working alongside Jesus, Mary and Joseph. We can pause to consider the many details of affection they must have shared with one another in the course of their daily family life.

Let us ask ourselves today whether our homes reflect in some way the cheerful and friendly atmosphere of the Holy Family in Nazareth. Do we keep up a spirit of service through attention to detail? Do we strive to go out of our way to make life pleasant for other members of our family? Are we making an effort to keep Jesus at the centre of our minds and hearts? Do we tolerate the friction of little quarrels, or get too engrossed in what pertains strictly to our personal well-being? Do we practise with true piety the Christian customs which help us to be more aware of God's presence in our lives, including Mass on Sundays and special feast days, blessings at meals and other prayers said in common?

54.3 Making life agreeable for those we live with.

What a wonderful model of daily living the Holy Family offers us!, states Leo XIII. *These three provide us with the perfect example of a Christian home. Each person lives with a tremendous simplicity in carrying out daily responsibilities while pursuing common goals with genuine mutual affection. There is no time for disordered or selfish pursuits. Each one carries out his or her particular responsibilities with such human and supernatural affection that others are edified to behold it.*[8] We look to the model of the Holy Family so that we can continually learn how to imitate the example of Jesus, Mary and Joseph in our own family life.

---

[7] Bl. Paul VI, *Address,* 5 January 1964
[8] Leo XIII, Encyclical, *Laetitiae sanctae,* 3

Affection in the family largely depends on the heart of the mother whose role is hard to replace. It also depends on the personal gift of self of each member of the family. Every one of us is called continually to be aware of the needs of others and to safeguard the particular customs and traditions we treasure at home. It is important that we carry out our tasks in such a way that we always have some element of sacrifice in them that we can offer up for the others when we are finished. Our homes will thus take on the flavour of family life found in the Holy Family at Nazareth. Seldom are there ever any extraordinary events there, since everything happens with complete naturalness. God awaits us also in the everyday services we are capable of rendering one another.

The Lord is not asking us for spectacular sacrifices, but He does expect us to show our dedication to him through the thousand and one details of service we render to the others in our family life – greeting with a smile the one who is most tired, carrying out punctually the many small duties living together entails, refraining from over-reacting to issues that are not very important, controlling our moods and so in general promoting a cheerful family atmosphere. Finally, we can strive to remember the birthdays and special anniversaries of the members in our family so that we may quietly mark and celebrate these special days together.

St John Paul II prayed at the Sanctuary of Loreto: *Accept, O Blessed Mother of the House of Loreto, my pilgrimage and that of all of us, as a common prayer for the family life of all the men and women of our age. We pray for the well-being of these homes, that they may prepare the sons and daughters of all to enter into the heavenly dwelling place of our common Father in heaven.*[9]

---

[9] John Paul II, *loc. cit.*

We entrust our own home to the Blessed Mother, so that she may help us to take care of it as though it were the house of God himself. May each person at home be able to grow in the practice of the human and supernatural virtues. May we be able to find there a place of refuge in which to regain our strength so that we may return to our work and apostolate with renewed vigour. We pray that the place where each of our families stays may be *a home resplendent with loving mutual concern, so that each day every member of it can be nourished with the warmth and affection of the others.*[10] May our family life be a foretaste of heaven, an anticipation of eternal life.

---

[10] *idem,* Apostolic Exhortation, *Familiaris Consortio,* 37

12 December

55. OUR LADY OF GUADALUPE

Memorial

The Blessed Virgin Mary appeared to Juan Diego on Tepayac hill near Mexico City on the 9th of December 1531 to ask for the construction of a church there in her honour. After the miraculous cure of his uncle, Bernardo, this Indian peasant brought to his Bishop some roses that he received from Our Lady as a sign of her request. As the flowers fell from his cloak to the ground before the astonished Prelate, the image of the Blessed Virgin, which is venerated in the Basilica of Guadalupe to this day, was miraculously impressed on the simple garment before their eyes.

55.1 The apparition of the Blessed Virgin to Juan Diego.
Devotion to Our Lady of Guadalupe began at the outset of evangelization in that country when there were still few Christians in Mexico. At this time, Our Lady having appeared to the Indian peasant Juan Diego had sent him to the Bishop to express her desire for a church to be built and dedicated in her honour on Tepayac hill. During the first apparition, Our Lady said to him: *Since I am truly your merciful Mother, and that of all men, I will grant everyone who visits the sanctuary the fruit of my affection, my compassionate attention, my help and salvation. I will hear your cries of distress so as to cure all your sufferings and ills.*[1] Mary delivered another message to Juan Diego that could well be addressed to all Christians: *I, who am your Mother, stand before you. You remain always under the shelter of my protection. Be aware of how fortunate you*

---

[1] *Nican Mopohua*, Mexico 1981, pp.28-32

are to have access to my motherly care at all times. We never have any reason to fear, since Mary the Mother of Jesus accompanies us, and she is the Mother of all men.

The local Bishop had asked for a sign as proof of Mary's petition before granting Juan Diego's request. Our Lady appeared again later and directed the amazed peasant to cut a bouquet of long-stemmed roses that were growing nearby on the arid hillside to be presented to the Bishop. This miraculous event took place in the dead of winter, in the month of December, two thousand feet above sea level. When Juan Diego spread out his white cloak to deliver the roses, *the beloved image of the Blessed Virgin Mary appeared, impressed upon it, as is plain for any observer to see today.*[2] This image of Our Lady of Guadalupe, a young dark-skinned woman surrounded by a radiant light, gradually appeared in full colour on the Indian's simple cloak, a garment woven together out of common vegetable fibres.

A remarkable wave of conversions in the entire Aztec territory, extending from Central America to the Philippine islands, took place following Our Lady's apparition on Tepayac hill. *Our Lady of Guadalupe continues to be a great sign of Christ's nearness to us today. She extends an invitation to all men and women to enter into communion with the Father. At the same time, Mary encourages all of us to enter into greater communion with one another...*[3] Our Lady's efficacious intercession has always prepared the way for the work of evangelization of nations. We cannot even imagine carrying out the apostolate of friendship and confidence without the help of Our Lady. Therefore when the Vicar of Christ on earth, the Pope, calls all the faithful to participate in a new evangelization

---

[2] *ibid.*, pp.181-183
[3] John Paul II, *Address,* 13 December 1987

of Europe and of the world, we look to the intercession of Our Lady, so that she will *show us, who belong to the Church, the best way to carry out this awesome task we are entrusted with. We implore from her the grace to dedicate ourselves with renewed missionary zeal to this sublime undertaking.*[4] She will show us the most efficacious way of drawing our friends closer to God, since she herself will prepare them to receive the grace of God fruitfully.

55.2 Our Lady prepares the souls of our friends, as she also prepares for all apostolate.

Through fervent piety and an efficacious desire to serve others we will be able to carry out the re-evangelization of the world. St John Paul II prayed: *Blessed Virgin of Guadalupe, Mother of the Americas... behold how great the harvest is. Intercede before the Lord for us so that our hunger for sanctity in the world may increase...*[5] May we give all we can to carrying out this task, especially to the people we find at our side every day. The harvest is still great and the labourers to gather it in continue to be few. The Holy Father continues: *May all the faithful strive to follow Christ closely. May the life of each one be filled with loving and humble service, carried out for the glory of God and the good of all souls.*[6] People from all walks of life hunger to know the truth, but have no one to teach it to them. Many seek to know the path to God, yet do not know the way. Each one of us, in our specific place in society, can point out to many others the straight path to union with Christ through devotion to Our Lady. Our word and our example of devotion to her will be the most efficacious witness we can render.

---

[4] *ibid.*
[5] *idem, Prayer of petition,* 27 January 1979
[6] *ibid.*

The Faith on the American continent had its origin in Europe. Many men and women of diverse races have found the way to salvation through the heroic and self-sacrificing efforts of the first missionaries to arrive there. During their period of history the Blessed Virgin prepared the way for them, as she will do for us now. In spite of all the difficulties they experienced in carrying out this divine task, the first Christians in these lands were able to proclaim the profound mysteries of the Faith in their milieu, through consistent effort, patience and supernatural spirit. *Now in Europe, however, we find a growing temptation and tendency toward atheism and scepticism. There is widespread uncertainty concerning morality itself. In the wake of this ignorance has come the disintegration of the family and the wholesale deterioration of the Christian way of life. A dangerous trend of ideas and practices conspires to stifle the expression of Christian life in society.*[7] Many countries of profound Christian tradition seem to be returning to a kind of paganism comparable in magnitude to the ones they were freed from in the past. Whereas in former times the light of the faith used to spread from these ancient countries to the rest of the world, currently *it is the poison of a new paganism that is being passed on.*[8]

We Christians are called to be leaven in the very heart of society. The strength of the Faith has not diminished over the course of twenty centuries. It is constantly being renewed. For this reason we cannot relax the intensity of our struggle as if everything had already been accomplished. In the face of the evil that threatens to destroy the seed which Christ desires to sow and cultivate in the heart of every man, we need to be more persistent than ever in helping to bring Christ's salvific mission to completion. If

---

[7] *idem, Address,* 6 November 1981
[8] A. del Portillo, *Pastoral Letter,* 25 December 1985

the early Christians had allowed themselves to become intimidated by the enormous challenge before them, if they had relied on human efforts alone, they would not have accomplished anything in those first centuries throughout those early pagan societies. The Lord encourages us to renew continually our efforts in the face of so urgent a task. Each of us is called to participate fully in this effort with the means we have at hand. *This undertaking is truly a fascinating adventure, both from a human and a supernatural point of view.*[9]

Today we may consider, with the support of Our Lady of Guadalupe, what we can contribute in our everyday circumstances in order to bring the task of re-Christianization to fruition. Do we foment an active interest in bringing our family and friends closer to Christ? Do we take advantage of every occasion, without missing opportunities, to speak courageously about the faith we carry in our heart? Do we take our own Christian formation seriously? Could we offer our time to teach catechism or to engage in other works of mercy? Do we lend financial assistance to sustain projects that contribute toward the human and supernatural development of people in need?

We cannot rest content under the impression that there is little we can do in the course of our everyday professional work to promote the re-evangelization of the world. God will multiply enormously the effect of apparently small offerings of work well done, of prayer and initiatives that we can offer him. Besides, when many people do what falls within the scope of their capabilities, entire countries can be converted, as happened in the earliest centuries.

---

[9] *ibid.*

55.3 Taking advantage of every opportunity of contributing to re-evangelization.

Go, therefore, and make disciples of all nations.[10] These words of the Lord are universally applicable, to every time and place, and are addressed to every individual of every nation. The Apostles received this commission from Jesus, and we in turn are entrusted with the same task. In a world where the customs and habits of millions to all intents and purposes are pagan, *we have the splendid responsibility of working to bring the divine message of salvation to all men.*[11] To carry out this commission from the Lord, we can count on the efficacious assistance He promised us: *I will be with you always, until the consummation of the world.*[12]

God acts directly in the soul of each person through grace. One Gospel account among many shows us that God wants some men to be instruments in working out the salvation of others: *Go therefore to the crossroads and invite to the marriage feast whomever you shall find.*[13] St John Chrysostom comments on this verse: *All noble human professions, like the study and teaching of philosophy or the calling of a soldier, for example, are circumstances in which men and women can help to draw others closer to the Lord.*[14] Business trips and recreational expeditions can no less be opportunities for spreading the teachings of Christ.[15]

There are countless occasions on which the laity can exercise an apostolate of evangelization and sanctification.[16]

---

[10] Mark 16:1

[11] Second Vatican Council, *Apostolicam actuositatem*, 3

[12] Matt 28:19

[13] Matt 22:9

[14] St John Chrysostom in *Catena Aurea*, III, p.63

[15] Second Vatican Council, *loc. cit.*, 14

[16] *ibid.*, 16

Family ties, sickness, friendly social visits to the homes of our friends, sending Christmas cards, and letters to newspapers can all provide good opportunities for doing apostolate. Each one of us must be able to say with St Thérèse of Lisieux: *Until the consummation of the world, while there are still souls to save, I will not be able to rest.*[17] We too live among souls still longing to be saved though they may not yet be aware of it. We encounter them in our own homes, at our places of work, and in our own neighbourhood.

Let us ask the Blessed Virgin for an ever-growing desire to be courageous and daring in sowing the good seed of Christ's doctrine. May we strive to contribute towards having the person and teachings of Christ proclaimed in every corner of the globe, without ever giving in to human respect.[18] May we cast aside all pessimism, ever confident of the ultimate triumph of good over evil. The effect of our good deeds will have an immeasurable impact on society. With the grace of the Lord we will be like the stone that falls into the lake and produces one ripple and then another and another until the end of time.[19] Truly Jesus grants supernatural efficacy to all our words and deeds in a way that we are most of the time unaware of.

Today we ask Our Lady of Guadalupe to show herself to be our compassionate Mother. May she help us to proclaim the Gospel through our behaviour in our everyday actions. May we make every effort to understand other people by sharing in their joys and in whatever may be sources of anxiety in their lives. Only by making an effort to live all the human virtues will we be able to draw our friends towards living the fullness of supernatural life, beginning here and now. *Queen of Apostles, accept our*

---

[17] St Thérèse of Lisieux in *Complete Works*
[18] St. J. Escrivá, *The Forge,* 716
[19] *idem, The Way*, 831

complete readiness to work for the restoration and fulfilment of your Son's kingdom. May we not withhold anything at all in helping to bring his salvific Will to fruition. May we be completely dedicated to the cause of the Gospel and of ultimate peace in the world. May our struggle be firmly grounded on justice, and be a stimulus for reciprocal charity among men and women and all nations.[20]

---

[20] John Paul II, *Address,* 27 January 1979

Index to Quotations from the Fathers, Popes and the Saints

Note: References are to **Volume**/Chapter.Section

Acts of Thanksgiving
St Augustine, **5**/39.2
St Bede, **5**/78.1
St Bernard, **5**/10.1, **5**/39.3
St Francis de Sales, **4**/84.1
St John Chrysostom, **2**/71.1
St Thomas Aquinas, **5**/78.2

Advent
St Bernard, **1**/1.3

Almsgiving
St Leo the Great, **5**/67.2
St Thomas Aquinas, **3**/17.3

Angels
Origen, **2**/9.3
St Bernard, **7**/30.3
St John Chrysostom, **2**/7.1
St John of the Cross, **2**/7.2
St Peter of Alcantara, **3**/51.2
St John Paul II, **2**/7.1, **2**/30.3, **7**/27

Apostolate
Benedict XV, **2**/85.1
Bl. Alvaro, **2**/29.1,
Bl. Paul VI, **6**/57.2, **7**/25.3
John Paul I, **3**/3.2
Letter to Diognetus, **2**/70.2
St Ambrose, **4**/87.1
St Augustine, **1**/8.3, **2**/59.1, **4**/92.3, **5**/52.1, **5**/87.3
St Cyril of Alexandria, **5**/62.1
St Gregory the Great, **3**/88.2, **4**/69.1
St Ignatius of Antioch, **5**/37.3
St John Chrysostom, **1**/4.3, **2**/85.1, **2**/94.1, **3**/88.2, **3**/89.3, **4**/87.1, **7**/42.2
St John Paul II, **1**/45.3, **2**/11.3,

3/13.3, **4**/37.3, **4**/69.1, **4**/87.3, **5**/10.2, **5**/20.1, **5**/57.1, **5**/68.3, **6**/57.3, **7**/2.3
St Teresa, **5**/68.3
St Thomas Aquinas, **1**/9.2, **3**/5.2, **7**/4.3
St Thomas of Villanueva, **4**/40.3
Tertullian, **2**/70.1, **4**/40.2

Ascetical struggle
Cassian, **2**/67.2
St Ambrose, **2**/22.3
St Augustine, **3**/3.1, **3**/18.2, **4**/25.1, **4**/80.2
St Bernard, **5**/50.2, **6**/12.2
St Cyprian, **5**/34.2
St Francis de Sales, **1**/12.3, **4**/25.1
St Gregory the Great, **2**/4.2, **4**/25.2
St Ignatius of Antioch, **4**/96.1
St John Chrysostom, **1**/12.2, **2**/22.3, **4**/14.1, **4**/59.1, **5**/34.2, **5**/50.2, **5**/61.2
St John Climacus, **2**/67.2
St John Paul II, **4**/14.3, **6**/20.1
St Peter Damian, **3**/92.2
St Peter of Alcantara, **1**/13.2
St Teresa, **1**/1.3, **2**/12.2
St Vincent of Lerins, **1**/6.3

Aspirations
St Teresa, **2**/35.3

Atonement
St Bernard, **6**/50.2

Baptism
Origen, **2**/70.3
St Augustine, **1**/51.1
St Cyril of Alexandria, **1**/50.1

St John Chrysostom, **2**/5.1
St John Paul II, **5**/43.2, **5**/59.2,
  6/3.2
St Leo the Great, **1**/51.1
St Thomas Aquinas, **6**/3.3

Blessed Trinity
St Augustine, **6**/40.3
St John of the Cross, **6**/40.1
St Teresa, **6**/40.2, **6**/40.3

Catechism
St John Paul II, **3**/13.2, **4**/86.2

Character
Cassian, **1**/11.1

Charity
St Alphonsus Liguori, **2**/22.2
St Augustine, **3**/52.2, **5**/23.1,
  5/52.1
St Bernard, **4**/85.3
St Cyprian, **2**/94.2, **5**/94.3
St Francis de Sales, **3**/100.1
St Jerome, **5**/23.1
St John Chrysostom, **4**/21.2
St Teresa, **3**/100.1
St Thomas Aquinas, **2**/44.2,
  4/1.2, **5**/15.3
Tertullian, **6**/4.3, **6**/52.3

Chastity
St Jean Vianney, **1**/23.3
St John Chrysostom, **1**/23.3,
  4/62.2, **4**/62.3
St John Paul II, **1**/23.1, **4**/62.2,
  4/83.2, **4**/83.3, **5**/90.3, **6**/22.1
St Leo the Great, **1**/16.3

Christ
Bl. Paul VI, **5**/18.3
Origen, **5**/31.2
Pius XI, **5**/91.1
Pius XII, **5**/52.2, **6**/49.3, **6**/50.1
St Ambrose, **5**/91.3
St Augustine, **1**/2.2, **1**/32.2,
  5/3.2, **5**/31.1, **5**/56.2
St Bernard, **5**/56.1
St Hippolytus, **5**/47.1

St John Chrysostom, **5**/6.1
St John of the Cross, **5**/96.2
St John Paul II, **5**/2.3, **5**/31.1,
  5/64.1, **6**/49.1, **6**/50.3
St Leo, **7**/12.2
St Teresa, **5**/61.3, **7**/35.2
St Thomas Aquinas, **1**/40.1,
  7/12.1

Church
Bl. Alvaro, **6**/18.3
Bl. Paul VI, **4**/18.3, **5**/47.2,
  6/8.1
Gregory XVI, **4**/73.3
Pius XI, **3**/10.2, **6**/8.2
Pius XII, **4**/37.3, **6**/8.2
St Ambrose, **4**/73.3, **5**/5.2
St Augustine, **5**/5.2
St Cyprian, **3**/10.2, **4**/13.3
St Cyril of Jerusalem, **3**/10.2
St Gregory the Great, **3**/10.2
St John Chrysostom, **5**/31.2
St Leo the Great, **4**/73.2
St John Paul II, **4**/37.2, **5**/28.1,
  5/41.2, **7**/40.3
St John XXIII, **3**/10.2

Civic Duties
St Ambrose, **4**/58.1
St Justin, **2**/33.2, **2**/70.2, **4**/58.2
St John Paul II, **5**/21.3
Tertullian, **4**/58.2

Communion of saints
St Ambrose, **5**/68.1
St John Paul II, **1**/10.3, **5**/68.1
St Teresa, **2**/66.1
St Thomas Aquinas, **5**/71.3, **6**/8.3

Compassion
Bl. Paul VI, **5**/15.1
St Augustine, **1**/4.3
St John Paul II, **1**/3.2, **1**/10.1,
  1/10.2, **5**/15.1, **5**/31.3
St Thomas Aquinas, **4**/64.2

Confession
Bl. Alvaro, **3**/7.2, **5**/27.2

Bl. Paul VI, **5**/27.2
St Ambrose, **2**/34.2
St Augustine, **3**/7.3, **4**/60.2
St Bede, **3**/4.1
St Gregory the Great, **2**/39.2
St Jean Vianney, **2**/55.2
St John Chrysostom, **2**/21.1,
  2/34.3
St John Paul II, **1**/4.2, **2**/1.1,
  2/18.3, **2**/34.1, **2**/34.3, **4**/46.3,
  5/5.3
St Thomas Aquinas, **2**/8.3,
  2/21.1
Conscience
St John Paul II, **2**/13.1
Contrition
St Augustine, **2**/41.2
St John Chrysostom, **4**/60.1
St Teresa, **5**/16.2
Conversation
St Augustine, **5**/15.3
St Gregory of Nyssa, **3**/19.2
St John Chrysostom, **5**/9.3
St John Paul II, **5**/6.2
Conversion
St Augustine, **7**/20
St John Paul II, **1**/10.1
Cowardice
St Basil, **2**/69.3
St John Chrysostom, **3**/89.3
Cross
St Athanasius, **3**/56.3
St Augustine, **4**/82.1
St Gregory the Great, **2**/12.1
St Irenaeus, **5**/28.3
St John Damascene, **7**/23.1
St John Paul II, **4**/82.1, **5**/22.2
St Thomas Aquinas, **5**/19.3
Death
Bl. Alvaro, **5**/97.3
Leo X, **5**/80.3
St Bede, **4**/2.2
St Ignatius Loyola, **5**/80.3

St Jerome, **4**/2.3
St John Paul II, **4**/2.1
Dedication
St Augustine, **5**/9.2, **5**/12.1
St Jerome, **3**/86.2
St John Paul II, **3**/104.2
Detachment
St Augustine, **5**/21.3
St Francis de Sales, **5**/24.2
St John of the Cross, **2**/16.1
St John Paul II, **5**/21.3, **5**/38.3
St Teresa, **2**/16.3
St Thomas Aquinas, **7**/50.3
Devil
Cassian, **2**/6.2
St Irenaeus, **2**/6.1
St Jean Vianney, **2**/6.2
St John of the Cross, **2**/6.3
St John Paul II, **2**/6.1, **2**/6.3,
  5/42.1
Tertullian, **5**/42.2
Difficulties
Bl. Alvaro, **4**/54.2
Bl. Paul VI, **2**/2.1
John Paul I, **5**/44.3
Pius XII, **2**/60.2, **5**/53.2
St Alphonsus Liguori, **5**/69.2
St Athanasius, **4**/3.1
St Augustine, **1**/32.1, **2**/24.3,
  2/64.3, **3**/98.3, **4**/8.1, **4**/25.1,
  5/16.2
St Bernard, **4**/96.1, **7**/43.2
St Cyprian, **1**/36.3
St Francis de Sales, **4**/25.1,
  6/30.2
St Gregory Nazianzen, **1**/13.1
St Gregory the Great, **3**/98.2,
  4/96.3, **5**/9.2, **5**/85.1
St Jean Vianney, **5**/61.1
St John Chrysostom, **1**/32.1,
  1/43.3, **2**/5.1, **2**/64.1, **2**/64.2,
  2/92.3, **4**/50.3
St John of the Cross, **4**/25.1

St John Paul II, **2**/29.3
St Teresa, **1**/32.3, **4**/25.3
St Theophilus of Antioch,
    5/53.2
St Thomas Aquinas, **2**/60.1

Divine filiation
St Athanasius, **5**/59.1
St Cyprian, **5**/33.1
St Cyril of Jerusalem, **6**/3.2
St Hippolytus, **6**/3.2
St John Chrysostom, **4**/24.3,
    7/5.2
St John Paul II, **1**/17.1, **4**/32,
    5/59.1, **5**/59.2
St Teresa, **5**/60.3
St Thomas Aquinas, **1**/24.3, **1**/36.2,
    1/36.3, **4**/32.1, **4**/98.1, **5**/33.1,
    5/59.1, **5**/59.2, **5**/64.2, **5**/75.3
Tertullian, **5**/33.2

Docility
St John Paul II, **7**/5.1

Doctrine
St Pius X, **7**/5.1

Duties
John Paul I, **5**/51.2
St Gregory the Great, **2**/13.3

Early Christians
St Clement, **6**/58.2
St John Chrysostom, **5**/79.1,
    6/58.2
St John Paul II, **5**/2.1, **5**/8.2
St Justin, **2**/70.2

Ecumenism
Bl. Paul VI, **6**/5.2
St John Paul II, **6**/4.3

Eucharist
Bl. Alvaro, **3**/46.2
Bl. Paul VI, **1**/2.2, **1**/2.3,
    2/44.1, **2**/49.2, **2**/65.1, **2**/65.2,
    3/4.3, **4**/43.2, **4**/56.2, **5**/89.3,
    6/5.1, **6**/41.3, **6**/43.1, **6**/45.3
Cassian, **6**/47.2
St Alphonsus Liguori, **1**/2.1,

6/44.2, **6**/47.1
St Ambrose, **5**/40.2, **5**/40.3,
    6/46.2
St Augustine, **2**/56.2, **4**/47,
    6/42.2, **6**/45.2, **6**/47.1
St Cyril of Jerusalem, **4**/47.2,
    4/56.2, **6**/43.1
St Fulgentius, **2**/65.3
St Gregory the Great, **4**/70.3
St Ignatius of Antioch, **2**/65.3
St Irenaeus, **4**/65.2
St Jean Vianney, **2**/65.3, **4**/65.3
St John Chrysostom, **1**/2.1,
    4/70.1
St John of the Cross, **5**/7.3
St John Paul II, **2**/51.2, **4**/46.3,
    4/47.1, **4**/65.3, **4**/70.2, **4**/70.3,
    6/41.1, **6**/41.2
St Pius X, **1**/2.3
St Teresa, **6**/45.2
St Thomas Aquinas, **2**/65.3,
    3/4.1, **3**/103.2, **4**/43.3, **6**/43.2,
    6/46.1 **6**/46.3, **6**/47.1

Evangelisation
Bl. Paul VI, **5**/20.2, **5**/20.3,
    6/9.2, **6**/13.2
St John Paul II, **2**/32.1, **2**/32.3,
    4/87.3, **5**/12.2, **6**/12.3, **6**/18.2

Examination of conscience
Bl. Alvaro, **4**/93.1
St Augustine, **1**/19.2
St John Chrysostom, **4**/57.2
St John Climacus, **4**/93.2
St John of the Cross, **4**/93.1
St Teresa, **4**/93.3

Example
St Ambrose, **5**/13.2
St Gregory the Great, **2**/32.2
St Ignatius of Antioch, **5**/1.2
St John Chrysostom, **4**/40.2,
    4/72.1, **4**/72.2, **5**/62.2
St John Paul II, **4**/4.3, **4**/73.1
St Teresa, **5**/62.2

Faith
Bl. Alvaro, **6**/18.3
Bl. Paul VI, **6**/6.2
Pius XII, **3**/55.2, **5**/53.2
St Ambrose, **1**/6.1, **4**/13.1,
  5/64.2
St Augustine, **2**/54.3, **4**/54.1,
  4/55.3, **5**/4.2, **5**/48.3, **5**/51.3
St Gregory Nazianzen, **5**/26.1
St Gregory the Great, **2**/54.2,
  2/54.3, **6**/45.1
St Jean Vianney, **3**/44.2
St John Chrysostom, **2**/63.1,
  3/55.1, **3**/89.1, **4**/55.3
St John Paul II, **1**/44.3, **2**/67.1,
  6/6.2, **6**/13.2, **7**/1.3, **7**/12.2
St Justin, **6**/52.1
St Vincent of Lerins, **6**/6.1
St Teresa, **4**/55.1

Family life
St Augustine, **7**/19.1
St John Chrysostom, **2**/70.3
St John Paul II, **1**/31.2, **2**/14.3,
  3/95.1, **4**/91.1, **4**/91.3, **5**/29.3,
  7/6.2, **7**/19, **7**/28.2, **7**/54.3
St Thomas Aquinas, **5**/29.3

Fear
St Augustine, **3**/99.1
St John Chrysostom, **6**/12.3
St John Paul II, **2**/93.3, **5**/82.2
St Teresa, **2**/93.1, **2**/93.3

Forgiveness
St Ambrose, **3**/5.1
St Augustine, **1**/37.2
St John Chrysostom, **3**/54.2,
  4/61.3, **5**/41.3
St John of the Cross, **5**/1.1
St John Paul II, **5**/1.3
St Therese of Lisieux, **5**/3.1
St Thomas Aquinas, **4**/60.2

Fraternity
Bl. Paul VI, **5**/20.3
St Augustine, **3**/52.2

St Cyprian, **5**/41.3
St Francis de Sales, **5**/78.3
St Gregory the Great, **5**/78.2
St John Chrysostom, **5**/79.1,
  5/88.3
St Leo the Great, **4**/10.2
St John Paul II, **5**/78.3,
Tertullian, **4**/79.2

Freedom
St John Paul II, **4**/74.2, **4**/74.3

Friendship
Bl. Paul VI, **2**/80.2
St Ambrose, **4**/41.2, **4**/41.3,
  4/89.3
St Bernard, **4**/89.1
St Teresa, **1**/36.1
St Thomas Aquinas, **2**/80.2,
  3/5.2

Generosity
Pastor of Hermas, **5**/92.2
St Ambrose, **4**/94.1
St Augustine, **5**/67.2, **5**/74.3,
  5/92.1
St Gregory the Great, **1**/26.2
St Ignatius of Antioch, **4**/97.1
St John Chrysostom, **5**/74.1
St John Paul II, **1**/18.3, **5**/8.3
St Teresa, **1**/26.3, **5**/74.3
St Thomas Aquinas, **5**/74.2

Good Shepherd
St Ambrose, **2**/4.3
St Augustine, **1**/7.2
St Thomas of Villanueva, **1**/7.2

Grace
St Augustine, **5**/77.2, **6**/12.2
St Bede, **4**/99.2
St Irenaeus, **1**/51.1
St John Chrysostom, **4**/97.2
St Teresa, **6**/12.2
St Thomas Aquinas, **2**/17.3,
  4/2.2, **5**/30.1

Heaven
St Augustine, **2**/82.3

St Cyprian, **3**/97.1
St Cyril of Jerusalem, **2**/82.1
St John Chrysostom, **2**/12.2
St John Paul II, **3**/58.2
St Leo the Great, **2**/86.2

Hell
St Teresa, **3**/58.2, **5**/73.2
St Thomas Aquinas, **5**/90.1,
  5/97.2, **5**/97.3

Holy Spirit
Bl. Paul VI, **2**/87.1
Leo XIII, **2**/83.1
St Augustine, **2**/95.3
St Cyril of Jerusalem, **2**/95.3,
  2/96.2
St Francis de Sales, **2**/96.2
St John Paul II, **5**/45.1
St Thomas Aquinas, **2**/90.3,
  3/5.3, **5**/45.1

Hope
John Paul I, **5**/93.3
St Ambrose, **5**/66.3
St Augustine, **1**/4.1, **2**/74.1
St Bernard, **2**/74.3
St John Paul II, **4**/57.1

Human dignity
St John Paul II, **7**/28.3

Humility
John Paul I, **5**/47.3
Leo XIII, **1**/27.1
St Ambrose, **5**/77.1
St Augustine, **1**/2.2, **1**/27.2,
  1/47.3, **5**/21.1, **5**/39.2, **5**/57.2,
  5/60.2
St Bede, **3**/4.1
St Bernard, **3**/45.2
St Cyril of Alexandria, **1**/50.1
St Francis de Sales, **1**/27.2,
  4/84.1, **4**/84.3
St Gregory the Great, **1**/8.2
St Jean Vianney, **1**/27.2
St John Chrysostom, **4**/84.1
St John Paul II, **1**/27.1, **5**/74.2

St Thomas Aquinas, **1**/27.2

Ignorance
St John XXIII, **2**/32.1
St John Chrysostom, **3**/18.2

Incarnation
St Augustine, **3**/3.1

Instruments of God
Cassian, **2**/20.2
John Paul I, **5**/2.1, **5**/65.2
Leo XIII, **5**/77.1
St Augustine, **5**/51.3, **5**/54.2
St Gregory the Great, **3**/98.2
St John Chrysostom, **2**/14.1,
  3/88.2, **4**/55.3
St Pius X, **5**/77.3
St Thomas Aquinas, **2**/70.1,
  5/12.3
St John Paul II, **5**/43.2
Theophylact, **5**/54.2

Interior Life
Bl. Alvaro, **4**/30.1
St John Paul II, **6**/4.3

Joy
Bl. Paul VI, **2**/26.2, **2**/48.3,
  5/27.1
St Basil, **4**/67.3
St Bede, **2**/12.2
St John Chrysostom, **4**/26.1
St Leo the Great, **1**/30.3
St John Paul II, **1**/30.2, **2**/77.1,
  3/15.3
St Thomas Aquinas, **2**/48.3,
  2/94.1, **3**/15.3, **7**/47.2
St Thomas More, **1**/39.2

Justice
Bl. Paul VI, **4**/12.3
St Cyril of Jerusalem, **5**/83.2
St John Chrysostom, **4**/85.2
St John XXIII, **4**/77.1
St John Paul II, **1**/35.3, **2**/75.1,
  3/19.1, **4**/12.2, **4**/16.3, **4**/77.3
St Thomas Aquinas, **2**/75.1,
  4/77.2, **5**/17.3, **5**/27.2, **5**/55.2

Leisure
Bl. Paul VI, **5**/17.1
St Augustine, **4**/29.1, **4**/29.2
St Gregory Nazianzen, **4**/29.1
St Teresa, **4**/29.2

Lent
St John Paul II, **2**/1.1, **2**/8.2

Little things
St Augustine, **1**/16.2
St Bernard, **5**/39.2
St John Chrysostom, **2**/22.3
St Francis de Sales, **4**/57.2

Love
St Augustine, **3**/52.2
St Gregory of Nyssa, **2**/93.2
St John Chrysostom, **4**/71.2
St John of the Cross, **2**/14.3,
    4/1.2
St John Paul II, **4**/1.2, **5**/8.2,
    5/64.2, **5**/64.3, **5**/88.1
St Teresa, **2**/14.3, **5**/55.2
St Thomas Aquinas, **4**/97.2

Love of God
Clement of Alexandria, **5**/3.1
John Paul I, **2**/24.3, **5**/53.3,
    5/65.1
St Alphonsus Liguori, **4**/66.1
St Ambrose, **5**/28.2
St Augustine, **2**/49.2, **4**/1.3,
    4/92.3, **5**/65.2
St Bernard, **3**/99.1
St Catherine of Siena, **3**/50.2
St Francis de Sales, **5**/77.2
St John Chrysostom, **2**/24.1,
    5/39.2
St John of the Cross, **2**/69.2,
    3/104.2, **4**/95.2
St John Paul II, **3**/104.3, **4**/95.1,
    5/5.1, **5**/5.3, **5**/38.2, **5**/66.2,
    5/75.3
St Teresa, **2**/4.1, **2**/69.1, **2**/69.2,
    5/14.1, **5**/57.3, **5**/92.3, **5**/95.3
St Thomas Aquinas, **4**/66.2,

    5/65.2

Lukewarmness
St Augustine, **5**/3.3
St Gregory the Great, **1**/12.2,
    5/55.1
St John Chrysostom, **4**/19.3, **4**/54.3
St John of the Cross, **4**/19.2,
    5/76.2
St Pius X, **3**/102.3
St Teresa, **4**/19.2
St Thomas Aquinas, **5**/30.1

Marxism
Bl. Paul VI, **2**/33.3

Marriage
John Paul I, **5**/29.2
St Francis de Sales, **4**/62.1
St John Chrysostom, **4**/62.2
St John Paul II, **4**/62.2, **5**/29.1

Mass
Bl. Paul VI, **2**/30.2
Pius XII, **5**/52.2, **5**/92.2
St Augustine, **2**/36.3
St Ephraim, **4**/26.2
St Gregory the Great, **2**/66.2
St Jean Vianney, **2**/30.2, **4**/7.1,
    4/7.3
St John Chrysostom, **4**/26.2
St John Paul II, **2**/30.2, **2**/30.3

Materialism
Bl. Alvaro, **4**/82.2
Bl. Paul VI, **5**/49.1
John Paul I, **5**/46.3
St Augustine, **5**/58.2
St Gregory the Great, **5**/58.2
St John Paul II, **4**/82.2, **5**/25.1,
    7/2.1
St John XXIII, **2**/58.2

Mercy
Clement of Alexandria, **5**/3.1
St Augustine, **5**/15.2, **5**/93.2
St Bernard, **5**/56.2
St Francis de Sales, **5**/93.2
St John Paul II, **4**/85.1, **5**/1.3,

5/3.2, 5/5.1, 5/5.2, 5/81.2
St Therese of Lisieux, 5/3.3
St Thomas Aquinas, 3/42.1,
   5/5.1, 5/17.3, 5/41.2, 5/70.2,
   5/81.2

Morning Offering
St Bernard, 2/79.1
Cassian, 2/79.2

Mortification
Bl. Paul VI, 2/15.2, 2/19.1
St Augustine, 4/8.1
St Francis de Sales, 2/1.1
St Jean Vianney, 5/26.1
St John Chrysostom, 2/15.2,
   4/8.2
St John of the Cross, 2/2.1,
   2/19.2
St Leo the Great, 2/19.1
St Peter of Alcantara, 3/101.2
St Teresa, 2/19.2

Obedience
Cassian, 2/20.2
St Augustine, 1/49.1
St Gregory the Great, 1/5.2,
   1/49.2, 5/19.3
St John Chrysostom, 1/5.3,
   1/45.1
St Teresa, 1/49.3, 5/19.1, 5/19.3
St Thomas Aquinas, 4/88.2,
   5/19.2
St John Paul II, 4/94.3, 7/12.2

Optimism
St Teresa, 4/49.1
St Thomas Aquinas, 4/49.2

Our Lady
Benedict XV, 3/105.2, 7/13.2
Bl. Alvaro, 3/28.2
Bl. Paul VI, 1/38.3, 2/48.3,
   2/84.1, 2/84.3, 2/95.1, 2/95.3,
   3/40.3, 3/105.3, 7/3.2
Leo XIII, 2/25.3, 3/45.3,
   5/18.1, 7/26.3, 7/34.1
Origen, 3/105.3

Pius IX, 1/25.1, 7/17.2
Pius XII, 2/95.1, 7/3.1, 7/14.2,
   7/17.2
St Alphonsus Liguori, 1/21.3,
   3/9.1, 4/99.2, 5/81.3, 7/9.2,
   7/9.3, 7/41.3, 7/49.3
St Amadeus of Lausanne,
   7/14.1
St Ambrose, 1/50.3
St Andrew of Crete, 7/22.1
St Augustine, 1/23.1, 1/47.3
St Bernard, 1/18.3, 1/38.3,
   1/40.3, 2/9.3, 2/74.3, 2/79.1,
   3/42.2, 3/98.3, 5/48.2, 5/92.3,
   6/1.1, 6/1.2, 6/15.2, 6/16.1,
   6/31.2, 7/11.3, 7/15.3, 7/43.3
St Bonaventure, 7/22.1
St Catherine of Siena, 6/28.3
St Cyril of Alexandria, 1/38.1,
   7/11.2
St Ephraim, 7/17.1
St Francis de Sales, 5/63.2
St Germanus of Constantinople,
   5/18.2
St Ildephonsus of Toledo, 7/15.2
St Jean Vianney, 2/30.2, 5/63.1
St John Damascene, 2/46.3,
   7/6.1, 7/14.2
St John Paul II, 1/22.3, 1/31.3,
   1/38.2, 2/47.3, 2/56.3, 2/84.3,
   2/95.1, 3/9.2, 3/38.3, 3/42.1,
   4/90.2, 4/90.3, 4/94.3, 4/99.1,
   4/99.3, 5/14.2, 5/18.1, 5/36.1,
   6/10.1, 6/10.3, 6/28.2, 6/31.1,
   6/51.3, 7/3.2, 7/3.3, 7/6.3,
   7/9.1, 7/11.1, 7/15.2, 7/24.3
St Peter Damian, 4/90.1, 7/22.3
St Teresa, 6/31.3, 7/3.2
St Thomas Aquinas, 1/41.1,
   4/90.1, 4/99.3, 5/18.1, 7/43.2
St Vincent Ferrer, 7/3.2

Passion
St Alphonsus Liguori, 2/37.1

St Augustine, 2/39.2, 2/45.1
St John Chrysostom, 2/37.1
St John Paul II, 5/22.2
St Leo the Great, 2/37.1
St Thomas Aquinas, 2/37.1

Patience
St Augustine, 5/94.1
St Francis de Sales, 5/94.2
St Gregory Nazianzen, 5/54.3
St John Chrysostom, 2/28.1,
  2/28.3
St John of the Cross, 5/5.1
St Thomas Aquinas, 5/94.2

Peace
Bl. Paul VI, 2/33.1, 4/12.3
St Augustine, 2/77.2, 2/94.1,
  3/98.3
St Gregory Nazianzen, 2/56.2
St Irenaeus, 2/56.2
St John Chrysostom, 1/3.2
St John of the Cross, 4/25.1
St John Paul II, 1/3.1, 1/3.3

Penance
Bl. Paul VI, 2/3.1
St Ambrose, 3/90.3
St Cyril of Jerusalem, 5/75.2
St Gregory the Great, 3/90.1
St John Chrysostom, 3/90.2
St John Paul II, 3/85.2, 5/1.3,
  5/41.1

Perseverance
Cassian, 2/39.1
St Augustine, 5/4.3, 5/81.1,
  5/86.3
St Gregory the Great, 7/4.1
St John Chrysostom, 4/80.2
St John Paul II, 5/57.1, 5/86.2
St Teresa, 2/92.2, 5/57.3
St Thomas Aquinas, 2/92.2

Poverty
St Augustine, 5/24.3, 7/31.2
St Gregory the Great, 2/16.2,
  2/16.3

St John Chrysostom, 4/48.2
St Leo the Great, 2/1.2

Prayer
Bl. Paul VI, 5/14.3
St Alphonsus Liguori, 2/12.3,
  2/81.3, 5/48.1, 5/57.2, 7/9.1
St Augustine, 2/9.3, 4/39.2,
  4/64.1, 4/64.2, 5/48.1, 5/48.3,
  5/56.2, 5/81.1, 5/95.2
St Bernard, 5/48.1
St Cyprian, 3/94.1
St Gregory the Great, 3/40.3
St Jean Vianney, 2/9.1, 3/40.1,
  7/35.1
St John Chrysostom, 2/68.2,
  4/64.3
St John of the Cross, 3/51.1
St John Paul II, 1/29.2, 3/93.1,
  4/39.1, 39.3, 4/91.1, 4/91.3,
  4/95.2, 5/33.1, 5/57.1, 7/32.1
St Peter of Alcantara, 3/51.2,
  5/57.3
St Teresa, 1/29.2, 1/29.3, 2/9.3,
  2/15.1, 2/27.1, 2/27.3, 3/51.2,
  3/94.1, 4/95.2, 5/14.1, 5/34.1,
  5/57.1, 5/57.3, 6/18.2, 7/35.1
St Thomas Aquinas, 3/40.2,
  4/64.2, 4/80.3

Presence of God
St Alphonsus Liguori, 5/61.1
St Augustine, 2/76.1, 2/76.2,
  4/30.1
St Basil, 5/72.2
St Gregory the Great, 2/76.2
St John of the Cross, 2/76.2
St John Paul II, 2/61.2, 5/83.1

Pride
Cassian, 2/14.1, 5/63.3
St Ambrose, 5/54.1
St John Chrysostom, 2/25.2,
  2/63.1, 2/63.3, 5/33.3
St Gregory the Great, 2/63.2
St Thomas Aquinas, 5/55.1

Priesthood
Bl. Alvaro, **1**/51.3, **5**/11.2
St Ambrose, **7**/10.3
St Catherine of Siena, **4**/20.3
St Ephraim, **5**/71.1
St John Paul II, **1**/7.2, **4**/20.1,
  5/57.1, **6**/9.3, **7**/10.1, **7**/10.2

Providence, divine
Cassian, **5**/33.2
St Augustine, **5**/60.2
St Bernard, **3**/96.3
St Jerome, **3**/97.2
St John Paul II, **3**/96.1
St Thomas Aquinas, **3**/96.2

Prudence
St Augustine, **4**/17.1
St John Paul II, **4**/17.1, **4**/17.2
St Teresa, **5**/93.2

Purgatory
St Catherine of Genoa, **7**/39.1
St John Paul II, **7**/39.1
St Teresa, **7**/39.1

Purity
St Ambrose, **5**/90.1
St John Paul II, **3**/8.1, **5**/75.3

Reading of the Gospel
St Augustine, **2**/73.1, **2**/73.3,
  4/86.3, **5**/96.3
St Cyprian, **5**/96.3
St Jerome, **7**/8.3
St John Chrysostom, **5**/96.1
St John Paul II, **4**/86.2

Responsibility
St Augustine, **5**/9.3
St Gregory the Great, **2**/63.2,
  5/68.2
St Ignatius of Antioch, **5**/79.2
St Thomas Aquinas, **5**/51.2

Roman Pontiff
St Ambrose, **6**/7.2
St Augustine, **6**/19.1, **6**/19.3
St Catherine of Siena, **6**/7.2
St Cyprian, **6**/19.1

St John Paul II, **6**/7.3
St Leo the Great, **6**/7.2, **6**/19.2

Rosary
Bl. Paul VI, **2**/81.1, **2**/81.2,
  5/18.3, **5**/36.2
Pius XI, **5**/36.2, **7**/32.3
Pius XII, **2**/81.1
St John Paul II, **2**/81.2, **5**/36.2,
  5/36.3
St John XXIII, **2**/81.1, **7**/33.1

Sacraments
St Augustine, **2**/46.1
St John Chrysostom, **4**/36.1
St Pius X, **4**/46.3

Saints, devotion to
St Catherine of Siena, **6**/32.1
St Jerome, **3**/72.2
St John Paul II, **3**/72.2, **6**/2

St John the Baptist
St Augustine, **1**/8.1
St John Chrysostom, **6**/55.3

St Joseph
Leo XIII, **4**/15.2, **6**/20.1, **6**/26.3
St Ambrose, **1**/22.1
St Augustine, **1**/22.2
St Bernard, **4**/15.3
St Bernardine of Siena, **1**/40.3,
  6/20.3, **6**/25.3
St Francis de Sales, **6**/25.2
St John Chrysostom, **6**/24.1
St John Paul II, **5**/64.3, **5**/84.3,
  6/20.2, **6**/26.3, **6**/27.3
St John XXIII, **6**/26.3
St Teresa, **1**/45.2, **4**/15.2,
  6/26.1, **6**/26.3

St Thomas More, **6**/54.3

Sanctity
Cassian, **5**/32.3
St John Paul II, **3**/7.3, **4**/4.3,
  5/58.3, **6**/21.3, **7**/38.1

Search for God
St Augustine, **5**/16.3, **5**/37.2,
  7/4.2

St Bernard, **5**/50.3
St Ignatius of Antioch, **5**/32.3
St John of the Cross, **2**/10.2
St John Paul II, **5**/66.1

Self-giving
St Augustine, **5**/3.3
St Gregory the Great, **5**/92.1
St John Paul II, **1**/26.1, **5**/90.3

Service
St Augustine, **5**/3.3
St John Chrysostom, **2**/24.1
St John Paul II, **2**/15.3, **5**/47.3

Simplicity
St Jerome, **1**/24.3
St John Chrysostom, **1**/24.3

Sin
Bl. Paul VI, **1**/51.1
Origen, **5**/93.1
St Augustine, **2**/17.3, **2**/21.3,
    5/31.1, **5**/45.2, **5**/93.1
St Bede, **5**/31.1
St Francis de Sales, **2**/17.3
St Gregory the Great, **5**/9.1
St Jean Vianney, **2**/17.1, **3**/44.2
St John Chrysostom, **4**/85.2
St John of the Cross, **4**/2.2,
    5/45.3
St John Paul II, **2**/17.1, **2**/17.3,
    2/18.2, **2**/29.2, **3**/56.3, **4**/2.2,
    4/34.1, **4**/34.2, **5**/3.2, **5**/41.1,
    5/45.1, **5**/45.2, **5**/70.1, **5**/71.2

Sincerity
St Augustine, **7**/18.2, **7**/18.3
St Francis de Sales, **2**/23.3
St John Chrysostom, **2**/23.1
St Thomas Aquinas, **5**/44.2

Society
Bl. Alvaro, **4**/12.2
Bl. Paul VI, **1**/35.1
Pius XI, **3**/37.1
St John Chrysostom, **3**/52.1

Spiritual childhood
Cassian, **5**/34.1

St Alphonsus Liguori, **5**/57.2
St Ambrose, **4**/63.3
Spiritual direction
St John Climacus, **1**/7.3
St John of the Cross, **4**/76.1,
    5/85.2
St Teresa, **5**/85.2
St Thomas Aquinas, **5**/19.3
St Vincent Ferrer, **4**/92.3
Spiritual reading
St Augustine, **3**/18.2
St Basil, **3**/43.2, **3**/43.3
St Jerome, **7**/36.3
St John Chrysostom, **7**/8.2
St John Eudes, **7**/8.3
St Peter of Alcantara, **7**/8.3
Suffering
St Augustine, **5**/69.2
St Bede, **7**/20.2
St Francis de Sales, **2**/31.2
St John Chrysostom, **2**/64.3,
    5/31.1
St John Paul II, **2**/31.3, **5**/15.1,
    5/15.2, **5**/22.2, **5**/69.1, **6**/17.3,
    6/22.1
St Teresa, **5**/69.3
St Thomas More, **2**/38.3
Supernatural outlook
Bl. Paul VI, **5**/83.3
Pius XII, **3**/55.2
St Augustine, **5**/34.1, **5**/80.1
St Bede, **4**/69.2
St Gregory the Great, **4**/80.2
St John Chrysostom, **4**/82.1
St John Paul II, **5**/58.3, **5**/97.1
St John XXIII, **5**/89.3
St Teresa, **5**/76.3
St Theophilus, **3**/55.2
Temperance
St John Paul II, **4**/35
St Peter Alcantara, **4**/35.1
Temptations
St Athanasius, **4**/3.1

St Basil, **5**/9.2

St Thomas Aquinas, **5**/42.2, **6**/3.3

Time

Bl. Paul VI, **5**/17.1

St Augustine, **4**/65.3

Trust in God

Tertullian, **5**/42.2

St Augustine, **2**/4.3, **5**/67.2, **5**/93.1

St Cyprian, **5**/35.2

St Francis de Sales, **5**/43.3

St Teresa, **5**/60.3, **5**/65.1

St Thomas Aquinas, **5**/33.2

St Thomas More, **5**/61.3

Truth

St Augustine, **4**/18.3

St John Chrysostom, **4**/28.2

St Thomas Aquinas, **5**/44.2

Understanding

St Augustine, **2**/21.2

St Gregory the Great, **2**/72.2

St Jerome, **2**/72.1, **4**/27.3

St John Paul II, **7**/18.2

St Teresa, **2**/87.2

Unity

Aristides, **2**/56.3

Bl. Paul VI, **2**/56.2, **6**/5.2

Cassian, **3**/72.2

Pius XI, **5**/87.3, **5**/91.2

St Augustine, **2**/56.3, **2**/78.3, **4**/92.1

St Cyprian, **4**/13.3

St Irenaeus, **2**/56.1, **2**/56.2

St John Chrysostom, **2**/56.1, **3**/50.7

St John Paul II, **2**/56.1, **2**/56.2, **3**/57.1, **5**/32.2, **5**/68.2, **6**/18.1

St Thomas Aquinas, **2**/56.2

Virtues

Bl. Alvaro, **2**/22.2, **4**/33.1

Pius XI, **4**/33.1

St Augustine, **3**/19.3, **3**/100.1

St Francis de Sales, **3**/6.2

St Gregory the Great, **4**/25.2

St Jerome, **3**/86.3

St John Chrysostom, **3**/52.1

St Teresa, **3**/54.3, **3**/100.1

St Thomas Aquinas, **3**/6.2

Visit to the Blessed Sacrament

Bl. Paul VI, **4**/56.3

Pius XII, **2**/51.2

St Alphonsus Liguori, **2**/51.3, **4**/56.3

St John Chrysostom, **2**/51.3

St Teresa, **2**/51.3

Vocation

Bl. Alvaro, **2**/32.1,

John Paul I, **1**/45.1

Pius XI, **4**/22.2

St Bernard, **4**/22.1

St Bernardine of Siena, **6**/20.3

St Gregory the Great, **3**/88.2

St John Chrysostom, **7**/25.1

St John Paul II, **4**/22.3, **5**/38.2, **5**/43.1, **5**/90.2, **7**/29.2, **7**/45.1

St Thomas Aquinas, **6**/20.2, **7**/45.2

Will of God

St John Paul II, **5**/43.1

St Augustine, **5**/35.1

St Teresa, **5**/57.2, **5**/35.3

Worldly Respect

St Bede, **5**/44.2

St Jean Vianney, **2**/62.1

St Thomas Aquinas, **5**/30.1

Work

Bl. Alvaro, **4**/30.3

Didache, **4**/78.1

St John Chrysostom, **1**/43.1, **3**/41.2

St John Paul II, **1**/46.2, **3**/11.2, **5**/13.2, **5**/32.2, **5**/84.3

St John XXIII, **3**/11.2

SUBJECT INDEX

Abandonment
  and responsibility, **3**/96.2, **7**/46.2
  confidence in God's Will, **3**/61.1, **3**/96.1, **5**/35, **5**/53.1, **5**/58.1
  healthy concern for *today*, **3**/61.3
  omnia in bonum, **3**/96.3, **5**/58.3, **5**/60.2
  unnecessary worries, **3**/61.2, **5**/17.3, **5**/82.3

Advent
  expectation of second coming, **1**/20.1
  joy of, **1**/2.1
  meaning of, **1**/1.3
  period of hope, **1**/21.1
  period of joy, **1**/15.1
  preparation for Christmas, **1**/1.1

Affability
  3/6.1, **3**/6.2, **3**/6.3

Angels
  7/27, **7**/28, **7**/29, **7**/30

Anger
  can be just and virtuous, **1**/11.3

Anointing of the Sick
  2/31.3, **3**/31

Apostolate
  a duty, **2**/53.1, **2**/85.1, **3**/21.3, **3**/69.1, **4**/40.3, **5**/10.2, **5**/25.1, **5**/51.3, **5**/87.3, **6**/30.3, **7**/2.3
  ad fidem, **1**/44.3, **4**/21.1
  and difficulties, **1**/9.2, **1**/41.3, **2**/32.3, **2**/53.2, **2**/62.2, **3**/89.2, **5**/52.1, **6**/52.3, **6**/57.3, **6**/58.2
  and doctrine, **4**/18.1, **5**/46.3

and example, **2**/32.2, **4**/44.3, **5**/13.1, **5**/51.2, **5**/76.3, **6**/58.1
and faith, **3**/5.1, **7**/34.3
and God's help, **1**/9.2, **2**/59.2, **5**/26.1, **5**/52, **6**/34.3
and humility, **1**/8.2, **5**/57.2
and joy, **1**/15.3, **3**/68.3, **3**/69.1, **5**/25.3, **5**/27.2, **5**/55.1, **5**/55.3, **7**/4.3
and meekness, **1**/11.3
and optimism, **2**/53.3, **3**/21.2
and patience, **2**/52.2, **2**/52.3, **3**/21.2, **5**/94.3
and prayer, **3**/3.1, **3**/88.2, **5**/57.1, **7**/46.3
and prudence, **3**/5.2
and proselytism, **2**/62.2, **5**/10.2, **7**/46.2
and worldly respect, **2**/62.3, **3**/89.3, **4**/44, **5**/30.1, **5**/44.2, **5**/62, **5**/72.3
basis of, **1**/9.1, **3**/3.3, **3**/35.2, **3**/68.1, **5**/10.2
being instruments, **3**/21.1, **3**/36.3, **5**/51.3, **5**/52
constancy in, **1**/12.2, **2**/85.2, **4**/69.2, **5**/20.2, **5**/50.2, **5**/68.3, **5**/94.3, **6**/2.3, **7**/55.3
fruits of, **2**/85.2, **3**/21.3, **5**/52.2, **5**/68.3, **5**/91.3
how to do it, **2**/52.3, **2**/59.3, needs formation, **2**/54.3
of friendship, **1**/8.3, **1**/9.2, **2**/53.3, **5**/25.2, **7**/42.2
of public opinion, **4**/45.2, **4**/45.3, **5**/44, **6**/32.2, **7**/2.2
part of the Christian vocation,

1/8.1, 2/53.1, 2/86.3, 3/69.2,
5/72.2

role of women, 2/85.3, 5/8,
7/36.1

universal meaning of, 1/44.3,
5/37.3, 5/43.1, 6/58.3, 7/25.3

upright intention, 2/62.3

virtues required, 3/36.1, 3/36.2,
3/36.3, 4/33.3, 5/20.1, 6/11.2

witnesses to Christ, 1/6.2,
1/8.3, 3/35.2, 4/66.3, 5/66.3,
5/87.3, 6/53, 7/2

Ascetical Struggle
beginning again, 1/12.2, 1/12.3,
1/24.3, 2/28.2, 4/14.3, 5/9.3,
5/50.2, 5/60.2, 5/70.2, 6/30.2,
7/20.2

constancy, 2/28.1, 4/14.1,
5/42.3, 5/48.1, 5/70.2, 5/94

develop a spirit of, 1/13.3,
1/19.1, 1/43.3, 5/34.2, 5/43.2

expect defeats, 1/12.3, 4/14.2,
5/93.3

fortitude in the face of
weaknesses, 1/12.1, 1/45.3,
4/11.2, 5/42.2, 5/61.2, 5/70.2,
5/93

until the last moments, 1/12.1,
5/97.3

Aspirations
1/29.3, 1/40.2, 1/40.3, 2/35.3

remembering to say, 2/35.2

Atonement
6/35.3, 49.3, 6/50.2

Baptism
effects of, 1/51.2, 5/43, 5/59,
5/71.2

gratitude for having received it,
1/51.1

incorporation into the Church,
1/51.3, 4/13.2

institution of, 1/51.1

of children, 1/51.3

Beatitudes
3/25.1, 3/25.2

Blessed Trinity
2/76.1, 6/3.1, 6/39, 6/40

Calumny
3/19.1, 3/19.2, 3/19.3

Celibacy
see Chastity, Virginity

Charity
and forgiveness, 2/21.1, 2/21.2,
2/21.3, 5/1.1

and judgements, 2/72.1, 5/41.3

effectiveness of, 2/72.3, 4/10.1,
5/20.3, 5/68.2, 5/94.3

its essence, 3/27.1, 3/27.2,
5/23.1, 5/31.3, 5/52.1, 5/79.3,
6/50.3

ordered, 1/25.3, 3/81.2, 4/21.3

sins of omission, 4/21.2

understanding, 2/72.1, 2/72.2,
3/52.1, 3/52.2, 3/81.3, 5/11.2,
5/6.1, 5/15.3, 5/67.3, 5/93.2

Chastity
and little things, 1/16.2, 5/90.3

clean of heart shall see God,
1/16.3, 3/8.1, 3/48.1, 5/16.1,
5/53.2, 5/75.3, 5/90

fruits of purity, 1/23.2, 5/63.3,
5/75.3, 5/90

guard of the heart, 1/16.2,
5/90.3

purity of heart, 1/16.1, 1/19.3,
1/23.1, 4/62.3, 5/90

ways of living purity well,
1/23.3, 3/8.2, 3/8.3, 5/90.3

Christians
early, 2/70.1, 5/52.3, 5/62.3,
5/68.3, 5/71.1, 5/74.2, 5/79.1,
5/84.1, 5/86.2

exemplary, 2/29.1, 2/70.2, 3/74,
3/102

Christmas
a call to interior purification,
1/16.1
humility and simplicity in
knowing Christ, 1/30.2
joy at, 1/30.3
receiving Christ, 1/30.1
the *Chair of Bethlehem,* 1/30.2
Church
characteristics of, 3/10.1,
3/57.3, 4/37.1, 5/5.2, 6/8
indefectibility, 2/60.1, 4/37.2,
4/37.3
its institution, 3/47.1, 6/4.1
love for, 2/59.2, 3/10.3, 4/13.1,
4/13.3, 7/16.3
mission of, 4/16.1, 4/16.2,
5/1.3, 5/28.1, 5/31.2, 5/41.1,
5/47.2, 5/48.2, 5/75.3, 5/87.1
prayer for, 3/47.2, 6/4.2, 7/27.3
Civic Duties
4/58.1, 5/21, 5/51.2, 5/67, 5/74
Commandments of God
first, 3/76.1, 3/76.2, 3/76.3,
5/55.2, 5/65.1
fourth, 3/38.1, 3/38.2, 3/38.3
ninth, 3/86.1, 3/86.2, 3/86.3
second, 5/34
Communion
confession, a preparation for,
1/2.3, 5/7.3
dispositions for, 1/2.1, 1/2.2,
5/7.3
effects of, 2/65.3, 3/29.3,
4/46.2, 4/47.3, 4/56, 4/65.3,
5/40.3, 6/46.3
preparation for, 1/2.3, 4/46.3,
5/7.2, 5/7.3, 5/95.2
spiritual communions, 3/29.1,
3/29.2
Viaticum, 4/56.1
see Eucharist
Communion of the Saints

and optimism, 4/49.3
and penance, 2/10.2
entry into, 1/51.2, 2/66.2
gaining merit for others, 1/10.3,
2/66.1, 5/5/33.3, 5/68
indulgences, 2/66.3, 5/71.3
Compassion
4/10.2, 4/27.3, 5/7.1, 5/15.1,
5/31, 5/33.1, 5/58.1, 5/62.1,
5/88.1
Concupiscence
1/1.2, 5/58.2
Confession
a good for the whole church,
1/10.3
and contrition, 1/37.2, 1/47.3,
2/41.2, 2/41.3, 3/90.2, 4/9.2,
5/5.3
and peace, 1/3.1, 5/27.2
and the Good Shepherd, 1/7.2
apostolate of, 1/9.1, 2/34.2,
5/5.3
frequent, 1/10.2, 1/16.2, 3/7.3,
4/9.3, 5/5.3, 5/27.2
fruits of, 2/4.2, 2/8.3, 2/18.3,
5/1.3, 5/27.2
institution of, 4/60.1, 5/3.2,
5/93.2
need for and importance of,
1/10.1, 5/7.3, 5/53.2
penance, 2/34.3, 5/5.3
personal, auricular and
complete, 1/10.1
preparation for, 1/9.3, 2/8.2,
2/8.3, 3/7.2, 4/9.3
preparation for Communion,
1/1.2, 5/7.3
respect, gratitude and
veneration for, 1/9.3, 4/60.2,
5/39.2
the power of forgiving, 1/9.3,
2/8.2, 2/34.1, 4/60.3, 5/.1,
5/41.2

Confidence in God
  and divine filiation, 1/36.2,
    2/60.3, 4/5.2, 4/5.3, 5/9.3,
    5/33.2, 5/81, 7/7.1
  its never too late, 1/36.2,
    4/55.3, 5/60, 5/93

Consumerism
  1/6.2, 5/25.1, 5/46.3, 5/49.1,
    5/55.2, 5/58.2, 7/31.3

Contrition
  4/9.2, 5/5.3, 5/9.1, 5/16.2,
    5/28.2, 5/60.2

Conversion
  1/18.3, 2/1.1, 5/9.3, 5/15.3,
    5/54.3, 5/70.2, 7/20.1

Culture
  7/2.1

Death
  3/63.1, 3/63.2, 3/63.3, 5/71,
    5/75, 5/80, 5/97.1, 5/97.3,
    6/25.1

Dedication
  4/3.1, 4/3.3, 5/9.2, 5/12.1, 5/86,
    7/41.2

Detachment
  examples, 2/16.2, 3/28.3,
    3/64.2, 5/24.2, 5/24.3
  its need, 1/28.1, 2/16.1, 3/17.1,
    4/19.2, 4/48.3, 5/24.1
  our practice, 2/16.3, 3/17.2,
    3/17.3, 3/65.2, 4/6.2, 5/21.3,
    5/38.3, 5/49.2

Devil
  2/6.1, 2/6.2, 2/6.3, 5/42.1,
    5/42.2

Difficulties
  and faith, 4/50.2, 5/61.1,
    5/85.1, 7/21.3
  current forms of, 1/32.2, 5/42.1
  Christian reaction to, 1/32.2,
    1/36.1, 1/41.3, 4/25.2, 5/56.1,
    5/59.2, 5/60.2, 5/61.2, 5/69.2,
    5/82.3, 5/93, 7/12.3, 7/16.2

  develop hope, 1/32.3, 4/5.3,
    4/25.3, 5/85.1, 7/5.2
  suffered for Christ, 1/32.1,
    1/32.3, 4/25.1, 4/96.2, 5/31.3,
    7/12.1, 7/23.2

Dignity, human
  3/11.1, 3/11.2, 3/11.3, 5/3.2,
    5/75, 5/76, 7/22.2, 7/28.2

Dispositions, interior
  humility, 2/20.1, 2/20.2
  need for, 1/18.1, 5/16.1, 5/53.2

Divine filiation
  and fraternity, 1/39.2, 4/98.3,
    5/33.1, 5/79.3
  and petition, 4/39.2, 4/39.3,
    5/60.3
  consequences of, 1/39.2, 3/2.2,
    4/24.2, 4/24.3, 4/63.2, 4/98.2,
    5/33.2, 5/46.3, 5/59.3, 5/60.2,
    5/72, 5/75.3
  everything is for the good,
    1/36.3, 3/96.3, 5/22.1, 5/58.3,
    5/65.1
  foundation for peace and joy,
    1/3.3, 1/39.3, 5/27.2, 5/33.1,
    5/59.2
  God is our Father, 1/24.3,
    1/36.3, 3/2.1, 3/56, 4/24.1,
    4/39.1, 4/58, 4/98.1, 5/3.2,
    5/33.2, 5/59, 5/60.1, 5/64
  gratitude for, 1/39.1
  truly sons, 1/39.1, 3/62.2,
    5/33.1, 5/47.1, 5/59.1

Docility
  a virtue, 1/24.3, 1/43.2, 7/5.1
  and spiritual guidance, 2/20.3,
    5/45.3

Doctrine
  and piety, 6/14
  giving it, 4/28.2, 4/28.3, 5/46.3,
    7/16.1
  need for, 7/13.1

Ecumenism
6/4, 6/5, 6/6, 6/7, 6/8
Education
7/6.3
Eucharist
Adoro te devote, 2/65.1, 3/4.1,
3/4.3, 3/4.2, 4/43.3, 4/97.2,
5/61.1, 5/95.2, 5/95.3
and adoration, 1/44.1, 5/40.3,
5/61, 5/89.3
and faith, 6/45
institution of, 2/44.2, 4/26.1,
4/26.2
pledge of Heaven, 4/65.1,
4/65.2, 5/40.3, 6/48
real presence, 4/43, 5/7.3,
5/16.3, 6/41, 6/42, 6/43, 6/44,
6/46
true food, 4/46, 4/47, 4/65.1,
5/40.2, 5/61
see Communion
Examination of Conscience
a means against evil
inclinations, 1/19.2, 5/41.3
a meeting with God, 1/14.2
and hope, 4/57.2
and self-knowledge, 1/14.1,
5/54.2, 5/73.3
contrition and resolutions,
1/14.3
fruits of, 1/14.1, 5/73.3
how to do it, 1/14.3
particular, 2/67.1, 2/67.2,
2/67.3, 4/19.3, 5/23.3
Example
3/34, 3/74.1, 4/4.3, 4/10.1,
4/40.2, 4/58.2, 5/1.2, 5/13.2,
556.3, 5/62.2, 5/68.3, 5/76.3

Faith
and apostolate, 1/9.2
and charity, 6/52.3
and Christ, 1/43.3, 2/20.1,
3/16.1, 3/67.1, 4/50.1, 4/50.2,
4/55.2, 4/55.3, 5/38.3, 5/56.2,
5/64.2, 6/54, 7/1.1, 7/37.2
and optimism, 4/49.2
docility in spiritual guidance,
1/43.2, 1/43.3, 5/45.3
firmness in, 1/43.1, 3/73.2,
4/54.1, 5/4.3, 5/30.2, 5/48,
5/85.1, 6/52.1, 7/1.3
giving it to others, 1/14.3,
6/6.3, 6/13.3, 6/52.2
need for it, 1/6.1, 5/30.3
of Our Lady, 1/6.3, 3/43.3,
3/55.3, 4/54.3, 5/51.3, 5/64.2
operative, 2/54.2, 2/60.3,
2/62.1, 3/12.3, 3/67.1, 4/54.3,
5/48.3, 5/60.2
ways to conserve and increase
it, 1/6.1, 1/6.2, 1/18.2, 3/55.1,
4/31.1, 4/54.2, 5/4.2, 6/6.1,
6/13
Faithfulness
a virtue, 3/104.1, 3/104.2, 5/86,
7/14.3
in little things, 2/50.2, 3/104.3,
5/91.3
Family
domestic church, 1/31.3,
3/95.1, 5/29.3, 5/55.3, 7/19.1
mission of parents, 1/31.2,
3/95.2, 7/6.2, 7/19.1, 7/28.2,
7/54.2
of Jesus, 4/32, 7/54.1
prayer in the, 3/95.3, 7/6.3,
7/19.2, 7/19.3
Family, Holy
example for all families, 1/31.3,
7/6.1, 7/54.1
love in the, 1/22.2, 1/27.3,
5/64.3
meeting with Simeon, 1/41.1
Redemption rooted here, 1/31.1
simplicity and naturalness,

1/42.2

Fear
1/36.1, 2/93, 3/99, 5/82.2

Feasts
2/61.1, 2/61.2, 2/61.3, 3/71.1
and Sundays, 3/71.2, 3/71.3

Formation, doctrinal
and interior life, 3/13.3, 3/18.3
in the truths of the faith, 3/13.1,
3/18.1
need to receive and to give it,
3/13.2, 3/18.2

Fortitude
gift of, 2/92.1
in daily life, 1/45.3, 3/32.2,
3/32.3, 3/97.3, 5/94.2
in difficult moments, 2/64.2,
7/21.1
virtue of, 3/32.1, 3/97.3, 4/44.2,
5/94.1

Fraternal correction
1/7.2, 3/24.1, 3/24.2, 3/24.3

Freedom
1/35.1

Friendship
and apostolate, 2/80.3, 4/41.3
qualities of a true friendship,
2/80.2, 5/6.2, 5/78.2
true friendship, 2/80.1, 6/11.1
with God, 4/41, 4/55, 5/4.2,
5/61.3, 5/88.1, 7/7.2, 7/7.3

Generosity
prize for it, 1/26.3
towards God, 3/46.1, 4/67.1,
4/98.1, 5/38.3, 5/55.2, 5/67.2,
5/72.3, 5/74, 5/92
with others, 1/26.2, 5/8.3,
5/66.2, 5/67

God's Love for men
gratuitous, 3/62.1, 5/3.2, 5/65.2
infinite and eternal, 2/24.1,
2/24.2, 3/62.1, 4/66.1, 5/1,

5/74.3

personal and individual, 3/62.3,
5/3.1, 5/38.2, 5/66.2, 5/70.2,
5/88
returning his love, 2/57.1,
3/62.2, 3/62.3, 4/66.2, 5/9.3,
5/37.2, 5/39.3, 5/65.2, 5/87.3
unconditional reply expected,
2/24.3, 5/51.1

Goods of the Earth
supernatural end, 4/68.1, 5/21,
5/24, 5/38.2, 5/38.3, 5/49,
5/55.2

Good Shepherd
and spiritual guidance, 1/7.3,
1/43.2
in the Church, 1/7.2, 2/68.1
Jesus Christ is, 1/1, 2/68.1,
5/66.3, 5/70
role of every Christian, 1/7.2
virtues of, 1/7.2, 5/63.3

Gospel
reading of, 1/48.2, 2/73.1, 5/96,
7/36.3
teaching is current, 1/48.3,
5/96.2

Grace
corresponding to it, 2/40.2,
4/19.3, 5/9.3, 5/51.1, 6/2.1,
7/41.2
its effects and fruits, 3/23.2,
3/23.3, 3/84.1, 3/91.1, 5/77,
7/40.3
its nature, 3/23.2, 3/84.2,
3/91.2, 5/30.1

Guardian Angels
help us, 2/7.2, 3/77.2, 3/77.3,
5/42.3, 5/73.3, 5/77.3, 5/84.3
love and devotion for, 2/7.1,
2/7.3, 3/77.2, 3/77.3

Heaven
2/82.1, 2/82.2, 2/82.3, 5/21.1,

5/73.2, 5/83.3, 5/90, 5/97
hope of, 2/12.2, 2/82.1, 3/58.3,
4/48.2, 5/37.1, 5/80.1, 5/97.1,
7/12.2, 7/14.2, 7/15.3, 7/52.1
and the Eucharist, 4/65

Holy days of Obligation
4/29.3

Holy Spirit
and Mary, 2/95.2, 2/95.3,
7/44.1
and supernatural virtues, 2/83.1
devotion to, 2/76.3
fruits, 2/94, 5/23.2, 5/45, 5/52.1
gifts,
counsel, 2/90
fear, 2/93
fortitude, 2/92
knowledge, 2/88
piety, 2/91
understanding, 2/87
wisdom, 2/89

Hope
and discouragement, 1/21.1,
2/4.3, 2/74.2, 3/79.2, 5/23.1,
7/1.2
and heaven, 2/12.2, 5/37.1,
5/80.1, 5/97.1, 7/15.3
and Our Lady, 1/21.1, 2/74.3,
5/36.3, 5/73.3, 6/31.2, 7/14.2
confidence in Christ, 1/23.3,
1/21.3, 2/74.1, 5/49.3, 5/53.3,
5/66.3, 5/83.3, 6/12
in apostolate, 2/4.3
its object, 1/21.2, 3/79.1,
4/57.1, 5/93.3

Humility
and prayer, 1/29.3, 4/51.1,
5/4.1, 5/57.2
and pride, 2/25.1, 2/25.2,
3/45.2, 5/30.1, 4/51.2
and simplicity, 1/42.1, 1/47.3,
5/63.2
founded on charity, 1/27.2,

2/25.3, 5/63.3, 5/74.2
fruits of, 1/27.2, 3/50.1, 5/21.1,
5/47.3, 5/77.1, 5/93.3, 6/55.3
is truth, 1/27.1, 5/39.2, 5/63.2
needed for the apostolate, 1/8.2,
5/77.3
ways to achieve it, 1/27.3,
2/14.3, 2/25.3, 3/45.3, 3/50.3,
4/51.3, 5/9.2

Illness
2/31.1, 2/31.2, 5/69.3, 5/94.2

Jesus Christ
and Our Lady, 1/17.2, 5/18.3,
7/49.1
and the Cross, 1/20.1, 2/30.1,
4/36.1, 4/53.1, 5/2.3, 5/19.3,
5/22, 5/28.3, 5/69, 5/70.1,
7/12.2
divinity, 4/52.1, 6/28.1
growth of, 1/50.1
hidden life, 1/46.1, 1/46.2,
1/50.1, 4/45.1, 5/84.2
high priest, 6/38
humanity, 1/17.3, 1/50.1,
4/52.2, 5/16.2, 5/28.3, 5/31.2,
5/78.1, 5/84.3, 5/88, 6/28,
6/47.3, 6/49, 7/7.2, 7/35.2
humility, 1/30.2, 5/47.2, 5/52.2,
5/63.1
Kingship, 2/42.3, 5/34.2,
5/34.3, 5/83.2, 5/87, 5/91
merits of, 4/4.2
Name of, 1/40.1, 1/40.2, 5/34.1
Only-Begotten Son, 1/17.1,
5/59.1
our knowledge of, 1/17.3,
1/48.2, 5/53.3, 5/96
our Model, 1/17.3, 1/49.3,
4/52.3, 5/2.2, 5/15.2, 5/31.2,
5/47.1, 5/66.2, 5/78.1, 7/38.3
our support, 1/36.1, 3/73.1,

5/56.1, **5**/61.1, **5**/69.3, **5**/70.1
our Teacher, **1**/48.1, **5**/2.1
search for, **2**/12.3, **2**/49.3,
  5/16.3, **5**/32.2, **5**/37.2, **5**/38.3,
  5/56.2, **5**/66.1, **5**/83.1, **5**/85.1

Joseph, Saint
and work, **6**/33
devotion to, **4**/15.2, **6**/20, **6**/21,
  6/22, **6**/23, **6**/24, **6**/25, **6**/26,
  6/27
exemplar of virtues, **1**/45.2,
  4/15.3, **5**/63.3, **6**/21
his dealings with Jesus and
  Mary, **1**/22.2, **1**/22.3, **1**/31.1,
  4/15.2, **5**/64.3, **5**/84.3, **6**/22
his intercession, **1**/45.2
his mission, **1**/22.1, **4**/15.1
his obedience and fortitude,
  1/6.3, **1**/45.1
honour and veneration, **1**/22.3
invoking his name, **1**/40.3
ite ad, **4**/15.3
patron of the Church, **4**/15.2,
  4/15.3

Joy
and apostolate, **3**/15.3, **5**/25.3,
  5/55, **5**/76.3, **5**/78.3
and divine filiation, **1**/15.2,
  3/15.1, **5**/27.2, **5**/33.1, **5**/59.2
and generosity, **2**/26.3, **4**/67,
  5/27.2, **5**/38.3, **5**/55.2, **5**/67.2,
  5/74.3
and sadness, **2**/48.2, **3**/15.2,
  4/67.3, **5**/55.1, **7**/47.3
and suffering **2**/26.1, **2**/26.2,
  3/15.2, **4**/96.1, **7**/23.3
being close to Jesus, **1**/15.1,
  3/15.1, **3**/25.3, **4**/96.1, **7**/4.2,
  7/47.1
in the family, **3**/15.3
its foundation, **1**/15.2, **3**/15.1,
  5/5/27
spreading it, **2**/48.3, **5**/55.3

Judgement
particular, **1**/20.3, **5**/73.2
preparation for, **1**/20.3, **5**/73
universal, **1**/20.2, **5**/73.3, **5**/83

Justice
and charity, **1**/35.3
and mercy, **1**/35.3, **5**/17.3
and the individual, **2**/33.1,
  2/33.2
consequences of, **1**/35.2, **2**/75.1
its aim, **2**/75.3

Laity
role of, **7**/10.2

Leisure
and tiredness, **3**/33.1, **3**/33.3
learning to sanctify it, **3**/33.2,
  4/29, **5**/17.1

Little things
and ascetical struggle, **1**/12.1,
  1/19.2, **1**/50.2, **3**/78.1, **3**/78.2,
  3/78.3, **4**/38, **4**/57.3, **5**/39.2,
  5/50.2, **7**/20.3

Love
seeing God in ordinary things,
  1/33.3, **5**/32.2, **5**/50.2

Love of God
above all things, **4**/1, **5**/35.3,
  5/38.1, **5**/49.1, **5**/55.2, **5**/74.2,
  7/37.3
and the danger of
  lukewarmness, **1**/13.1, **5**/30.1,
  5/50.3
far-sighted, **1**/33.3
in daily incidents, **2**/24.3, **4**/58
leading to abandonment,
  2/57.3, **5**/55.2, **5**/60.3, **5**/77.2
with deeds, **2**/57.2, **4**/66.2,
  5/51.2, **5**/65.2, **5**/72.3, **5**/73.1,
  5/82.2, **5**/84, **7**/4.1

Loyalty
3/87.1, **3**/87.2, **3**/87.3, **5**/21.1,
  5/44.2, **5**/79.3, **5**/86

Lukewarmness
  causes of, 1/13.2, 1/15.1,
    5/28.2, 5/50.3
  consequences of, 1/13.1,
    1/47.2, 3/83.1, 5/3.3, 5/16.2,
    5/30.1, 5/55.1, 5/76.2
  remedy for, 1/13.3, 1/47.3,
    3/83.2

Magisterium
  God speaks through it, 1/48.3

Magnanimity
  3/54.1, 3/54.2, 3/54.3, 5/1.2,
    5/46.2, 5/64.2

Marriage
  3/59.1, 3/59.2, 3/59.3, 5/29,
    5/90
  dignity of, 4/62.1, 5/64.2, 5/90
  see Family life

Mass
  attendance at, 4/36.2, 4/36.3
  centre of interior life, 4/26.3,
    5/52.3
  its value, 2/30.2, 2/30.3, 3/49.1,
    4/7.1, 5/52.2
  fruits of, 3/103, 4/7.2, 4/7.3
  our offering, 1/44.2, 3/49.3,
    4/61.2, 5/92.2

Materialism
  7/2.1

Maturity
  1/50.3, 1/51.3

Meekness
  and peace, 1/11.1
  dealings with others, 1/11.1,
    5/1.1
  fruits of, 1/11.3
  is foundation, 1/11.2
  Jesus, model of, 1/11.1, 5/1,
    5/41.3
  need for it, 1/11.3

Mercy
  and justice, 1/35.3, 3/82.2,
    5/17.3

  fruits of, 3/82.3
  works of, 1/4.3, 4/16.3, 4/27.3,
    5/15

Mercy, divine
  an example, 1/4.1, 3/82.1,
    5/5.1, 5/66.3
  turn to it, 1/4.1, 5/3, 5/17.3,
    5/39.1, 5/45.2, 5/81, 5/93
  with men, 1/4.2, 4/27.1, 4/27.2,
    5/1.3, 5/3, 5/41.2, 5/56.2,
    5/70.2, 5/81.1

Merit
  of good works, 4/97

Morning Offering
  2/79

Mortification
  and purity, 1/16.3
  and the Cross, 2/2.1, 2/2.2,
    2/15.2, 2/43.2, 4/53.3, 5/75.3
  fasting, 2/3.1
  interior, 1/19.2, 1/19.3, 1/44.2,
    2/3.2, 2/55.1, 5/26.1
  of imagination, 2/55.2, 2/55.3
  small sacrifices, 2/2.3, 2/3.3,
    4/8, 5/26, 5/28.3

Obedience
  and docility, 1/24.3
  and faith, 1/12.3, 1/45.1
  and freedom, 1/49.3, 5/19.2
  and God's Will, 1/5.2
  and humility, 1/5.2
  because of love, 1/49.3, 5/11.2,
    5/19.1
  fruits of, 1/49.2
  model of, 1/49.1, 5/11.3, 5/19.3

Optimism
  4/49, 5/61.3, 5/78.3

Our Lady
  and confession, 7/51.1
  and faithfulness, 7/14.3
  and God's Will, 1/25.3, 4/99.1,
    6/29.2, 7/45.3

and joy, **7**/47
and St John, **1**/33.2
and the Mass, **3**/105, **6**/48.3
and the Old Testament, **7**/5.1
and the Trinity, **6**/1.2
birth of, **7**/22.1
co-redemptrix, **1**/41.2, **3**/105.2,
  5/18, **7**/24.2
devotion, **1**/33.2, **1**/40.3, **1**/38.3,
  2/84.2, **7**/3.1, **7**/9.1, **7**/11,
  734.1, **7**/53.3
full of grace, **4**/99.2, **4**/99.3
generosity, **1**/26.1, **7**/41.1
her gifts, **7**/44.2, **7**/44.3
her help, **1**/38.2, **3**/9.1, **5**/36.1,
  5/48.2, **5**/81.3, **6**/16, **7**/3.2,
  7/34.2, **7**/49.3, **7**/52.3
her vocation, **1**/25.1, **5**/14.1,
  6/29, **7**/6.1, **7**/41.3, **7**/45.3
Immaculate Heart of, **6**/35.3,
  6/51
humility, **1**/27.1, **5**/14.2, **5**/63,
  6/27.3
invoke her name, **1**/40.3, **3**/9.1,
  3/42, **5**/81.3, **5**/92.3, **7**/5.3
mediatrix, **7**/9.2, **7**/9.3, **7**/11.3
Mother of God, **1**/17.2, **1**/38.1,
  5/18.3, **5**/81.3, **6**/1, **7**/11.2,
  7/26.3
our guide, **7**/43.2
our Mother, **1**/38.2, **2**/84.1,
  5/36.3, **5**/63.2, **6**/1.3, **7**/3.3,
  7/11.2, **7**/14.1, **7**/15, **7**/49.2
Queen, **7**/17
pilgrimages, **2**/84.3, **6**/31.1,
  6/35
rosary, **2**/38.3, **2**/79.3, **2**/81.1,
  2/81.2, **2**/81.3, **5**/18.3, **5**/27.3,
  5/36.2, **5**/36.3, **7**/13.2, **7**/13.3,
  7/32.3, **7**/33.1, **7**/48.3
service, **1**/26.1
to Jesus through Mary, **6**/37.2,
  7/52.1

Parables of the Gospel
banquet, **5**/37
good Samaritain, **4**/21, **5**/31
grain of wheat, **5**/34.2
leaven in dough, **4**/40
lost sheep, **4**/59. **5**/70.2
mustard seed, **5**/34.2
pearl of great value, **4**/42
Pharisee and tax-collector,
  5/57.2
prodigal son, **5**/3, **5**/41.1
shrewd steward, **5**/12
sowing seed, **4**/19, **5**/9
talents, **5**/51, **5**/82, **5**/87
two sons sent out, **5**/19
unjust judge, **5**/48, **5**/81.1
vineyard, **5**/10.2, **5**/28.1, **5**/54
virgins, **5**/73
wheat and cockle, **4**/28
working in vineyard, **4**/69,
  5/10, **5**/94.3

Patience
2/28.2, **2**/28.3, **5**/11.1, **5**/9.3,
  5/54, **5**/94
see Meekness

Peace
and Christ, **1**/3.1, **2**/77.1
causes, lack of, **1**/3.1, **4**/12.2,
  5/14.3
foundation of, **1**/3.3, **1**/35.3,
  5/59.3
fruits of, **1**/3.2
gift of God, **1**/3.1, **2**/77.2,
  4/12.1
source of, **1**/3.2, **4**/12.3

Penance
and Fridays, **3**/85.2
characteristics of, **3**/85.3, **5**/1.3,
  5/5.3, **5**/26.2, **5**/41, **5**/75.2

Persecution
see Difficulties

Perseverance
2/39.1, **2**/40.3, **5**/4.3, **5**/43.3,

5/57, 5/81, 5/86, 7/4.1

Piety
2/91
Way of the Cross, 2/3.2
see Our Lady, rosary

Pope
2/68.2, 2/68.3, 5/64.1, 6/7,
6/19.3, 6/32.2, 7/16.3

Poverty
and sobriety, 1/28.3
evangelical poverty, 1/28.2
Jesus' example, 1/28.1
ways of practising it, 1/28.3,
4/68.2, 5/24, 7/31.1, 7/31.2,
7/50.3

Prayer
and humility, 1/29.3
and St Joseph, 1/29.3, 3/93.3,
5/64.3, 5/84.3
and thanksgiving, 7/32
dealings with Jesus, 1/29.2,
3/51.1, 5/56.2, 7/35.2, 7/48.1
fruits of, 4/95.1, 5/33.3, 5/57.3,
5/71.1
how to pray, 1/29.3, 2/27.2,
2/27.3, 2/55.3, 3/40.1, 3/55.3,
3/93.2, 4/64.2, 5/4.2, 5/33,
5/40.1, 5/48, 5/96, 7/48.2
mental prayer, 7/34.3
need for it, 1/29.2, 2/38.2,
3/93.1, 5/9.2, 5/14, 5/48.3,
5/81, 7/9.1, 7/35.1
of petition, 2/9.1, 2/9.2, 2/9.3,
3/9.3, 3/40.3, 4/5.1, 4/39.2,
4/39.3, 4/64.1, 4/64.3, 7/32.3
vocal prayers, 3/94.1, 3/94.2,
3/94.3, 4/95.3, 5/94, 5/34.1,
5/95

Presence of God
2/12.3, 2/76.2, 5/57.3, 5/61.1,
5/72.2, 5/83.1

Priesthood, 2/44.2
identity and mission, 4/20.1,

4/20.2. 5/48.2, 5/57.1, 5/71.1,
6/9, 6/38, 7/10.1
love for, 7/10.3
prayer for, 4/20.3, 7/10.2

Prudence
essence of, 4/17.1, 5/93.2
false, 4/17.3
seeking advice, 4/17.2

Purgatory
7/39.1

Purification
interior mortification, 1/19.3,
5/26

Purity
see Chastity

Recollection, interior
union with God, 4/19.1, 5/14
Our Lady's example, 1/29.1,
5/14

Rectitude of intention
2/63, 5/11.1, 5/57.1, 5/67, 5/72,
5/74.3

Redemption
2/29.2, 2/36.1, 2/36.2, 2/36.3,
5/52.1, 5/56.3, 5/69.1, 5/75,
5/80.2

Resurrection
of the body, 3/75.2, 3/75.3,
5/75, 5/90.1, 5/97.2

Sacraments
4/13.2, 4/36.1

Saints
as intercessors, 3/72.1, 7/50.1
cult to, 3/72.2
veneration of relics, 3/72.3

Sanctity
consequences of, 1/35.2, 4/4.1,
5/68.1, 5/87.1
developing talents, 4/68.2,
4/68.3, 5/12.2, 5/51.2, 5/82,
5/84

in ordinary life, 1/46.1, 2/11.2,
2/57.1, 2/69, 3/16.2, 3/16.3,
3/92.2, 4/6.3, 4/40.1, 4/45.3,
5/10.3, 5/32, 5/57.3, 5/72,
6/9.2, 7/38.1, 7/55.2
principal enemies of, 1/1.2,
5/50.2
universal call to, 3/92.1, 5/10.2,
5/37.3, 5/43.1, 6/9.1, 7/38.2

Serenity
3/98

Service, spirit of
2/14.1, 2/14.3, 3/66.3, 5/3.3,
5/67, 5/87.2, 6/37.1

Simplicity
and humility, 1/42.1
and spiritual childhood, 1/24.3,
1/42.2
fruits of, 1/42.3
in dealings with God, 1/42.2,
5/57.2, 7/18.3
opposite of, 1/42.3
rectitude of intention, 1/42.2,
4/17.1

Sin
consequences of, 2/10.1,
2/17.1, 2/18.1, 2/41.1, 3/80.2,
4/2, 4/34.2, 5/28.2, 5/31.1,
5/41.1, 5/45, 5/69.1, 5/71.2,
5/85.1
forgiveness of, 3/44.2, 5/41.2,
5/70.3
reality of, 1/47.2, 3/26.2, 4/23.1,
4/34.1, 5/3.2, 5/45.3, 5/93.1
sorrow for, 4/23.2, 4/23.3,
5/9.1, 5/28.2
see Confession

Sin, venial
deliberate, 2/17.3, 3/26.3,
4/34.3
does damage, 1/10.2

Sincerity
2/23, 3/60, 4/18.2, 5/44, 7/18.2

Society
and human solidarity, 3/37.2,
4/58.3, 5/46.1, 5/68
obligations to, 3/37.3, 3/53.3,
4/58.1, 5/39.3, 5/44.3, 5/46.1,
5/51.2
service to, 3/53, 4/58.3, 5/67,
5/74

Spiritual childhood
and divine filiation, 1/24.2,
4/63.2, 5/34, 5/59, 5/64
and humility, 1/27.2, 3/100.1,
4/63.3, 5/57.2
consequences of, 1/42.2,
5/33.2, 5/46.3, 5/59.3, 5/60.2,
5/72, 5/75.3
nature, 1/24.1, 5/64
need for, 1/7.3
virtues associated with it,
1/24.3, 3/60.2, 3/100.2

Spiritual guidance
and joy, 1/15.3
need for, 1/7.3, 1/43.2, 4/31.3,
5/19.3, 5/43.1, 5/85

Spiritual reading
7/8
advice for, 7/8.3

Suffering
and consolation, 1/34.3
and divine filiation, 1/24.2,
5/59.2, 5/60.2
cross of each day, 1/34.2,
4/53.1, 7/23.2, 7/23.3
fruits of, 2/26.2, 2/64.1, 4/53.2,
7/5.1
helping others through, 1/34.3,
5/15, 5/22.3, 5/31.3, 5/60.3
in the world, 1/34.1, 5/22.2,
5/69.1
Our Lady's example, 1/41.1,
1/41.3, 5/69.3, 6/17, 7/24.3
redeeming and purifying value,
1/34.2, 5/69, 5/94

Supernatural life
 and apostolate, 2/78.3
 and ascetical struggle, 1/1.3,
  3/9.2, 3/22, 5/60.2
 and human maturity, 1/50.3
 practice of virtues, 1/50.1, 5/84,
  5/87.3
Supernatural outlook
 and God's calling, 1/18.2, 5/87
 examining situations with,
  1/18.2, 5/12.3, 5/17.1, 5/32.2,
  5/53.1, 5/58.3, 5/82.3, 5/84

Temperance, 3/101, 4/35
Temptations
 4/3.3, 4/11.1, 4/11.3, 5/9.2,
  5/42, 5/69.2, 5/90.3
Thanksgiving, acts of
 1/37.2, 1/51.1, 2/71.1, 2/71.3,
  5/101.1, 5/39, 5/60.2, 5/78,
  5/95
 after Communion, 2/71.3,
  3/29.3, 5/95.2, 5/95.3
 human virtue of gratitude,
  2/71.2, 4/61.1, 4/61.3, 5/39,
  5/60.2, 5/78.2
Time, good use of
 acts of contrition, 1/37.2
 acts of thanksgiving, 1/37.2,
  5/95
 Christian value, 1/37.3, 5/8.2,
  5/17.1
 our life is short, 1/37.1, 4/48.2,
  4/48.3, 5/54.2, 5/82.3, 5/84.1
Trust
 4/5.2
Truth
 2/23.2, 2/23.3
 love for, 4/18.1, 4/31.2, 5/44
 speaking, 4/18.3, 5/44

Unity
 2/56, 5/32.2, 5/68.1, 5/87.3,

 5/91.2, 6/4.3, 6/5, 6/7
Unity of life
 2/29, 3/74.2, 4/16.3, 5/122.2,
  5/13.3, 5/32, 5/46.2, 5/72,
  5/79, 5/84, 5/87, 6/54.3

Vigilance
 against evil inclinations, 1/19.2,
  5/42.3, 5/76.2
 Come Lord Jesus, 1/19.1,
  5/83.1
 in waiting for Christ, 1/19.1,
  5/49.2, 5/73.2, 5/80, 5/97.3
 the means, 1/19.2, 5/43.3
Virginity
 apostolic celibacy, matrimony
  and, 1/23.1, 4/62.2, 5/63.3,
  5/64.2, 5/90
 free choice, 1/23.1
 of Our Lady, 1/23.1, 5/64.2
Virtues
 1/50.3, 2/22.1, 2/22.3, 3/6.3,
  4/3.3, 5/78, 5/79.3
Visit to the Blessed Sacrament
 2/51.2, 2/51.3, 4/43.3, 4/56.3,
  5/61.1, 5/88.1
Vocation
 and apostolate, 7/25.3, 7/29.3
 and freedom, 4/22.1, 5/37.1
 and joy, 7/25.2
 and parents, 4/22.3
 grace for, 6/36.2, 7/45.2
 of each person, 1/8.1, 1/33.1,
  1/51.3, 5/37.3, 6/36.3
 of Our Lady, 1/25.1, 7/41.3
 of St Andrew, 7/42.1
 of St Bartholomew, 7/18.1
 of St John, 1/33.1, 5/23.1
 of St John the Baptist, 1/8.1,
  5/13.1, 6/55
 of St Matthew, 7/25.1
 prayer to St Joseph, 6/25.3
 responding to it, 1/25.2, 3/14.3,

4/22.2, 4/22.3, 4/42.3, 5/38.2,
  5/43, 5/51.1, 7/42.3
signs of, 1/18.2, 1/18.3
special calling, 1/25.2, 3/14.1,
  4/22.1, 4/42.2, 5/43.1, 5/90.2,
  6/34.1, 6/36.1, 6/56.1, 6/57,
  7/37.1

Will of God
  above earthly plans, 1/47.3,
    5/10.1
  and peace of soul, 1/5.3
  and sanctity, 1/5.1, 5/35
  embracing it, 1/5.1, 1/5.3,
    1/18.3, 2/15.1, 3/20.3, 3/70.3,
    5/35, 5/94.2, 7/45.3
  its manifestation, 1/5.1, 3/20.2
Work
  and prayer, 4/30.3, 5/84.3

in God's presence, 4/30, 5/84.2,
  7/22.3
  its dignity, 1/46.3, 5/84, 6/33.1
  of Jesus, 1/46.1, 1/46.2, 3/1.1,
    3/30.2, 3/41.1, 5/84.1, 5/88.2
  sanctification of, 1/46.2, 1/46.3,
    3/1, 3/30, 3/39, 3/41, 5/13.2,
    5/17.2, 5/32.2, 5/51.2, 5/84,
    6/33, 7/36.1
Works of mercy
  see Mercy
World
  justice in the, 1/35.1, 5/60.3
  re-evangelisation of, 2/58.2,
    2/58.3 , 5/12.2, 5/20, 5/25,
    5/87, 6/18
Worship, divine
  3/46.2, 3/46.3, 5/65.3, 5/89,
  5/92.2

EPILOGUE

FROM THE PUBLISHERS

This volume, the seventh in the series, completes the work IN CONVERSATION WITH GOD. The original Spanish edition was finished on 25 January 1991. The translation of the English edition was completed on 9 January 1993.

The publishers wish to acknowledge the very many letters we have received since the first volume was published in 1988.

These have come from Trinidad to Taiwan, from San Francisco to Singapore, Saligao to Sydney, from Lagos to London. With sales in very many English-speaking countries, they reflect the tremendous help this work has been for daily meditation in everyday life on every continent. It would seem that many have taken to heart *L'Osservatore Romano*'s review of the first volume: *As a source of suggestions for meditation on various aspects of Christian life, the series is to be highly recommended* (11 December 1989).

We are all grateful to the author for the quality of his effort and to the sources of his spirituality.

14 February 1993

We have also seen, since the first volume was published, the canonization of authors frequently quoted in this series like John XXIII, Paul VI, John Paul II, J. H. Newman and Opus Dei's founder, Josemaría Escrivá; and the beatification of Alvaro del Portillo.

28 November 2019